Unsanctifying Human Life

Unsanctifying Human Life

Essays on Ethics

Peter Singer

Edited by *Helga Kuhse*

Blackwell
Publishing

BLACKWELL PUBLISHING
350 Main Street, Malden, MA 02148-5020, USA
9600 Garsington Road, Oxford OX4 2DQ, UK
550 Swanston Street, Carlton, Victoria 3053, Australia

First published 2002 by Blackwell Publishing Ltd

2   2005

Library of Congress Cataloging-in-Publication Data has been applied for.

ISBN-13: 978-0-631-22506-5 (hardback)
ISBN-10: 0-631-22506-4 (hardback)
ISBN-13: 978-0-631-22507-2 (paperback)
ISBN-10: 0-631-22507-2 (paperback)

A catalogue record for this title is available from the British Library.

Set in 10.5 / 12.5 pt Bembo
by Kolam Information Services Pvt Ltd, Pondicherry, India
Printed and bound in India
by Replika Press Pvt Ltd, Kundli

The publisher's policy is to use permanent paper from mills that operate a sustainable forestry policy, and which has been manufactured from pulp processed using acid-free and elementary chlorine-free practices. Furthermore, the publisher ensures that the text paper and cover board used have met acceptable environmental accreditation standards.

For further information on
Blackwell Publishing, visit our website:
www.blackwellpublishing.com

Contents

Introduction: The Practical Ethics of Peter Singer

Helga Kuhse

You start with six albino rabbits. You take each animal and check that its eyes are in good condition. Then, holding the animal firmly, you pull the lower lid away from one eyeball so that it forms a small cup. Into this cup you drop 100 milligrams of whatever it is you want to test. You hold the rabbit's eyelids closed for one second and then let it go. A day later you come back and see if the lids are swollen, the iris inflamed, the cornea ulcerated, the rabbit blinded in that eye.

This is how, in 1981, Peter Singer described the Draize test. Named after John H. Draize, a former chief of the skin and toxicity branch of the US Food and Drug Administration, the test was commonly defended by the claim that it is necessary to test substances that might get into people's eyes, to protect them from harm. But, for nearly three decades, Singer has forcefully argued that the harm to animals is often conveniently and inexcusably ignored when it comes to conferring benefits on humans.

At the time, Singer, then a professor of philosophy at Australia's Monash University in Melbourne, was telling readers of the daily newspaper *The Age* about an announcement by the cosmetics giant Revlon that it was committing 750,000 dollars to research that would allow the testing of new cosmetics without the use of animals. Singer hailed this as an important victory not only for the leader of the US campaign against Revlon, Henry Spira, and the still infant animal liberation movement, but also as a first step towards the equal consideration of the interests of *all* sentient beings. After all, Singer asked, "Don't we have enough cosmetics already?" and in what sense "[c]an a painful test on a rabbit's eye be 'necessary' if the product itself is manifestly unnecessary?"[1]

Peter Singer is almost certainly the best-known and most widely read of all contemporary philosophers. He may also, as Dale Jamieson and Colin McGinn have suggested, be one of the most influential ones, who has changed more lives than any other twentieth-century philosopher.[2] His 1975 book *Animal Liberation*, translated into thirteen languages, has sold more than half a million copies. It has turned many otherwise unimpassioned readers into vegetarians and even animal rights activists. Not counting second editions, the 55-year-old Peter Singer has so far written, co-written, edited, or co-edited thirty books, produced one video-documentary, and written a few hundred articles and reviews for either professional or general publications.

The sheer volume of Singer's writings alone cannot, of course, explain the impact of his work; nor can the impressive analytical and critical skills that Singer shares with other less well-known and less influential philosophers. Rather, as James Rachels has noted in a review of one of Singer's books, "[t]he impact of Peter Singer's writing is due as much to his gift for moral rhetoric as to the quality of his arguments . . . I know of no other writer whose work combines intellectual analysis and moral persuasion so compellingly."[3]

"Famine, Affluence, and Morality" (chapter 10, pp. 145–56), one of Singer's first full-length professional publications, written when he was only 25 years old, is a particularly powerful example of this kind of writing. While it is less well known among members of the general public, Gilbert Harman considers it to be one the most famous articles written in moral philosophy.[4] Its publication, in the first volume of the journal *Philosophy and Public Affairs* in 1972, established the young Singer as a formidable and revolutionary thinker amongst his colleagues. It provides compelling arguments as to why it is morally wrong for well-to-do citizens to enjoy their wealth and comfort while others, in remote parts of the world, are dying from lack of food and other necessities of life. It challenged readers to radically alter their attitudes and way of life. For Singer, this was not a matter of charity, of feeding beggars with the crumbs that fall from our well-laden tables, but of giving to the point of marginal utility, that is, to the point "at which by giving more one would cause oneself and one's dependents as much suffering as one would prevent in Bengal" (chapter 10, p. 149) On reading the article, James Rachels reports "one felt intellectual interest in the argument, but also guilt for not having contributed more money to relieve starvation."[5]

A special challenge was extended to philosophers, who, Singer argued, ought not only to give materially like everybody else, but also to take a position on important practical matters, such as world hunger. "If philosophy is to deal with matters that are relevant to both teachers and students, this is an issue that philosophers should discuss" (chapter 10, p. 155).

The reverberations of Singer's powerful arguments in that article can still be felt today. Already at the time "convinced of the essential soundness of, and the enormous importance of the essay's main ideas," Peter Unger, now a professor of philosophy at New York University, credits "Singer's thinking . . . more than any other contemporary philosopher's" with having influenced the book *Living High and Letting Die: Our Illusion of Innocence*, which he wrote two and a half decades later.[6]

But Peter Singer's writings are not always well received. His central ideas, and the unapologetic and direct way in which he expresses them, are frequently experienced not only as an intellectual and practical challenge, but also as a threat. Written in clear prose, free from philosophical jargon and comforting obfuscation, Singer's writings threaten cozy values and beliefs, including the belief that we are entitled to dispose of our money as we see fit and eat what we like. Eating meat is not, Singer tells his readers, one of life's innocent pleasures, but amounts to complicity in the infliction of serious suffering on animals reared in factory farms; it carries in its wake environmental destruction, pollution, and degradation (chapter 20, pp. 297–305). When profiling Peter Singer for the Australian *Independent Monthly*, Michael Duffy reports that he had long felt morally uncomfortable about eating meat, but had so far successfully dismissed the thought of giving it up with "hearty jokes about lentil burgers and the rights of vegetables":

> It explains why my heart sank soon after I began work on this article. Once you come on Singer's utilitarian train it is difficult to deny that vegetarianism seems to be one of its destinations. . . It does seem difficult to use reason (unassisted by religion) to justify the horrors of factory farming.[7]

Singer has been the subject of many opprobrious, vitriolic, and even abusive attacks, particularly over his challenges to the so-called doctrine of the sanctity of human life. According to Singer, what is important is not whether a life is human or nonhuman; rather, what is of central importance from an ethical perspective is what interests and capacities a being has. Based on the principle of the equal consideration of interests (chapter 5, pp. 79–94), Singer thus argues against the privileged status of humans and the conventional assumption that we are, simply because we are human, justified in overriding the interests of nonhuman animals when they conflict with our own. To do so, he says, is "speciesism," that is, species-selfishness akin to racism. For Singer, as for his intellectual forebear, the classical utilitarian Jeremy Bentham, "From an ethical perspective, we all stand on an equal footing – whether we stand on two feet, or four, or none at all."[8] Racism is now universally condemned and, the young Singer was confident, so would speciesism be one day soon.

The principle of the equal consideration of interests does not, of course, entail that all lives are of equal worth – that the life of a lettuce has the same value as the life of a normal adult human being. Rather, Singer says, what is important is whether a being has the capacity to experience pain and happiness, and the kinds of mental state that make it a "person" with a right to life. As Singer explains in "Killing Humans and Killing Animals" (chapter 7, pp. 112–22), while a being's capacity to experience pain makes that being morally considerable, only in the case of persons, that is, beings with the mental wherewithal to see themselves as existing over time, is killing directly wrong. While all normal adult human beings and some nonhuman animals, such as the great apes (chapters 8 and 9, pp. 123–41), are persons, many animals and some human beings, such as newborn infants and the severely brain-damaged, are not persons in a moral sense. Their capacity to experience pain makes them morally considerable, but killing them painlessly is not directly wrong.

This view has far-reaching implications (see the readings in part V). While it will often be wrong, for example, to use healthy animals in research, it may not be wrong to use anencephalic infants or patients in a persistent vegetative state for these purposes. Add to this Singer's rejection of a being's potential, and his dismissal of the moral relevance of the distinction between killing and letting die, and you have a position that shakes the very foundations of the sanctity of human life view. Not only are human embryos, fetuses, and newborn infants lacking a "right to life," but it will often be better, Singer holds, for a severely disabled infant that is unwanted by its parents to be killed, rather than allowed to die slowly and under distressing circumstances. Infants are replaceable, and "[t]he replaceability principle would allow [parents] to kill the defective infant and then go ahead with another pregnancy" (chapter 7, p. 120).

Put like this, and out of context, Singer's position has struck many as too shocking and extreme to warrant serious consideration. But is it really as shocking and extreme as all that? Singer does not stand alone in thinking that infants and some other humans lack personhood and the right to life, and that an embryo's or infant's potential to become a person one day is in itself morally irrelevant to how it ought to be treated. Many contemporary philosophers share this view. Many contemporary philosophers also share with Singer the view that the distinction between killing and letting die has no intrinsic moral significance. More than that: in light of modern medicine's enormous potential to keep patients alive, it has become common medical practice, sometimes supported by the law, to allow some hopelessly ill patients to die, or to expedite their demise. Abortion is now widely condoned, and in many places legally sanctioned; and destructive embryo experimentation is becoming an accepted option. In other words, Peter Singer is not the first or the only one to suggest that the doctrine of the sanctity of life – largely already undermined in practice – is "terminally ill" (chapter 17, pp. 246–61).

It is, however, primarily Singer – not his philosopher colleagues, medical practitioners, or judges – who has attracted the wrath of outraged members of the public, of various community groups, such as the disabled, and of some philosophers. Why? There are a number of reasons for this. Singer does not limit himself to scholarly articles, but will often speak publicly and write for medical and other journals, and for the popular press. Also, as already noted, his writings are always clear and accessible and sometimes deliberately confrontational. Debra Galant, writing for the *New York Times*, describes Singer as a thinker who "is consistent, clear, and as subtle as a tank rolling over a wheelchair."[9] This may be exaggerated; but Singer likes "to puncture comfortable beliefs"[10] and clearly sees himself as standing in the Socratic tradition, according to which it is the role of philosophers to question the basic assumptions of their age.[11]

Singer is good in this role. He removes fig leaves wherever he finds them and reveals what is hidden underneath them. Sometimes people don't like what they see and will avert their eyes and close their minds. No wonder, then, that Singer – often unread and misquoted – provokes strong reactions. Idolized by members of the animals rights movement, Singer is sometimes treated with disrespect and scorn by those who see themselves as inhabiting a different moral universe. The Archbishop of Melbourne, George Pell, for example, has called Singer "Herod's propaganda minister," and the *Wall Street Journal* has compared him to Hitler's deputy, Martin Bormann.[12] In German-speaking countries, where discussions about medical end-of-life decisions are still conducted in the shadow of Germany's horrendous Nazi extermination programs, Singer – himself the child of Austrian Jews – has been shouted down and physically assaulted (chapter 4, pp. 66–76), and, following threats of violence, the large German publishing house Rowohlt decided against bringing out the nearly completed German translation of the book *Should the Baby Live?*[13] More recently, when Singer's appointment as the new Ira W. DeCamp Professor of Bioethics at Princeton University was announced, the University was reeling under public and internal opposition, with one member of the class of '38 describing the hiring of Peter Singer as epitomizing the decline of Western civilization.[14]

One would be well justified in rejecting responses such as those above as unreflective and over-emotional, but some of the concerns underpinning them also arise at the level of ethical theory and form the basis of criticisms of Singer's writings by colleagues. Peter Singer's work is largely and unashamedly revisionist.[15] As he put it in his 1974 *New York Times Magazine* article "Philosophers are back on the job," "moral positions should be discussed and argued about, not accepted on the authority of God or god-professor." Nor should they, according to Singer, take too much account of people's moral intuitions:

"No conclusions about what we ought to do can validly be drawn from a description of what most people in our society think we ought to do" (chapter 3, pp. 63, 62). Rather, Singer has been unwavering in the view that we should start with "undeniable fundamental axioms" and follow moral principles wherever they lead us.[16] The mere fact that this will sometimes lead to consequences that are contrary to our moral intuitions is not, for Singer, a valid reason for changing our moral views:

> If we have a soundly based moral theory we ought to be prepared to accept its implications even if they force us to change our moral views on major issues. Once this point is forgotten, moral philosophy loses its capacity to generate radical criticism of prevailing moral standards, and serves only to preserve the status quo. (chapter 3, p. 62)

Many contemporary philosophers consider this methodological approach, and the utilitarianism which underpins it, outdated and wrongheaded. It is nowadays often said that an impartialist strongly principle-driven maximizing approach is unable to deal with the complexities of human life, cannot take sufficient account of the emotions, of personal integrity, is "masculine" and dismissive of women's moral experiences, and is too austere and demanding. It would require us, for example, to give the same moral consideration to those distant from us as to those to whom we are close, in the various senses of that term.

Singer has put much weight on impartiality. As he wrote in "Famine, Affluence, and Morality," "If we accept the principle of impartiality, universalizability, equality, or whatever, we cannot discriminate against someone merely because he is far away from us (or we are far away from him)" (chapter 10, p. 147). This puts Singer squarely in the tradition of William Godwin, who is today best remembered for his dismissal of partialist concerns.

Writing some 200 years ago, Godwin believed that morality consists in acting so as to bring about the greatest possible benefit, viewed from an impartial perspective. In this context he presented an example that was to become notorious. Being able to save only one of two people from a burning house, Godwin held that "that life ought to be preferred which will be most conducive to the general good." In his example, this meant that the worthy Archbishop Fénelon – whose writings were bringing happiness to millions – should be saved, rather than the chambermaid. Godwin then went on to ask whether the situation would change if the chambermaid had been the rescuer's wife or mother, and concluded that it would not. As he famously asked, "What magic is there in the pronoun 'my' to overturn the decisions of everlasting truth?" (chapter 11, p. 159).

Commentators have found Godwin's conclusion monstrous, and Singer's writings have at times elicited similar responses. Like Godwin, Singer has sometimes written as if he firmly believes that morality requires an unadulterated impartialist maximizing perspective – that we should leave our mother to burn, in circumstances where the saving of a contemporary Fénelon would maximize utility. But, based on the two-level view of utilitarianism espoused by R. M. Hare, one of the most important twentieth-century ethical theorists, Singer has in his later writings made it clear that such an approach must be somewhat muted to capture the complex elements that contribute to human happiness and the good life. He now explicitly argues that it would be a mistake to ask people to give up all partialist concerns. Rather, it might be best to foster habits and dispositions that take account of people's deeply felt sentiments, such as love and attachments to their parents, children, wives, husbands, lovers, and friends, while at the same time recognizing that from a critical, impartialist perspective a different act would have been better. As he puts it in "William Godwin and the Defence of Impartialist Ethics":

> In the end it is from an agent-neutral standpoint that we determine whether an action was right; but it is a mistake to focus always on the rightness of individual actions, rather than on the habits or intuitive ways of thinking that can be expected, over a lifetime, to do the most good. (chapter 11, p. 174)

In other words, Singer argues for what he calls a "muted impartialism," an impartialism that would not require us to be impartialist in everyday life. We would not, on an intuitive level, be required to save Fénelon rather than our mother, because to become the kind of person who would leave her or his mother to the flames, "we would have to give up too much else of value." This means, for Singer, that "the only tenable position is one that recognizes the importance of both elements," that is, partialism and impartialism (chapter 11, p. 174).

Singer is applying a similarly muted utilitarianism to question of the allocation of scarce resources. While utilitarianism would, at first blush, seem to support a straightforward maximizing approach, Singer points out that matters may be more complicated than that:

> There is more to overall utility than health-related QALYs (Quality Adjusted Life Years), and it is plausible to suppose that tilting the balance of health care towards the more disadvantaged members of society will reinforce feelings of concern and sympathy, and lead to a more compassionate society. This in turn may be a society with more community feelings and therefore one that provides

a higher level of general welfare than a less compassionate society. (chapter 19, p. 292)

The question is, of course, whether such a sophisticated utilitarianism can retain its revisionist force and, ultimately, whether the view can still properly be called utilitarian.

Peter Singer has not engaged himself deeply in these kinds of debate. Rather, he has always been somewhat impatient with the more abstract, theoretical questions. He is not, as someone has remarked somewhere, a philosophers' philosopher, and freely admits that he has not, for example, provided the world with a new ethical theory. His contributions to the discipline lie, he says, in the attention he has devoted to specific, practically relevant issues.[17]

Singer has always found metaphysics a bit dry. Questions such as "How do we know that there is a table in front of us?" he says, "can be debated for quite a while."[18] But in the meanwhile there is unnecessary and unrelieved suffering in the world and millions of people are dying. Some philosophers, such as Socrates, Machiavelli, Adam Smith, and Karl Marx, have changed the world, Singer says, but twentieth-century philosophers have often devoted themselves to abstract – even sterile – intellectual concerns.[19] Already as a young philosopher, he felt that "philosophy was too detached and remote an occupation, I couldn't spend my life doing it. The question was whether it would change, or whether I was to do it. Fortunately it did change."[20]

Some of the titles of Singer's early writings have a somewhat abstract, philosophical ring, but this is deceptive. Even here, the concerns were practical. In his 1973 article "The triviality of the debate over 'is–ought' and the definition of 'moral'" (chapter 1), the aim was, Singer recently explained, to argue

> that the debates then dominating moral philosophy, over the possibility of deducing an "ought" from an "is" and over the proper way to define "moral", were merely terminological, and hence trivial. Instead of wasting time on such debates, I suggested, we could simply stipulate what we mean by the moral terms, and then move on to consider more important issues.[21]

A similarly practical motivation appears to have been behind the 1974 publication "Sidgwick and reflective equilibrium" (chapter 2, pp. 27–50). For Singer, it was necessary to make clear that there were real dangers in following John Rawls (who had recently published his famous *A Theory of Justice*) in accepting particular moral judgments as data against which particular moral theories are to be tested. For Singer, intent on changing the world, such an approach would have been far too uncritical and conservative. Intuitive judgments, he wrote, "are likely to be derived from discarded religious systems, from warped views of sex and bodily functions, or from customs necessary for the survival of the group in social and economic circumstances that now lie in the distant past." Hence, in pitching the utilitarian Henry Sidgwick against Rawls, Singer concluded that "it would be best to forget all about our particular moral judgments" and to proceed as Sidgwick had done: "search for fundamental moral axioms, and build a moral theory from them" (chapter 2, p. 48).

Peter Singer is not afraid to go where his theory and moral axioms have led him – both in a theoretical and in a practical sense. This has, at times, meant political and subversive action. Using his high profile in Australia to draw public attention to important practical issues, Singer has demonstrated in Melbourne streets, sat in a cage to make vivid the plight of battery hens, and has been arrested on an intensive pig farm, partly owned by the then Prime Minister, Paul Keating. As he told the media at the time, the piggery did not give animals room to turn and walk freely, did not give them access to pastures and suitable bedding, and the pigs were subjected to routine mutilations, including tail docking, ear notching, and the clipping of needle teeth. "Because Paul Keating is our national leader, the condition of his pigs is properly a national issue."[22]

Singer was born in Melbourne in 1946, as the son of well-to-do Jewish immigrants, who had fled their native Austria in the late 1930s. He attended prestigious progressive and Christian private schools, and rejected any kind of religion at a relatively young age. At school and university he did well, and after rejecting the study of law in favour of philosophy, graduated from the University of Melbourne with a Master's degree in 1969, at the age of 23.

In a massive 246-page thesis, Singer examined the question "Why should I be moral?" – a question that would continue to occupy him for many years to come. At the time Singer reluctantly reached the conclusion that the question, "despite its age-old importance, has yet to be answered." To the extent that being moral might conflict with rational self-interest, it remained unclear why an individual should choose morality rather than immorality.[23]

In the last chapter of *Practical Ethics*[24] Singer returned to that question and, in *How Are We to Live?*[25] and "Coping with global change: the need for new values" (chapter 22, pp. 324–37), argues that even though the egoist is not making a mistake in the strict sense, there are nonetheless good reasons why people would be well advised to choose morality over immorality. The reason is that they are more likely to be happy. A life devoted to the unquestioning pursuit of individual self-interest, Singer suggests, will often not be fulfilling. We tend to see ethics as opposed to self-interest, but this view may well be mistaken. As he explains,

> The pursuit of self-interest, as standardly conceived, is a life without meaning beyond our pleasure or individual satisfaction. Such a life is often a self-defeating enterprise. The ancients knew of the "paradox of hedonism," according to which the more explicitly we pursue our desire or pleasure, the more elusive we will find its satisfaction...Here ethics returns to complete our picture. An ethical life is one in which we identify ourselves with other, and larger goals, thereby giving meaning to our lives. If we understand both ethics and self-interest properly, they may not be at odds after all. (Chapter 22, p. 335)

But what does it mean to lead an "ethical life"? Does it entail, as the article "Famine, affluence, and morality" (Chapter 10) seemed to suggest, that we must give everything away – money, time, our life projects and plans – right up to the level of marginal utility? The answer, for Singer, is once again "yes," but the "yes" now sounds a little more muted than it did in the past. While giving until it really hurts is what is strictly required of us, Singer would not want to blame those who make some effort when others do much less. As he recently explained, "well-off Americans, who are giving away but 10 percent of their income to overseas aid organizations are so far ahead of most of their equally comfortable citizens that I wouldn't go out of my way to chastise them for not doing more." Nonetheless, the fact remains that most of us could, and should, give much more than that.

> Evolutionary psychologists tell us that human nature just isn't sufficiently altruistic to make it plausible that many people will sacrifice so much for strangers. On the facts of human nature, they might be right, but they would be wrong to draw moral conclusions from those facts...If we don't do it, then we should at least know that we are failing to live a morally decent life – not because it is good to wallow in guilt but because knowing where we should be going is the first step toward heading in that direction.[26]

More generally, Peter Singer, whose ethics has always recognized the importance of facts, has recently reiterated the view that ethical prescriptions and political aspirations must take closer note of human nature. While Marx was correct when he thought of human nature as malleable, it is in some senses less malleable than Marx thought; rather, as Darwin and those who followed him have shown, human nature is carved out of hardwood by evolution, and cannot as easily be shaped by social institutions and arrangements, as the Left has traditionally believed. But, Singer points out, human beings have evolved not only as selfish beings, but also as beings with the capacity for (kin) altruism. The Left, intent on social change, must, Singer suggests, pay more attention to Darwin and to our natural proclivities – harnessing our potential for altruism, while not forgetting about some of our other less admirable tendencies (chapters 24, pp. 358–66, and 23, pp. 341–57).

Singer himself seems less optimistic now than he was in his youth that the changes he envisaged can be achieved. In 1980, a headline in the Australian newspaper, *The Age*, read "Animal Liberation shakes the land,"[27] and Singer was still confident that the prediction he had made in *Animal Liberation* in 1975 would soon come true: "Surely one day our children will feel the same sense of horror and incredulity [toward our treatment of animals] that we now feel when we read about the atrocities of the Roman gladiatorial conquests."[28] Since then, at least one generation of children has grown up and, in 1999, Singer indicated that he was "somewhat disappointed." While he acknowledges that his writings have had "effects around the margins," he now thinks "they have mostly been minor":

> When I wrote [*Animal Liberation*], I really thought the book would change the world. I know it sounds a little grand now, but at the time the sixties still existed for us. It looked as if real changes were possible, and I let myself believe that this would be one of them. All you have to do is walk around the corner to McDonald's to see how successful I have been.[29]

Peter Singer has been accused of being cold-hearted and excessively rational, and it is true, as Singer explained to a reporter, that for him it is generally reason first, and emotion second.[30] This view about the role of reason and morality in his life is well-captured in the quasi-fictional contribution to a volume on "The Lives of Animals":

> "Lay off with the 'You reason so you don't feel stuff', please. I feel but I also think about what I feel. When people say we should *only* feel . . . I am reminded of Göring, who said, 'I think with my blood.' See where it led him."[31]

Recently, Singer has been accused of "thinking with his blood" when (instead of doing what his critics said his philosophy would demand), he did not kill his mother, who had advanced Alzheimer's disease and whose care was consuming money that could, those critics said, more profitably be spent elsewhere.

Singer has never denied that there is a gap between what pure reason would seemingly demand that people should do and what is practically feasible, given their particular circumstances in certain social environments. His response to his mother's illness may thus have been not so much the result of Singer "thinking with his blood" as living according to a kind of "muted" utilitarianism that incorporates various relational responsibilities, and takes cognizance of the law.

In a similar vein, Peter Singer has also been accused of not living at the level of marginal utility, but of maintaining, despite his disregard for some trappings of modern life, a relatively comfortable lifestyle. But again, Singer has never claimed that his life matches the strict dictates of his ethics. Some years ago, when asked by a German magazine to list his greatest weaknesses, he accorded the first place to "selfishness." But, by having devoted much of his life to attempts to relieve unnecessary suffering and death in the world, and by giving more than 20 percent of his income[32] to organizations such as Community Aid Abroad, it is very likely that Peter Singer is approximating his ethical ideal far more closely than many, if not most, of his critics.

During his last two years or so in Australia, before taking up his present professorship at Princeton University in 1999, Peter Singer's primary attention – perhaps a result of his less optimistic views about the realistic possibility of achieving fundamental change – had been somewhat introspective. He researched the life of his maternal grandfather, an enthusiastic teacher and a prominent participant in the intellectual life of Vienna during the early twentieth century, until his dismissal by the Nazis. While the resultant, as yet unpublished, book is unlikely to disappoint, I conclude this introduction with the hope that Peter Singer, who now has the potential to be not only the most prominent practical philosopher in the United States but also the most effective one, will once again turn his full attention to revisionist practical ethics. It may be disappointing if the walls of Jericho[33] refuse to fall quickly, but they may yet come tumbling down.

This has not been a critical introduction to Peter Singer's work. Those looking for criticisms of Singer's views are well advised to look elsewhere.[34] They are unlikely to find them in the introduction to a selection of what this writer herself considers to be some of Singer's best writings. Nor are they likely to find them in the pages of someone who has collaborated closely with Peter Singer for many years, shares many of his fundamental views, and regards him as her friend.

Some of the articles included in this volume are collaborations between Peter Singer and myself. After years of working together and many discussions, it is sometimes difficult to untangle intellectual responsibility for particular ideas. I have not tried to do so. This book is about Peter Singer's work, and the question of whatever responsibility I may have had in a particular piece of work is unimportant in the present context. Many ideas were spelled out by Peter Singer, in embryonic form, as early as 1974 (chapter 3, pp. 53–65), and I have written as if all the articles were entirely attributable to Peter Singer alone – leaving him, hopefully not too unfairly, not only with the possible credit but also with the possible blame.

Notes

1   Peter Singer, "How the bunny lobby terrorized Revlon," *The Age* (February 21, 1981), p. 26.

2   Dale Jamieson, "Singer and the Practical Ethics Movement" in Dale Jamieson (ed.), *Singer and His Critics* (Oxford and Malden, MA: Blackwell, 1999), p. 1. Colin McGinn, quoted by Michael Specter, "The Dangerous Philosopher," *New Yorker* (September 6, 1999), p. 52.

3   James Rachels, "Sociobiology and the 'Escalator' of Reason," review of *The Expanding Circle: Ethics and Sociobiology*, by Peter Singer, in *Hastings Center Report*, 11 (1981), p. 45.

4   Debra Galant, "Peter Singer Settles In, and Princeton Looks Deeper," *New York Times* (March 5, 2000), p. 9.

5   James Rachels, "Sociobiology and the 'Escalator' of Reason," p. 45.

6   Peter Unger, *Living High and Letting Die: Our Illusion of Innocence* (Oxford: Oxford University Press, 1996).

7   Michael Duffy, "The Vegetarian Philosopher," *Independent Monthly* (September 1990), p. 37.

8   Interview with Peter Singer: "Animals join man's 'circle of ethics'," *Monash Reporter* (April 1983), p. 8.

9   Debra Galant, "Peter Singer Settles In, and Princeton Looks Deeper," p. 1.

10 Peter Singer quoted by Rod Usher in "Saintly or Satanic? Peter Singer, Australia's best-known public philosopher, is finding it easier to liberate animals than to free human minds," *Time* (Australian edition, November 20, 1989), p. 88.

11 Janet Ardnov, "Philosopher in the Tradition of Sophocles," *The Age* (Melbourne), (December 10, 1983).

12 See Michael Specter, "The Dangerous Philosopher," p. 49.

13 The German translation was subsequently published under the title *Muss dieses Kind am Leben bleiben? Das Problem schwerstgeschädigter Neugeborener* (Erlangen: Harald Fischer Verlag, 1993).

14 Michael Specter, "The Dangerous Philosopher," p. 52.

15 See Dale Jamieson, "Singer and the Practical Ethics Movement."

16 Peter Singer, "A Response" in Dale Jamieson (ed.), *Singer and His Critics*, pp. 516–17.

17 Jeff Sharlett, "Why are we Afraid of Peter Singer?" *Chronicle of Higher Education*, XLVI, no. 27 (March 10, 2000), p. A21.

18 Michael Specter, "The Dangerous Philosopher," p. 50.

19 Debra Galant, "Peter Singer Settles in, and Princeton Looks Deeper," p. 9.

20 Jane Sullivan, "Thinker who shocks," *The Age* (Melbourne), (June 25, 1980).

21 Peter Singer, "A Response," in Dale Jamieson (ed.): *Singer and his Critics*, p. 273.

22 Gareth Boreham, "PM's piggery cruel, say protesters," *The Age*, n.d.a.

23 Peter Singer, "Why Should I Be Moral?" a thesis submitted to the Department of Philosophy, University of Melbourne for the degree of Master of Arts, July 1969.

24   Chapter 10, "Why act morally?" Peter Singer, *Practical Ethics* (Cambridge: Cam-
      bridge University Press, 1979), pp. 201–20.
25   Peter Singer, *How are we to Live? Ethics in an Age of Self-interest* (Melbourne: Text
      Publishing, 1993).
26   "The Singer Solution to World Poverty" in Peter Singer, *Writings on an Ethical Life*
      (New York: Ecco Press, 2000), pp. 123–4. (The article was first published in the
      New York Times Magazine, September 5, 1999.)
27   Ted Cavey, "Animal Lib shakes the land", *The Age* (Melbourne), (July 21, 1980).
28   Jane Sullivan, "Thinker who shocks."
29   Michael Specter, "The Dangerous Philosopher," p. 50.
30   Jane Sullivan, "Thinker who shocks."
31   As quoted by Michael Specter, "The Dangerous Philosopher," p. 53.
32   Michael Specter, "The Dangerous Philosopher," p. 53.
33   Peter Singer on his initial expectations, in Janet Ardnov, "Philosopher in the
      Tradition of Sophocles."
34   A good place to start would be Dale Jamieson's *Singer and his Critics*.

Part One

From Philosophical to Practical Ethics

One

The Triviality of the Debate over "Is–ought" and the Definition of "Moral"

"The central problem in moral philosophy is that commonly known as the *is–ought* problem." So runs the opening sentence of the introduction to a recent volume of readings on this issue.[1] Taken as a statement about the preoccupations of moral philosophers of the present century, we can accept this assertion. The problem of how statements of fact are related to moral judgments has dominated recent moral philosophy. Associated with this problem is another which has also been given considerable attention – the question of how morality is to be defined. The two issues are linked, since some definitions of morality allow us to move from statements of fact to moral judgments, while others do not. In this article I shall take the two issues together, and try to show that they do not merit the amount of attention they have been given. I shall argue that the differences between the contending parties are terminological, and that there are various possible terminologies, none of which has, on balance, any great advantage over any other terminology. So instead of continuing to regard these issues as central, moral philosophers could, I believe, "agree to disagree" about the "is–ought" problem, and about the definition of morality, provided only that everyone was careful to stipulate how he was using the term "moral" and was aware of the implications and limitations of the definition he was using. Moral philosophers could then move on to consider more important issues.

It has long been a commonplace in the debate about the definition of morality that moral terms are used in many different ways at different times

First published in the *American Philosophical Quarterly*, 10 (1973), pp. 51–6.

and by different people. The search for a definition, therefore, is not a search for the one true definition which expresses all that anyone has ever meant by the term. On the contrary, the search has been for the best definition, the definition that will express the most important or the most useful of the various meanings that moral terms have in ordinary speech. We are, then, to some extent at liberty to choose our definition from among the various definitions which could be given some justification from ordinary usage. On what basis should we make this choice? Provided a definition is not too much at odds with ordinary usage, so that it is still a definition of morality, and not of some newly invented concept, it seems to be generally agreed that the consequences for practical discourse of a particular definition are crucial. The kind of criticisms that are made of particular definitions bear this out. The emotivists, for example, were criticized for making morality a matter of personal whim, in which reason has no part to play, while they accused their opponents of restricting the possibilities of moral discourse by inserting their own values into the definition of morality. The real basis for choosing or rejecting a definition was, and is: how would that definition affect practical disputes? Will it allow sufficient scope, so that all dissenting opinions can be subject to discussion, without being ruled out from the start? Will it allow a sufficient role to reason, so that agreed principles of conduct can emerge, provided only that men are rational? The proponents of different definitions, some of which allow the move from "is" to "ought," and some of which do not, assume that it does make a difference which definition of morality is accepted. This assumption needs to be examined.

I shall begin by considering two possible views on the meaning of the moral "ought," and its relation to matters of fact. These two positions are at opposite ends of the spectrum of positions which can be taken on this issue.

The first position has often been called "subjectivism" but this is a misleading term and, extravagant as it may seem to invent yet another label, I shall call it "form-and-content neutralism," or, for brevity, just "neutralism," because the chief characteristic of this position is its complete neutrality about both the form and the content of moral principles. According to this position, there are no limits on the kind of principle which can be held as a moral principle. A moral principle can have any content whatsoever – that is, it is not restricted to a certain kind of subject matter, like suffering and happiness, or the satisfaction of wants, needs, or interests. "Clasp your hands three times every hour" might seem to have no connection with anything we value; nevertheless it could, on the neutralist view, be a moral principle. There are also no restrictions on the form a moral principle can take, so long as it is intelligible, not self-contradictory, and so on. By this I mean that to count as a moral principle, a principle does not have to satisfy any of the formal requirements that have sometimes been proposed, such as being able to be willed as a universal law, being acceptable to an impartial observer, being able to be formulated without the use of proper names, personal pronouns, or other singular terms. For example, the principle of pure egoism: "Everyone ought to do what is in my interest" fails the test of universalizability as propounded by R. M. Hare because it contains the singular term "my." According to the neutralist, however, this does not preclude it from being held as a moral principle.

Of course, there must be some way in which even the neutralist distinguishes a man's moral principles from other principles which he may hold. For the neutralist, a man's moral principles are the principles, whatever they may be, which that man takes to be overriding. This is made true by definition. In support of the definition, the neutralist can refer to usages like "They gave up everything for Art; Art was their morality" or: "His morality was just egoism, for he cared about nothing but himself."

The neutralist view, then, is that whether a principle is a moral principle for a particular person is determined solely by whether that person allows the principle to override any other principles which he may hold. Any principle at all is capable of being a moral principle for a person, if that person should take it as overriding.[2]

The strength of this account of morality is that it provides a very close logical connection between the moral principles a man holds and the way he acts. It is often said that we can tell what a man's moral principles are by observing how he acts. Certainly we feel uneasy in saying of a man who owns three cars that his moral principles dictate that every rich man should give whatever he can to the poor. The neutralist is able to explain why, if a man acts on the basis of a coherent set of principles at all, he will act in accordance with his moral principles. If a man recognizes that a certain action is prescribed by his overriding principles, he surely will do that action, if he can. There are, of course, instances in which a man does not do what is in accord with his own overriding principles, but in these cases we look for some explanation, such as succumbing to temptation, kleptomania, addiction, or whatever the case may be. This is the sort of explanation that we look for when a man does not act rationally, and it is clear that behavior that has to be explained in this way does not count against saying that the man who acts against his overriding principles has all the reason that he could possibly have for doing the opposite.

The significance of the sort of tie between moral principles and action which the neutralist account provides can be seen in a situation of the following sort: Jack is trying to persuade Bill to do something which he, Jack, thinks would be a morally good thing to do – say, give money to famine relief. If Jack can convince Bill that giving the money is in accordance with Bill's own moral principles, then, so long as Bill continues to act on his own overriding principles, that is, so long as he continues to make rational decisions about what to do, and carries out these decisions, he will give money to famine relief. There is no step between accepting the view that an action is in accord with his moral principles and the decision to do that action.

On the other hand, the neutralist position has a less welcome consequence, which can also be illustrated by the above example. Whatever facts Jack mentions in his attempt to convince Bill that giving to famine relief is demanded by Bill's own moral principles, Bill can always retort that no moral conclusions follow from these facts. Jack might, for instance, refer to the immense amount of suffering that will be relieved by a substantial donation, and compare this with the relatively trivial difference in pleasure that Bill will get if he uses the money to buy a Mercedes rather than a Morris. Bill could reply that according to his moral principles, suffering matters only when experienced by himself, his family, or friends. Jack would have no effective counter to this reply – he could not argue, for example, that Bill would not be prepared to accept his own moral principles if he were one of the victims of a famine. Bill could reject this argument as simply irrelevant, since there is no reason why a moral principle should conform to such a requirement. This the neutralist must accept. So the only role which reason has to play in the choice of moral principles is that role which it has in all areas of life, associated with correct beliefs about what is the case, what ends are attainable, the best means to them, and so on. When any principle at all can be a moral principle, there can be no special kind of reasoning applicable to moral principles.

At the other end of the meta–ethical spectrum there is the kind of position which R. M. Hare has termed "descriptivism." It is often called "naturalism," but since the intuitionist account of morality cannot really be called naturalist, but may, for our purposes, be grouped together with naturalist theories, I shall use Hare's term. Descriptivism is the direct opposite of neutralism in that for a principle to be a moral principle, as the descriptivist defines the term, it must satisfy criteria of both form and content. Thus, to give just one example of the many possible forms of descriptivism, it might be said that moral judgments are logically tied to suffering and happiness, impartially assessed. In other words, a judgment is not a moral judgment unless it is somehow connected to suffering and happiness, and a judgment is also not a moral judgment unless it is an impartial judgment, in the sense that it does not arbitrarily place more importance on the suffering and happiness of a particular person or group of persons than on the suffering and happiness of any others.

The strength of the descriptivist view is that once the definition of morality is accepted, watertight reasoning from statements of fact to moral conclusions is possible. This means that (to continue with the example used earlier) from the fact that Bill's money will reduce suffering and increase happiness to a greater extent if given to famine relief rather than if spent on a Mercedes, Jack can argue that Bill ought, morally, to give the money to famine relief rather than buy the more expensive car. If the descriptivist is right in tying morality to suffering and happiness, impartially assessed, Bill has no way of resisting this argument, for the conclusion follows deductively from the definition of morality and the facts of the case. Of course, most descriptivist views are not as straightforward as the example I have given, and so the argument may be more complicated. Nevertheless, to the extent that the descriptivist gives definite form and content to his definition of morality, he is able to show that reason has a prominent role in moral argument, and that moral arguments are objective.

Unfortunately the significance of this conclusion is reduced by the fact that descriptivism, strong where neutralism is weak, is also weak where neutralism is strong. To show that an action is required by a moral principle does not, if the descriptivist view is accepted, have the consequences it would have if moral principles were necessarily overriding. We are not, on the descriptivist view, free to form our own opinion about what is and what is not a moral principle; but we are free to refuse to concern ourselves about moral principles. Bill has to grant that if morality is tied to suffering and happiness, it follows that he is morally obliged to give to famine relief, but he may say that if that is what morality is about, he is not interested in acting according to moral principles. The descriptivist cannot tie morality to action, as the neutralist did, because he has tied it to form and content. So morality may become irrelevant to the practical problem of what to do.

We have, then, two quite opposed views about the meaning of moral judgments and their relations to statements of fact. These two views differ as much as any of the contending views that have been put forward in the "is–ought" controversy. Yet on the issue of how statements of fact are connected with reasons for acting in general (and not just moral reasons for acting) neutralism and descriptivism do not differ at all. To go from the statement of fact: "Giving money to famine relief will reduce suffering and increase happiness to a greater extent than spending the money on a more expensive car" to the practical conclusion of giving the money away is neither easier nor more difficult if we adopt one position rather than the other. The arguments which we might use are, in fact, substantially the same in either case, although the way we express them may differ. Thus if a person accepts, on the basis of an argument from a descriptivist definition of morality, that morally he ought to give to famine relief, but asks what reason there is for taking any notice of morality, we may answer by appealing to the feelings of sympathy and benevolence which, in common with most of mankind, he probably has to some extent. We may talk of the fulfillment and real happiness that can come through knowing that one has done what one can to make the world a little better, and contrast this with the disappointments and ultimate sense of futility which are likely to come from a self-centered existence devoted to nothing but selfish concerns. We might mention the value of friendship between open people who respect each other, a kind of friendship impossible for the narrowly egoistical man or woman. These are just some of the considerations we might mention, and they may or may not be valid reasons for leading a life which the descriptivist would say was morally good. Whether these are valid reasons is not my concern here; it might depend on the person to whom they are addressed. My point is that the neutralist could use exactly the same reasons in an attempt to persuade the man whose overriding, that is, moral, principles take no account of the happiness or suffering of people other than himself, his family, and friends, to widen his area of concern, and so, perhaps, to adopt principles which would involve giving to famine relief.[3]

I hope it is now clear that the issue that really matters, that is of practical significance, is how statements of fact are connected with reasons for acting, and not how statements of fact are connected with moral judgments. The latter question is encompassed by the former. To hold, as the neutralist does, that action follows from moral judgments but moral judgments do not follow from facts, is to place morality close to the "action" side of the "fact-action" or "reason-action" gap, while to hold, as the descriptivist does, that moral judgments follow from facts but action does not follow from moral judgments, is to place morality on the opposite side. The dispute between the neutralist and the descriptivist, therefore, is a dispute about where, within a limited framework, morality shall be placed. Since nothing of any practical significance hangs on the placing of this term within this framework – the prospects for going from facts to action are the same in either case – the dispute is merely terminological.[4]

I said earlier that neutralism and descriptivism are at opposite ends of the spectrum of positions which can be taken over the "is-ought" issue. If this is true, it would mean that other positions differ from each other, and from the two extreme positions, even less than the two just discussed, so that if the difference between neutralism and descriptivism is of no real importance, the differences between any other positions will be no more significant. Yet it might be thought that a middle position between neutralism and descriptivism could combine the strengths and avoid the weaknesses of the extreme positions – that is, that it could preserve the tie between action and morality as well as the tie between fact and morality. If this could be done, such a position would differ significantly from both neutralism and descriptivism, for it would eliminate the gap between facts and action.

The difficulty which must be faced by any attempt to combine the advantages of neutralism and descriptivism without their disadvantages should be obvious from what has already been said. If we insist that the principles a person acts upon are, by definition, his moral principles, we must recognize that people can act on all sorts of principles without committing any logical error. How can we claim a necessary connection between a person's moral principles and the way he acts, while simultaneously denying that some conceivable principles of action can be moral principles?

Let us consider one way in which it might be thought possible to deny the status "moral principle" to at least some principles of action, while preserving the tie between the way a person acts and what we regard as his moral principles. It might be thought that one can maintain that moral principles are, by definition, prescriptive, so that to assent to a moral principle is to commit oneself to acting upon it when it is appropriate to do so, and at the same time maintain that, while a moral principle can have any content whatsoever, it must satisfy the formal requirement of universalizability.[5] Does this position overcome the difficulty I mentioned?

First, what advantage does such a position have over ordinary neutralism? It will be remembered that the position I have been referring to as neutralism was neutral as to both the form and the content a moral principle could have. The position we are now considering is neutral as to content, but not as to form. This means that there are some principles on which people might act which are not moral principles. This restriction on the form a moral principle can take makes it possible to develop a more effective form of moral argument than was possible with form-and-content neutralism. To illustrate, using the same example as before: Jack can ask Bill how he would feel about other people indulging in luxuries while he starved to death. So long as Bill continues to claim that he acts on moral principles, he cannot deny the relevance of this question, for if he cannot prescribe universally that people who feel inclined to spend their money on luxuries should do so, even when others (including, perhaps, Bill himself) are starving, then he cannot defend his purchase of the Mercedes on moral grounds. This argument is not quite as watertight as the direct argument from a descriptivist definition of "moral," for it is at least logically possible that Bill will reply that, according to his moral principles, suffering, whether his own or anyone else's, is not very important. He might say that the ideal of "standing on one's own two feet," and not being dependent on anyone else, is more important than suffering, or there may be some other ideal for which he would be prepared to suffer, and thinks others should, if necessary, suffer for too. Nevertheless, as a matter of fact, few people are prepared to starve to death for an ideal, and so the universalization argument does provide a means of linking moral conclusions with statements about suffering, happiness, and other matters which may, with some reservations, be termed "factual."

The composite position, then, does allow a more powerful form of moral argument than is possible for the neutralist. Does it avoid the disadvantage of descriptivism? It would seem that it does, for by defining moral principles so that they are necessarily prescriptive, it seems to make it logically impossible for anyone to say that, while he can see that from the moral point of view he ought to do a particular act, he is not interested in acting according to moral principles. So this position appears to have advantages over both the positions we considered earlier.

Unfortunately, this impression is not sustained on closer examination. To see this, we only have to ask what a defender of the composite position would say about a person whose overriding principle of action is non-universalizable – for instance, a person who acts on the principle of pure egoism, mentioned earlier. The only thing that can be said about such a person, consistent with the composite position, is that he does not hold any moral principles at all, for there are no universalizable principles which he holds prescriptively. The restriction on the form a moral principle can take is incompatible with the view that whatever principles of conduct a person espouses are his moral principles. So, on this account of morality, it is possible to "opt out" of acting on moral principles, and thus there is still a gap between action and morality. Certainly, to opt out of morality defined in this way is not quite the same as opting out of morality as defined by a descriptivist. To opt out of morality as defined by a typical descriptivist one would have to deny that one is concerned, say, about suffering and happiness, impartially assessed. To opt out of universal prescriptive morality, one would have to deny that one is concerned to act on judgments which one is prepared to universalize. Still, it is possible to do this, and there are no doubt many people whose overriding principles are selfish ones, which they would not be prepared to universalize. If we were to try to persuade these people to act only on judgments which they are prepared to universalize, we should have to use arguments the same as or similar to those already mentioned, which the descriptivist could use in attempting to persuade people to act on moral principles as he defines them, and which the neutralist could use to get an egoist to take the interests of others into account.

Does the middle position have any advantage over descriptivism, then? It may be – depending, I think, on just what account is given of the notion of universalizability – that there are some people who are prepared to act on universalizable judgments, but not on judgments which are tied to suffering and happiness, or whatever other content the descriptivist gives to his definition of morality. For these people, on the middle position, but not on the descriptivist position, there still is a logical tie between action and morality. But is this really a gain? It is doubtful if it is. For it is precisely these people – people who are prepared to universalize their judgments but do not concern themselves with the suffering or happiness of others – who will hold ideals which allow them to remain unmoved by the "how would you like it if you were in that position?" argument. To see this requires only a little reflection. The person who, because he holds the ideal of "standing on one's own two feet" is able to resist the universalization argument and buy his Mercedes while others starve, is just the sort of person who would not be prepared to act on moral principles, if "moral" were defined in terms of suffering and happiness, but would be prepared to act on moral principles, defined so that they must be universalizable but can have *any* content. A person who does not hold ideals which he considers more important than suffering and happiness, and is prepared to act only on universalizable principles, could be moved by the universalization argument, but would also, presumably, be prepared to act on moral principles defined as a descriptivist might define them, in terms of suffering and happiness.

So the middle position does not seem to have any advantage over the other two positions. The only advantage it seemed to have over descriptivism was that there are some people for whom it can show a logical tie between action and morality, while descriptivism cannot, but it turns out to be just these people for whom the middle position cannot provide a tie between reason, or fact, and morality. Nor does the middle position have any real advantage over neutralism, for, as we have seen, to get an egoist to act according to moral, that is, universalizable, principles, an advocate of the middle position would have to use the same arguments that a neutralist can use to get an egoist to take into account considerations other than his own interests.

I have not, of course, considered every possible account of the meaning of moral concepts, nor every way of either overcoming or preserving the "is-ought" gap. Nevertheless, I think that the three positions I have examined are illustrative of the kinds of account that can be offered and have been offered in recent years. I have tried to show, by examining these positions, that there are limits to what any account of morality can do. No definition of morality can bridge the gap between facts and action. Nor does any one definition of morality have any important overall advantages as against the other plausible definitions that have been suggested. It follows that the disputes over the definition of morality and over the "is-ought" problem are disputes over words which raise no really significant issues.

In conclusion, I should perhaps add that I am not denying that lack of clarity about the meaning of words is an important source of error, both in philosophy and in practical argument. Confusion is likely to occur unless both parties to a discussion are sure about what the use of a word implies. It is not difficult to see how, if one did not make the way in which one was using the term "moral" clear, errors could happen. It might be thought that one could argue that moral principles must be concerned with suffering and happiness, impartially considered, and then maintain that if a person is to act on a coherent set of principles at all, he must act on moral principles, since moral principles are necessarily overriding. This would be a particularly obvious slide from the descriptivist to the neutralist definition of morality, but such moves can be better disguised. It is therefore necessary, before embarking on a discussion of morality, to make quite clear in what sense one is using terms like "moral judgment," and what follows and what does not follow from such a use of the term. This is an essential preliminary; but it is only a preliminary. My complaint is that what should be regarded as something to be got out of the way in the introduction to a work of moral philosophy has become the subject matter of almost the whole of moral philosophy in the English-speaking world.

Notes

1   *The Is-Ought Question*, ed. W. D. Hudson (New York, 1969).
2   I have described a possible position, and it is not necessarily the precise position of any particular moral philosopher. The fullest recent statement of a position which is neutralist in all important respects is to be found in D. H. Monro's (*Empiricism and Ethics*, New York, 1967).
3   D. H. Monro does in fact use reasons of this sort in showing that his neutralist account of morality leaves a place for argument (*Empiricism and Ethics*, pp. 231–3).
4   This point is not entirely new. The existence of the gap between reason and action was the basis of Hume's arguments that moral judgments are not derived from reason. For Hume thought that moral judgments must be connected with action, while reason alone cannot lead to action. Had someone suggested that "moral judgment" be defined in a way not necessarily connected with action, Hume would no doubt have been prepared to grant that, so defined, moral judgments could be derived from reason. See *A Treatise of Human Nature*, Bk. III, Pt. I, § I; and *An Enquiry Concerning the Principles of Morals*, Appendix I.
5   This position has been advocated by R. M. Hare in *The Language of Morals* (Oxford, 1952) and *Freedom and Reason* (Oxford, 1963). See also P. H. Nowell-Smith, *Ethics* (Baltimore, 1954), pp. 307–9.

Two

Sidgwick and Reflective Equilibrium*

In his book *A Theory of Justice*, John Rawls introduces and employs the concept of "reflective equilibrium" as a method of testing which of rival moral theories is to be preferred.[1] The introduction of this concept is plainly a significant event for moral philosophy. The criterion by which we decide to reject, say, utilitarianism in favour of a contractual theory of justice (or vice versa) is, if anything, even more fundamental than the choice of theory itself, since our choice of moral theory may well be determined by the criterion we use.

Moral philosophy is an ancient subject. It would be surprising if someone were suddenly to propose a new way of deciding between competing moral theories, implying thereby that all the moral philosophers of the past have been mistaken about the nature of a successful moral theory. Rawls does not see his proposal in this way. Far from being an innovation, the method of reflective equilibrium, he claims, goes back to Aristotle, and can be followed down through the classical writers at least as far as Sidgwick. Rawls quotes from Sidgwick (and from no other classical writer) to show that this is Sidgwick's own method of doing moral philosophy.

I do not intend to examine the moral philosophy of Aristotle, or of any other moral philosopher between Aristotle and Sidgwick. But I shall examine the

* I have greatly benefited from comments on an earlier version from: B. Barry, R. M. Hare, J. L. Mackie, D. Parfit, J. B. Schneewind, and K. Watts. This paper has been read at Johns Hopkins University and Princeton University, and I am grateful to faculty and students there for valuable discussion.

First published in *The Monist*, 58 (1974), pp. 490–577. Copyright © 1974, The Monist, Peru, Illinois 61354. Reprinted by permission of The Monist.

evidence for the view that Sidgwick uses the method of reflective equilibrium as a test for the validity of moral theories; and, to anticipate the result of this examination, I shall deny that Sidgwick does use this method. I shall then try to say what, for Sidgwick, the ultimate test of a moral theory is. Thus this article is in part an attempt to correct Rawls's interpretation of Sidgwick; nevertheless, my concerns are not limited to the desire to refute a few peripheral sentences of *A Theory of Justice*. The issue is important because of the need to decide on the correct method in moral philosophy. Rawls believes that reflective equilibrium is the correct method, and he also thinks it the method of the classical philosophers, including Sidgwick. My own view is that it is not Sidgwick's method, and it is not the correct method either. If it can be shown that Sidgwick uses some other means of testing moral theories, we can ask what that method is, and whether it is preferable to reflective equilibrium. Since Sidgwick is among the clearest and most careful thinkers in the field, and had a profound knowledge of the history of moral philosophy, whatever method he employs is likely to be worth serious consideration.

I

The first question to ask, then, is what this method of reflective equilibrium is. Although Rawls first introduced this idea in his article "Outline of a Decision Procedure for Ethics,"[2] I shall use only the more recent account in *A Theory of Justice*.

Rawls begins with our "moral capacity" – that is, the skill we acquire, in normal circumstances, of judging things to be just or unjust, and, presumably, right or wrong, good or bad, as well. He then says:

> Now one may think of moral philosophy at first (and I stress the provisional nature of this view) as the attempt to describe our moral capacity; or, in the present case, one may regard a theory of justice as describing our sense of justice. This enterprise is very difficult. For by such a description is not meant simply a list of the judgments on institutions and actions that we are prepared to render, accompanied with supporting reasons when these are offered. Rather, what is required is a formulation of a set of principles which, when conjoined to our beliefs and knowledge of the circumstances, would lead us to make these judgments with their supporting reasons were we to apply these principles conscientiously and intelligently. A conception of justice characterizes our moral sensibility when the everyday judgments we do make are in accordance with its principles. [*ATOJ*, p. 46]

At this point Rawls offers an instructive comparison between this method of doing moral philosophy and Chomsky's undertaking of "describing the sense of grammaticalness that we have for the sentences of our native language." The aim here, Rawls tells us, is to formulate principles "which make the same discriminations as the native speaker."

Rawls then adds an important qualification to what has been said so far, by introducing the idea of "considered judgments" which are "those judgments in which our moral capacities are most likely to be displayed without distortion." In other words, we exclude judgments made without real confidence, or under stress, or when we may have been swayed by undue consideration of our own interests. The relevant judgments then, are "those given under conditions favorable for deliberation and judgment in general" (*ATOJ*, p. 48).

We now come to the final statement of reflective equilibrium itself, and it is necessary to quote the central passage in full:

> According to the provisional aim of moral philosophy, one might say that justice as fairness is the hypothesis that the principles which would be chosen in the original position are identical with those that match our considered judgments and so these principles describe our sense of justice. But this interpretation is clearly oversimplified. In describing our sense of justice an allowance must be made for the likelihood that considered judgments are no doubt subject to certain irregularities and distortions despite the fact that they are rendered under favorable circumstances. When a person is presented with an intuitively appealing account of his sense of justice (one, say, which embodies various natural and reasonable presumptions), he may well revise his judgments to conform to its principles even though the theory does not fit his existing judgments exactly. He is especially likely to do this if he can find an explanation for the deviations which undermine his confidence in his original judgments, and if the conception presented yields a judgment which he finds he can now accept. From the standpoint of moral philosophy, the best account of a person's sense of justice is not the one which fits his judgments prior to his examining any conception of justice, but rather the one which matches his judgments in reflective equilibrium. As we have seen, this state is one reached after a person has weighed various proposed conceptions and he has either revised his judgments to accord with one of them or held fast to his initial convictions (and the corresponding conception). [*ATOJ*, p. 48]

Thus Rawls's view is that a normative moral theory is like a scientific theory.[3] As in science, the aim of the theory is to explain all the data; but, also as in science, if a promising theory conflicts with only one or two observations, the observations may be jettisoned and the theory retained, rather than the other way around. In science this is achieved by introducing additional hypotheses, or assuming that an instrument was faulty, or some disturbance overlooked; in moral theory, what was previously thought to be a considered moral judgment may after all have been a result of distorted thinking, and so may be explained away. In both cases, although there are no "brute" facts, there are facts, and the successful theory is the one that provides a plausible systematization of them. So Rawls says:

> I wish to stress that a theory of justice is precisely that, namely, a theory. . . . There is a definite if limited class of facts against which conjectured principles can be checked, namely our considered judgments in reflective equilibrium. [*ATOJ*, p. 51]

These passages may give rise to differing interpretations of the notion of reflective equilibrium. Most importantly: is the fact that a moral theory matches a set of considered moral judgments in reflective equilibrium, to be regarded merely as *evidence* of the validity of the moral theory, or is it then valid *by definition* – in other words, is the achievement of a stable reflective equilibrium what Rawls means by "valid," as applied to moral theories, or would he allow that there is a meaningful sense of "valid" that goes beyond this? My belief is that Rawls has left no room for any idea of validity that is independent of achieving reflective equilibrium. The passages I have quoted all point in this direction. Thus we are to start by thinking of moral philosophy as an attempt to describe our moral capacity – and there is no sense in which a description can be correct that is independent of the way it fits what it describes. Admittedly, this starting point is provisional, but I take this to be a reference to the fact that the procedure is not as one-sided as the provisional idea indicates, since our moral capacity may itself alter under the influence of a plausible theory. There is still nothing to suggest room for a notion of validity beyond the conjunction of theory and revised moral capacity. Next, we have the analogy with the attempt to describe the sense of grammaticalness of the native speaker – again, a perfect fit is not merely evidence that the theory of grammar is correct, it is what is meant by a "correct" theory. Finally there is the analogy with science, and in particular with Quine's model of science. This too gives no sense to the idea of a correct theory other than the theory that best fits the data, after that data has been subject to possible revision in the light of plausible theories.

If I am right in attributing this version of the reflective equilibrium idea to Rawls, then Rawls is a subjectivist about morality in the most important sense of this often misused term.[4] That is, it follows from his views that the validity of a moral theory will vary according to whose considered moral judgments the theory is tested against. There is no sense in which we can speak of a theory being objectively valid, no matter what considered moral judgments people happen to hold. If I live in one society, and accept one set of considered moral judgments, while you live in another society and hold a quite different set, very different moral theories may be "valid" for each of us. There will then be no sense in which one of us is wrong and the other right.[5]

This point is not affected by the question of whether there is one unique reflective equilibrium for all men or not (a question upon which Rawls refuses to speculate). Even if everyone shared the same considered moral judgment, this would only mean that a theory might have intersubjective validity: it would not make for objective validity. People might have judged differently, and then a different moral theory would have been "valid."

The second issue of interpretation left unresolved by the passages quoted is whether a moral theory is supposed to match the considered moral judgments of an individual, or of some larger group, such as a society. Rawls, after refusing to discuss whether there is a unique reflective equilibrium for all men, goes on to say: "for the purposes of this book, the opinions of the reader and the author are the only ones that count. The opinions of others are used only to clear our heads" (*ATOJ*, p. 50).

This is a clear statement, but can Rawls really mean it? Throughout the book, some consensus seems to be presupposed. Rawls always writes of "our" judgments, never "mine" or "yours"; this may only be a matter of style, but the assurance with which he assumes that the reader shares his own intuitions can only be based on the assumption that there is a wide consensus about, for example, what is just and what unjust.[6] For the purposes of comparison with Sidgwick, this vacillation need not be forced into one or other interpretation. It needs only to be noted, and will be referred to again after we have examined Sidgwick's own method.

Other points of interpretation will best be dealt with when they come up in the course of the discussion of whether Sidgwick uses the reflective equilibrium method. To this we may now turn.

II

The evidence Rawls himself gives for the claim that Sidgwick does use the method of reflective equilibrium is scanty, though Rawls cannot be blamed for feeling that his book is sufficiently long without adding purely historical digressions. Rawls gives one quotation from Sidgwick, which does look like a description of a procedure similar to Rawls's "reflective equilibrium" idea. Apart from this, he relies on a reference to an article by J. B. Schneewind, entitled "First Principles and Common Sense Morality in Sidgwick's Ethics."[7]

If we follow up the reference to Schneewind's article, we find a clearly written account, backed with numerous quotations, of Sidgwick's methodology;

moreover, it is an account that does support the contention that Sidgwick uses a method rather like reflective equilibrium. Since Schneewind's account is so much fuller than anything Rawls says, and since it merits attention in its own right (and would surely have received more attention had it not appeared in a periodical little read by English-language moral philosophers) I now proceed to a discussion of Schneewind's account of Sidgwick's methodology.

Schneewind sees *The Methods of Ethics* as an elaborate attempt to "prove," in a special sense, the truth of utilitarianism. The argument proceeds, according to Schneewind, in two stages – but in order to understand Schneewind's account, we must first ask in what sense of "proof" Sidgwick is supposed to be trying to prove utilitarianism to be true. As Schneewind points out, Sidgwick, like Mill, is clear that it is impossible to prove a first principle "if by proof we mean a process which exhibits the principle in question as an inference from premises upon which it remains dependent for its certainty; for these premises, and not the inference drawn from them, would then be the real first principles."[8] So what possibilities are left? The following passage is crucial both for an understanding of Schneewind's interpretation of Sidgwick, and for my argument that this interpretation is mistaken:

> Nay, if Utilitarianism is to be *proved* to a man who already holds some other moral principles – whether he be an Intuitional moralist who regards as final the principles of Truth, Justice, Obedience to authority, Purity, etc., or an Egoist who regards his own interest as the ultimately reasonable end of his conduct, – it would seem that the process must be one which establishes a conclusion actually *superior* in validity to the premises from which it starts. For the Utilitarian prescriptions of duty are *prima facie* in conflict, at certain points and under certain circumstances, both with rules which the Intuitionist regards as self-evident, and with the dictates of Rational Egoism; so that Utilitarianism, if accepted at all, must be accepted as overruling Intuitionism and Egoism. At the same time, if the other principles are not throughout taken as valid, the so-called proof does not seem to be addressed to the Intuitionist or Egoist at all. How shall we deal with this dilemma? How is such a process – clearly different from ordinary proof – possible or conceivable? Yet there clearly seems to be a general demand for it. Perhaps we may say that what is needed is a line of argument which on the one hand allows the validity, to a certain extent, of the maxims already accepted, and on the other hand shows them to be not absolutely valid, but needing to be controlled and completed by some more comprehensive principle. [*ME*, pp. 419–20. Italics in original.]

According to Schneewind, Sidgwick is here proposing a two-stage argument. The first part (actually mentioned second in the final sentence of the passage quoted) is an attempt to show that "the principles of Truth, Justice, etc.

have only a dependent and subordinate validity"; they require some further principle which is unconditionally and independently valid, to justify exceptions, settle cases on which the subordinate principle is vague or indeterminate, and resolve conflicts between subordinate principles. The second stage, the "systematization argument," is to the effect that the utilitarian principle "affords a principle of synthesis, and a method for binding the unconnected and occasionally conflicting principles of common moral reasoning into a complete and harmonious system" (*ME*, pp. 421, 422). The overall procedure, then, is first to show that our ordinary moral judgments – "the morality of Common Sense," in Sidgwick's terminology – need some further principle for their completion, and then to show that this further principle is none other than the principle of utility.

Now it may seem that since in expounding Schneewind's version of Sidgwick, I have illustrated the exposition with quotations from Sidgwick himself, I can hardly deny that this is in fact the method Sidgwick employs. It is true that these, and many other passages in *The Methods of Ethics*, can be cited in support of the Schneewind/Rawls interpretation. Yet there is something puzzling here, for contrary passages can be quoted with equal ease. For example, on the very first page of the book, Sidgwick says that he prefers to call the subject of ethics a "study" rather than a "Science" because "it is widely thought that a Science must necessarily have some department of actual existence for its subject-matter." Rawls, surely, would say that ethics, like linguistics or other sciences, does have a "department of actual existence" as its subject – namely, our considered moral judgments. So we seem to have contradictory passages in a writer who has the reputation of being one of the most clear-headed and consistent of ethical thinkers.

The contradiction, however, is only a superficial appearance of contradiction, and Sidgwick's reputation can easily be vindicated. Although there are many passages in which Sidgwick uses arguments that look as if they are appealing to our ordinary moral judgments, pruned and refined in various ways, as a test of the validity of moral theories, an examination of the context in which these arguments appear reveals that Sidgwick uses them, not as a criterion of the truth of a theory such as utilitarianism, but as some kind of confirmation of a result independently arrived at, and in particular as an *ad hominem* argument addressed to the supporter of common sense morality. In other words, the appeal to common sense morality is in no way an appeal to a "decision-procedure for ethics." It is, rather, a means by which the utilitarian might win certain kinds of opponents over to his own views.

That the two-stage argument Schneewind describes is one kind of *ad hominem* argument can be seen by recalling the first line of the long passage on how utilitarianism might be proved (quoted above) and by considering the way in which Sidgwick continues after this passage. The first line speaks of proving utilitarianism "to a man who already holds some other moral principles," whether intuitionist or egoist. Then, continuing after the quotation breaks off, Sidgwick refers immediately to a line of argument that might be addressed to an egoist. About this line of argument I shall have more to say later, but for the moment all that needs to be said is that it has nothing at all to do with common sense morality. The upshot of this line of argument, Sidgwick believes, is that "starting with his own principle" the egoist "may be brought to accept Universal happiness or pleasure as that which is absolutely and without qualification Good or Desirable." Only after giving this summary of how the utilitarian might proceed when confronted with an egoist does Sidgwick go on to outline the two-stage argument that a utilitarian might address to an intuitionist (Sidgwick refers to the philosophical representative of common sense morality as an "intuitionist"). Here Sidgwick carefully notes that a different mode of argument is required because, "as addressed to the Intuitionist," the argument recommended for dealing with the egoist proves only that the utilitarian principle is *one* axiom of morality; it does not prove that it is the sole or supreme moral axiom. The reason for this difference lies in "the premises from which the Intuitionist starts." We must address our argument to what the intuitionist himself already accepts, if we are to win him over to utilitarianism. Commonly, the intuitionist will accept as self-evident independent moral axioms not only the utilitarian principle of rational benevolence, but also principles like Truth, Justice, and so on. Therefore:

> The Utilitarian must, in the first place, endeavour to show to the Intuitionist that the principles of Truth, Justice, etc. have only a dependent and subordinate validity: arguing either that the principle is really only affirmed by Common Sense as a general rule admitting of exceptions and qualifications, as in the case of Truth, and that we require some further principle for systematising these exceptions and qualifications; or that the fundamental notion is vague and needs further determination, as in the case of Justice; and further, that the different rules are liable to conflict with each other, and that we require some higher principle to decide the issue thus raised; and again, that the rules are differently formulated by different persons, and that these differences admit of no Intuitional solution, while they show the vagueness and ambiguity of the common moral notions to which the Intuitionist appeals. [*ME*, p. 421]

This passage could, out of context, be taken as a description of how Sidgwick intends to establish the validity of utilitarianism; as such, it would resemble an application of Rawls's "reflective equilibrium" procedure. In context, however, we can see that Sidgwick regards the argument outlined not as a means of establishing the validity of utilitarianism, but as a means of winning over to utilitarianism one who happens to hold a particular moral position, opposed to utilitarianism – namely, the philosophy of common sense morality, or intuitionism.

Whether the appeal to common sense morality is the ultimate test of the validity of utilitarianism, or an *ad hominem* argument for it, makes a fundamental difference to the nature of ethics as Sidgwick conceived it. Although Schneewind accepts that Sidgwick's arguments "are addressed... to those who take the morality of common sense to be valid and binding, at least to some extent,"[9] Schneewind does not appreciate the significance of this point, for later he writes:

> It [the utilitarian principle] is valid because it is demanded by our actual moral principles (cf. *ME* 420). In a world that was very different from ours, in which very different moral principles were commonly accepted, some other principle might be the independent first principle.[10]

This would be an accurate statement of Sidgwick's method if Sidgwick were using the reflective equilibrium procedure. Yet it is exactly what Sidgwick's appeal to common sense morality does not imply. Nothing whatsoever about the validity of a principle follows from the fact that an *ad hominem* argument may be made against a particular opponent of the principle. Moreover, what Schneewind says here would make nonsense of a point he himself makes about Sidgwick's belief in the objectivity of moral judgments. Schneewind notes that Sidgwick believes moral judgments to be objective, and as evidence cites the reason Sidgwick gives for avoiding the use of the term "moral sense" – because it "suggests a capacity for feelings which may vary from A to B without either being in error, rather than a faculty of cognition: and it appears to me fundamentally important to avoid this suggestion" (*ME*, p. 34).[11] That Sidgwick means by this more than the mere intersubjective sense of truth and falsity that is compatible with a relativistic denial of objectivity between different societies or different worlds is confirmed by the following paragraph, in which he states that "ought," in its ethical sense, applies to "rational beings as such."

This point is worth emphasizing. Sidgwick's belief in the objectivity of moral judgments is in itself enough to show that he does not go along with the idea of "reflective equilibrium," because that idea, as we have seen, does imply that if A and B live in very different "worlds" (societies?) they might espouse different ultimate ethical principles without either of them being in error: and this is the very suggestion Sidgwick thinks it "fundamentally important" to avoid.[12]

On the other hand, to appeal to common sense morality as part of an *ad hominem* argument is quite compatible with belief in objective truth in morals. Sidgwick is in effect saying to the intuitionist: "Look, if it is going to be a choice between common sense morality and utilitarianism, the latter has the advantage of being able to show that common sense morality requires an independent first principle like the principle of utility; and furthermore, the utilitarian principle systematizes and makes coherent all the diverse judgments of common sense morality." To argue in this way is to take common sense morality as valid for the purpose of the argument, but it does not commit one to accepting common sense morality in arguments with those who do not themselves accept it, and it does not debar one from holding that the principle of utility would be valid even if it were quite inconsistent with common sense morality. If there were this inconsistency, it would be much more difficult for a utilitarian to convince a supporter of common sense morality, but it would not mean that the utilitarian was wrong.

Why do Schneewind and Rawls miss the importance of the *ad hominem* nature of the argument? The reason may be a general misconception of the intentions of *The Methods of Ethics* – a misconception that appeared in print soon after the book first appeared, and has survived the intervening century despite an explicit rebuttal by Sidgwick in his preface to the second edition. This misconception Sidgwick describes as follows:

> There is, however, one fundamental misunderstanding, on which it seems desirable to say a few words. I find that more than one critic has overlooked or disregarded the account of the plan of my treatise, given in the original preface and in §5 of the introductory chapter: and has consequently supposed me to be writing as an assailant of two of the methods which I chiefly examine, and a defender of the third. Thus one of my reviewers seems to regard Book iii (on Intuitionism) as containing mere hostile criticism from the outside: another has constructed an article on the supposition that my principal object is "the suppression of Egoism": a third has gone to the length of a pamphlet under the impression (apparently) that the "main argument" of my treatise is a demonstration of Universalistic Hedonism. I am concerned to have caused so much misdirection of criticism: and I have carefully altered in this edition the passages which I perceive to have contributed to it. [*ME*, p. xx]

Alas, Sidgwick's careful alterations have been in vain. The mistaken impression of the pamphleteer is today the standard view of Sidgwick's book. Schneewind begins his article by a reference to the arguments Sidgwick uses "to establish the utilitarian principle,"[13] and Rawls, in his frequent references to Sidgwick, also appears to accept unquestioningly the view that *The Methods of Ethics* is basically an attempt to demonstrate the superiority of utilitarianism over other moral theories. Admittedly, there is no doubt that Sidgwick was a utilitarian (a term he uses interchangeably with "Universalistic Hedonism"). We would know this from his other writings, and from the autobiographical note printed in the preface to the sixth edition of *The Methods of Ethics*, even if it were not apparent from the body of that work. So the standard view is a natural one. Nevertheless, Sidgwick's deliberate intention was "to put aside temporarily the urgent need which we all feel of finding and adopting the true method of determining what we ought to do; and to consider simply what conclusions will be rationally reached if we start with certain ethical premises, and with what degree of certainty and precision" (*ME*, p. vi). This intention explains the title and structure of the book: the three "methods of ethics" Sidgwick discusses are the procedures most commonly used, both by ordinary men and philosophers, for obtaining reasoned convictions about what ought to be done, and the book is a critical exposition of these three methods. Naturally, in the course of this exposition Sidgwick is led "to discuss the considerations which should, in my opinion, be decisive in determining the adoption of ethical first principles," but, as he reiterates, "it is not my primary aim to establish such principles" (*ME*, p. 14).

So *The Methods of Ethics* is an investigatory work. No doubt, Sidgwick hoped that if he impartially examined the major methods one of them would emerge with a superior claim to validity. No doubt, too, Sidgwick expected and hoped that if one method did distinguish itself in this way, it would be the utilitarian method. Nevertheless, to see the whole work as a single-minded attempt to establish utilitarianism is to misunderstand it, and consequently to risk misunderstanding the function of the various arguments that occur in it.

The express primary aim of *The Methods of Ethics*, then, is to define and unfold the methods of ethics implicit in our ordinary moral reasoning, and to point out their relations to each other. The three methods are, of course, Egoistic Hedonism, Intuitionism, and Utilitarianism. It should be noted that although there is a reference here to "ordinary moral reasoning," this does not suggest that the validity of a moral theory depends on it being in accordance with these ordinary methods. These methods, being the most popular ones, are merely the ones that Sidgwick chose as the most likely candidates for the position of the correct method. Even if they could all be perfectly harmonized this would not mean that the resulting harmonization was necessarily valid. It might be that all the popular methods are irrational, and some quite esoteric method the only rational one.

A further difference from the reflective equilibrium model is that it is not the *results* of our ordinary moral reasoning, not our particular moral judgments, but the methods we use in reaching these judgments that Sidgwick thinks worth examining. The validity of a method would seem to depend on the self-evidence of the "primary intuition" and the soundness of the reasoning used in its application, not on whether its results match our considered moral judgments.[14]

If this is so, it is natural to ask why the book does contain so much discussion of common sense morality – for that it does contain a very detailed, even repetitious, discussion of it is undeniable. Part of the answer to this question has already been given. The discussion in chapter 3 of Book IV, entitled "The Relation of Utilitarianism to Common Sense," is an *ad hominem* argument by which a Utilitarian might try to prove the superiority of his principle to one committed to common sense morality. The far lengthier discussion which comprises almost the whole of Book III serves a different purpose. This is apparent immediately we reject the idea that Book III is one stage of an argument for utilitarianism. The aim of Book III is to examine a particular method of reaching moral conclusions – the method Sidgwick calls "Intuitionism," which is the view that we can discover what we ought to do simply by consulting our conscience, or, as it used to be called, our "Moral Faculty." The immediate outcome of this method is the set of judgments Sidgwick calls "the morality of Common Sense." So, as Sidgwick says in reviewing his survey of this morality, "I wish it to be particularly observed that I have in no case introduced my own views insofar as I am conscious of their being at all peculiar to myself: my sole object has been to make explicit the implied premises of our common moral reasoning" (*ME*, p. 338).

Still, it might be suggested, though not, I think, by those who have, in reading Sidgwick, come to feel an almost personal acquaintance with him, that Sidgwick was being less than candid in his avowals of his aims: alternatively, it might be thought that he was himself deceived about his real intentions. Yet there is evidence that neither of these possibilities was the case. The evidence comes from Sidgwick's discussion of the method of Egoistic Hedonism. As we have seen, Sidgwick's own sympathies are with the utilitarian, or universalistic hedonist method; nevertheless, his examination of the method of egoistic hedonism is not a refutation of that method, nor is it a demonstration of the superiority of utilitarianism. On the contrary, Sidgwick's final verdict in the concluding chapter of the whole book is that the aim of furthering one's own interest stands on just as rational a basis as the aim of furthering the universal interest; and that the two methods lead to incompatible results, except on the hypothesis that there is a Supreme Being who ensures that it is in our own interest to follow the universal interest (Sidgwick himself was very doubtful about the truth of this hypothesis). So, even if we disregard the author's explicit denial, it is impossible to regard *The Methods of Ethics* as an argument for utilitarianism. The most that could be said is that it is an argument for both egoistic and universalistic hedonism against intuitionism. This would be an odd aim for any book, however, and it is much more plausible to accept the view that the book is concerned to unfold the implications of the three methods, rather than to argue for any one (or two!) of them. If Sidgwick hoped by this unfolding to discover the correct method, the result is impressive testimony to his fair-mindedness, for he considers himself unable to establish the rational superiority of the utilitarian method. The result of unfolding the method happens to be that the method of intuitionism and the method of utilitarianism are shown to be reconcilable, because the judgments of common sense morality turn out to require the utilitarian principle to fall back on as an underlying self-evident first principle, and a means of settling conflicts, resolving vagueness, and so on. On the other hand, divine interference apart, the opposition between egoism and utilitarianism leaves an "ultimate and fundamental contradiction in our apparent intuitions of what is Reasonable in conduct" (*ME*, p. 508).

So Sidgwick's conclusion about egoistic hedonism is independent evidence of the intentions of his book. At the same time, it is further evidence of a fairly direct kind against the claim that Sidgwick used the method of reflective equilibrium to judge between rival theories. For while Sidgwick thought that utilitarianism coincides with intuitionism, that is, with the philosophical position based on our ordinary moral judgments, egoism remains the odd man out. Sidgwick clearly believes that egoism is, at least in some circumstances, incompatible with both utilitarianism and common sense morality (since he believes that these last two coincide, if egoism is incompatible with one it must also be incompatible with the other). Thus, Sidgwick sums up the chapter in which he discusses the compatibility of happiness and duty by saying:

> although the performance of duties towards others and the exercise of social virtue seem to be *generally* the best means to the attainment of the individual's happiness, and it is easy to exhibit this coincidence between Virtue and Happiness rhetorically and popularly; still when we carefully analyse and estimate the consequences of Virtue to the virtuous agent, it appears improbable that this coincidence is complete and universal. [*ME*, p. 175. Italics in original.]

This conclusion, as we have seen, is repeated in the concluding chapter (*ME*, pp. 503, 508) and is also brought out clearly in the autobiographical sketch in the preface to the sixth edition.

If Sidgwick were using the reflective equilibrium procedure to test moral theories, the incompatibility of egoism and common sense morality would be a decisive point against egoism. We could argue simply: the test of a moral theory is whether it matches our considered moral judgments in reflective equilibrium; egoistic hedonism is incompatible with at least some of our considered moral judgments and cannot be brought into equilibrium with them; therefore egoistic hedonism is not an acceptable moral theory. But Sidgwick does not argue in this way; indeed, he does not regard the incompatibility between egoism and our considered moral judgments even as a consideration that counts against egoism. Instead he sees the reasonableness of egoism as quite independent of the extent to which it matches our moral judgment – it is based on the plausibility of its starting point, of which Sidgwick says:

> It would be contrary to Common Sense to deny that the distinction between any one individual and any other is real and fundamental, and that consequently "I" am concerned with the quality of my existence as an individual in a sense, fundamentally important, in which I am not concerned with the quality of the existence of other individuals: and this being so, I do not see how it can be proved that this distinction is not to be taken as fundamental in determining the ultimate end of rational action for an individual. [*ME*, p. 498; see also pp. 7, 119–20, 419][15]

I hope that I have now offered sufficient evidence to convince the reader that Sidgwick does not use the reflective equilibrium procedure to test moral theories. What, then, is the significance of the coincidence of utilitarianism and common sense morality for Sidgwick, and what is his attitude to common sense morality in general? A brief discussion of these questions may help to clear up any remaining doubts about the passages that appear to favor the reflective equilibrium interpretation.

On the basis of what has already been said, the significance of the coincidence of utilitarianism and common sense morality can be stated briefly. It does not prove the truth of utilitarianism, but it does mean that utilitarianism is doubly supported. It is supported both on its own terms – that is, by the initial plausibility of its assumptions and the absence of any inconsistency or indeterminacy in their unfolding – and it receives the additional support of whatever plausibility is possessed by common sense morality, or more strictly, by the method of intuitionism. For, according to Sidgwick's account of intuitionism, any supporter of this method will have to admit that the only pertinent self-evident intuition, and the one to which all his more particular intuitions lead him, is the intuition that it is right to do whatever promotes the greatest happiness for all. Thus he will be led to become a utilitarian, though on an intuitionist basis.[16]

This is, as I have been saying, an *ad hominem* argument; nevertheless, it must be admitted that for Sidgwick it has a significance not possessed by any other parallel argument, for instance, that directed against the egoist. Sidgwick had a great deal of respect for common sense morality. He refers to it as "a marvellous product of nature, the result of long centuries of growth." At the same time, Sidgwick was sufficiently skeptical of his own primary method of testing the truth of moral theories – which was, as we shall see, based on the alleged self-evidence of certain ethical axioms – to realize that it was fallible. Accordingly, he looked to common sense morality as a safeguard against error. If an apparently self-evident moral principle has consequences at odds with common sense morality, this should be a warning to us that we may be mistaken in our intuition of self-evidence. Sidgwick stated this view clearly in an article explicitly directed to the question of how first principles are to be established in ethics:

> If we have once learnt, either from personal experience or from the history of thought, that we are liable to be mistaken in the affirmation of apparently self-evident propositions, we may surely retain this general conviction along with the special impression of the self-evidence of any proposition which we may be contemplating; and thus however strong this latter impression may be, we shall still admit our need of some further protection against the possible failure of our faculty of intuition. Such a further guarantee we may reasonably find in "general consent"; for though the protection this gives is not perfect – since there are historical examples of untrue propositions generally accepted as self-evident – it at least excludes all such error as arises from the special weaknesses and biases of individual minds, or of particular sections of the human race. A proposition which presents itself to my mind as self-evident, and is in harmony with all the rest of my intuitions relating to the same subject, and is also accepted by all other minds that have been led to contemplate it *may after all turn out to be false*: but it seems to have as high a degree of certainty as I can hope to attain under existing conditions of human thought.[17]

This passage shows well the similarities and differences between Sidgwick and Rawls. Common sense morality, representing as it does the accumulated experience of mankind, is a useful check on our intuitions of self-evident moral axioms; but even when it is in harmony with our own intuitions we may after all be mistaken. It is this possibility, which I have italicized in the original passage, that marks the distinction between the two authors – for on Rawls's view, one could not even make sense of such a possibility. For Rawls, reaching this kind of harmony is the goal of moral philosophy; it is the definition of "valid" so far as moral theories are concerned: for Sidgwick, it is the best possible insurance against error, but because our target is a moral theory that is true, and not merely in harmony with our intuitions and with common sense morality, we may still be in error.

We may summarize the prominence Sidgwick gives to common sense morality by saying that it plays three different roles: firstly, it is in itself a method of moral reasoning, though one that may be reconciled with utilitarianism; secondly, its reduction to utilitarianism is the foundation on which a utilitarian may construct an *ad hominem* argument in favor of his own principle, which is thereby doubly supported; thirdly, it is an important check on our intuitions of self-evidence about ethical first principles.[18]

III

If Sidgwick did not believe that the truth of a moral theory is shown by its success in systematizing our considered moral judgments, how did he think a moral theory could be shown to be correct?

The short and simple answer is that, as he himself states in the autobiographical sketch already referred to, he is an intuitionist. In this sketch Sidgwick tells how, under the influence first of Kant and then of Butler, he was led to see that:

> The utilitarian method – which I had learnt from Mill – could not, it seemed to me, be made coherent and harmonious without this fundamental intuition . . . the supreme rule of aiming at the general happiness, as I had come to see, must rest on a fundamental intuition, if I was to recognise it as binding at all . . . I was then a Utilitarian again, but on an Intuitional basis. [*ME*, pp. xvi–xx]

There is, however, more to be said than this simple answer reveals. Though from the point of view of what Sidgwick sometimes called "abstract philosophy" he would probably have thought that the self-evidence of the utilitarian principle was the primary reason for accepting it, Sidgwick is not content to stop at abstract philosophy. He is much more interested in the sort of argument that can win over opponents, and in his book he considers various arguments by which a proponent of one of the methods of ethics might try to convince a proponent of another. We have already seen how he thinks a utilitarian might demonstrate the superiority of utilitarianism to a supporter of common sense morality. What, though, would a utilitarian say to someone who had no great respect for our ordinary judgments?

In the short chapter entitled "The Proof of Utilitarianism," before he begins the *ad hominem* argument against the proponent of common sense morality, Sidgwick indicates what a utilitarian might say against a different kind of opponent. What he says there, however, is brief, because many of the points have come up in earlier chapters, to which the reader's attention is directed. The argument needs to be put together from these earlier chapters.

We begin with the search for "real ethical axioms – intuitive propositions of real clearness and certainty" (*ME*, p. 373). This search is in fact the final stage of the unfolding of the intuitionist method, after the intuitions with which we started – those of common sense morality – have been shown to lack the status of self-evident axioms. Putting aside those apparently self-evident principles which turn out, on examination, to be nothing more than tautologies (e.g. "It is right that the lower parts of our nature should be governed by the higher") Sidgwick finds three, and only three, genuine axioms. The first is an axiom of impartiality, in some sense: "whatever action any of us judges to be right for himself, he implicitly judges to be right for all similar persons in similar circumstances" (*ME*, p. 379).[19] The second axiom is an element in the idea of rational self-interest, or prudence: it is the idea of impartial concern for all parts of our conscious life, so that we do not prefer a smaller present good to a greater future good, once any difference in the certainty of gaining the good has been taken into account. This, Sidgwick says, is an axiom about the good for any single individual; but when we consider the notion of universal good, we obtain the "self-evident principle that the good of any one individual is of no more importance, from the point of view (if I may say so) of the Universe, than the good of any other." Here we have more or less reached the third axiom, which is also stated as "it is evident to me that as a rational being I am bound to aim at good generally, ... not merely at a particular part of it" (*ME*, p. 382).

It is to this third axiom that Sidgwick refers when, in the chapter on the "proof" of utilitarianism, he considers to what extent the principle of utilitarianism might be proved to the egoistic hedonist. Sidgwick's point is that:

> When ... the Egoist puts forward, implicitly or explicitly, the proposition that his happiness or pleasure is Good, not only *for him* but from the point of view of the Universe ... it then becomes relevant to point out to him that *his* happiness cannot be a more important part of Good, taken universally, than the equal happiness of any other person. And thus, starting with his own principle, he may be brought to accept Universal happiness or pleasure as that which is absolutely and without qualification Good or Desirable: as an end, therefore, to which the action of a reasonable agent as such ought to be directed. [*ME*, pp. 420–1. Italics in original.]

On the other hand, Sidgwick does not think it possible to prove utilitarianism to an egoist who "confines himself to stating his conviction that he ought to take his own happiness or pleasure as his ultimate end"; under these circumstances "there seems no opening for any line of reasoning to lead him to Universalistic Hedonism as a first principle; it cannot be proved that the difference between his own happiness and another's happiness is not *for him* all-important" (*ME*, p. 420. Italics in original).

This seems to me an important and correct statement. It is analogous with R. M. Hare's mode of argument in *Freedom and Reason*. The analogy may be brought out by putting Sidgwick's point in this way: if a person is concerned only with his own interest, and is not concerned to do what is good in a universal sense, there is no argument we can produce which will force him to concern himself with the interests of others; but if he claims to be aiming at what is morally good, then because of the universalizability inherent in this claim, we can argue that he cannot, consistently, give greater consideration to his own interests, simply on the ground that they are *his* interests, than he gives to the interests of others.[20]

Against the egoistic hedonist, no more can be done, which is why, in his concluding chapter, Sidgwick recognizes that egoism and utilitarianism are conflicting fundamental intuitions, and the egoist can avoid the "proof" of utilitarianism by limiting his concern to what is the rational ultimate end for himself, thereby disclaiming any concern for what is good in a universal sense (*ME*, 497–8).

What if the utilitarian's opponent is not even an egoistic hedonist? The universalizing argument just discussed leads to universalistic hedonism (as distinct from some broad utilitarian position that would include varieties of ideal utilitarianism) only if it is already admitted that happiness or pleasure is the only thing ultimately good and desirable. Once this is admitted, the question is merely whether the goal is one's own happiness, or that of every sentient being (no intermediate position having the status of a self-evident axiom). But what if the hedonistic assumption is denied? Can an opponent be brought to admit it?

On this issue Sidgwick refers us back to Book III, chapter 14, the chapter entitled "Ultimate Good." The argument of this chapter follows on directly from that of the previous chapter, in which the three self-evident ethical axioms were stated. At the conclusion of that chapter, Sidgwick thought, the rigorous demand for really self-evident intuitions had led the intuitionist to a kind of utilitarianism, but only in the broad sense of a principle which judges actions by their tendency to promote "Universal Good" rather than some specific form of universal good, like happiness. Now Sidgwick faces the question whether only happiness is ultimately good in itself. He explicitly rejects the standard utilitarian argument for this conclusion, attributed to Bentham and Mill, which is based on the psychological theory that no one ever does desire anything but happiness. Sidgwick does not think this theory true. What other arguments remain?

The way in which the intuitionist is led from the general notion of universal good to its specific hedonist form illustrates Sidgwick's approach to ultimate questions. The chapter contains both argument and appeals to intuition. The role of the argument is to support the intuition Sidgwick feels to be correct, and in particular to explain why apparently contrary intuitions are not to be taken at face value. In this way the idea that virtue is good in itself, apart from its effects on consciousness, is dismissed, and ultimate good is narrowed down to nothing other than "Desirable Consciousness." This notion still includes more than happiness, since it might be said that knowing the truth, or contemplating beauty or virtue, are desirable forms of consciousness independently of their tendency to promote happiness. Sidgwick does not think this view can be refuted by any decisive argument, but he regards it as a view which, to give his own characteristic phrase, "ought not to commend itself to the sober judgment of reflective persons." To persuade the reader of this he appeals firstly to the reader's own intuitive judgment "after due consideration of the question when fairly placed before it," and secondly to a comparison of the judgments of common sense. In this second appeal, argument again has its place in showing how the superficial aversion common sense sometimes has to regarding happiness as the sole ultimate end of right conduct is compatible with a real acceptance of happiness as the sole end. The appeal to common sense here is, again, not a *test* of the validity of hedonism – if it were, then this appeal alone would be decisive, and the prior appeal to the reader's intuitions would have been superfluous – but is based on the assumption that common sense morality represents the accumulated experience of mankind, and so is worthy of considerable respect.

A final argument for universal hedonism is that if happiness is regarded not as the sole ultimate good, but as only one among ultimate goods, then we need, in practice, to compare and balance these goods with each other, and how we are to go about doing this is a problem to which no one has produced a coherent answer.[21]

Since my present concern is with the method Sidgwick uses for testing the validity of a moral theory, rather than with the arguments for particular theories to be found in his book, I will not discuss the merits of the arguments for utilitarianism. What I have tried to show is that though, for Sidgwick, the ultimate appeal is to the carefully considered intuitive judgment of the reader, this is a very different procedure from one which aims at matching a moral theory with the considered moral judgments either of the reader, or of some widely accepted moral consensus. Even if everyone should agree that the fundamental principle of utilitarianism is a clear and certain rational intuition, this would not, on Sidgwick's view, actually establish the truth of utilitarianism. Agreement, no matter how widespread it may be, is not a criterion for the truth or validity of a normative theory. Sidgwick would admit that, in the end, we have nothing to fall back on other than careful consideration of whether some fundamental principle really is intuitively clear and certain (though we may be able to support our intuitions to some extent by a comparison with common sense morality), but he does not *define* validity for a moral theory in terms of agreement with our ultimate intuitions or in terms of a match with our particular judgments. Therefore he is not committed to the kind of subjectivism that is consequent upon any such definition of validity for a moral theory.

IV

How are we, as moral philosophers, to decide between the two ways of doing moral philosophy represented by Sidgwick and Rawls? This question can appear mind-boggling, for it requires us to establish the criteria for the correct choice of criteria for the correct choice of moral theory. Yet I think we can come to a decision by reflection on what it is that we, as moral philosophers, are trying to do.

The historical task of moral philosophy has been to develop theories that serve as guides to conduct. So long as there are grounds for hoping that discussion, argument, and the careful consideration of moral theories can help us to decide how to act, the importance of this historical task cannot be denied. Sidgwick, obviously, was engaged on this task. Can the same be said for Rawls? In a sense, yes. Rawls clearly intends his theory to be a guide to conduct; yet at the same time, his use of the reflective equilibrium idea means that he is on the verge of slipping off into an altogether different activity, that of systematizing the considered moral judgments of some unspecified moral consensus. This latter task, while it may be of some interest, is, like the linguistic and scientific investigations on which it is modelled, a descriptive task from which, without supplementation from other sources, no normative or action-guiding consequences can be derived. We cannot test a normative theory by the extent to which it accords with the moral judgments people ordinarily make. Insofar as Rawls frequently does seem to be testing his own theory in this way, the theory fails to be normative and Rawls cannot be regarded as pursuing the same task as Sidgwick and most other moral philosophers.[22]

Now it is true that Rawls does not really propose that normative theories should be tested by comparison with the moral judgments people ordinarily make. He says, as we have seen, that he appeals directly to the reader's own considered moral judgments. The reader's own considered moral judgments are relevant for normative purposes. If the reader simply cannot accept a moral judgment that follows from a moral theory, he must modify the theory, or else drop it altogether. Otherwise he is being inconsistent. To this extent the reflective equilibrium method is sound. But why should the reader be unable to accept any consequence of a theory that is based on a fundamental axiom that seems to him clear and undeniable? This is a question which Rawls never asks, and he never asks it because from the start he thinks of moral philosophy in the wrong way. Thus he says: "Now one may think of moral philosophy at first (and I stress the provisional nature of this view) as the attempt to describe our moral capacity" (*ATOJ*, p. 46). Even if this is only provisional, it is a misleading provisional starting point. It leads to the assumption that we have a certain moral capacity, and that at least some of the moral judgments we make will, after consideration, remain as fixed points against which theories can be tested. Why should we not rather make the opposite assumption, that all the particular moral judgments we intuitively make are likely to derive from discarded religious systems, from warped views of sex and bodily functions, or from customs necessary for the survival of the group in social and economic circumstances that now lie in the distant past? In which case, it would be best to forget all about our particular moral judgments, and start again from as near as we can get to self-evident moral axioms.

Rawls could maintain that even this last hypothesis is compatible with "reflective equilibrium." It is simply the limiting case, in which there are no moral judgments that survive consideration, and so there are no considered moral judgments. Again, this is strictly correct, but it is a result that one is very unlikely to arrive at if one starts off by thinking about moral philosophy in the way that Rawls suggests. We are unlikely to arrive at it because we start from a position in which we are trying to produce a theory that will match our moral judgments; but there is another reason as well. We have all been making moral judgments about particular cases for many years before we begin moral philosophy. Particular views have been inculcated into us by parents, teachers and society from childhood. Many of them we act upon every day – telling the truth, not stealing when we have the opportunity to do so, and so on. These judgments sink deep, and become habitual. By contrast, when we read Sidgwick for the first time we are suddenly called upon to decide whether certain fundamental moral principles, which we may never have explicitly thought about before, are self-evident. If it is then pointed out to us that this fundamental moral principle is incompatible with some of the particular moral judgments we are accustomed to making, and that therefore we must either reject the fundamental principle, or else abandon our particular judgments, surely the odds are stacked against the fundamental principle. Most of us are familiar with lingering guilt feelings that occur when we do something that we are quite certain is right, but which we once thought to be wrong. These feelings make us reluctant to abandon particular moral views we hold, but they in no way justify these views.

The reflective equilibrium conception of moral philosophy, then, by leading us to think of our particular moral judgments as data against which moral theories are to be tested, is liable to mislead in two ways: first, it slides easily into the view that moral theories are to be tested against the moral judgments made by some group or consensus, and no normative significance can be attached to the judgments of any group; second, even when the "reflective equilibrium" method says no more than that one cannot consistently accept a moral theory while holding particular judgments incompatible with it, it puts this truth in a way that tends to give excessive weight to our particular moral judgments.

That these dangers are real enough is evidenced by the great weight placed on particular intuitive judgments, both those of an assumed consensus and those of the author himself, in *A Theory of Justice*. It seems preferable to proceed as Sidgwick did: search for undeniable fundamental axioms; build up a moral theory from them; and use particular moral judgments as supporting evidence, or as a basis for *ad hominem* arguments, but never so as to suggest that the validity of the theory is determined by the extent to which it matches them.

Notes

1 John Rawls, *A Theory of Justice* (Oxford: Clarendon Press; Cambridge, MA: Harvard University Press, 1972). Hereinafter abbreviated in the text to *ATOJ*.

2 John Rawls, "Outline of a Decision Procedure for Ethics," *Philosophical Review*, 60 (1951), pp. 177–97.

3 This analogy was explicit in "Outline of a Decision for Ethics," and Rawls states that what he now says is in accord with that (pp. 46n., 579n.). He now refers as well to Quine's view of justification, though without explicitly comparing his own to it (p. 579n.).

4 R. M. Hare reaches the same conclusion in his "Rawls' Theory of Justice – I," *Philosophical Quarterly*, 23 (1973), pp. 144–7.

5 Perhaps there is room for some doubt about this subjectivist interpretation. Certainly, on pp. 516–17, Rawls appears to claim objectivity for his theory. A careful reading of this passage suggests, however, that it is only the elimination of personal bias, and not real objectivity that Rawls has in mind here.

6 Hare, "Rawls' Theory of Justice – I," has pointed out how frequent and deep-rooted the appeal to consensus is for Rawls.

7 *ATOJ*, p. 51n. The full reference for Schneewind's article is *Archiv für Geschichte der Philosophie*, 45 (1963), pp. 137–56.

8 *The Methods of Ethics*, 7th edn. (London: Macmillan, 1907), p. 419. Hereinafter abbreviated in the text to *ME*. The sixth and seventh editions are practically identical; they differ considerably from the first edition, but the differences are not crucial for present purposes.

9 "First Principles and Common Sense Morality," p. 140. This is true only of *some* of Sidgwick's arguments – not, of course, of those addressed to the egoist.

10 "First Principles and Common Sense Morality," p. 150.

11 The passage is quoted by Schneewind, "First Principles and Common Sense Morality," p. 150.

12 Rawls seems to accept the fact that reflective equilibrium implies this kind of relativism. See the reference to Quine mentioned in n. 3 above.

13 "First Principles and Common Sense Morality," p. 137; but for Schneewind's present view, see "Sidgwick and the Cambridge Moralists" in *The Monist*, 58 (1974), pp. 371–404.

14 It has been suggested to me that if we interpret the reflective equilibrium model so that it is not only our particular judgments that the moral theory is to match, but also our ordinary methods of reasoning, Sidgwick and Rawls are not so far apart after all. Rawls himself appears to be thinking primarily of a match with our particular intuitive judgments (*ATOJ*, pp. 19, 49), and indeed the suggested alteration would cause difficulties for his conception, since our ordinary method of reasoning might itself be a candidate moral theory, and would then be measured up against itself – an unfair advantage, we might well think. In any case, though, the difference pointed out in the previous paragraph still stands, and it is crucial to the nature of the enterprise.

It is, incidentally, the methods of reasoning, and not particular judgments, that are the "primary intuitions" mentioned in the passage from Sidgwick quoted by Rawls, *ATOJ*, p. 51n.

15 Schneewind recognizes that "Sidgwick can see no rational way of proving one of these principles [egoistic and universalistic hedonism] to the exclusion of the other" but claims that this shows how little weight Sidgwick is prepared to put on intuition unsupported by considerations like the systematization of our ordinary moral judgments. Schneewind goes on to point out that other philosophers, like Butler and Whewell, were prepared to say that we can simply *see* conscience to be superior in authority to self-love ("First Principles and Common Sense Morality," pp. 155–6). It is true that Sidgwick does not make this move against egoistic hedonism, but that is because, as is evident from the passage just quoted, he thought the "intuition" of the rationality of egoism was as self-evident as any other. What Schneewind fails to address himself to is why, if Sidgwick places great weight on the systematization argument, the superiority of utilitarianism in this respect is not enough to oust the rival principle. While Sidgwick does, as Schneewind notes, think that egoism and common sense morality are compatible in many circumstances, it cannot be denied that he thought that this match breaks down in a way that the match between utilitarianism and common sense morality does not – otherwise how would one explain the fact that egoism is the odd man out in the concluding chapter?

16 On this, see the discussion of Sidgwick's own position, Section III below.

17 "The Establishment of Ethical First Principles," *Mind*, 4 (1879), p. 108. (The italics are mine.) For a recent statement of a similar position, see R. M. Hare, "The Argument from Received Opinion" in Hare, *Essays on Philosophical Method* (London: Macmillan, 1971).

18   There is also a fourth role for common sense morality in *ME*, which is less relevant to our purposes: since Sidgwick believes common sense morality to be not only the result of the accumulation of practical wisdom over the centuries, but also, in its essentials, "unconsciously utilitarian," common sense morality can serve the utilitarian as a valuable, though imperfect, guide to the promotion of the general happiness.

19   Sidgwick takes this axiom from earlier writers, including Clarke and Kant; it also resembles Hare's principle of universalizability: see Hare, *Freedom and Reason* (London: Oxford University Press, 1965), especially chapter 2.

20   In view of this parallel, it is not surprising that Hare should now acknowledge a much closer connection between his own position and utilitarianism than had previously been recognized: see "Wrongness and Harm" in *Essays on the Moral Concepts* (London: Macmillan, 1972); cf. *Freedom and Reason*, chapter 7. J. L. Mackie has convinced me, however, that Sidgwick's argument is limited to those who try to justify their conduct in terms of objective *goodness*; it does not hold for those who claim a deontological justification for their conduct, expressed in terms of the moral "ought." This is because "Everyone ought to further his or her own interests exclusively," held not as a kind of laissez-faire theory for bringing about the universal good, but as a theory of right conduct, is universalizable. A person who holds this position is not committed to saying anything about objective goodness at all. He may even deny that it is meaningful to talk of goodness except in the sense of "good for someone."

G. E. Moore attacked Sidgwick's argument on the grounds that no intelligible meaning can be given to the idea of "good for him" which distinguishes it from Universal Good (*Principia Ethica* [Cambridge University Press, 1903], pp. 96–105); but this is surely a perverse refusal to understand an expression with a perfectly clear sense. Thomas Nagel's *The Possibility of Altruism* (Oxford: Clarendon Press, 1970) appears to be based on a similar denial of the intelligibility of goodness in any subjective sense. As Nagel says on p. 90: "The principle behind altruism is that values must be objective, and that any which appear subjective must be associated with others that are not." The difference between Moore and Nagel, on the one hand, and Sidgwick, on the other, is that only Sidgwick admits that the use of the argument against egoism is conditional on the egoist attempting to justify his position in terms of objective values.

21   This may have been true when Sidgwick wrote, but today it is perhaps the least convincing of his points. Both Rawls in *ATOJ* and Brian Barry in *Political Argument* (London: Routledge & Kegan Paul, 1965), pp. 3–8, have shown how it is possible to deal coherently with values as different from each other as justice and welfare.

22   On this point see R. M. Hare, "The Argument From Received Opinion," in Hare, *Essays on Philosophical Method* (London: Macmillan, 1971). See also n. 4 above.

Part Two

The Role of Philosophers

Three

Philosophers are Back on the Job

While watching Tom Stoppard's play *Jumpers* – recently performed on Broadway – I wondered what the audience, consisting predominantly of people outside professional philosophy, were making of it. They were surely missing a few philosophical "in" jokes, but that did not matter. It might be more perplexing, I thought, to be unable to judge how close to reality Stoppard's portrayal of philosophers in a modern university had come. The play's central character, George Moore, is a professor of moral philosophy who spends most of the play trying to write a lecture he must deliver on the topic: "Man – good, bad or indifferent?" Is the lecture, which we hear him dictate to his patient secretary, as wild a parody of academic philosophy as the vice-chancellor's team of gymnasts from which the play takes its name?

Many of those in the audience, had they pondered this, would have had to admit that they know less about philosophy than they know about almost any other academic discipline. We all studied history and physics in high school, and although we might not have the faintest idea of the kind of work that is being done by researchers in these fields now, their general aim is straightforward enough. But what is the aim of philosophy? The origin of the word suggests that the philosopher is one who loves wisdom – but doesn't everybody? And what does the philosopher do to manifest his special love of wisdom?

Some think that today philosophy is a study of the wisdom of the past. Philosophers, according to this conception of the subject, are all long dead,

First published in the *New York Times Magazine* (July 7, 1974), pp. 6–7, 17–20.

except perhaps for rare specimens to be found in Parisian cafes or among the Yaqui Indians. Those who teach philosophy in the universities are not philosophers themselves. They try merely (merely?) to pass on the wisdom of the philosophers to each new generation of students.

Maybe *Jumpers* will do something to dispel this fallacy. George Moore is trying to solve philosophical problems, and it is clear that he must answer them himself, by constructing an argument that leads to a conclusion one way or the other, rather than by reporting what someone else said about the matter long ago. This is the central philosophical activity: attempting to construct a solution to a problem (although the title of Moore's lecture poses a broader issue, and one more closely tied in with matters of fact, than most of the problems philosophers discuss).

Of course, the central philosophical problems are ancient, and many of the philosophical "greats" have had something to say about them. This something may be worth discussing, if only to see why it is inadequate. Courses on Plato, Aristotle, Descartes, Hume, and Kant still make up a large part of what is taught in university philosophy departments; but the primary concern is with unsolved problems, and the history of philosophy is important to most philosophers not for its own sake, but because it may help us with these problems.

Why is it that ancient philosophical problems remain unsolved? Why is it that what Aristotle wrote about ethics is still of interest to the student of moral philosophy, while the budding zoologist, say, can safely ignore the same author's writings on animals. And why is it that the much-vaunted "revolutions" in English-speaking philosophy that have occurred in the present century have been unable to clear up the old problems finally?

A brief answer to the first of these queries is that philosophical problems are just those residual problems that we are left with when we have answered all the problems that can be answered by the discovery of new facts. Physics, for example, was a branch of philosophy ("natural philosophy") until it became possible to solve its problems by experiment and observation. Philosophical problems require reasoned argument, not the assembling of new information. Our knowledge has expanded greatly since Aristotle, but our reasoning powers have not.

How can there be problems that would still be unsolved even if we knew all the relevant facts? Perhaps any problems that seemed to persist would not be real problems, but some kind of misconception or illusion? The two aforementioned "revolutions" – logical positivism and linguistic analysis – are variations on this theme.

The logical positivists thought that any utterance that could not, even in principle, be verified by some observation was meaningless. The task of philosophy was to expose the unverifiable gibberish of the traditional metaphysicians for what it is, extract anything that could be verified and hand that over to the scientists to test, discarding all the rest on the garbage heap of history. As A. J. Ayer wrote in *Language, Truth and Logic*, a book that served as a kind of manifesto for logical positivism, all the philosopher can do is provide definitions. Presumably, though, this could only be done for a limited time before we had all the definitions we were likely to need. No doubt philosophers would then find something other than philosophy to occupy themselves with.

Logical positivism was a hard-headed movement that looked to physics as a model of clarity and progress and wished to imitate its methods. Its attitude to the concepts embedded in ordinary language was uncompromising: They had to become scientific, or go.

After a time it became clear that ordinary concepts would not vanish at the invocation of the verification principle; and philosophers, led by Ludwig Wittgenstein, whom the positivists had previously regarded as one of their guiding spirits, began to accept that there are areas in which statements may be meaningful even if they are not verifiable. This the positivists could hardly deny, since it was now a commonplace that the verification principle was itself unverifiable.

The next major philosophical movement, linguistic analysis or "ordinary-language philosophy," grew out of this objection to logical positivism. The problem with which it started was: If the meaning of an utterance is not to be found in the observable states of affairs that would verify or falsify it, where is meaning to be found? Ordinary-language philosophy took its answer from Wittgenstein's view that the meaning of a term is to be found in the way it is used in a language, and the role that language plays in what Wittgenstein called a "form of life." (Wittgenstein himself, however, became contemptuous of the method of doing philosophy that he had inspired. Yet his influence has survived its demise. Since his death in 1951, his work has been subject to a fresh examination and his ideas are still influential, particularly in such areas as philosophy of the social sciences and philosophy of religion.)

So philosophers began to pay more attention to how words are used. In its moderate form, all this movement claimed was that such attention would enable us to understand what was really problematical and what was a mere linguistic confusion in philosophical discussions. Soon, though, a more extreme position became influential. Once we understood how ordinary language functioned, some philosophers said, we could see that, far from needing the ruthless reform the logical positivists had wanted to impose on it, ordinary language was perfectly all right as it was. All that was needed was a careful analysis that would reveal the subtle nuances of concepts like knowledge, truth, goodness, freedom, God and so on. Everything that earlier philosophers had thought to be a philosophical problem was now seen by this new school of philosophy to be no more than a confusion resulting from the misuse of ordinary language. For instance, the ancient controversy over whether we have free will was "dissolved" by the observation that we may properly say of the smiling bridegroom embracing his sweetheart that he marries "of his own free will." Since there is a proper use for the term (a "paradigm case," as it was called), to deny that there is free will must be to misuse the term; and since meaning was held to depend on use, anyone who misused a term was changing its meaning, and perhaps emptying it of any meaning at all. Philosophical problems, it was held, arose when words with clear meanings in their ordinary contexts were used outside their normal habitat.

By now it is apparent to most philosophers that the standard philosophical problems have not been dissolved by the linguistic analysts. After we have distinguished, as Moore does in *Jumpers* and real-life philosophers have done in articles and books, between knowledge in the sense of having-experience-of, and knowledge in the sense of being-acquainted-with, and knowledge in the sense of comprehending truths, there still remains the skeptic's old question: Since we might always be mistaken, can we ever rightly claim to know anything? And however much a bridegroom may smile, if we discover a complete causal explanation of his behavior on the basis of which we could have predicted his decision to marry, we will not be able to think of that decision as a decision made "of his own free will" in the way we did formerly.

The failure of ordinary-language philosophy to dissolve major philosophical problems, coupled with growing unease about accounting for the meaning of an expression in terms of its use, led philosophers to look elsewhere for solutions to their problems. Abused by leftists like Marcuse, who regarded it as a bourgeois ideology that protected the status quo from criticism, and deserted by others who simply thought it trivial by comparison with the momentous events of the sixties, ordinary-language philosophy passed away unmourned, although no clear solution had been found to the basic problem of meaning which had given it its impetus.

The departure of linguistic analysis brought a number of changes in the philosophical world. Most striking is the change of style. In this respect *Jumpers* is already out of date. In the heyday of linguistic analysis, philosophy was, for those who had acquired the taste, something to be savored, like a wine that was pleasing only to the trained palate of the connoisseur. A satisfying discussion might consist of a few people puzzling away at what we mean when we say of someone, "He is in pain," and offering each other new tidbits like, "If I have a toothache after the pain-killer wears off, can I say that it is the same toothache I had before?"

The center of the philosophical world at this time was undoubtedly Oxford, and the philosophical mannerisms that were carried by Oxford graduates to America and the British Commonwealth reflected the urbane discussions that took place over dinner at Oxford high tables, where wit and style are highly prized. Today Oxford has changed. Although the ripples it sent out a few years ago have not quite died away on distant shores, Oxford philosophers are again grappling with philosophical issues directly, rather than via the subtleties of ordinary language.

In any case, Oxford no longer sets the style for other philosophers. There are now a number of important philosophy departments rather than a single leading university. If the philosophical world has a center at all, it is in the northeastern United States, somewhere between Harvard and Princeton; but the pre-eminence of this region lies mainly in its high density of fine philosophers, and equally talented figures can be found more widely dispersed elsewhere.

Because there are more philosophers in America than anywhere else, Oxford's loss of pre-eminence means that for the first time in the history of the subject, there is more important new work being done here than anywhere else in the world. It is the American journals – like Columbia University's *Journal of Philosophy*, and Cornell's *Philosophical Review* – that are setting the trends, and not the British journal *Mind*, which used to be *the* place to be published in the golden age of linguistic philosophy.

So the old Oxford elegance has given way to a characteristic American bluntness. It is a refreshing change. There is far more hard argument than there used to be. There is also, however, far more specialization, and one result of attempts to make philosophy more exact is that large areas of it now assume a level of knowledge of technical terms, definitions, and methods of notation that can be acquired only by an extensive reading of the related literature. Moreover, there is a tendency for a new approach to develop its own terminology and its own literature, based on the work of some leading figure, who will be a professor at one of the major universities. Adherents of the same approach have no difficulty in understanding each other, but it becomes difficult to keep up with several of these "schools" simultaneously, and so communication problems arise. The effect of this is to make a good deal of recent work in philosophy inaccessible not only to the general public, but to undergraduates studying philosophy as well.

So it is difficult, if not impossible, to give a short, simple account of the work that is now being done in subdivisions like philosophy of language, epistemology, metaphysics, philosophy of mind, and many of the other areas in which philosophers are actively pursuing solutions to old and new problems. Fortunately, however, this technical style does not dominate all philosophy. For those who want the subject to have something to say to people outside academic life, there is ample compensation for the inaccessibility of some areas in the resurgence of interest in the side of philosophy most closely connected with problems that nonphilosophers also face: moral philosophy, or ethics, and political philosophy. In reviving these subjects, philosophers have not, by and large, succumbed to the temptation of making their work appear more profound by developing an esoteric terminology or incorporating superfluous logical formulas.

Today it already seems strange that such obviously important subjects as ethics and political philosophy should recently have been in need of revival. Yet 20 years ago these subjects were the ones at which the positivists had delivered a stunning blow: Since moral judgments could not be verified, it was thought that they could not be true or false; at most, they were expressions of emotional attitudes. This view, known as "emotivism," tended to discount the value of serious reasoning about ethical questions. Building on earlier arguments that we cannot derive judgments of value from judgments of fact, the emotivists claimed that we can reason only about the latter, and that once disagreements over matters of fact have been cleared away, any ethical disagreement that remains depends on attitudes which, like matters of taste, are personal and not based on considerations that can properly be reasoned or argued about. Since, then, fundamental ethical disagreements would not yield to the characteristic philosophical methods of analysis, reason and argument, all the moral philosopher could do was to discuss the meaning of moral terms and the nature of moral language. This, at least, was supposedly a morally neutral activity. To get involved in any other questions in ethics or political philosophy, one would have had to introduce value judgments, and since these were merely expressions of one's own emotional attitudes, it was thought improper to allow them to intrude into a respectable academic discipline.

For a time it became a platitude that "the job of the moral philosopher is not that of the moralist." C. D. Broad expressed a widely accepted view when he wrote in "Ethics and the History of Philosophy": "Moral philosophers, as such, have no special information not available to the general public about what is right and what is wrong; nor have they any call to undertake those hortatory functions which are so adequately performed by clergymen, politicians, leader-writers...." Even a man as committed to moral and political philosophy as Russell felt constrained to say that when he wrote on these questions he was writing as an ordinary citizen and not as a philosopher. By denying themselves the most stimulating sections of ethics in this way, moral philosophers turned their field into a minor province of ordinary-language philosophy.

Political philosophy, too, seemed headed for extinction. What had formerly been thought to be political philosophy could now be divided, it was held, into two subjects, neither suitable for philosophers: moral judgments applied to the political arena (excluded for the same reason that value judgments were excluded from moral philosophy); and questions of fact about the consequences of various social and political arrangements (suitable topics for political scientists, sociologists, and futurologists generally, but not for philosophers). Again, all that was left for the philosopher was the analysis of political terms like "authority," "obligation," "legitimate government" and so on. As Peter Laslett wrote in an introduction to an influential collection of articles that appeared in 1956: "For the moment, anyway, political philosophy is dead."

The first sign that death might be temporary came with the decline of emotivism, a decline which paralleled that of the overall positivism that had made emotivism so popular. Emotivism was not overthrown suddenly, and it still has some adherents today, but a steadily growing number of books and articles suggesting that there is more to morality than the expression of emotional attitudes began to appear.

There were strong grounds for discontent with the idea that morality is just a matter of taste, or nonrational attitude. If I say that it is wrong for those with plenty to allow others short of food to starve, I am not merely expressing my dislike of allowing people to starve, as I might express my dislike of gin. Maybe moral judgments are not verifiable; maybe they are not even true or false as statements of fact are; nevertheless, they are still based on reason, and we can argue about them in a way in which it would be pointless to argue about whether we like the taste of gin. Recognizing this, philosophers began to reconsider the structure of ethical argument and the part that logic and reason play in it.

Of particular importance in this reconsideration was the revival of an idea that goes back to Kant and ultimately to the Biblical Golden Rule – the idea that an ethical judgment should be universal in form, so that if I claim that I'm morally justified in my actions toward you, I must be prepared to allow that you would be similarly justified if our positions were reversed. Although the significance and interpretation of this idea are still controversial, it was a first step away from the position that when we discuss moral issues "anything goes" and no one's opinion is any better than anyone else's.

Moral philosophers do not agree on the role of reason in moral argument, but there is now a general consensus for a view of ethics that, while in no sense a return to traditional ideas of absolute moral laws written up in heaven for all to see, does make a distinction between sound and unsound argument, and so allows us to claim that in discussing moral questions we are doing more than expressing arbitrary preferences.

By going beyond emotivism, philosophers made it possible for themselves to bring the scrutiny of real moral issues within the scope of moral philosophy.

The impetus that actually brought them to do this on a large scale, however, came from outside the profession. Suddenly issues like racial equality, human rights, the morality of war, and the justifiability of disobeying the law became matters of public concern. This and the related pressure of student demands for "relevant" courses seem to have been decisive in breaking down the earlier, more restricted view of moral and political philosophy. Many teachers of philosophy, especially the younger ones, were more than willing to go along with the students. They were bored with analyzing moral terms. They were inclined to be politically radical, and they wanted to connect their professional activities with broader social goals. Traditionally, moral and political philosophers had written about the issues now in the public spotlight. The obvious thing for philosophers to do, therefore, was to drop their neutral stance and see if they had anything useful to say about these issues.

Old habits die hard, and for a time it looked as if philosophy did not have much to contribute after all. Lengthy articles began to appear on civil disobedience, for instance, but the articles rarely got beyond discussing how the concept should be defined. Only gradually did assessments of the moral arguments on this and other controversial issues gain acceptability in the learned journals. Once this happened, however, interest grew quickly. By 1971 it had become so keen that a new journal, *Philosophy and Public Affairs*, was created to promote the philosophical discussion of matters of public concern, and to bridge the gap that exists between philosophers and those in other disciplines, or in no academic discipline at all, who are working on questions that raise philosophical issues. The journal has maintained a high level of discussion from the start, publishing articles on such topics as the morality of war and responsibility for war crimes, civil disobedience, the obligations of the affluent to the starving, preferential hiring and compensatory discrimination for disadvantaged groups, freedom of expression, the nature of justice, the problem of "getting your hands dirty" in politics, and a whole spate of articles and replies on the morality of abortion (with some provocative sidelights on infanticide as well).

All this has shown that many problems that have been well worked over have by no means been worked out. One might think, for example, that so much has been said about equality that nothing new could possibly turn up; but the discussions of preferential hiring and compensatory discrimination show that there are still implications of our ideas of equality waiting to be unraveled and discussed. The same is true of many other issues, especially the heated question of abortion, a question about which only a few philosophers have appreciated that the crucial issue is not, as many people assume, "When does the fetus become a human being?" but rather, "What are the characteristics of a being that make it wrong to kill that being?" It is by no means obvious that being a member of the species *Homo sapiens* is what counts in the answer to this second question. Sentience, or even a certain measure of self-awareness, might be more appropriate characteristics to choose. In any case, this deeper approach to the question opens a new line of investigation that has been substantially overlooked by both philosophers and nonphilosophers until quite recently.

Another indication of the new strength of moral and political philosophy is the extraordinary reception that greeted the publication of John Rawls's new book, *A Theory of Justice*, in 1971. The book immediately became the most discussed single item on the philosophical scene, a position it continues to hold. Of course, by the standards of philosophical publishing there had been unusual advance publicity. The author is a Harvard professor, and many of his former students are now in philosophy departments throughout the country. The core of the theory the book proposes had already appeared in articles in the journals and had been widely argued about. Early versions of the book had been circulated in mimeographed form to friends and critics. None of this, however, would have been enough to make the book the philosophical best seller it has been, had there not been great interest in the topic, and no major new work prior to *A Theory of Justice* on which that interest could focus.

The early rave reviews that appeared in magazines and newspapers when the book first appeared have now given way to more sober and much more critical studies in the journals, but there is no doubt that the merits of Rawls's theory will be debated for some time to come. There is already a long bibliography for the Rawls scholar to keep up with and it is growing fast. In some respects all this is unfortunate, since the book does not represent moral and political philosophy at its best. It has many good things in it, but it is so long, and the basic themes are so often repeated and qualified in so many different ways, that it is difficult to grasp as a whole, and consequently difficult to teach to undergraduates.

A more serious objection is that the book embodies a questionable view of the nature of moral philosophy. Rawls sees the aim of the subject as, at least in part, the systematizing of our moral intuitions. We all possess, Rawls says, the capacity to make moral judgments on a number of particular matters – we can say: "That would be unjust... This would be just..." and so on in particular circumstances. Rawls thinks moral philosophy should take the firmest of these particular judgments as data, and try to produce a plausible general moral theory that will yield the same judgments in those particular situations. Thus Rawls's theory of justice seeks to unify our particular intuitions about justice in much the same way as a scientific theory seeks to unify the data of particular observations.

This approach leads Rawls to rely heavily on moral intuitions that he thinks the reader accepts and to avoid subjecting common intuitions to rigorous criticism. The basic idea of Rawls's theory is that we can discover what principles and institutions are just by asking what principles and institutions rational self-interested people would agree to under certain hypothetical con-- ditions which eliminate personal biases and inequality of bargaining power. We might expect that this method, with its egalitarian starting point, would lead to a conception of justice that was radically different from the usual one (for instance, in respect of the disparity that the commonly accepted view of justice tolerates between the standard of living in affluent nations and elsewhere in the world). Rawls, however, in this and other instances, blunts the radical impli- cations of his own starting point and so arrives at a theory of justice that justifies a kind of society apparently not so very different from our own liberal- democrat free-enterprise system, and says almost nothing about the demands of justice in distribution between nation-states. So justice is made to accord with most of the moral intuitions most people already accept.

Admittedly, Rawls's conception of the subject is compatible with a certain amount of criticism of common moral intuitions, but the extent to which he himself, in the book, is prepared to tinker with the basic theory in order to make it conform to these intuitions could set a trend which would take moral philosophy in the same direction as the kind of ordinary-language philosophy that refused to challenge our ordinary preconceptions. This tendency would be particularly regrettable in moral and political philosophy, since these areas of the subject have practical consequences if they are taken seriously. No conclu- sions about what we ought to do can validly be drawn from a description of what most people in our society think we ought to do. If we have a soundly based moral theory we ought to be prepared to accept its implications even if they force us to change our moral views on major issues. Once this point is forgotten, moral philosophy loses its capacity to generate radical criticism of prevailing moral standards, and serves only to preserve the status quo.

As long as moral philosophy avoids this danger, I do not think the renewed interest in substantive questions will be a temporary phenomenon. It shows no signs of ebbing now that students have become less insistent – and much less intimidating – in their demands for relevance. Thoughtful discussions of ethical issues meet a need that is felt outside academic circles. Although Mr. Nixon has said that the President is the moral leader of the nation, no one else would now describe the provision of moral guidance, as Broad did, as a task "so adequately performed" by politicians.

Clergymen, too, do not make entirely satisfactory moralists. When contro- versial moral issues arise, religious leaders are routinely asked their opinions; but since only a minority of the population regularly attends church or synagogue, the result is a distorted impression of moral attitudes in the com- munity. Clerical pronouncements on moral issues give undue importance to sexual morality, so much so that terms like "loose morals" are now automatically taken to refer to sexual conduct rather than, say, tax evasion, although the latter may be the more serious offense. To restore balance, secular moralists should be consulted as often as religious moralists – and who is better qualified as a secular moralist than a moral philosopher?

This suggestion is not meant to imply that moral philosophers should pontificate from their professorial chairs while the masses dutifully obey. Moral positions should be discussed and argued about, not accepted on the authority of God or god-professor. The moral philosopher does not present his views as derivations from authority or from ancient books. The philosopher's aim is to show that reasoning and argument favor one position rather than another. It may not always be possible to achieve this aim. Sometimes moral arguments do break down in a disagreement that reason seems unable to resolve. But at other times quite rigorous argument against certain views will be possible. Philosophers may be able to locate an inconsistency between two positions that someone wants to hold simultaneously. By using their understanding of the nature of moral concepts and, above all, by probing more deeply and taking less for granted than others do, philosophers may be able to raise the standard of moral discussion from its present depressingly low level.

Some of the best examples of debates about moral issues that are in need of the clarification and rigor that a philosopher can provide occur in the field of medical ethics. New medical procedures and changing attitudes have produced a growing number of ethical problems that some medical practitioners must face daily. Doctors, however, are uncomfortable making these decisions. Many prefer to see themselves as technicians, plumbers of the human body happy to repair a fault but not equipped to set policy. Indeed, it is true that doctors are no better qualified to make ethical decisions than most other people. Yet the American Medical Association is extremely influential in setting ethical standards. The results can be confusing and even incoherent. It is worth looking at an example, both for the intrinsic interest of the issue raised, and as an illustration of how collaboration with moral philosophers might avoid mistakes.

Last year, the House of Delegates of the AMA approved a policy statement condemning "the intentional termination of the life of one human being by another" – as in mercy killing – as "contrary to that for which the medical profession stands." The same statement goes on, however, to condone "the cessation of the employment of extraordinary means to prolong the life of the body. . . ." The implication is that these are different actions; but if a doctor turns off a machine that is keeping a patient alive, knowing that this will result in the patient's death, what is he doing if it is not "the intentional termination of the life of one human being by another"?

No competent philosopher could have written this statement without noticing its inconsistency. Perhaps the distinction between killing a patient with an incurable, painful disease, and letting the same patient die can be drawn in some other way, but it is clear that the House of Delegates did not formulate its view coherently. If the delegates had struggled with the problem of finding a coherent formulation, they might have begun to question whether, even if the distinction can be properly drawn, much moral weight should be given to it. The topic is one that philosophers have been discussing recently and their discussions have shown that when we get down to particular cases that embody a distinction between killing and letting die, without any other irrelevant considerations to influence our judgment, it becomes implausible to say that there is a great moral difference between the act and the omission. Either way, we must take responsibility for what we do. We cannot claim that we are "playing God" in one case but not in the other, since a decision not to do something is as much a decision as one to do something, and we cannot wash our hands of the responsibility for that decision.

This is a conclusion that challenges many people's beliefs. We feel intuitively that it is worse to kill directly than to allow to die. But if upon reflection and after discussion of possible cases most people agree that this intuitive feeling is unreliable (and this has been my experience when discussing the issue with both students and nonphilosophers) then it seems that philosophical methods can help to resolve practical dilemmas.

Granted, in the example I have chosen the issue is not settled by what I have said so far. If we decide to abandon the distinction between killing and letting die, we must still decide whether we now accept direct mercy killing, or go to the other extreme and treat the withdrawal of any life-sustaining support from any patient as equivalent to murder. There is a lot more to be said on this topic, more than it would be appropriate to say here, since I am using the topic only as an example. Briefly, though, I think the avoidance of pointless suffering must take precedence over a rigid adherence to a prohibition on killing. If a doctor accepted the argument against attributing great moral weight to the distinction between killing and allowing to die, he would, when faced with a patient in pain, dying slowly and wanting to be put out of pain, use whatever method involved less suffering for his patient. Sometimes that would mean direct killing rather than "allowing to die." At present, of course, this is illegal, but it might not remain illegal long if doctors were to withdraw their support.

This is only one example of a discussion to which philosophers can usefully contribute. Whatever conclusion one reaches on the particular issue, it is absurd to leave the moral philosopher out of the debate. His training makes him more than ordinarily competent in assessing arguments and detecting fallacies. He has studied the nature of moral concepts and the logic of moral argument. His views are tested by his colleagues at seminars, conferences, and in the learned journals. Most important of all, he has the precious advantage of ample time to reflect on and discuss ethical issues, since this is his occupation and not a hobby that must always yield to more pressing commitments. This is why I believe that the entry of philosophers into areas of ethical concern from which they have hitherto excluded themselves is the most stimulating and potentially fruitful of all the recent development in philosophy.

Four

Bioethics and Academic Freedom

Two years ago, in a "Report from Germany" entitled "Euthanasia after the Holocaust – Is it Possible?," M. H. Kottow described the shadow still cast by Nazism over the issue of euthanasia in the Federal Republic of Germany.[1] The so-called "euthanasia" program carried out under official Nazi directives between 1939 and 1941 has made it impossible for Germany to contemplate changes of the kind which have occurred in the neighboring Netherlands. Kottow did point to forces working against this inhibition of discussion of euthanasia: the development of medical technology, which has increasingly made the process of dying a more complex, protracted, and "medically managed" event; and also the coming of age of a generation of Germans who bear no responsibility for the crimes of the Nazi era. Nevertheless, Kottow concluded: "In the foreseeable future and possibly for a long time to come, pro-euthanasia arguments will be nipped in the bud by pointing an accusatory and perhaps overzealous finger at associations with the not too distant past."

In June 1989 I attempted to lecture on the subject of euthanasia for severely disabled newborn infants in Germany. My intention was to defend the view that it may be ethically permissible to take active steps to end the lives of infants where, because of a severe disability, death is considered to be best for the infant; and perhaps also in some cases (for example, where there is no acceptable alternative to the child staying with the family) where the infant's death is considered best for the family as a whole.[2] My experiences in trying to talk

First published in *Bioethics*, 4 (1990), pp. 33–44. Reprinted with permission of Blackwell Publishers.

about this issue bore out Kottow's words in an unpleasantly vivid manner. They also illustrate the grave danger posed to academic freedom by intolerance, even in a modern liberal democracy. Bioethics, as a discipline (or perhaps better, as an interdisciplinary activity) has taken for granted the freedom to challenge conventional moral beliefs. It is hard to imagine bioethics surviving as a worthwhile activity without this freedom. Yet events in Germany last summer threaten our complacent assumption that we shall always be free to follow arguments where they may lead in sensitive areas of morality. We may need to dust off the old arguments used by our forebears to defend academic freedom and freedom of expression.

The story begins in February 1988, when I accepted an invitation to speak at a European Symposium on "Bio-engineering, Ethics, and Mental Disability," organized jointly by Lebenshilfe, a large German organization for parents of intellectually disabled infants, and the Bishop Bekkers Institute, a Dutch organization in the same field. The program specified that the symposium would be held under the auspices of the International League of Societies for Persons with Mental Handicap, and the International Association for the Scientific Study of Mental Deficiency. It was to take place in June, 1989, in Marburg, a Germany university town. The program was to be opened by the German Minister of Family Affairs, and the list of speakers included the Canadian geneticist Joseph Berg and bioethicist Edward Keyserlingk, the Dutch health lawyer H. J. Leenan, the English theologian Gordon Dunstan, the French geneticist Jerome Lejeune, and many other experts in related fields from Europe and North America.

During the next year I let a few colleagues know that I would be in Europe in the spring of 1989. As a result Dr Christoph Anstoetz, a professor of special education at the University of Dortmund, invited me to give a lecture at his university on the subject: "Do severely disabled newborn infants have a right to life?"

Nine days before the symposium was due to open, I received by facsimile a letter from Lebenshilfe cancelling my invitation to speak at the conference. The reason given was that the announcement of my lecture at the University of Dortmund had caused trouble for Lebenshilfe. They were now confronted, they wrote, with the argument that they were providing the means for me to promote my views on euthanasia in Germany. The letter drew a distinction between my discussing these views "behind closed doors with critical scientists who want to convince you that your attitude infringes human rights" and my promoting my position "in public." It also indicated that the German Minister of Family Affairs had announced that she would withdraw her promise to open the symposium if I took part, and that the Ministry of Social Affairs, which was subsidizing the symposium, had given "strong advice" that my invitation should be cancelled. A postscript added that several organizations of handi-capped persons were planning protest demonstrations in Marburg and Dort-mund against me, and against Lebenshilfe for having invited me.

I flew to Europe anyway; I had several other lectures arranged, in Italy and Britain as well as Germany, and could not cancel them all at short notice. On arrival I learned that the storm of criticism against Lebenshilfe for initiating a discussion of euthanasia had spilled over into the popular press. Although led by organizations for the disabled, the protests were supported by a range of other groups, including the Greens, the German Society for Social Psychiatry, and various alliances of students and women against genetic engineering and repro-ductive technology. Even the "Anti-Atom Office" joined the coalition (without enquiring about my views on nuclear issues). Selected quotations from one of my books, *Practical Ethics* (which had appeared in German in 1984) were being circulated and cited in the press.[3] The influential magazine *Der Spiegel*, which has a position in Germany similar to that of *Time* in the United States, published a long article written by Franz Christoph, the leader of the "Cripples Movement," a militant organization of disabled people.[4] The article was a vehement attack on my views, on Lebenshilfe, and on Professor Anstoetz for inviting me to speak. It was illustrated by photographs of the transportation of "euthanasia victims" in the Third Reich, and of Hitler's "Euthanasia Order." A spokesperson for a group of disabled people was quoted as justifying the protests by saying: "We cannot tolerate that people should speak about whether we may live or not." The article went on to say that this was "The only legitimate answer to any setting up of a pro and contra debate on the theme of euthanasia." It failed to point out that my views are no threat to anyone capable of expressing a preference for continued life, and thus obviously no threat to anyone capable of commenting on what I have written or said. This and other press articles gave little or no account of the ethical basis on which I had reached the views so bluntly presented in brief quotations. My suggestion that some lives might be so full of suffering as not to be worth living, from the perspective of the individual whose life it is, was always cast in the Nazi terminology "lebensunwertes Leben," which in Nazi jargon conveyed the very different idea that some life was not "worthy of living" because it was racially or genetically impure and thus unworthy to be part of the Aryan "Volk."

The cancellation of my own invitation to speak at the symposium in Marburg proved insufficient to placate the protesters. They now organized themselves against what they called the "Euthanasia Congress." The pressure proved too much; shortly before the symposium was due to open, Lebenshilfe and the Bishop Bekkers Institute cancelled the entire event. Similar pressure had been turned on the University of Dortmund. Though Anstoetz worked in the field of special education, he was clearly surprised and shaken by the reaction to the announcement of the lecture he had sponsored. He knew that there were groups in Germany very much opposed to any attempts to judge one life as more worth living than another (in Germany there is even opposition, on these grounds, to genetic counselling) but he had never expected such vehement protests. Arriving at his office one morning, he found a label saying "Schreibtischtaeter," a term which translates literally as "Desk-doer," and is used to refer to bureaucrats like Eichmann who organized the dispatch of people to the gas chambers. The protesters made it clear that if the lecture were not cancelled, they would seek to stop it by physical means. As a result the Faculty of Special Education at Dortmund resolved that the lecture must not proceed.

Meanwhile Professor Georg Meggle, Professor of Philosophy at the University of Saarbruecken, had read of the cancellation of my lectures and invited me to lecture at his university in order to show that it was possible to discuss the ethics of euthanasia rationally in Germany. When I arrived at the lecture theatre, however, there was a group waiting at the door, trying to block my entry. We managed to get in through another door and tried to get the lecture under way. Professor Meggle got through his introduction without interruption. I came to the lectern, planning to say that I understood the sensitivity to the issue of euthanasia in Germany, but what I was suggesting was entirely different from what the Nazis did. I was not proposing that the state should decide who could live or die, but that parents, in consultation with doctors, should be able to decide when, in the interests of their child, and of their family as a whole, it was better that a severely disabled infant should not live.[5] I wanted to point out that the only logical alternative – to do everything possible to preserve life at any cost – was extremely cruel in those cases where the only prospect was months of suffering before a premature death. A decision not to do everything possible to preserve life, on the other hand, already involves an implicit judgment that the quality of that life is so poor that it is not worth prolonging it – in other words, a judgment that some lives are not worth living. Once such a decision has been taken, it might be kinder to take active steps to end life quickly, rather than to allow an infant to die from dehydration, or from an infection.

That was my lecture plan. As soon as I began to speak, however, a chorus of whistles, of the sort used by football umpires, began. It was soon obvious that I was not going to be heard. This was an intensely frustrating moment. Looking at the people whistling and chanting, I thought that most of them seemed people to whom I could easily relate. They looked like the people with whom, at home, I work politically on a range of environmental and social issues. Did they really imagine that I was some kind of Nazi? Could they possibly have read anything of *Practical Ethics* beyond the oft-quoted sentences? Had they thought at all about whether we should keep severely disabled infants alive in all cases, even if the parents want no further treatment? Did they believe that withdrawing antibiotics from a severely disabled baby with an infection was only "letting nature take its course," and therefore intrinsically different from giving a lethal injection? What would the feminists among them (and there clearly were some) say about a woman's right to an abortion when prenatal testing had shown that the pregnancy would result in a disabled infant? If only I could discuss these matters with them, I thought, surely these people would realize that their hostility was misdirected. But how can one have a reasonable discussion with someone who just whistles?

In the end Professor Meggle did persuade the protesters in Saarbruecken to participate in a discussion with me, during which some of these questions were raised. More significant, however, was the unleashing of the discussion on a national level by Germany's leading liberal weekly newspaper, *Die Zeit*. Their coverage of the question began with a short article on "Can Euthanasia be Ethically Grounded?"[6] followed up a week later with a much longer discussion both of the issue and of the taboo which prevented it being discussed.[7] Here it was reported that – as anyone with knowledge of modern neonatal medicine would have expected – in Germany as elsewhere, some severely disabled newborn infants are allowed to die, and there are guidelines, approved by the Federal Chamber of Medicine, which recognize that doctors are not under a duty to prolong life by all possible means.

As a result of these articles, *Die Zeit* also became the target of protests. Franz Christoph, the leader of the Cripples Movement who had written the article in *Der Spiegel*, chained his wheelchair to the newspaper's editorial offices. Subsequently *Die Zeit* invited him, Dr Josef Schaedle of the German Society for Social Psychiatry, and Bishop Ulrich Wilckens, to a debate with editors from *Die Zeit* about whether the question of euthanasia should be raised. The debate was recorded, and published in another "Dossier," this time over four pages.[8] The discussion was opened by Franz Christoph stating why he thought the question should not be discussed:

> "Do the severely handicapped have a right to life?" We oppose the putting of this question by Mr Singer, and are also opposed to the fact that such a thing is now publicly discussed, that Mr Singer is invited to lecture, and that such thoughts become more established. We say: our right to life is not open to discussion. For we think that putting the question, whether in some situations disabled people may be killed, makes a "yes" or "no" possible, and thus also gives a little more credence to the affirmative answer.

To this Theo Sommer, editor of *Die Zeit*, responded that while the right to life of handicapped people might not be open to discussion, the problem of euthanasia must be discussed, because the discussion was already going on. He added " . . . there are no opinions that one should hold to be fundamentally not worthy of being discussed or not permissible to discuss." Bishop Wilckens then intervened, but not to defend the view that the issue should not be discussed. Instead he criticized *Die Zeit* for having failed to bring out the distinction between passive and active assistance in dying. From this point the discussion moved away from the question of whether euthanasia should be discussed, and instead discussed it.

Die Zeit also published a page and a half of readers' letters, showing a spread of opinion both about the euthanasia issue and about whether it should be discussed.[9] The debate then moved to television. The popular German television program *Panorama* did a special documentary in which it showed that in Germany too, doctors allow severely disabled infants to die. In Austria, I took part in a two-hour television debate with a theologian, a journalist from *Die Zeit*, and several representatives of the disabled and their parents.

Thus the protesters succeeded in preventing me giving academic lectures, but ensured that millions of readers and television viewers would get to know about my views. That is an old story (could any publicity agent have done as much for sales of *The Satanic Verses* as the Ayatollah Khomeini?) and it is the most positive aspect of the events I have described. Perhaps now the debate over euthanasia really has commenced in Germany. But the darker side of these events is that they show that intolerance of controversial views is still strong in Germany, even in the universities. The opponents of my views were not satisfied with the cancellation of the symposium in Marburg and the lecture in Dortmund. A meeting in Hamburg, called by some of the groups that had opposed the lectures, resolved to find out where else I was speaking in Europe, and to attempt to prevent those lectures taking place. (By the time this occurred, however, I had no further lectures planned for Germany, and had almost completed my engagements in Europe, so there were no more disruptions.)

More serious was an open campaign for the dismissal of Anstoetz from his university chair. Petitions were circulated, and letters written to the Minister of Science and Research for the State of Nordrhein-Westfalen (which includes Dortmund). One example is an open letter dated June 1989 to the Minister, Mrs Anke Brunn, circulated by staff of the Pestalozzi School for the Intellectually Handicapped, in Essen. The letter refers to my planned lecture at the University of Dortmund, and expresses satisfaction that students and others prevented the lecture taking place. It then states that Professor Anstoetz has not as yet distanced himself from my views, and claims that Professor Anstoetz is therefore acting contrary to the constitution of the Federal Republic of Germany, which states that every person has a right to life. Finally the letter asks the Minister to examine these circumstances, and concludes with the statement that if this examination confirms the situation described above:

> then we endorse the suggestion of numerous teachers and students of the University of Dortmund, that Professor Anstoetz's teaching duties be immediately withdrawn, and that he be suspended from service.

As a result of such complaints, Anstoetz was asked by an official acting for the Minister to explain his invitation to me and what consequences he drew, as far as the ethic of rehabilitative education was concerned, from my ethical stance.[10]

Thus the clear implication of the campaign against Anstoetz is that university teachers have a duty, not merely to abide by the constitution, but also to maintain that the constitution is sound and there is nothing in it to be improved. Since the Minister appears to have taken the complaints seriously, the Minister must herself have regarded this as at least a defensible view of the duty of teachers. If so, the threat to academic freedom is a real one.

Constitutions themselves normally provide for constitutional means of amendment. There could certainly be no suggestion that by inviting me to lecture, Anstoetz had actually breached the constitution, or suggested that the constitution should be breached. It is entirely consistent with my views that no acts of euthanasia should take place until the law is amended to permit and regulate such conduct. How can one even consider whether the constitution should be amended if one does not permit discussion about whether the views implicit in it are morally sound? To prohibit such discussion is to entrench forever the ideas held four decades ago, when the constitution was adopted.

When government officials, particularly those responsible for the universities, express such views, we need to remind ourselves of John Stuart Mill's classic arguments in defence of freedom of speech and expression:

> There is the greatest difference between presuming an opinion to be true, because, with every opportunity for contesting it, it has not been refuted, and assuming its truth for the purpose of not permitting its refutation. Complete liberty of contradicting and disproving our opinion is the very condition which justifies us in assuming its truth for purposes of action; and on no other terms can a being with human faculties have any rational assurance of being right.[11]

To this Mill added a second consideration, which holds even if we assume that the opinion in question is unquestionably true:

> However unwillingly a person who has a strong opinion may admit the possibility that his opinion may be false, he ought to be moved by the consideration that, however true it may be, if it is not fully, frequently, and fearlessly discussed,

it will be held as a dead dogma, not a living truth . . . so essential is this discipline [of fearless discussion] to a real understanding of moral and human subjects, that if opponents of all important truths do not exist, it is indispensable to imagine them, and supply them with the strongest arguments which the most skilful devil's advocate can conjure up . . . not only the grounds of the opinion are forgotten in the absence of discussion, but too often the meaning of the opinion itself.[12]

German professors with teaching chairs do have tenure, and academic freedom is explicitly guaranteed in the German constitution. Yet Anstoetz and, to a lesser extent, Meggle have been put under very considerable pressure to distance themselves from my views, and the academic climate is clearly not a healthy one for freedom of opinion on this topic.

Although Anstoetz and Meggle received individual letters of support from other academics against these attacks, there was a disappointing failure of those teaching in German universities to close ranks against this grave attack on academic freedom and freedom of expression. In Britain, when news of the situation in Germany reached Professor R. M. Hare, he wrote immediately expressing support for free discussion of euthanasia; and subsequently he was instrumental in moving the following motion, which was passed by the annual general meeting of the Aristotelian Society on July 16, 1989, at Swansea:

> The Aristotelian Society of Great Britain expresses concern that the Australian philosopher Peter Singer was prevented from presenting his views at a number of West German seminars and affirms its concern for freedom of speech, academic freedom, and the rational discussion of important practical issues.

No similar motions have, at the time of writing, been passed by any German academic organization. A number of German bioethicists attending a course at the Kennedy Center of Bioethics, in Washington, DC, did sign a statement of support for freedom of discussion. On balance, though, the preponderance of academic influence in Germany has gone in the opposite direction. German academics in the field of special education had been prominent among those calling for the cancellation of the lecture at Dortmund; and when a professor of special education at the University of Cologne sent Anstoetz a letter of support for his right to organize a discussion with me, he had to report in a covering letter that he had been unable to gain any additional signatories to his letter among the professors at his university. Long after the lecture had been cancelled, when the calls for the dismissal of Anstoetz were mounting, the Director of the Institute for Special and Rehabilitative Education at the Free University of Berlin added support to such moves by circulating a letter condemning as "highly irresponsible" the presentation of positions like mine in university education.[13]

The arguments for the dismissal of Anstoetz were presented in one magazine as follows:

> Because the freedom of research and teaching in no way includes the right to deny other humans the entitlement to exist or to justify infanticide; because we do not want to know that our taxes are used for professors who speculate more or less openly about killing, instead of respecting, those humans whom their discipline should serve; therefore numerous organizations, among them the DGSP [German Society for Social Psychiatry] have, at a protest meeting in Dortmund, advocated that Christoph Anstoetz should be dismissed from his position as one entitled to examine at the Dortmund Faculty of Education for the Intellectually Disabled.[14]

In response to such views, it is important to reiterate that it is precisely in those cases where ideas strike at widely and firmly held moral beliefs, that freedom of thought and expression are most in need of protection. Freedom of speech that is unable to challenge social consensus is not worthy of the name. The test of a truly liberal society is its tolerance of views that most members of the society regard as profoundly wrong. But it is also curious to note that those who have claimed (mistakenly) to find in my writings a narrowly economic view of human life, according to which life is to be preserved only if it is socially useful, themselves take a narrow view of the value of a university; namely that the taxes used to support professors are not best regarded as fostering free intellectual inquiry but rather entitle us to insist on those on the university payroll advocating specific socially accepted values.

One explanation for the lack of academic support for free discussion is the understandable German sensitivity about the Nazi past. The protesters claimed that my views could erode respect for human life, and so lead to a return of the mentality that made the Nazi atrocities possible. Yet this is only a partial explanation. One irony that did not escape some of those who wrote letters to *Die Zeit* is that the protesters have themselves shown the kind of fanaticism and lack of respect for rational debate that was also a necessary precondition of the Nazi atrocities. Perhaps what really was instrumental in preparing the Nazi path to genocide, and has not yet been eradicated in the modern Germany, is not the euthanasia movement at all, but the kind of fanatical certainty in one's own rectitude that refuses to listen to, or engage in rational debate with, anyone who harbors contrary views. (In Austria, where discussion of the issue of euthanasia was a little more relaxed, several people with whom I discussed what had happened in Germany made deprecating noises about the tendency of their northern neighbors to take everything to extremes.)

Here the study of applied or practical ethics, in general, and of bioethics in particular, may have a role to play. In English-speaking countries the views I hold about severely disabled newborn infants are no longer extraordinary, at least not among philosophers and bioethicists. Jonathan Glover, Michael Tooley, John Harris, James Rachels, and Helga Kuhse are among those who have argued for similar views.[15] What strikes an outsider as truly extraordinary about the many leaflets and articles written by those Germans against my views is that it never seems to occur to any of them that there are arguments here which need to be rebutted if their own position is to be shown to be tenable. Instead, again and again, the mode of attack is to take a quotation and display it, as if its intuitive shock value were sufficient to prove its falsity and to show that any attempt to defend it by rational argument must be mere cunning sleight of hand. There appears to be a near-total lack of a tradition of rational argument in practical ethics in Germany. Of course, there are a few exceptions, a few philosophers struggling to develop such a tradition. Meggle is one of them and Anstoetz, though not by profession a philosopher, another. But they and the others in this field in Germany are a small minority. Thus bioethics cannot grow, as it has in many other countries, on a soil already tilled by philosophers working in a tradition of rational argument about particular problems in ethics. In English-speaking countries we may sometimes despair at the failure of what we take to be rational argument to win over opponents, or to persuade the politicians to adopt the most reasonable solution. When we look at Germany, however, we can see that these failures are relatively insignificant compared with problems posed by the absence of a real tradition of rational debate in bioethics.

I have emphasised the distinctive local character of the events I have described. In doing so, there is always a danger of over-generalization and exaggeration of national tendencies. To redress the balance, I shall close by pointing out that these events are probably not so much different in kind, as in degree, from what could happen, and perhaps already has happened, elsewhere. Bioethics is a discipline that leads to the questioning of values and ethical doctrines that had previously been treated as sacrosanct. Often these doctrines are closely connected with religious beliefs, and we did not need Khomeini to remind us that religious fundamentalism is often intolerant of free speech. Obviously such intolerance can also have a political basis. Even if opposition to those who hold radical views in bioethics does not go to the extreme of denying them freedom of expression, it may manifest itself in more subtle ways, including efforts to restrict funding to those organizations which allow such views to be expressed. There is a clear need to develop a broader appreciation of the importance of an atmosphere of support for rational discussion of controversial ideas, in bioethics and elsewhere. One step towards doing this would be an institutional means – such as an international association of bioethics – which could show the united support of bioethicists from all over the world, whatever their views, for the right to discuss freely issues in bioethics.

Notes

1   *Bioethics*, 2 (1988), pp. 58–69.
2   For a full defence of this position, see Helga Kuhse and Peter Singer, *Should the Baby Live?* (Oxford: Oxford University Press, 1985).
3   *Practical Ethics* (Cambridge: Cambridge University Press, 1979; German translation, *Praktische Ethik*, Stuttgart: Reclam, 1984).
4   "Kein Diskurs über 'lebensunwertes Leben,'" *Spiegel*, 43: 23 (June 5, 1989).
5   See Helga Kuhse and Peter Singer, *Should the Baby Live?* This book is not available in German.
6   Hans Schuh, "Läßt sich Euthanasie ethisch begründen?" *Die Zeit* (June 16, 1989), p. 78.
7   Reinhard Merkel, "Der Streit um Leben und Tod"; and Hans-Harald Braeutigam and Class Thomsen, "Was heißt lebensfähig?" *Die Zeit* (June 23, 1989), pp. 13–15.
8   "Exzess der Vernunft oder Ethik der Erlösung," *Die Zeit* (July 14, 1989), pp. 9–12.
9   July 14, 1989, pp. 54–5; further letters were published in *Die Zeit* on August 11, 1989.
10 Letter from Herr Pelzner, Minister der Wissenschaft und Forschung des Landes Nordrhein-Westfalen, to Professor Christoph Anstoetz, July 12, 1989.
11 John Stuart Mill, *On Liberty* (London: J. M. Dent, 1960; first published 1859), p. 81.
12 *On Liberty*, pp. 95, 97–8, 99.
13 Circular Letter of July 12, 1989, from Professor O. Sasse, Free University of Berlin.
14 Lothar Evers, "Bio-Ethik?" *Dr. med. Mabuse*, 14: 61 (August/September 1989) p. 39.
15 See Jonathan Glover, *Causing Death and Saving Lives* (Harmondsworth: Penguin, 1977); Michael Tooley, *Abortion and Infanticide* (Oxford: Oxford University Press, 1988); John Harris, *The Value of Life* (London: Routledge and Kegan Paul, 1985); James Rachels, *The End of Life* (Oxford: Oxford University Press, 1986); Helga Kuhse, *The Sanctity of Life Doctrine in Medicine: A Critique* (Oxford: Oxford University Press, 1987).

Part Three

The Idea of Equality

Five

All Animals are Equal[1]

In recent years a number of oppressed groups have campaigned vigorously for equality. The classic instance is the Black Liberation movement, which demands an end to the prejudice and discrimination that has made blacks second-class citizens. The immediate appeal of the Black Liberation movement and its initial, if limited success made it a model for other oppressed groups to follow. We became familiar with liberation movements for Spanish-Americans, gay people, and a variety of other minorities. When a majority group – women – began their campaign, some thought we had come to the end of the road. Discrimination on the basis of sex, it has been said, is the last universally accepted form of discrimination, practiced without secrecy or pretense even in those liberal circles that have long prided themselves on their freedom from prejudice against racial minorities.

One should always be wary of talking of "the last remaining form of discrimination." If we have learnt anything from the liberation movements, we should have learnt how difficult it is to be aware of latent prejudice in our attitudes to particular groups until this prejudice is forcefully pointed out.

A liberation movement demands an expansion of our moral horizons and an extension or reinterpretation of the basic moral principle of equality. Practices that were previously regarded as natural and inevitable come to be seen as the result of an unjustifiable prejudice. Who can say with confidence that all his or her attitudes and practices are beyond criticism? If we wish to avoid being

First published in *Philosophical Exchange*, 1:5 (1974), pp. 103–16.

numbered amongst the oppressors, we must be prepared to rethink even our most fundamental attitudes. We need to consider them from the point of view of those most disadvantaged by our attitudes, and the practices that follow from these attitudes. If we can make this unaccustomed mental switch we may discover a pattern in our attitudes and practices that consistently operates so as to benefit one group – usually the one to which we ourselves belong – at the expense of another. In this way we may come to see that there is a case for a new liberation movement. My aim is to advocate that we make this mental switch in respect of our attitudes and practices towards a very large group of beings: members of species other than our own – or, as we popularly though misleadingly call them, animals. In other words, I am urging that we extend to other species the basic principle of equality that most of us recognize should be extended to all members of our own species.

All this may sound a little far-fetched, more like a parody of other liberation movements than a serious objective. In fact, in the past the idea of "The Rights of Animals" really has been used to parody the case for women's rights. When Mary Wollstonecraft, a forerunner of later feminists, published her *Vindication of the Rights of Woman* in 1792, her ideas were widely regarded as absurd, and they were satirized in an anonymous publication entitled *A Vindication of the Rights of Brutes*. The author of this satire (actually Thomas Taylor, a distinguished Cambridge philosopher) tried to refute Wollstonecraft's reasonings by showing that they could be carried one stage further. If sound when applied to women, why should the arguments not be applied to dogs, cats, and horses? They seemed to hold equally well for these "brutes"; yet to hold that brutes had rights was manifestly absurd; therefore the reasoning by which this conclusion had been reached must be unsound, and if unsound when applied to brutes, it must also be unsound when applied to women, since the very same arguments had been used in each case.

One way in which we might reply to this argument is by saying that the case for equality between men and women cannot validly be extended to nonhuman animals. Women have a right to vote, for instance, because they are just as capable of making rational decisions as men are; dogs, on the other hand, are incapable of understanding the significance of voting, so they cannot have the right to vote. There are many other obvious ways in which men and women resemble each other closely, while humans and other animals differ greatly. So, it might be said, men and women are similar beings, and should have equal rights, while humans and nonhumans are different and should not have equal rights.

The thought behind this reply to Taylor's analogy is correct up to a point, but it does not go far enough. There *are* important differences between humans and other animals, and these differences must give rise to *some* differences in the rights that each have. Recognizing this obvious fact, however, is no barrier to the case for extending the basic principle of equality to nonhuman animals. The differences that exist between men and women are equally undeniable, and the supporters of Women's Liberation are aware that these differences may give rise to different rights. Many feminists hold that women have the right to an abortion on request. It does not follow that since these same people are campaigning for equality between men and women they must support the right of men to have abortions too. Since a man cannot have an abortion, it is meaningless to talk of his right to have one. Since a pig can't vote, it is meaningless to talk of its right to vote. There is no reason why either Women's Liberation or Animal Liberation should get involved in such nonsense. The extension of the basic principle of equality from one group to another does not imply that we must treat both groups in exactly the same way, or grant exactly the same rights to both groups. Whether we should do so will depend on the nature of the members of the two groups. The basic principle of equality, I shall argue, is equality of consideration; and equal consideration for different beings may lead to different treatment and different rights.

So there is a different way of replying to Taylor's attempt to parody Wollstonecraft's arguments, a way which does not deny the differences between humans and nonhumans, but goes more deeply into the question of equality, and concludes by finding nothing absurd in the idea that the basic principle of equality applies to so-called "brutes." I believe that we reach this conclusion if we examine the basis on which our opposition to discrimination on grounds of race or sex ultimately rests. We will then see that we would be on shaky ground if we were to demand equality for blacks, women, and other groups of oppressed humans while denying equal consideration to nonhumans.

When we say that all human beings, whatever their race, creed, or sex, are equal, what is it that we are asserting? Those who wish to defend a hierarchical, inegalitarian society have often pointed out that by whatever test we choose, it simply is not true that all humans are equal. Like it or not, we must face the fact that humans come in different shapes and sizes; they come with differing moral capacities, differing intellectual abilities, differing amounts of benevolent feeling and sensitivity to the needs of others, differing abilities to communicate effectively, and differing capacities to experience pleasure and pain. In short, if the demand for equality were based on the actual equality of all human beings, we would have to stop demanding equality. It would be an unjustifiable demand.

Still, one might cling to the view that the demand for equality among human beings is based on the actual equality of the different races and sexes. Although humans differ as individuals in various ways, there are no differences between the races and sexes *as such*. From the mere fact that a person is black, or a woman, we cannot infer anything else about that person. This, it may be said, is what is wrong with racism and sexism. The white racist claims that whites are superior to blacks, but this is false – although there are differences between individuals, some blacks are superior to some whites in all of the capacities and abilities that could conceivably be relevant. The opponent of sexism would say the same: a person's sex is no guide to his or her abilities, and this is why it is unjustifiable to discriminate on the basis of sex.

This is a possible line of objection to racial and sexual discrimination. It is not, however, the way that someone really concerned about equality would choose, because taking this line could, in some circumstances, force one to accept a most inegalitarian society. The fact that humans differ as individuals, rather than as races or sexes, is a valid reply to someone who defends a hierarchical society like, say, [the former state of] South Africa, in which all whites were superior in status to all blacks. The existence of individual variations that cut across the lines of race or sex, however, provides us with no defense at all against a more sophisticated opponent of equality, one who proposes, say, the interests of those with ratings above 100. Would a hierarchical society of this sort really be so much better than one based on race or sex? I think not. But if we tie the moral principle of equality to the factual equality of the different races or sexes, taken as a whole, our opposition to racism and sexism does not provide us with any basis for objecting to this kind of inegalitarianism.

There is a second important reason why we ought not to base our opposition to racism and sexism on any kind of factual equality, even the limited kind that asserts that variations in capacities and abilities are spread evenly between the different races and sexes: we can have no absolute guarantee that these abilities and capacities really are distributed evenly, without regard to race or sex, among human beings. So far as actual abilities are concerned, there do seem to be certain measurable differences between both races and sexes. These differences do not, of course, appear in each case, but only when averages are taken. More important still, we do not yet know how much of these differences is really due to the different genetic endowments of the various races and sexes, and how much is due to environmental differences that are the result of past and continuing discrimination. Perhaps all of the important differences will eventually prove to be environmental rather than genetic. Anyone opposed to racism and sexism will certainly hope that this will be so, for it will make the task of ending discrimination a lot easier; nevertheless it would be dangerous to rest the case against racism and sexism on the belief that all significant differences are environmental in origin. The opponent of, say, racism who takes this line will be unable to avoid conceding that if differences in ability did after all prove to have some genetic connection with race, racism would in some way be defensible.

It would be folly for the opponent of racism to stake his whole case on a dogmatic commitment to one particular outcome of a difficult scientific issue which ·is still a long way from being settled. While attempts to prove that differences in certain selected abilities between races and sexes are primarily genetic in origin have certainly not been conclusive, the same must be said of attempts to prove that these differences are largely the result of environment. At this stage of the investigation we cannot be certain which view is correct, however much we may hope it is the latter.

Fortunately, there is no need to pin the case for equality to one particular outcome of this scientific investigation. The appropriate response to those who claim to have found evidence of genetically based differences in ability between the races or sexes is not to stick to the belief that the genetic explanation must be wrong, whatever evidence to the contrary may turn up; instead we should make it quite clear that the claim to equality does not depend on intelligence, moral capacity, physical strength, or similar matters of fact. Equality is a moral ideal, not a simple assertion of fact. There is no logically compelling reason for assuming that a factual difference in ability between two people justifies any difference in the amount of consideration we give to satisfying their needs and interests. The principle of the equality of human beings is not a description of an alleged actual equality among humans: it is a prescription of how we should treat humans.

Jeremy Bentham incorporated the essential basis of moral equality into his utilitarian system of ethics in the formula: "Each to count for one and none for more than one." In other words, the interests of every being affected by an action are to be taken into account and given the same weight as the like interests of any other being. A later utilitarian, Henry Sidgwick, put the point in this way: "The good of any one individual is of no more importance, from the point of view (if I may say so) of the Universe, than the good of any other."[2] More recently, the leading figures in contemporary moral philosophy have shown a great deal of agreement in specifying as a fundamental presupposition of their moral theories some similar requirement which operates so as to give everyone's interests equal consideration – although they cannot agree on how this requirement is best formulated.[3]

It is an implication of this principle of equality that our concern for others ought not to depend on what they are like, or what abilities they possess – although precisely what this concern requires us to do may vary according to the characteristics of those affected by what we do. It is on this basis that the case against racism and the case against sexism must both ultimately rest; and it is in accordance with this principle that speciesism is also to be condemned. If possessing a higher degree of intelligence does not entitle one human to use another for his own ends, how can it entitle humans to exploit nonhumans?

Many philosophers have proposed the principle of equal consideration of interests, in some form or other, as a basic moral principle; but, as we shall see in more detail shortly, not many of them have recognized that this principle applies to members of other species as well as to our own. Bentham was one of the few who did realize this. In a forward-looking passage, written at a time when black slaves in the British dominions were still being treated much as we now treat nonhuman animals, Bentham wrote:

> The day *may* come when the rest of the animal creation may acquire those rights which never could have been witholden from them but by the hand of tyranny. The French have already discovered that the blackness of the skin is no reason why a human being should be abandoned without redress to the caprice of a tormentor. It may one day come to be recognized that the number of the legs, the villosity of the skin, or the termination of the *os sacrum*, are reasons equally insufficient for abandoning a sensitive being to the same fate. What else is it that should trace the insuperable line? Is it the faculty of reason, or perhaps the faculty of discourse? But a full-grown horse or dog is beyond comparison a more rational, as well as a more conversable animal, than an infant of a day, or a week, or even a month, old. But suppose they were otherwise, what would it avail? The question is not, Can they reason? nor Can they *talk*? but, *Can they suffer?*[4]

In this passage Bentham points to the capacity for suffering as the vital characteristic that gives a being the right to equal consideration. The capacity for suffering – or more strictly, for suffering and/or enjoyment or happiness – is not just another characteristic like the capacity for language, or for higher mathematics. Bentham is not saying that those who try to mark "the insuperable line" that determines whether the interests of a being should be considered happen to have selected the wrong characteristic. The capacity for suffering and enjoying things is a prerequisite for having interests at all, a condition that must be satisfied before we can speak of interests in any meaningful way. It would be nonsense to say that it was not in the interests of a stone to be kicked along the road by a schoolboy. A stone does not have interests because it cannot suffer. Nothing that we can do to it could possibly make any difference to its welfare. A mouse, on the other hand, does have an interest in not being tormented, because it will suffer if it is.

If a being suffers, there can be no moral justification for refusing to take that suffering into consideration. No matter what the nature of the being, the principle of equality requires that its suffering be counted equally with the like suffering – insofar as rough comparisons can be made – of any other being. If a being is not capable of suffering, or of experiencing enjoyment or happiness, there is nothing to be taken into account. This is why the limit of sentience (using the term as a convenient, if not strictly accurate, shorthand for the capacity to suffer or experience enjoyment or happiness) is the only defensible boundary of concern for the interests of others. To mark this boundary by some characteristic like intelligence or rationality would be to mark it in an arbitrary way. Why not choose some other characteristic, like skin color?

The racist violates the principles of equality by giving greater weight to the interests of members of his own race, when there is a clash between their interests and the interests of those of another race. Similarly the speciesist allows the interests of his own species to override the greater interests of members of other species.[5] The pattern is the same in each case. Most human beings are speciesists. I shall now very briefly describe some of the practices that show this.

For the great majority of human beings, especially in urban, industrialized societies, the most direct form of contact with members of other species is at mealtimes: we eat them. In doing so we treat them purely as means to our ends. We regard their life and well-being as subordinate to our taste for a particular kind of dish. I say "taste" deliberately – this is purely a matter of pleasing our palate. There can be no defense of eating flesh in terms of satisfying nutritional needs, since it has been established beyond doubt that we could satisfy our need for protein and other essential nutrients far more efficiently with a diet that replaced animal flesh by soy beans, or products derived from soy beans, and other high-protein vegetable products.[6]

It is not merely the act of killing that indicates what we are ready to do to other species in order to gratify our tastes. The suffering we inflict on the animals while they are alive is perhaps an even clearer indication of our speciesism than the fact that we are prepared to kill them.[7] In order to have meat on the table at a price that people can afford, our society tolerates methods of meat production that confine sentient animals in cramped, unsuitable conditions for the entire duration of their lives. Animals are treated like machines that convert fodder into flesh, and any innovation that results in a higher "conversion ratio" is liable to be adopted. As one authority on the subject has said, "cruelty is acknowledged only when profitability ceases."[8] So hens are crowded four or five to a cage with a floor area of 20 inches by 18 inches, or around the size of a single page of the *New York Times*. The cages have wire floors, since this reduces cleaning costs, though wire is unsuitable for the hens' feet; the floors slope, since this makes the eggs roll down for easy collection, although this makes it difficult for the hens to rest comfortably. In these conditions all the birds' natural instincts are thwarted: they cannot stretch their wings fully, walk freely, dust-bathe, scratch the ground, or build a nest. Although they have never known other conditions, observers have noticed that the birds vainly try to perform these actions. Frustrated at their inability to do so, they often develop what farmers call "vices," and peck each other to death. To prevent this, the beaks of young birds are often cut off.

This kind of treatment is not limited to poultry. Pigs are now also being reared in cages inside sheds. These animals are comparable to dogs in intelligence, and need a varied, stimulating environment if they are not to suffer from stress and boredom. Anyone who kept a dog in the way in which pigs are frequently kept would be liable to prosecution, in England at least, but because our interest in exploiting pigs is greater than our interest in exploiting dogs, we object to cruelty to dogs while consuming the produce of cruelty to pigs. Of the other animals, the condition of veal calves is perhaps worst of all, since these animals are so closely confined that they cannot even turn around or get up and lie down freely. In this way they do not develop unpalatable muscle. They are also made anemic and kept short of roughage, to keep their flesh pale, since white veal fetches a higher price; as a result they develop a craving for iron and roughage, and have been observed to gnaw wood off the sides of their stalls, and lick greedily at any rusty hinge that is within reach.

Since, as I have said, none of these practices cater for anything more than our pleasures of taste, our practice of rearing and killing other animals in order to eat them is a clear instance of the sacrifice of the most important interests of other beings in order to satisfy trivial interests of our own. To avoid speciesism we must stop this practice, and each of us has a moral obligation to cease supporting the practice. Our custom is all the support that the meat industry needs. The decision to cease giving it that support may be difficult, but it is no more difficult than it would have been for a white Southerner to go against the traditions of his society and free his slaves; if we do not change our dietary habits, how can we censure those slaveholders who would not change their own way of living?

The same form of discrimination may be observed in the widespread practice of experimenting on other species in order to see if certain substances are safe for human beings, or to test some psychological theory about the effect of severe punishment on learning, or to try out various new compounds just in case something turns up. People sometimes think that all this experimentation is for vital medical purposes, and so will reduce suffering overall. This comfortable belief is very wide of the mark. Drug companies test new shampoos and cosmetics that they are intending to put on the market by dropping them into the eyes of rabbits, held open by metal clips, in order to observe what damage results. Food additives, like artificial colorings and preservatives, are tested by what is known as the "LD_{50}" – a test designed to find the level of consumption at which 50 percent of a group of animals will die. In the process, nearly all of the animals are made very sick before some finally die, and others pull through. If the substance is relatively harmless, as it often is, huge doses have to be force-fed to the animals, until in some cases sheer volume or concentration of the substance causes death.

Much of this pointless cruelty goes on in the universities. In many areas of science, nonhuman animals are regarded as an item of laboratory equipment, to be used and expended as desired. In psychology laboratories experiments devise endless variations and repetitions of experiments that were of little value in the first place. To quote just one example, from the experimenter's own account in a psychology journal; at the University of Pennsylvania, Perrin S. Cohen hung six dogs in hammocks with electrodes taped to their hind feet. Electric shock of varying intensity was then administered through the electrodes. If the dog learnt to press its head against a panel on the left, the shock was turned off, but otherwise it remained on indefinitely. Three of the dogs, however, were required to wait periods varying from 2 to 7 seconds while being shocked before making the response that turned off the current. If they failed to wait, they received further shocks. Each dog was given from 26 to 46 "sessions" in the hammock, each session consisting of 80 "trials" or shocks, administered at intervals of one minute. The experimenter reported that the dogs, who were unable to move in the hammock, barked or bobbed their heads when the current was applied. The reported findings of the experiment were that there was a delay in the dogs' responses that increased proportionately to the time the dogs were required to endure the shock, but a gradual increase in the intensity of the shock had no systematic effect in the timing of the response. The experiment was funded by the National Institutes of Health, and the United States Public Health Service.[9]

In this example, and countless cases like it, the possible benefits to mankind are either nonexistent or fantastically remote; while the certain losses to members of other species are very real. This is, again, a clear indication of speciesism.

In the past, argument about vivisection has often missed this point, because it has been put in absolutist terms: would the abolitionist be prepared to let thousands die if they could be saved by experimenting on a single animal? The way to reply to this purely hypothetical question is to pose another: would the experimenter be prepared to perform his experiment on an orphaned human infant, if that were the only way to save many lives? (I say "orphan" to avoid the complication of parental feelings, although in doing so I am being overfair to the experimenter, since the nonhuman subjects of experiments are not orphans.) If the experimenter is not prepared to use an orphaned human infant, then his readiness to use nonhumans is simple discrimination, since adult apes, cats, mice, and other mammals are more aware of what is happening to them, more self-directing and, so far as we can tell, at least as sensitive to pain as any human infant. There seems to be no relevant characteristic that human infants possess that adult mammals do not have to the same or a higher degree. (Someone might try to argue that what makes it wrong to experiment on a human infant is that the infant will, in time and if left alone, develop into more than the nonhuman, but one would then, to be consistent, have to oppose abortion, since the fetus has the same potential as the infant – indeed, even contraception and abstinence might be wrong on this ground, since the egg and sperm, considered jointly, also have the same potential. In any case, this argument still gives us no reason for selecting a nonhuman, rather than a human with severe and irreversible brain damage, as the subject for our experiments.)

The experimenter, then, shows a bias in favor of his own species whenever he carries out an experiment on a nonhuman for a purpose that he would not think justified him in using a human being at an equal or lower level of sentience, awareness, ability to be self-directing, etc. No one familiar with the kind of results yielded by most experiments on animals can have the slightest doubt that if this bias were eliminated the number of experiments performed would be a minute fraction of the number performed today.

Experimenting on animals, and eating their flesh, are perhaps the two major forms of speciesism in our society. By comparison, the third and last form of speciesism is so minor as to be insignificant, but it is perhaps of some special interest to those for whom this paper was written. I am referring to speciesism in contemporary philosophy.

Philosophy ought to question the basic assumptions of the age. Thinking through, critically and carefully, what most people take for granted is, I believe, the chief task of philosophy, and it is this task that makes philosophy a worthwhile activity. Regrettably, philosophy does not always live up to its historic role. Philosophers are human beings and they are subject to all the preconceptions of the society to which they belong. Sometimes they succeed in breaking free of the prevailing ideology: more often they become its most sophisticated defenders. So, in this case, philosophy as practiced in the universities today does not challenge anyone's preconceptions about our relations with other species. By their writings, those philosophers who tackle problems that touch upon the issue reveal that they make the same unquestioned assumptions as most other humans, and what they say tends to confirm the reader in his or her comfortable speciesist habits.

I could illustrate this claim by referring to the writings of philosophers in various fields – for instance, the attempts that have been made by those interested in rights to draw the boundary of the sphere of rights so that it runs parallel to the biological boundaries of the species *Homo sapiens*, including infants and even mental defectives, but excluding those other beings of equal or greater capacity who are so useful to us at mealtimes and in our laboratories. I think it would be a more appropriate conclusion to this paper, however, if I concentrated on the problem with which we have been centrally concerned, the problem of equality.

It is significant that the problem of equality, in moral and political philosophy, is invariably formulated in terms of human equality. The effect of this is that the question of the equality of other animals does not confront the philosopher or student as an issue in itself – and this is already an indication of the failure of philosophy to challenge accepted beliefs. Still, philosophers have found it difficult to discuss the issue of human equality without raising, in a paragraph or two, the question of the status of other animals. The reason for this, which should be apparent from what I have said already, is that if humans are to be regarded as equal to one another, we need some sense of "equal" that does not require any actual, descriptive equality of capacities, talents, or other qualities. If equality is to be related to any actual characteristics of humans, these characteristics must be some lowest common denominator, pitched so low that no human lacks them – but then the philosopher comes up against the catch that any such set of characteristics which covers *all* humans will not be possessed *only by humans*. In other words, it turns out that in the only sense in which we can truly say, as an assertion of fact, that all humans are equal, at least some members of other species are also equal – equal, that is, to each other and to humans. If, on the other hand, we regard the statement "All humans are equal" in some nonfactual way, perhaps as a prescription, then, as I have already argued, it is even more difficult to exclude nonhumans from the sphere of equality.

This result is not what the egalitarian philosopher originally intended to assert. Instead of accepting the radical outcome to which their own reasonings naturally point, however, most philosophers try to reconcile their beliefs in human equality and animal inequality by arguments that can only be described as devious.

As a first example, I take William Frankena's well-known article "The Concept of Social Justice."[10] Frankena opposes the idea of basing justice on merit, because he sees that this could lead to highly inegalitarian results. Instead he proposes the principle that:

> . . . all men are to be treated as equals, not because they are equal, in any respect but simply because they are human. They are human because they have emotions and desires, and are able to think, and hence are capable of enjoying a good life in a sense in which other animals are not.

But what is this capacity to enjoy the good life which all humans have, but no other animals? Other animals have emotions and desires, and appear to be capable of enjoying a good life. We may doubt that they can think – although the behavior of some apes, dolphins, and even dogs suggests that some of them can – but what is the relevance of thinking? Frankena goes on to admit that by "the good life" he means "not so much the morally good life as the happy or satisfactory life," so thought would appear to be unnecessary for enjoying the good life; in fact, to emphasize the need for thought would make difficulties for the egalitarian since only some people are capable of leading intellectually satisfying lives or morally good lives. This makes it difficult to see what Frankena's principle of equality has to do with simply being *human*. Surely every sentient being is capable of leading a life that is happier or less miserable than some alternative life, and hence has a claim to be taken into account. In this respect the distinction between humans and nonhumans is not a sharp division, but rather a continuum along which we move gradually, and with overlaps between the species, from simple capacities for enjoyment and satisfaction, or pain and suffering, to more complex ones.

Faced with a situation in which they see a need for some basis for the moral gulf that is commonly thought to separate humans and animals, but can find no concrete difference that will do the job without undermining the equality of humans, philosophers tend to waffle. They resort to high-sounding phrases like "the intrinsic dignity of the human individual";[11] they talk of the "intrinsic worth of all men" as if men (humans?) had some worth that other beings did not,[12] or they say that humans, and only humans, are "ends in themselves," while "everything other than a person can only have value for a person."[13]

This idea of a distinctive human dignity and worth has a long history; it can be traced back directly to the Renaissance humanists, for instance, to Pico della Mirandola's *Oration on the Dignity of Man*. Pico and other humanists based their estimate of human dignity on the idea that man possessed the central, pivotal position in the "Great Chain of Being" that led from the lowliest forms of matter to God himself; this view of the universe, in turn, goes back to both classical and Judeo-Christian doctrines. Contemporary philosophers have cast off these metaphysical and religious shackles and freely invoke the dignity of mankind without needing to justify the idea at all. Why should we not attribute "intrinsic dignity" or "intrinsic worth" to ourselves? Fellow–humans are unlikely to reject the accolades we so generously bestow on them, and those to whom we deny the honor are unable to object. Indeed, when one thinks only of humans, it can be very liberal, very progressive, to talk of the dignity of all human beings. In so doing, we implicitly condemn slavery, racism, and other violations of human rights. We admit that we ourselves are in some fundamental sense on a par with the poorest, most ignorant members of our own species. It is only when we think of humans as no more than a small subgroup of all the beings that inhabit our planet that we may realize that in elevating our own species we are at the same time lowering the relative status of all other species.

The truth is that the appeal to the intrinsic dignity of human beings appears to solve the egalitarian's problems only as long as it goes unchallenged. Once we ask *why* it should be that all humans – including infants, mental defectives, psychopaths, Hitler, Stalin and the rest – have some kind of dignity or worth that no elephant, pig, or chimpanzee can ever achieve, we see that this question is as difficult to answer as our original request for some relevant fact that justifies the inequality of humans and other animals. In fact, these two questions are really one: talk of intrinsic dignity or moral worth only takes the problem back one step, because any satisfactory defense of the claim that all and only humans have intrinsic dignity would need to refer to some relevant capacities or characteristics that all and only humans possess. Philosophers frequently introduce ideas of dignity, respect, and worth at the point at which other reasons appear to be lacking, but this is hardly good enough. Fine phrases are the last resource of those who have run out of arguments.

In case there are those who still think it may be possible to find some relevant characteristic that distinguishes all humans from all members of other species, I shall refer again, before I conclude, to the existence of some humans who quite clearly are below the level of awareness, self-consciousness, intelligence, and sentience, of many nonhumans. I am thinking of humans with severe and irreparable brain damage, and also of infant humans. To avoid the complication of the relevance of a being's potential, however, I shall henceforth concentrate on permanently retarded humans.

Philosophers who set out to find a characteristic that will distinguish humans from other animals rarely take the course of abandoning these groups of humans by lumping them in with the other animals. It is easy to see why they do not. To take this line without rethinking our attitudes to other animals would entail that we have the right to perform painful experiments on retarded humans for trivial reasons; similarly it would follow that we had the right to rear and kill these humans for food. To most philosophers these consequences are as unacceptable as the view that we should stop treating nonhumans in this way.

Of course, when discussing the problem of equality it is possible to ignore the problem of mental defectives, or brush it aside as if somehow insignificant.[14] This is the easiest way out. What else remains? My final example of speciesism in contemporary philosophy has been selected to show what happens when a writer is prepared to face the question of human equality and animal inequality without ignoring the existence of mental defectives, and without resorting to obscurantist mumbo-jumbo. Stanley Benn's clear and honest article "Egalitarianism and Equal Consideration of Interests"[15] fits this description.

Benn, after noting the usual "evident human inequalities" argues, correctly I think, for equality of consideration as the only possible basis for egalitarianism. Yet Benn, like other writers, is thinking only of "equal consideration of human interests." Benn is quite open in his defence of this restriction of equal consideration:

> ... not to possess human shape *is* a disqualifying condition. However faithful or intelligent a dog may be, it would be a monstrous sentimentality to attribute to him interests that could be weighed in an equal balance with those of human beings ... if, for instance, one had to decide between feeding a hungry baby or a hungry dog, anyone who chose the dog would generally be reckoned morally defective, unable to recognize a fundamental inequality of claims.
>
> This is what distinguishes our attitude to animals from our attitude to imbeciles. It would be odd to say that we ought to respect equally the dignity or personality of the imbecile and of the rational man ... but there is nothing odd about saying that we should respect their interests equally, that is, that we should give to the interests of each the same serious consideration as claims to considerations necessary for some standard of well-being that we can recognize and endorse.

Benn's statement of the basis of the consideration we should have for imbeciles seems to me correct, but why should there be any fundamental inequality of claims between a dog and a human imbecile? Benn sees that if equal consideration depended on rationality, no reason could be given against using imbeciles for research purposes, as we now use dogs and guinea pigs. This will not do: "But of course we do distinguish imbeciles from animals in this regard," he says. That the common distinction is justifiable is something Benn does not question; his problem is how it is to be justified. The answer he gives is this:

> ... we respect the interests of men and give them priority over dogs not *insofar* as they are rational, but because rationality is the human norm. We say it is *unfair* to exploit the deficiencies of the imbecile who falls short of the norm, just as it would be unfair, and not just ordinarily dishonest, to steal from a blind man. If we do not think in this way about dogs, it is because we do not see the irrationality of the dog as a deficiency or a handicap, but as normal for the species. The characteristics, therefore, that distinguish the normal man from the normal dog make it intelligible for us to talk of other men having interests and capacities, and therefore claims, of precisely the same kind as we make on our own behalf. But although these characteristics may provide the point of the distinction between men and other species, they are not in fact the qualifying conditions for membership, or the distinguishing criteria of the class of morally considerable persons; and this is precisely because a man does not become a member of a different

species, with its own standards of normality, by reason of not possessing these characteristics.

The final sentence of this passage gives the argument away. An imbecile, Benn concedes, may have no characteristics superior to those of a dog; nevertheless this does not make the imbecile a member of "a different species" as the dog is. *Therefore* it would be "unfair" to use the imbecile for medical research as we use the dog. But why? That the imbecile is not rational is just the way things have worked out, and the same is true of the dog – neither is any more responsible for their mental level. If it is unfair to take advantage of an isolated defect, why is it fair to take advantage of a more general limitation? I find it hard to see anything in this argument except a defense of preferring the interests of members of our own species because they are members of our own species. To those who think there might be more to it, I suggest the following mental exercise. Assume that it has been proven that there is a difference in the average, or normal, intelligence quotient for two different races, say whites and blacks. Then substitute the term "white" for every occurrence of "men" and "black" for every occurrence of "dog" in the passage quoted; and substitute "high IQ" for "rationality" and when Benn talks of "imbeciles" replace this term by "dumb whites" – that is, whites who fall well below the normal white I.Q. score. Finally, change "species" to "race." Now reread the passage. It has become a defence of a rigid, no-exceptions division between whites and blacks, based on IQ scores, *notwithstanding an admitted overlap* between whites and blacks in this respect. The revised passage is, of course, outrageous, and this is not only because we have made fictitious assumptions in our substitutions. The point is that in the original passage Benn was defending a rigid division in the amount of consideration due to members of different species, despite admitted cases of overlap. If the original did not, at first reading, strike us as being as outrageous as the revised version does, this is largely because although we are not racists ourselves, most of us are speciesists. Like the other articles, Benn's stands as a warning of the ease with which the best minds can fall victim to a prevailing ideology.

Notes

1   Passages of this article appeared in a review of *Animals, Men and Morals*, edited by S. and R. Godlovitch and J. Harris (London: Gollancz and Taplinger, 1972) in the *New York Review of Books*, April 5, 1973. The whole direction of my thinking on this subject I owe to talks with a number of friends in Oxford in 1970–1, especially Richard Keshen, Stanley Godlovitch, and, above all, Roslind Godlovitch.

2   *The Methods of Ethics* (7th edn.), p. 382.

3   For example, R. M. Hare, *Freedom and Reason* (Oxford: Oxford University Press, 1963) and J. Rawls, *A Theory of Justice* (Cambridge, MA: Harvard University Press, 1972); for a brief account of the essential agreement on this issue between these and other positions, see R. M. Hare, "Rules of War and Moral Reasoning," *Philosophy and Public Affairs*, vol. I, no. 2 (1972).

4   *Introduction to the Principles of Morals and Legislation*, ch. XVII.

5   I owe the term "speciesism" to Dr. Richard Ryder.

6   In order to produce 1 lb. of protein in the form of beef or veal, we must feed 21 lbs. of protein to the animal. Other forms of livestock are slightly less inefficient, but the average ratio in the US is still 1:8. It has been estimated that the amount of protein lost to humans in this way is equivalent to 90% of the annual world protein deficit. For a brief account, see Frances Moore Lappe, *Diet for a Small Planet* (New York: Friends of the Earth/Ballantine, 1971), pp. 4–11.

7   Although one might think that killing a being is obviously the ultimate wrong one can do to it, I think that the infliction of suffering is a clearer indication of speciesism because it might be argued that at least part of what is wrong with killing a human is that most humans are conscious of their existence over time, and have desires and purposes that extend into the future – see, for instance, M. Tooley, "Abortion and Infanticide," *Philosophy and Public Affairs*, vol. 2, no. 1 (1972). Of course, if one took this view one would have to hold – as Tooley does – that killing a human infant or mental defective is not in itself wrong, and is less serious than killing certain higher mammals that probably do have a sense of their own existence over time.

8   Ruth Harrison, *Animal Machines* (London: Stuart, 1964). This book provides an eye-opening account of intensive farming methods for those unfamiliar with the subject.

9   *Journal of the Experimental Analysis of Behavior*, vol. 13, no. 1 (1970). Any recent volume of this journal, or of other journals in the field, like the *Journal of Comparative and Physiological Psychology*, will contain reports of equally cruel and trivial experiments. For a fuller account, see Richard Ryder, "Experiments on Animals" in *Animals, Men and Morals*.

10 In R. Brandt (ed.), *Social Justice* (Englewood Cliffs, NJ: Prentice Hall, 1962); the passage quoted appears on p. 19.

11 W. K. Frankena, "The Concept of Social Justice," in R. Brandt (ed.), *Social Justice*, p. 23.

12 H. A. Bedau, "Egalitarianism and the Idea of Equality" in *Nomos IX: Equality*, ed. J. R. Pennock and J. W. Chapman (New York 1967).

13 G. Vlastos, "Justice and Equality" in Brandt, *Social Justice*, p. 48.

14 E.g. Bernard Williams, "The Idea of Equality," in *Philosophy, Politics and Society* (second series), ed. P. Laslett and W. Runciman (Oxford: Blackwell, 1962), p. 118; J. Rawls, *A Theory of Justice*, pp. 509–10.

15 *Nomos IX: Equality*; the passages quoted are on pp. 62ff.

Six

Is Racial Discrimination Arbitrary?

1 Introduction

There is nowadays wide agreement that racism is wrong. To describe a policy, law, movement, or nation as "racist" is to condemn it. It may be thought that since we all agree that racism is wrong, it is unnecessary to speculate on exactly what it is and why it is wrong. This indifference to moral fundamentals could, however, prove dangerous. For one thing, the fact that most people agree today that racism is wrong does not mean that this attitude will always be so widely shared. Even if we had no fears for the future, though, we need to have some understanding of what it is about racism that is wrong if we are to handle satisfactorily all the problems we face today. For instance, there is the contentious issue of "reverse discrimination" or discrimination in favor of members of oppressed minority groups. It must be granted that a university which admits members of minority groups who do not achieve the minimum standard that others must reach in order to be admitted is discriminating on racial lines. Is such discrimination therefore wrong?

Or, to take another issue, the efforts of Arab nations to have the United Nations declare Zionism a form of racism provoked an extremely hostile reaction in nations friendly to Israel, particularly the United States, but it led to virtually no discussion of whether Zionism is a form of racism. Yet the charge is not altogether without plausibility, for if Jews are a race, then Zionism promotes the idea of a state dominated by one race, and this has practical

First published in *Philosophia*, 8 (1978), pp. 185–203. Reprinted by permission of the editor.

consequences in, for instance, Israel's immigration laws. Again, to consider whether this makes Zionism a form of racism we need to understand what it is that makes a policy racist and wrong.

First it is necessary to get our terms clear. "Racism" is, as I have said, a word which now has an inescapable evaluative force, although it also has some descriptive content. Words with these dual functions can be confusing if their use is not specified. People sometimes try to argue: "X is a case of racial discrimination, therefore X is racist; racism is wrong, therefore X is wrong." This argument may depend on an equivocation in the meaning of "racist," the term being used first in a morally neutral, descriptive sense, and secondly in its evaluative sense.

To avoid this kind of confusion, I shall accept the usual evaluative force of the term "racist" and reserve it for practices that are judged to be wrong. Thus we cannot pronounce a policy, law, etc. "racist" unless we have decided that it is wrong. "Racial discrimination" on the other hand I shall use in a descriptive and morally neutral sense, so that to say that a policy or law discriminates racially is simply to point to the fact of discrimination based on race, leaving open the question of whether it can be justified. With this terminology it becomes possible to ask whether a given form of racial discrimination is racist; this is another way of asking whether it is justifiable.[1]

If we ask those who regard racial discrimination as wrong to say why it is wrong, it is commonly said that it is wrong to pick on race as a reason for treating one person differently from others, because race is irrelevant to whether a person should be given a job, the vote, higher education, or any benefits or burdens of this sort. The irrelevance of race, it is said, makes it quite arbitrary to give these things to people of one race while withholding them from those of another race. I shall refer to this account of what is wrong with racial discrimination as the "standard objection" to racial discrimination.

A sophisticated theory of justice can be invoked in support of this standard objection to racial discrimination. Justice requires, as Aristotle so plausibly said, that equals be treated equally and unequals be treated unequally. To this we must add the obvious proviso that the equalities or inequalities should be relevant to the treatment in question. Now when we consider things like employment, it becomes clear that the relevant inequalities between candidates for a vacant position are inequalities in their ability to carry out the duties of the position and, perhaps, inequalities in the extent to which they will benefit through being offered the position. Race does not seem to be relevant at all. Similarly with the vote, capacity for rational choice between candidates or policies might be held a relevant characteristic, but race should not be; and so on for other goods. It is hard to think of anything for which race in itself is a relevant characteristic, and hence to use race as a basis for discrimination is arbitrarily to single out an irrelevant factor, no doubt because of a bias or prejudice against those of a different race.[2]

As we shall see, this account of why racial discrimination is wrong is inadequate because there are many situations in which, from at least one point of view, the racial factor is by no means irrelevant, and therefore it can be denied that racial discrimination in these situations is arbitrary.

One type of situation in which race must be admitted to be relevant to the purposes of the person discriminating need not delay us at this stage; this is the situation in which those purposes themselves favor a particular race. Thus if the purpose of Hitler and the other Nazi leaders was, among other things, to produce a world in which there were no Jews, it was certainly not irrelevant to their purposes that those rounded up and murdered by the SS were Jews rather than so-called "Aryans." But the fundamental wrongness of the aims of the Nazis makes the "relevance" of race to those aims totally inefficacious so far as justifying Nazi racial discrimination is concerned. While their type of racial discrimination may not have been arbitrary discrimination in the usual sense, it was no less wrong for that. *Why* it was wrong is something that I hope will become clearer later in this article. Meanwhile I shall look at some less cataclysmic forms of racial discrimination, for too much contemporary discussion of racial discrimination has focused on the most blatant instances: Nazi Germany, [the former situation in] South Africa, and the American "Deep South" during the period of legally enforced racial segregation.[3] These forms of racism are not the type that face us now in our own societies (unless we live in South Africa) and to discuss racial discrimination in terms of these examples today is to present an oversimplified picture of the problem of racial discrimination. By looking at some of the reasons for racial discrimination that might actually be offered today in countries all over the world I hope to show that the real situation is usually much more complex than consideration of the more blatant instances of racial discrimination would lead us to believe.

2   Examples

I shall start by describing an example of racial discrimination which may at first glance seem to be an allowable exception to a general rule that racial discrimination is arbitrary and therefore wrong; and I shall then suggest that this case has parallels with other cases we may not be so willing to allow as exceptions.

Case 1. A film director is making a film about the lives of blacks living in New York's Harlem. He advertises for black actors. A white actor turns up, but the director refuses to allow him to audition, saying that the film is about blacks and there are no roles for whites. The actor replies that, with the appropriate wig and make-up, he can look just like a black; moreover he can imitate the mannerisms, gestures, and speech of Harlem blacks. Nevertheless the director refuses to consider him for the role, because it is essential to the director's conception of the film that the black experience be authentically portrayed, and however good a white actor might be, the director would not be satisfied with the authenticity of the portrayal.

The film director is discriminating along racial lines, yet he cannot be said to be discriminating arbitrarily. His discrimination is apt for his purpose. Moreover his purpose is a legitimate one. So the standard objection to racial discrimination cannot be made in this instance.

Racial discrimination may be acceptable in an area like casting for films or the theater, when the race of a character in the film or play is important, because this is one of the seemingly few areas in which a person's race is directly relevant to his capacity to perform a given task. As such, it may be thought, these areas can easily be distinguished from other areas of employment, as well as from areas like housing, education, the right to vote, and so on, where race has no relevance at all. Unfortunately there are many other situations in which race is not as totally irrelevant as this view assumes.

Case 2. The owner of a cake shop with a largely white and racially prejudiced clientele wishes to hire an assistant. The owner has no prejudice against blacks himself, but is reluctant to employ one, for fear that his customers will go elsewhere. If his fears are well-founded (and this is not impossible) then the race of a candidate for the position is, again, relevant to the purpose of the employer, which in this case is to maintain the profitability of his business.

What can we say about this case? We cannot deny the connection between race and the owner's purposes, and so we must recognize that the owner's discrimination is not arbitrary, and does not necessarily indicate a bias or prejudice on his part. Nor can we say that the owner's purpose is an illegitimate one, for making a profit from the sale of cakes is not generally regarded as wrong, at least if the amount of profit made is modest.

We can, of course, look at other aspects of the matter. We can object to the racial discrimination shown by customers who will search out shops staffed by whites only – such people do discriminate arbitrarily, for race is irrelevant to the quality of the goods and the proficiency of service in a shop – but is this not simply a fact that the shop-owner must live with, however much he may wish he could change it? We might argue that by pandering to the prejudices of his customers, the owner is allowing those prejudices to continue unchallenged; whereas if he and other shopkeepers took no notice of them, people would eventually become used to mixing with those of another race, and prejudices would be eroded. Yet it is surely too much to ask an individual shop-owner to risk his livelihood in a lone and probably vain effort to break down prejudice. Few of the most dedicated opponents of racism do as much. If there were national legislation which distributed the burden more evenly, by a general prohibition of discrimination on racial grounds (with some recognized exceptions for cases like casting for a film or play) the situation would be different. Then we could reasonably ask every shop-owner to play his part. Whether there should be such legislation is a different question from whether the shop-owner may be blamed for discriminating in the absence of legislation. I shall discuss the issue of legislation shortly, after we consider a different kind of racial discrimination that, again, is not arbitrary.

Case 3. A landlord discriminates against blacks in letting the accommodation he owns. Let us say that he is not so rigid as never to let an apartment to a black, but if a black person and a white person appear to be equally suitable as tenants, with equally good references and so on, the landlord invariably prefers the white. He defends his policy along the following lines:

> If more than a very small proportion of my tenants get behind in their rent and then disappear without paying the arrears, I will be out of business. Over the years, I have found that more blacks do this than whites. I admit that there are many honest blacks (some of my best tenants have been black) and many dishonest whites, but, for some reason I do not claim to understand, the odds on a white tenant defaulting are longer than on a black doing so, even when their references and other credentials appear equally good. In this business you can't run a full-scale probe of every prospective tenant − and if I tried I would be abused for invading privacy − so you have to go by the average rather than the individual. That is why blacks have to have better indications of reliability than whites before I will let to them.

Now the landlord's impression of a higher rate of default among blacks than among comparable whites may itself be the result of prejudice on his part. Perhaps in most cases when landlords say this kind of thing, there is no real factual basis to their allegations. People have grown up with racial stereotypes, and these stereotypes are reinforced by a tendency to notice occurrences which conform to the stereotype and to disregard those which conflict with it. So if unreliability is part of the stereotype of blacks held by many whites, they may take more notice of blacks who abscond without paying the rent than of blacks who are reliable tenants; and conversely they will take less notice of absconding whites and more of those whites who conform to their ideas of normal white behaviour.

If it is prejudice that is responsible for the landlord's views about black and white tenants, and there is no factual basis for his claims, then the problem becomes one of eliminating this prejudice and getting the landlord to see his mistake. This is by no means an easy task, but it is not a task for philosophers, and it does not concern us here, for we are interested in attempts to justify racial discrimination, and an attempted justification based on an inaccurate description of a situation can be rejected without raising the deeper issue of justification.

On the other hand, the landlord's impression of a higher rate of default among black tenants *could* be entirely accurate. (It might be explicable in terms of the different cultural and economic circumstances in which blacks are brought up.) Whether or not we think this likely, we need to ask what its implications would be for the justifiability of the racial discrimination exercised by the landlord. To refuse even to consider this question would be to rest all one's objections to the landlord's practice on the falsity of his claims, and thereby to fail to examine the possibility that the landlord's practice could be open to objection even if his impressions on tenant reliability are accurate.

If the landlord's impressions were accurate, we would have to concede, once again, that racial discrimination in this situation is not arbitrary; that it is, instead, relevant to the purposes of the landlord. We must also admit that these purposes – making a living from letting property that one owns – are not themselves objectionable, provided the rents are reasonable, and so on. Nor can we, this time, locate the origin of the problem in the prejudices of others, except insofar as the problem has its origin in the prejudices of those responsible for the conditions of deprivation in which many of the present generation of blacks grew up – but it is too late to do anything to alter those prejudices anyway, since they belong to previous generations.

We have now looked at three examples of racial discrimination, and can begin to examine the parallels and differences between them. Many people, as I have already said, would make no objection to the discriminatory hiring practice of the film director in the first of these cases. But we can now see that if we try to justify the actions of the film director in this case on the grounds that his purpose is a legitimate one and the discrimination he uses is relevant for his purpose, we will have to accept the actions of the cake-shop owner and the landlord as well. I suspect that many of those ready to accept the discriminatory practice in the first case will be much more reluctant about the other two cases. But what morally significant difference is there between them?

It might be suggested that the difference between them lies in the nature of what blacks are being deprived of, and their title to it. The argument would run like this: No one has a right to be selected to act in a film; the director must have absolute discretion to hire whomsoever he wishes to hire. After all, no one can force the director to make the film at all, and if he didn't make it, no one would be hired to play in it; if he does decide to make it, therefore, he must be allowed to make it on his own terms. Moreover, since so few people ever get the chance to appear in a film, it would be absurd to hold that the director violates someone's rights by not giving him something which most people will never have anyway. On the other hand, people do have a right to employment, and to housing. To discriminate against blacks in an ordinary employment situation, or in the letting of accommodation, threatens their basic rights and therefore should not be tolerated.

Plausible as it appears, this way of distinguishing the first case from the other two will not do. Consider the first and second cases: almost everything that we have said about the film director applies to the cake-shop owner as well. No one can force the cake-shop owner to keep his shop open, and if he didn't, no one would be hired to work in it. If in the film director's case this was a reason for allowing him to make the film on his own terms, it must be a reason for allowing the shop-owner to run his shop on his own terms. In fact, such reasoning, which would allow unlimited discrimination in restaurants, hotels, and shops, is invalid. There are plenty of examples where we would not agree that the fact that someone did not have to make an offer or provide an opportunity at all means that if he does do it he must be allowed to make the offer or provide the opportunity on his own terms. The United States Civil Rights Act of 1965 certainly does not recognize this line of argument, for it prohibits those offering food and lodgings to the public from excluding customers on racial grounds. We may, as a society, decide that we shall not allow people to make certain offers, if the way in which the offers are made will cause hardship or offense to others. In so doing we are balancing people's freedom to do as they please against the harm this may do to others, and coming down on the side of preventing harm rather than enlarging freedom. This is a perfectly defensible position, if the harm is sufficiently serious and the restriction of freedom not grave.[4]

Nor does it seem possible to distinguish the first and second cases by the claim that since so few people ever get the chance to appear in a film, no one's rights are violated if they are not given something that most people will never have anyway. For if the number of jobs in cake-shops was small, and the demand for such jobs high, it would also be true that few people would ever have the chance to work in a cake-shop. It would be odd if such an increase in competition for the job justified an otherwise unjustifiable policy of hiring whites only. Moreover, this argument would allow a film director to discriminate on racial lines even if race was irrelevant to the roles he was casting; and that is quite a different situation from the one we have been discussing.

The best way to distinguish the situations of the film director and the shop-owner is by reference to the nature of the employment offered, and to the reasons why racial discrimination in these cases is not arbitrary. In casting for a film about blacks, the race of the actor auditioning is intrinsically significant, independently of the attitudes of those connected with the film. In the case of hiring a shop assistant, race is relevant only because of the attitudes of those connected (as customers) with the shop; it has nothing to do with the selling of cakes in itself, but only with the selling of cakes to racially prejudiced customers. This means that in the case of the shop assistant we could eliminate the relevance of race if we could eliminate the prejudices of the customers; by contrast there is no way in which we could eliminate the relevance of the race of an actor auditioning for a role in a film about blacks, without altering the nature of the film. Moreover, in the case of the shop–owner racial discrimination probably serves to perpetuate the very prejudices that make such discrimination relevant and (from the point of view of the owner seeking to maintain his profits) necessary. Thus people who can buy all their cakes and other necessities in shops staffed only by whites will never come into the kind of contact with comparable blacks which might break down their aversion to being served by blacks; whereas if shop-owners were to hire more blacks, their customers would no doubt become used to it and in time might wonder why they ever opposed the idea. (Compare the change of attitudes toward racial integration in the American South since the 1956 United States Supreme Court decision against segregated schools and subsequent measures against segregation were put into effect.)[5]

Hence if we are opposed to arbitrary discrimination we have reason to take steps against racial discrimination in situations like Case 2, because such discrimination, while not itself arbitrary, both feeds on and gives support to discrimination by others which is arbitrary. In prohibiting it we would, admittedly, be preventing the employer from discriminating in a way that is relevant to his purposes; but if the causal hypothesis suggested in the previous paragraph is correct, this situation would only be temporary, and after some time the circumstances inducing the employer to discriminate racially would have been eliminated.

The case of the landlord presents a more difficult problem. If the facts he alleges are true his nonarbitrary reasons for discrimination against blacks are real enough. They do not depend on present arbitrary discrimination by others, and they may persist beyond an interval in which there is no discrimination. Whatever the roots of hypothetical racial differences in reliability as tenants might be, they would probably go too deep to be eradicated solely by a short period in which there was no racial discrimination.

We should recognize, then, that if the facts are as alleged, to legislate against the landlord's racially discriminatory practice is to impose a long-term disadvantage upon him. At the very least, he will have to take greater care in ascertaining the suitability of prospective tenants. Perhaps he will turn to data-collecting agencies for assistance, thus contributing to the growth of institutions that are threats, potential or actual, to our privacy. Perhaps, if these methods are unavailable or unavailing, the landlord will have to take greater losses than he otherwise would have, and perhaps this will lead to increased rents or even to a reduction in the amount of rentable housing available.

None of this forces us to conclude that we should not legislate against the landlord's racial discrimination. There are good reasons why we should seek to eliminate racial discrimination even when such discrimination is neither arbitrary in itself nor relevant only because of the arbitrary prejudices of others. These reasons may be so important as to make the disadvantage imposed on the landlord comparatively insignificant.

An obvious point that can be made against the landlord is that he is judging people, at least in part, as members of a race rather than as individuals. The landlord does not deny that some black prospective tenants he turns away would make better tenants than some white prospective tenants he accepts. Some highly eligible black prospective tenants are refused accommodation simply because they are black. If the landlord assessed every prospective tenant as an individual this would not happen.

A similar point is often made in the debate over alleged differences between blacks and whites in America in whatever is measured by IQ tests. Even if, as Jensen and others have suggested, there is a small inherited difference in IQ between blacks and whites, it is clear that this difference shows up only when we compare averages, and not when we compare individuals. Even if we accept the controversial estimates that the average IQ of American blacks is 15 points lower than the average IQ of American whites, there is still a tremendous amount of overlap between the IQs of blacks and whites, with many whites scoring lower than the majority of blacks. Hence the difference in averages between the races would be of limited significance. For any purpose for which IQ mattered – like entrance into higher levels of education – it would still be essential to consider each applicant individually, rather than as a member of a certain race.

There are plenty of reasons why in situations like admitting people to higher education or providing them with employment or other benefits we should regard people as individuals and not as members of some larger group. For one thing we will be able to make a selection better suited for our own purposes, for selecting or discarding whole groups of people will generally result in, at best, a crude approximation to the results we hope to achieve. This is certainly true in an area like education. On the other hand it must be admitted that in some situations a crude approximation is all that can be achieved anyway. The landlord claims that his situation is one of these, and that as he cannot reliably tell which individuals will make suitable tenants, he is justified in resorting to so crude a means of selection as race. Here we need to turn our attention from the landlord to the prospective black tenant.

To be judged merely as a member of a group when it is one's individual qualities on which the verdict should be given is to be treated as less than the unique individual that we see ourselves as. Even where our individual qualities would merit less than we receive as a member of a group – if we are promoted over better-qualified people because we went to the "right" private school – the benefit is usually less welcome than it would be if it had been merited by our own attributes. Of course in this case qualms are easily stilled by the fact that a benefit has been received, never mind how. In the contrary case, however, when something of value has been lost, the sense of loss will be compounded by the feeling that one was not assessed on one's own merits, but merely as a member of a group.

To this general preference for individual as against group assessment must be added a consideration arising from the nature of the group. To be denied a benefit because one was, say, a member of the Communist Party, would be unjust and a violation of basic principles of political liberty, but if one has chosen to join the Communist Party, then one is, after all, being assessed for what one has done, and one can choose between living with the consequences of continued party membership or leaving the party.[6] Race, of course, is not something that one chooses to adopt or that one can ever choose to give up. The person who is denied advantages because of his race is totally unable to alter this particular circumstance of his existence and so may feel with added sharpness that his life is clouded, not merely because he is not being judged as an individual, but because of something over which he has no control at all. This makes racial discrimination peculiarly invidious.

So we have the viewpoint of the victim of racial discrimination to offset against the landlord's argument in favor, and it seems that the victim has more at stake and hence should be given preference, even if the landlord's reason for discriminating is nonarbitrary and hence in a sense legitimate. The case against racial discrimination becomes stronger still when we consider the long-term social effects of discrimination.

When members of a racial minority are overwhelmingly among the poorest members of a society, living in a deprived area, holding jobs low in pay and status, or no jobs at all, and less well educated than the average member of the community, racial discrimination serves to perpetuate a divided society in which race becomes a badge of a much broader inferiority. It is the association of race with economic status and educational disadvantages which in turn gives rise to the situation in which there could be a coloring of truth to the claim that race is a relevant ground for discriminating between prospective tenants, applicants for employment, and so on. Thus there is, in the end, a parallel between the situation of the landlord and the cake-shop owner, for both, by their discrimination, contribute to the maintenance of the grounds for claiming that this discrimination is nonarbitrary. Hence prohibition of such discrimination can be justified as breaking this circle of deprivation and discrimination. The difference between the situations, as I have already said, is that in the case of the cake-shop owner it is only a prejudice against contact with blacks that needs to be broken down, and experience has shown that such prejudices do evaporate in a relatively short period of time. In the case of the landlord, however, it is the whole social and economic position of blacks that needs to be changed, and while overcoming discrimination would be an essential part of this process it may not be sufficient. That is why, if the facts are as the landlord alleges them to be, prohibition of racial discrimination is likely to impose more of a long-term disadvantage on the landlord than on the shop-owner – a disadvantage which is, however, outweighed by the costs of continuing the circle of racial discrimination and deprivation for those discriminated against; and the costs of greater social inequality and racial divisiveness for the community as a whole.

3   A Basic Principle

If our discussion of the three examples has been sound, opposition to racial discrimination cannot rely on the standard objection that racial discrimination is arbitrary because race is irrelevant to employment, housing, and other things that matter. While this very often will be true, it will not always be true. The issue is more complicated than that appealing formula suggests, and has to do with the effect of racial discrimination on its victims, and on society as a whole. Behind all this, however, there is a more basic moral principle, and at this more basic level the irrelevance of race and the arbitrariness of racial discrimination reappear and help to explain why racism is wrong. This basic moral principle is the principle of equal consideration of interests.

The principle of equal consideration of interests is easy to state, though difficult to apply. Bentham's famous "each to count for one and none for more than one" is one way of putting it, though not free from ambiguity; Sidgwick's formulation is more precise, if less memorable: "The good of any one individual is of no more importance, from the point of view (if I may say so) of the Universe, than the good of any other."[7] Perhaps the best way of explaining the effect of the principle is to follow C. I. Lewis's suggestion that we imagine ourselves living, one after the other, the lives of everyone affected by our actions; in this way we would experience all of their experiences as our own.[8]

R. M. Hare's insistence that moral judgments must be universalizable comes to much the same thing, as he has pointed out.[9] The essence of the principle of equal consideration of interests is that we give equal weight in our moral deliberations to the like interests of all those affected by our actions. This means that if only X and Y would be affected by a possible act, and if X stands to lose more than Y stands to gain (for instance, X will lose his job and find it difficult to get another, whereas Y will merely get a small promotion) then it is better not to do the act. We cannot, if we accept the principle of equal consideration of interests, say that doing the act is better, despite the facts described, because we are more concerned about Y than we are about X. What the principle is really saying is that an interest is an interest, whoever's interest it may be.

We can make this more concrete by considering a particular interest, say the interest we have in the relief of pain. Then the principle says that the ultimate moral reason for relieving pain is simply the undesirability of pain as such, and not the undesirability of X's pain, which might be different from the undesirability of Y's pain. Of course, X's pain might be more undesirable than Y's pain because it is more painful, and then the principle of equal consideration would give greater weight to the relief of X's pain. Again, even where the pains are equal, other factors might be relevant, especially if others are affected. If there has been an earthquake we might give priority to the relief of a doctor's pain so that he can treat other victims. But the doctor's pain itself counts only once, and with no added weighting. The principle of equal consideration of interests acts like a pair of scales, weighing interests impartially. True scales favor the side where the interest is stronger, or where several interests combine to outweigh a smaller number of similar interests; but they take no account of whose interests they are weighing.

It is important to understand that the principle of equal consideration of interests is, to adopt Sidgwick's suggestive phrase, a "point of view of the universe" principle. The phrase is, of course, a metaphor. It is not intended to suggest that the universe as a whole is alive, or conscious, or capable of having a point of view; but we can, without getting involved in any pantheist suppositions, imagine how matters would be judged by a being who was able to take in all of the universe, viewing all that was going on with an impartial benevolence.[10]

It is from this universal point of view that race is irrelevant to the consideration of interests; for all that counts are the interests themselves. To give less consideration to a specified amount of pain because that pain was experienced by a black would be to make an arbitrary distinction. Why pick on race? Why not on whether a person was born in a leap year? Or whether there is more than one vowel in his surname? All these characteristics are equally irrelevant to the undesirability of pain from the universal point of view. Hence the principle of equal consideration of interests shows straightforwardly why the most blatant forms of racism, like that of the Nazis, are wrong. For the Nazis were concerned only for the welfare of members of the "Aryan" race, and the sufferings of Jews, Gypsies, and Slavs were of no concern to them.

That the principle of equal consideration of interests is a "point of view of the universe" principle allows us to account for the fact that it is a principle upon which it seems virtually impossible to act. Who of us can live as if our own welfare and that of our family and friends were of no more concern to us than the welfare of anonymous individuals in far-away countries, of whom we know no more than the fact of their existence? Only a saint or a robot could live in this way; but this does not mean that only a saint or a robot can live in accordance with the principle of equal consideration of interests, for a principle which is valid from a universal point of view may yield subordinate principles to be acted upon by those who have limited resources and are involved in a particular segment of the world, rather than looking down upon the whole from a position of impartiality.

So subordinate principles giving members of families responsibility for the welfare of others in the family, or giving national governments responsibility for the welfare of their citizens, will be derivable from the principle of equal consideration, *if* everyone's interests are best promoted by such arrangements; and this is likely to be the case if, first, people are more knowledgeable about the interests of those close to them and more inclined to work to see that these interests are catered for, and, second, if the distribution of resources between families and between nations is not so unequally distributed that some families or nations are simply unable to provide for themselves the means to satisfying interests that could be satisfied with ease by other families or nations. In the world as it is presently constituted the first condition seems to hold, but not the second. For that reason I do not think that the subordinate principles mentioned correctly set out our present moral responsibilities, though they could do so if resources were more evenly distributed. Until then, we ought to strive to be more saint-like.[11]

Subordinate principles based on race, giving each race responsibility for the welfare of other members of that race are, I think, considerably less likely to be derivable from the principle of equal consideration than subordinate principles based on family or membership of a nation. For where they are not living together as a nation, races tend to be widely scattered; there is usually little knowledge of the circumstances of other members of one's race in different parts of the world, and there is nobody with the capacity to look after all members of a race as a national government can look after the interests of its citizens. There is, admittedly, often a degree of sentiment connecting members of a race, however widely they are separated. The contributions of American

Jews to the support of members of their race in Israel is a well-known example of this, and there are many others. But the intermingling of races still makes it very doubtful that interests could be generally promoted by dividing responsibilities along racial lines.

The fundamental principle of equal consideration of interests, then, pays no regard to the race of those whose interests are under consideration; nor can we plausibly derive from the basic principle a subordinate principle enjoining us to consider the interests of members of our own race before we consider the interests of others; yet it cannot be said that the principle rules out racial discrimination in all circumstances. For the principle is an abstract one, and can only be applied in a concrete situation, in which the facts of the situation will be relevant. For instance, I have heard it said that somewhere in ancient Hindu writings members of the Brahmin or priestly caste are claimed to be so much more sensitive than members of the lower castes that their pleasures and pains are twenty times as intense as those of lesser human beings. We would, of course, do well to be suspicious of such a claim, particularly as the author of the document would no doubt have been a Brahmin himself. But let us assume that we somehow discovered that this extraordinary difference in sensitivity did in fact exist; it would follow that Brahmins have a greater interest in having access to a source of pleasure, and in avoiding a source of pain, than others. It would be as if when a Brahmin scratches his finger he feels a pain similar to that which others feel when they dislocate their shoulder. Then, consistently with the principle of equal consideration of interests, if a Brahmin and an ordinary person have both scratched their fingers, and we have only enough soothing ointment to cover one scratch, we should favor the Brahmin – just as, in the case of two normal people, if one had scratched a finger while the other had dislocated a shoulder we should favor the person with the more painful injury.

Needless to say, the example is a fanciful one, and intended to show only how, within the confines of the principle of equal consideration of interests, factual differences could be relevant to racial discrimination. In the absence of any real evidence of racial differences in sensitivity to pleasure and pain, the example has no practical relevance. Other differences between races – if they were differences between all members of races, and not differences which showed up only when averages were taken – could also justify forms of discrimination which ran parallel to the boundary of race. Examples would be substantial differences in intelligence, educability, or the capacity to be self-governing. Strictly, if there were such differences then discrimination based on them would not be *racial* discrimination but rather discrimination on the ground of differences which happened to coincide with racial differences. But perhaps this is hair-splitting, since it would certainly be popularly known as racial discrimination. The kind of discrimination that such differences would justify would be only that to which these differences were relevant. For instance, a respectable argument for benevolent colonialism could be mounted if it really were true that certain races were so incapable of self-government as to be obviously better off on the whole when ruled by people of a different race. I hasten to add that the historical record gives no support to such a hypothesis, but rather suggests the contrary. Again, this fictional example shows only that, given peculiar enough factual assumptions, any acceptable principle of equality can lead to racial discrimination.

On the other hand, the principle of equal consideration of interests does underpin the decisions we reached when considering the three more realistic examples of racial discrimination in the preceding section of this article. Although the principle is too general to allow the derivation of straightforward and indisputable conclusions from it in complex situations, it does seem that an impartial consideration of the interests of all involved would, for reasons already discussed, rule out discrimination by the shop-owner and the landlord, though allowing that of the film director. Hence it is the arbitrariness of racial discrimination at the level of the principle of equal consideration of interests, rather than at the level of the particular decision of the person discriminating, that governs whether a given act of racial discrimination is justifiable.

This conclusion may be applied to other controversial cases. It suggests, for instance, that the problem of "reverse discrimination" or "compensatory discrimination," which arises when a university or employer gives preference to members of minority groups, should be discussed by asking not whether racial discrimination is always and intrinsically wrong, but whether the proposal is, on balance, in the interests of all those affected by it. This is a difficult question, and not one that can be answered generally for all types of reverse discrimination. For instance, if white communities have a far better doctor–patient ratio than black communities because very few blacks are admitted to medical school and white doctors tend to work in white communities, there is a strong case for admitting some black candidates to medical school ahead of whites who are better qualified by the standard entry procedures, provided, of course, that the blacks admitted are not so poorly qualified as to be unable to become competent doctors. The case for separate and easier entry would be less strong in an area where there is no equivalent community need, for instance, in philosophy. Here much would depend on whether black students who would not otherwise have been admitted were able to make up ground and do as well as whites with higher ratings on standard entry procedures. If so, easier entry for blacks could be justified in terms of the conventional goal of admitting those students most likely to succeed in their course; taking into account a student's race would merely be a way of correcting for the failure of standard tests to allow for the disadvantages that face blacks in competing with whites on such tests. If, on the other hand, blacks admitted under easier entry in a field like philosophy did not do as well as the whites they displaced could have been expected to do, discrimination in their favor would be much harder to justify.

Immigration policy, too, is an area in which the principle of equal consideration of interests suggests the kinds of facts we should look for, instead of giving a definite answer. The relevant questions are the extent to which an immigrant will be benefited by admission, and the extent to which the admitting nation will be benefited. Race certainly does not provide an answer to the first of these questions. A country which chooses to give only those of a certain race the benefit of permanent residence fails to give equal consideration to those not of the favored race who may have a greater interest in leaving their present country than others who are accepted because of their race. While this kind of racial discrimination would in itself be unjustifiable, it has been defended on the grounds that the alternative would be disastrous for citizens of the admitting nation, and ultimately for those admitted too. An extreme version of this kind of defense is the line taken by the British politician Enoch Powell, who prophesied "rivers of blood" if black immigration was not stopped and blacks who had already arrived were not encouraged to go back to where they had come from.[12] Here again, the facts are relevant. If Powell's claims had been soundly based, if it really were impossible for blacks and whites to live together without widespread bloodshed, then continued immigration would have been in the interests of neither blacks nor whites, and stopping immigration could not have been condemned as racist – though the epithet could have been applied to those Britons who were so hostile to blacks as to produce the situation Powell predicted. Despite occasional racial disturbances in Britain, however, there is no sign that Powell's predictions will come true. While a sudden influx of large numbers of immigrants of a different racial (or ethnic) group may cause problems, it is clear that people of different races can live together without serious strife. This being so, there is no justification for immigration policies that impose blanket prohibitions on people of a different race from that of the residents of the country. The most that can be defended in terms of the principle of equal consideration of interests is a quota system that leads to a gradual adjustment in the racial composition of a society.[13]

Notes

1 In popular usage, even the term "discrimination" is often used to suggest that the practice referred to is wrong; this is, of course, an abuse of language, for to discriminate is merely to distinguish, or differentiate, and we could hardly get along without doing that.

2 For a brief and clear statement of this idea of justice, see H. L. A. Hart, *The Concept of Law* (Oxford: Clarendon Press, 1961), pp. 156–8; see also Joel Feinberg, *Social Philosophy* (Englewood Cliffs, NJ: Prentice-Hall, 1973), ch. 7.

3 See, for instance, R. M. Hare, *Freedom and Reason* (Oxford: Clarendon Press, 1963), chs. 9, 11; Richard Wasserstrom, "Rights, Human Rights, and Racial Discrimination," *Journal of Philosophy*, vol. 61 (1964) and reprinted in James Rachels (ed.), *Moral Problems* (New York: Harper and Row, 1975).

4 See Feinberg, *Social Philosophy*, p. 78.

5 "In most southern communities...the adjustment to public desegregation following the enactment of the 1964 Civil Rights Act was amazing." Lewis M. Killian, *White Southerners* (New York: Random House, 1970). Similar comments have been made by many other observers; for a more recent report, see *Time*, September 27, 1976, especially the favorable comments of Northern blacks who have recently moved to the South (p. 44). That contact with those of another race helps to reduce racial prejudice had been demonstrated as early as 1949, when a study of US soldiers showed that the more contact white soldiers had with black troops, the more favorable were their attitudes to integration. See Samuel Stouffer et al., *The American Soldier: Adjustment During Army Life* (Princeton, NJ: Princeton University Press, 1949), p. 594. This finding was supported by a later study, "Project Clear," reported by Charles Moskos, Jr., "Racial Integration in the Armed Forces," *American Journal of Sociology*, 72 (1966), pp. 132–48.

6 The situation is different if it is because of a past rather than a present political connection that one is subjected to disadvantages. Perhaps this is why the hounding of ex-communists in the McCarthy era was a particularly shameful episode in American history.

7 Henry Sidgwick, *The Methods of Ethics*, 7th edn. (London: Macmillan, 1907), p. 382.

8 C. I. Lewis, *Analysis of Knowledge and Valuation* (La Salle, IL: 1946), p. 547; I owe this reference to R. M. Hare.

9 See Hare, "Rules of War and Moral Reasoning," *Philosophy and Public Affairs*, vol. 1 (1972).

10 See the discussion of the Ideal Observer theory in Roderick Firth, "Ethical Absolutism and the Ideal Observer," *Philosophy and Phenomenological Research*, vol. XII (1952) and the further discussion in the same journal by Richard Brandt, vol. XV (1955).

11 For a general discussion of this issue, see Sidgwick, *Methods of Ethics*, pp. 432–3; for considerations relevant to the present distribution of resources, see my "Famine, Affluence, and Morality," *Philosophy and Public Affairs*, vol. 1 (1972) and reprinted in James Rachels (ed.) *Understanding Moral Philosophy* (Encino, CA: Dickenson, 1976) and Paula and Karsten Struhl (eds.) *Philosophy Now*, 2nd edn. (New York: Random House, 1975).

12 *The Times* (London), April 21, 1968.

13 I am grateful to Robert Young for comments and criticism on this paper.

Seven

Killing Humans and Killing Animals

In setting out to write this paper, my intention was to fill a gap in my book *Animal Liberation.*[1] There I argued that the interests of animals ought to be considered equally with our own interests and that from this equality it follows that we ought to become vegetarian. The argument for vegetarianism is not based on any claim about the wrongness of killing animals – although some careless reviewers read this claim into my book, no doubt because they assumed that any moral argument for vegetarianism *must* be based on the wrongness of killing. Instead the argument for vegetarianism is based on the suffering that is, and as far as I can see always will be, associated with the rearing and slaughtering of animals on a large scale to feed urban populations. I explicitly avoided taking a position on the wrongness of killing animals, for I wanted the book to reach nonphilosophers, and the issue of killing cannot be dealt with briefly and simply.

So why is it wrong to kill? Since my basic ethical position is utilitarian, my initial approach is to ask what objections a utilitarian would have to killing. If we are considering killing a normal human being, the utilitarian can point to obvious bad effects that the killing of one normal human has on others. Killing leads to grief on the part of friends and relatives of the victim, and to fear and insecurity in the community generally. Nonutilitarians, however, regard these as mere "side-effects," not touching upon the real wrongness of killing; for, they say, it would be wrong to kill even if one's victim was a hermit whose death would never be discovered. I am not sure that we should, in the case of

First published in *Inquiry*, 22 (1979), pp. 145–56. Reprinted by permission of Taylor and Francis, Oslo, Norway.

normal human beings, allow these "side-effects" to be so lightly brushed aside – the use of fantastic examples can be misleading. In the case of at least some species of nonhuman animals, however, these side-effects cannot explain the wrongness of killing – if it is wrong – since the animals may lack sufficient knowledge of what is happening to feel fear and insecurity, and pair-bonding, maternal relations, or social relations may not be strong enough to give rise to any sense of loss among survivors. (I said in the case of *some* species – with others this may not be true.) This lack of knowledge, incidentally, will also be true of some human beings, namely infants and severe mental defectives.

So what should we say about the wrongness of killing beings to whom the "side-effects" argument does not apply? Here the most obvious answer for the utilitarian to give is that, provided the being is capable of pleasant experiences, to kill it is to reduce the amount of pleasure in the world. Since pleasure is good, this is, other things being equal, wrong. Of course, a similar argument about pain points in the opposite direction, and it is only when we believe that the pleasure a being is likely to experience outweighs the pain it is likely to suffer, that this argument counts against killing. So what this amounts to is that we should not cut short a pleasant life.

This seems simple enough: we value pleasure, killing those who lead pleasant lives eliminates the pleasure they would otherwise experience, therefore such killing is wrong. But stating the argument in this way conceals something which, once noticed, makes the issue anything but simple. There are two ways of reducing the amount of pleasure in the world: one is to eliminate pleasure from the lives of those leading pleasant lives; the other is to eliminate those leading pleasant lives. The former leaves behind beings who experience less pleasure than they otherwise would have. The latter does not. This means that we cannot move automatically from a preference for a pleasant life rather than an unpleasant one, to a preference for a pleasant life rather than no life at all. For, it might be objected, being killed does not make us worse off; it makes us cease to exist. Once we have ceased to exist, we shall not miss the pleasure we would have experienced.

Perhaps this seems sophistical. Well, then, consider the opposite case: a case not of reducing pleasure, but of increasing it. There are two ways of increasing the amount of pleasure in the world: one is to increase the pleasure of those who now exist; the other is to increase the number of those who will lead pleasant lives. If killing those leading pleasant lives is bad because of the loss of pleasure, then it would seem to be good to increase the number of those leading pleasant lives. We could do this by having more children, provided we could reasonably expect their lives to be pleasant, or by rearing large numbers of animals under conditions which would ensure that their lives would be pleasant. But would it really be good to create more pleasure by creating more pleased beings?

This perplexing issue was first raised by Henry Sidgwick and has since been revived by Jan Narveson and Derek Parfit.[2] There are at least three possible approaches. The first is simply to accept that it is good to increase the amount of pleasure in the world by increasing the number of pleased beings, and bad to reduce the amount of pleasure in the world by reducing the number of pleased beings. This approach, which Sidgwick favored, has the advantage of being straightforward and clearly consistent, but it requires us to hold that if we could increase the number of beings leading pleasant lives without making others worse off, it would be good to do so. To see whether you are troubled by this conclusion, it may be helpful to consider a specific case. Imagine that a couple are trying to decide whether to have children. Suppose that so far as their own happiness is concerned, the advantages and disadvantages balance out. Children will interfere with their careers at a crucial stage of their professional lives, and they will have to give up their favourite recreation, cross-country skiing, for a few years at least. On the other hand they know that, like most parents, they will get joy and fulfillment from having children and watching them develop. Suppose that if others will be affected, the good and bad effects will cancel each other out. Finally, suppose that since the couple could provide their children with a good start in life, it is probable that their children will lead pleasant lives. Should the couple count the likely future pleasure of their children as a significant reason for having children? If we accept this first approach, they should.

This approach is known as the "total" view since on this view we ought to increase the total surplus of pleasure over pain, irrespective of whether this is done by increasing the pleasure of existing beings, or increasing the number of beings who exist.

The alternative approach mentioned by Sidgwick is to aim at the highest possible *average* level of happiness. Sidgwick's assumption that this is the major alternative to the total view is still commonly made; but the "average" view is most implausible. It implies, as Richard Henson has pointed out, that other things being equal, it would be good to kill all those below the average level of happiness, since this would raise the average – but raising the average gives us a new group of people below the new average, who then also become eligible for elimination – and so on.[3]

If this is not enough there are other objections to the average view. On this view it would be wrong to bring into a world of extremely happy beings an additional being who would have a happy life, but not quite so happy as the already existing people; but why should this be wrong if all it does is create an additional happy life, making no one worse off? Similarly, on the average view, if the world consists only of utterly miserable beings, it would be good to bring into the world more beings who, though still very miserable, would not be quite so miserable as the already existing beings.[4]

For these reasons I shall not consider the average view any further.

A third approach, and a more plausible alternative to the total view, is to count only beings who already exist, prior to the decision we are taking, or who will exist independently of that decision. This is sometimes called a "person-affecting" view, but this is hardly an appropriate label when we are applying it to animals. I shall refer to it as the "prior existence" view. On this view there is no value in increasing pleasure by creating additional beings. This accords with the intuitive judgments most people seem to make about whether couples ought to have children because of the pleasant lives the children are likely to lead (other things being equal). But how do we square this view with our intuitions about the reverse case, when a couple are considering having a child who, perhaps because it will inherit a genetic defect, would lead a thoroughly miserable life and die before its second birthday? We would think it wrong for a couple knowingly to conceive such a child; but if the pleasure a possible child will experience is not a reason *for* bringing it into the world, why is the pain a possible child will experience a reason *against* bringing it into the world? A convincing explanation of this asymmetry has not, to my knowledge, been produced.[5]

It should now be apparent why I avoided the issue of killing in *Animal Liberation*. The issue forces us to choose between three possible versions of utilitarianism. One can be disregarded, but which of the other two should we choose? The difference is important. If we take the "prior existence" view we shall hold that it is wrong to kill any being whose life is likely to contain, or can be brought to contain, more pleasure than pain. This implies that it is normally wrong to kill animals for food, since we could bring it about that these animals had a few pleasant months or even years before they died – and the brief pleasure we get from eating them would not outweigh this.

The other view – the "total" view – can justify meat-eating. Leslie Stephen implicitly invoked it when he wrote:

> Of all the arguments for Vegetarianism none is so weak as the argument from humanity. The pig has a stronger interest than anyone in the demand for bacon. If all the world were Jewish, there would be no pigs at all.[6]

Stephen views animals as if they were replaceable, and with this those who accept the total view must agree. The total version of utilitarianism regards sentient beings as valuable only insofar as they make possible the existence of intrinsically valuable experiences like pleasure. It is as if sentient beings are receptacles of something valuable and it does not matter if a receptacle gets broken, so long as there is another receptacle to which the contents can be transferred without any getting spilt. Although meat-eaters are responsible for the death of the animal they eat and for the loss of pleasure experienced by that animal, they are also responsible for the creation of more animals, since if no one ate meat there would be no more animals bred for fattening. The loss meat-eaters inflict on one animal is thus balanced, on the total view, by the benefit they confer on the next. We may call this the "replaceability" argument.[7]

The first point to note about the replaceability argument is that even if it is valid when the animals in question have a pleasant life, it would not justify eating the flesh of animals reared in modern "factory farms," where the animals are so crowded together and restricted in their movements that their lives seem to be more of a burden than a benefit to them.[8]

A second point is that if it is good to create life, then presumably it is good for there to be as many people on our planet as it can possibly hold. With the exception of areas suitable only for pasture, the surface of our globe can support more people if we grow plant foods than if we raise animals.[9]

These two points greatly weaken the replaceability argument as a defense of meat-eating, but they do not go to the heart of the matter. Are sentient beings really replaceable?

Henry Salt, a nineteenth-century English vegetarian and author of a book called *Animals' Rights*, thought that the argument rested on a simple philosophical error:

> The fallacy lies in the confusion of thought which attempts to compare existence with non-existence. A person who is already in existence may feel that he would rather have lived than not, but he must first have the *terra firma* of existence to argue from: the moment he begins to argue as if from the abyss of the non-existent, he talks nonsense, by predicating good or evil, happiness or unhappiness, of that of which we can predicate nothing.[10]

When I wrote *Animal Liberation* I accepted Salt's view. I thought it absurd to talk as if one conferred a favor on a being by bringing it into existence, since at the time one confers this favor there is no being at all.[11] But now I am less confident, for three reasons.

First, as we have seen, we do seem to do something bad if we bring a miserable being into existence, and if this is so it is difficult to explain why we do not do something good when we bring a happy being into existence. At the time of writing *Animal Liberation* I thought I could overcome this and other difficulties in the way of an acceptable formulation of the prior-existence view. Derek Parfit has convinced me that the difficulties are more formidable than I had supposed.[12]

Secondly, although it would be wrong to bring into existence a being who will be thoroughly miserable, it does not seem wrong for the government of an underpopulated country to encourage its people to have more children so that the population will rise by, say, one million. Yet of this million, we can be sure that at least one will be thoroughly miserable. If it is not wrong to create the million, but would be wrong to create the single miserable being, the obvious explanation is that there is value in the creation of the 999,999 – or however many it will be – whose lives are happy.[13]

Thirdly, Salt and other advocates of the prior-existence view need to say something about the point at which a being comes into existence, for this, on their view, marks a morally crucial dividing line. Once a being is in existence, we must maximize its happiness; before it is in existence, there is supposed to be nothing at all to take into account. There is something puzzling about attributing such great moral significance to the moment of birth for, as opponents of abortion have often said, birth does not really make a crucial difference to the fetus. A premature newborn may be less developed than a fetus just before the normal time of delivery. On the other hand – as supporters of abortion have pointed out – it is equally puzzling to make conception mark the dividing line, since the zygote immediately after conception does not seem to have any morally relevant properties not possessed by the egg and sperm before they unite. Why should killing it be worse than using a contraceptive to prevent the egg and sperm uniting?[14]

It has been suggested that the development of consciousness, or the capacity to feel, is the essential criterion, but while I accept that the possession of consciousness makes it wrong to cause the conscious being to suffer, or to make its conscious states less pleasurable than they otherwise would be, it is not clear why mere consciousness should be crucial to the wrongness of killing.[15]

The search for a morally crucial dividing line leads me to a conclusion very different in its implications from Salt's. Is it possible that, as Michael Tooley has suggested, the important distinction so far as killing is concerned is the distinction between beings that are merely conscious and those that are also self-conscious, in the sense of being able to conceive of themselves as distinct entities, existing over time with a past and a future?[16] If we think of a living creature as a self-conscious individual, leading its own life and with a desire to go on living, the replaceability argument holds little appeal. Salt may be thinking of such beings himself, for he concludes his essay by claiming that Lucretius long ago refuted Stephen's "vulgar sophism" in the following passage of *De Rerum Natura*:

> What loss were ours, if we had known not birth?
> Let living men to longer life aspire,
> While fond affection binds their hearts to earth:
> But who never hath tasted life's desire,
> Unborn, impersonal, can feel no dearth.

This passage supports the claim that there is a difference between killing living beings who "to longer life aspire" and failing to create a being which, "unborn, impersonal," can feel no loss of life. But what of a being which, though alive, cannot aspire to longer life because it lacks the conception of itself as a being with a future? This kind of being is, in a sense, impersonal. Perhaps, therefore, in killing it one does it no personal wrong, although one does reduce the quantity of happiness in the universe. This wrong, however, can be counterbalanced by bringing into existence a similar being which will lead an equally happy life.

Classical hedonistic utilitarianism does not support this distinction between personal and impersonal life, but a different variety of utilitarianism, preference utilitarianism, does. This is the form of utilitarianism which Hare claims is implied by the universalizability of our moral concepts.[17] Whether or not one accepts this claim, it is clear that universalizability supports the distinction between self-conscious and merely conscious beings. If I imagine myself in turn as a self-conscious and a merely conscious being, it is only in the former case that I could have a desire to live which will not be fulfilled if I am killed. Hence it is only in the former case that my death is not balanced by the creation of a being with similar prospects of pleasurable experiences. Preference utilitarianism reflects this by taking into account the preferences of all affected by an action, and weighting them according to the strength of preference, under certain conditions of knowledge and reflection. Preference utilitarians count the killing of a being with a preference for continued life as worse than the killing of a being without any such preference. Self-conscious beings therefore are not mere receptacles for containing a certain quantity of pleasure, and are not replaceable.

To take the view that non–self-conscious beings are replaceable is not to say that their interests do not count. I have elsewhere argued that their interests do count. As long as a sentient being is conscious, it has an interest in experiencing as much pleasure and as little pain as possible.[18] Sentience suffices to place a being within the sphere of equal consideration of interests; but it does not mean that the being has a personal interest in continuing to live. For a non–self-conscious being, death is the cessation of experiences, in much the same way that birth is the beginning of experiences. Death cannot be contrary to a preference for continued life, any more than birth could be in accordance with a preference for commencing life. To this extent, with non–self-conscious life, birth and death cancel each other out; whereas with self-conscious beings the fact that once self-conscious one may desire to continue living means that death inflicts a loss for which the birth of another is insufficient gain.

This suggests a possible compromise between the two versions of utilitarianism. We might grant that the total view applies when we are dealing with beings that do not exist as individuals living their own lives. Here it is appropriate to consider only the total amount of happiness. When we switch our attention to self-conscious beings, however, there is more at stake than impersonal quantities of happiness. We are therefore justified in giving priority to self-conscious beings who exist now or, independently of our decisions, will exist at some future time, rather than to the creation of possible extra beings.

This is, of course, only a suggestion towards a utilitarian answer to the problem of killing. It is not an adequately worked-out answer, because it says nothing about the nature of the priority we give to self-conscious beings. Should it be a lexical priority, so that no loss to a self-conscious existing being is justified by the creation of any number of additional happy beings? Or is there a nonarbitrary way of trading off losses to self-conscious beings against the creation of extra happy beings? These questions need to be answered, but I am not going to attempt to answer them now. Instead I shall return to the practical issue from which I began. Even the incomplete answer to the problem of killing allows us to reach some practical conclusions about the killing of animals and humans.

So far as animals are concerned, it obviously becomes important to try to decide which animals are self-conscious, in the sense of being capable of desiring to go on living. Some philosophers have argued that only a language-user can be self-conscious. I do not find these arguments convincing, but the issue is too large to be considered here. In any case I would be prepared to concede that some of the animals commonly killed for food are not self-conscious – chickens could be an example.[19]

Given that an animal belongs to a species incapable of self-consciousness, it follows that it is not wrong to rear and kill it for food, provided that it lives a pleasant life and, after being killed, will be replaced by another animal which will lead a similarly pleasant life and would not have existed if the first animal had not been killed. This means that vegetarianism is not obligatory for those who can obtain meat from animals that they know to have been reared in this manner. In practice, I think this exemption will apply only to those who are able to rear their own animals, or have personal knowledge of the conditions under which the animals they eat were raised and killed. For the reasons given in *Animal Liberation*, I doubt if it would apply to commercially reared and slaughtered animals.

I am sure that some will claim that in taking this view of the killing of some nonhuman animals I am myself guilty of "speciesism" – that is, discrimination against beings because they are not members of our own species. My position is not speciesist, because it does not permit the killing of nonhuman beings on the ground that they are not members of our species, but on the ground that they lack the capacity to desire to go on living. The position applies equally to members of our own species who lack the relevant capacity.

This last consequence strikes many as shocking, for it amounts to saying that infants, for instance, are as replaceable as merely conscious animals. (Potential self-consciousness is not enough, for a potentially self-conscious being has never desired to go on living.) In real life we are not likely to want to kill and replace normal babies. Parents who do not wish to keep their infants can and would normally prefer to give them up for adoption. In the case of defective infants, however, replacement could be a desirable option. Suppose that a couple plan to have two children. Their first child is normal, but the second is diagnosed immediately after birth as a severe case of spina bifida. If it lives, the child will grow up paralyzed from the waist down, incontinent, and mentally retarded – though it might, for all that, have a tolerably pleasant existence if it is intensively cared for. Suppose that the couple do not wish to give the child up to an institution, fearing that it may not receive the best care there. Yet they are equally unhappy at the prospect of trying to bring up such a child. They still want two normal children. They feel that with the burden of a handicapped as well as a normal child to bring up, however, they cannot have another child. The replaceability principle would allow them to kill the defective infant and then go ahead with another pregnancy.

Is this conclusion too shocking to accept? Before answering, consider two currently accepted practices which are, in my view, not fundamentally different. The first is the practice of examining the amniotic fluid of pregnant women who have a higher than average risk of giving birth to a defective child. If the examination reveals that the fetus will have a defect such as spina bifida – or even a less serious defect like hemophilia – the woman is offered, and usually accepts, an abortion. She may then get pregnant again and repeat the process until the tests show that she is carrying a normal fetus. In other words the fetus is treated as replaceable. As I have already said, I do not think the moment of birth marks a morally crucial divide.

The second practice is that of allowing defective newborns to die. It is now perfectly standard – and recognized as such by the Department of Health in the United Kingdom – for the more severe cases of spina bifida to receive no medical treatment other than what is necessary to relieve pain. Operations which would enable the infants to live indefinitely are performed only on the less severely affected children. With the others the avowed aim of not operating is that the infant will die as swiftly and painlessly as possible. Because I agree with James Rachels, Jonathan Glover, and others that the distinction between killing and allowing to die is not of intrinsic moral significance, I do not think that this policy differs greatly from direct killing. (Insofar as it does differ, it probably is worse, since it prolongs the ordeal for infant, parents, and hospital staff.)[20]

Some may object to the two practices I have just described. I think our previous discussion of killing shows that they are justifiable, and that direct killing of the newborn infant can also be justifiable. So there is no discrimination on the basis of species. The replaceability principle applies, regardless of species, to beings who have never had the capacity to desire continued life.[21]

Notes

1　Peter Singer, *Animal Liberation* (New York; New York Review, 1975; London: Jonathan Cape, 1976).

2　See H. Sidgwick, *The Methods of Ethics*, 7th edn. (London: Macmillan, 1907), pp. 414–16; Jan Narveson, "Utilitarianism and New Generations," *Mind*, vol. 76 (1967) and "Moral Problems of Population," *The Monist*, vol. 57 (1973) and reprinted in M. Bayles (ed.), *Ethics and Population* (Cambridge, MA: Schenkman, 1976). Derek Parfit's extremely influential contribution was published in Part 4 of his *Reasons and Persons* (Oxford: Oxford University Press, 1984).

3　See Richard Henson, "Utilitarianism and the Wrongness of Killing," *Philosophical Review*, vol. 80 (1971). Henson's objection does not apply if the average view is interpreted as directing us to maximize the average amount of happiness *per life lived*, rather than the average level of happiness of those alive at any given instant. Probably Sidgwick had in mind happiness per life lived. The objections in the following paragraph, however, apply to both versions of the average view.

4　I owe these points to Derek Parfit.

5　I attempted to produce one in "A Utilitarian Population Principle" in M. Bayles (ed.), *Ethics and Population*, p. 93; but Parfit's reply ("On Doing the Best for Our Children" in the same volume, pp. 110–11) has convinced me that the attempt failed.

6　From *Social Rights and Duties*, quoted by Henry Salt, "The Logic of the Larder," which appeared in Salt's *The Humanities of Diet* (Manchester: The Vegetarian Society, 1914), and has been reprinted in T. Regan and P. Singer (eds.), *Animal Rights and Human Obligations* (Englewood Cliffs, NJ: Prentice-Hall, 1976).

7　Jonathan Glover discusses whether human beings are ever replaceable in *Causing Death and Saving Lives* (Harmondsworth: Penguin, 1977), pp. 72–3, 159–60, 163.

8　See *Animal Liberation*, ch. 3.

9　I owe this point – which assumes that people are better happiness-producers than nonhumans – to Roslind Godlovitch.

10　"The Logic of the Larder," in T. Regan and P. Singer (eds.), *Animal Rights*, p. 186.

11　*Animal Liberation*, pp. 240–2.

12　See the articles cited in note 5 above.

13　See R. I. Sikora, "Is it Wrong to Prevent the Existence of Future Generations?" in *Obligations to Future Generations*, edited by B. Barry and R. I. Sikora (Philadelphia: Temple University Press, 1978), pp. 112–66.

14　For a similar point see T. G. Roupas, "Abortion and Simple Consciousness," *Philosophy and Public Affairs*, 7 (1978), pp. 154–83 at p. 167.

15   The suggestion that simple consciousness is enough has been made by W. S.
      Pluhar, "The Value of Life," *Journal of Philosophy*, vol. 74 (1977), pp. 159–72.

16   "Abortion and Infanticide," *Philosophy and Public Affairs*, vol. 2 (1972); a revised
      version appears in J. Feinberg (ed.), *The Problem of Abortion* (Belmont, CA:
      Wadsworth, 1973).

17   See R. M. Hare, "Ethical Theory and Utilitarianism," in H. D. Lewis (ed.),
      Contemporary British Philosophy, 4th series (London: Allen & Unwin, 1976); for
      Hare's own views on the application of this theory to a situation involving taking
      life, see his "Abortion and the Golden Rule," *Philosophy and Public Affairs*, vol. 4
      (1975), pp. 201–22.

18   See *Animal Liberation*, ch. 1.

19   The fact that an animal struggles when an attempt to capture or kill it is made does
      not show that it desires to live; all it can show is that the animal in some way
      perceives the situation as undesirable, and tries to escape from it. On the other
      hand, it is difficult to establish that an animal does not have a desire to live and
      even in the case of a chicken there may be sufficient doubt for it to be better to
      give the chicken the benefit of the doubt.

20   See James Rachels, "Active and Passive Euthanasia," *New England Journal of
      Medicine*, vol. 292 (Jan 9, 1975); and Jonathan Glover, *Causing Death and Saving
      Lives*, ch. 7. For an opposed view by a doctor involved in the treatment of spina
      bifida infants see the comments by John Lorber, "Early Results of Selective
      Treatment of Spina Bifida Cystica," *British Medical Journal*, 4 (1973), esp. p. 204.

21   Portions of this paper appear in a book on *Practical Ethics* published by Cambridge
      University Press in 1979, second edition 1993. It has been read to several univer-
      sity departments, and I have received many helpful comments. Invidious as it is to
      single out one or two from all those who have helped, it would be worse still not
      to thank Michael Lockwood and Derek Parfit for their especially valuable assist-
      ance.

Eight

To Do or Not to Do?

In 1939 Otto Schmidt was working as a laboratory assistant at a distinguished medical research institute in Germany. He learned, through chance remarks and his own observation, that another unit of the institute was receiving mentally retarded patients from a nearby asylum, and using them as research subjects. The patients were exposed to various poisonous gases, including nerve gas, and then forced to continue walking up and down an inclined ramp. They frequently vomited, and showed other symptoms of illness; but if they stopped, they were beaten with sticks. After a few days, most patients died from the poison gases they had inhaled; the remainder were put to death.

Schmidt was horrified by his discovery. At first he assumed that the scientists carrying out this research were doing so without authority, and that if the authorities were informed, it would be stopped. But his initial attempts to act on this assumption failed when the director of the institute made it clear that he had special permission from the highest levels to carry out this research "in the interests of the German soldier, who may again be exposed to chemical warfare." Schmidt attempted to contact these higher authorities, but he received no response. He also tried to alert the relatives of the patients, but his inquiries revealed that only patients who had no contact with relatives were selected for the experiments.

There was little more, legally, that Schmidt could do, but the experiments were continuing, and he could not simply forget about them. Therefore he decided on the only course of action he could think of that stood a chance of

First published in the *Hastings Center Report*, 19: 6 (1989), pp. 42–4.

stopping the experiments. The unit conducting the experiments was housed in a separate and specially equipped building. One night, when neither staff nor experimental subjects were in the building, Otto obtained a supply of petrol and set fire to the building. His plan was entirely successful; the building was destroyed, and because of shortages of resources at the time, never rebuilt. No further experiments with poison gases were conducted at that research institute.

What attitude should we take to what Otto Schmidt did? In criticism of his actions, it might be argued that he broke the law of his own country. Although he had certainly attempted to use legal channels to stop the research, it could not be said that he had exhausted all legal channels, since he had not received a definite and final response to his letters to higher authorities. It may also be said that Schmidt caused the destruction of a costly scientific research facility, and stopped a scientific research project that was adding to our knowledge about the capacities of human beings to continue working after exposure to harmful chemicals. Schmidt was not qualified, it might plausibly be asserted, to assess the scientific value of this work, nor its importance to the German Army.

Yet I do not think many of us will find these criticisms convincing. Schmidt was witnessing an atrocity. While the subjects of the experiments were suffering every day, he could not be expected to wait indefinitely for an official response – especially since this response might well be that the project should continue. As for the claim that Schmidt was not qualified to judge the value of the project, in this particular situation it seems clear that the project was unjustifiable. Schmidt did indeed use his own moral judgment on this matter, but his judgment was sound. For this – and also, of course, for his personal courage – he deserves not criticism, but the highest praise.

Now consider a more recent incident. At a prestigious research institute in the United States, monkeys were trained to run in a cylindrical treadmill. The monkeys received electric shocks unless they kept the treadmill moving. Once the monkeys had completed initial training at keeping the treadmill in motion, they were subjected to varying doses of radiation. Monkeys receiving the higher doses vomited repeatedly. They were then put back into the treadmill to measure the effect of the radiation on their ability to keep it moving. During this period, if a monkey did not move the treadmill for one minute, shock intensity was increased to 10 mA. (This is an intense electric shock, causing severe pain.) Some monkeys continued to vomit while in the treadmill. The irradiated monkeys took up to five days to die.

Animal liberationists learned that the institute was conducting these experiments. For several years they protested against them through a variety of legal channels, without success. Then an animal activist – let us call her Olivia Smith – succeeded in entering the laboratory in which these experiments were carried out and caused such damage to the laboratory and its equipment that the experiments stopped and were not resumed.

What attitude should we take to what Olivia Smith did? If we think that Schmidt was a hero, should we also think of Smith in the same way?

The criticisms noted in relation to Otto Schmidt's action will also be pressed against Olivia Smith. Do they have greater validity in her case than in his? Those who want to argue that Schmidt was a hero, but at the same time want to condemn Smith, will probably appeal first to the fact that the victims for whom Schmidt acted were human beings, whereas those saved by Smith's act were monkeys. I have elsewhere argued – and many other philosophers now agree – that species *in itself* cannot be a basis for this kind of distinction. It may be legitimate to treat differently beings with different capacities; but the mere fact that one being is a member of our species, and another being is not, cannot justify us in inflicting pain and death on the latter in circumstances that would not justify us in inflicting pain and death on the former.[1]

So can we appeal to differences in the capacities of the beings involved in the experiments that took place in Germany and in the United States? We could only do this if our judgment about Schmidt's action was based on knowledge about the capacities of the subjects of the experiments he stopped. But we have no information on this matter – the subjects were described as mentally retarded, but how severely was not stated. Obviously, they were capable of walking, and of feeling pain. Equally obviously, so were the monkeys in the American experiment. There is no basis on which we can be confident that the human subjects were superior in respect of rationality, awareness, or any other possibly relevant capacity, to the nonhumans. In any case, if we were able to decide that Schmidt's actions were justified without inquiring more closely into the mental capacities of the human subjects, this strongly suggests that the existence of higher mental capacities – beyond the capacity to feel pain and to suffer from the poisonous gases – was not really relevant to our judgment. Accordingly, I conclude that our knowledge of any differences between the experimental subjects, whether in species or in capacities, is insufficient to serve as a basis for sharply differing judgments about what Schmidt and Smith did.

The other factor likely to be put forward in explanation of why Schmidt was fully justified but Smith was not, is that Germany in 1939 was not a democracy, and there was no proper channel for stopping the experiments; in the United States, on the other hand, there are adequate opportunities for bringing about change through the democratic process. The differences between the political systems is of immense significance. Although the United States is far from being a perfect democracy, we rightly treasure the opportunities it offers for peacefully and legitimately changing the laws of the country. In a society like the United States the obligation to try to bring about change by democratic means is very strong. If Olivia Smith's action had not been preceded by a long period of attempting to stop such experiments by lawful means, it would have been wrong. But such efforts *had* been made. They had been unavailing. The monkeys were continuing to go through extreme pain and suffering in the course of an experiment that was highly unlikely to bring significant benefits to humans or animals. In such circumstances, is the obligation to use only democratic means to bring about change an absolute one?

Though I am a strong supporter of democratic systems of government, even imperfect ones, I cannot believe that the obligation to use only democratic means is absolute. During the period of the civil rights marches, and later of protest against the Vietnam war, millions of Americans supported illegal forms of protest. Many of these involved breaches of racist segregation laws, and of the draft laws; some also caused damage to property, both private and government. It may be questioned whether such tactics were the most effective means possible to achieve civil rights for blacks, or to end the war in Vietnam; but this is a matter of strategy, not of ethics. If we can assume, for the sake of argument, that they were the *only* possible means of achieving those goals in a reasonable period of time, were they justified? I think they were. Even in a democracy, we can be justified in taking unlawful means to bring about change.

There is, I believe, a line to be drawn between acts that are illegal (including acts that cause specific and limited damage to property) and acts that inflict physical violence on others. A sound democracy can tolerate a certain amount of illegal protest; but violence against others is always likely to escalate quickly. More important still, when those who are acting on an ethical basis resort to violence, they obscure the clarity of their ethical stand and send a confused message to the public. Under a repressive dictatorship there may be no alternative to violence; but in a democracy, to resort to violence is to put in peril values that are greater than almost any cause.

Since Olivia Smith avoided inflicting physical violence on anyone, her act was not on the wrong side of this line. There may have been a much heavier burden of justification on Olivia Smith than on Otto Schmidt, but if her act, like his, was the only way to end an atrocity, she may also have been justified in what she did.

This is not a view I reach lightly. To encourage people to take the law into their own hands is a dangerous thing. There will be many people who regard as an atrocity acts that I do not see in the same light. Abortion is one obvious example. People who believe that a prenatal human being has the same right to life as an older human being are, in my view, misguided.[2] In that respect I see a greater difference between Otto Schmidt and a pro-life activist who burns down an abortion clinic than I do between Otto Schmidt and Olivia Smith. Yet it is impossible to convince many pro-life people that they are mistaken, and so from their perspective, they too are entitled to the praise we bestow upon Otto Schmidt.

Reflecting on the position of those who do not share our views about what is right and what is wrong is salutary, because it makes us realize how great a responsibility we are under to think and think again about the judgment that what is happening is not merely wrong, but *so* wrong that it justifies taking the law into one's own hands. But where that judgment is clear; where it is a judgment that other reasonable people, fully informed of the facts of the situation, will share; where there is no other way of halting a continuing atrocity; where care is taken to avoid physical violence against anyone; then, and only then, do I believe direct action to be justifiable.

Otto Schmidt and Olivia Smith are imaginary, as are the German experiments I described. But I did not invent the experiments on monkeys. My account is drawn from a paper entitled "Effects of Mixed Neutron-gamma Total-body Irradiation on Physical Activity Performance of Rhesus Monkeys," published in *Radiation Research* in 1985.[3] The experiments took place at the Armed Forces Radiobiology Institute, in Bethesda, Maryland. As far as I am aware, similar experiments are still continuing.

References

1 See *Animal Liberation* (New York: New York Review/Random House, 1975, rev. edn., 1989), ch. 1; or *Practical Ethics* (Cambridge: Cambridge University Press, 1979; 2nd edn., 1993), ch. 3.
2 See *Practical Ethics*, ch. 6.
3 Vol. 101, pp. 434–41.

Nine

The Great Ape Project

Paola Cavalieri and Peter Singer

The Great Ape Project was launched in London in June 1993. It is an idea, a book, and an organization. All three are built around a *Declaration on Great Apes*, which begins like this (Cavalieri and Singer 1993: 4):

> We demand the extension of the community of equals to include all great apes: human beings, chimpanzees, gorillas and orang-utans. "The community of equals" is the moral community within which we accept certain basic moral principles or rights as governing our relations with each other and enforceable at law. Among these principles or rights are the following: (1) The right to life. The lives of the members of the community of equals are to be protected. Members of the community of equals may not be killed except in very strictly defined circumstances, for example, self-defence. (2) The protection of individual liberty. Members of the community of equals are not to be arbitrarily deprived of their liberty; if they should be imprisoned without due legal process, they have the right to immediate release. The detention of those who have not been convicted of any crime, or of those who are not criminally liable, should be allowed only where it can be shown to be for their own good, or necessary to protect the public from a member of the community who would clearly be a danger to others if at liberty. In such cases, members of the community of equals must have the right to appeal, either directly or, if they lack the relevant capacity, through an advocate, to a judicial tribunal. (3) The prohibition of torture. The

First published in *Ape, Man, Apeman: Changing Views since 1600*, ed. Raymond Corbey and Bert Theunissen (Leiden University, Department of Prehistory, 1995), pp. 367–76. Reprinted by permission of Universiteit Leiden.

deliberate infliction of severe pain on a member of the community of equals, either wantonly or for an alleged benefit to others, is regarded as torture, and is wrong.

In this paper, we shall discuss some of the key ideas raised by the Great Ape Project. First, however, we need to provide some philosophical background.

Applied Ethics and Cultural Change

The growth of applied ethics during the past two decades ranks among the most significant developments in philosophy in the present century. While different areas of knowledge employ moral theories of various sorts to settle questions within their fields, or even to justify their existence and pursuits, philosophy is the sole discipline which expressly includes the study of ethical theory amongst its peculiar themes. Traditionally, philosophers have been engaged in the attempt to scrutinize and uphold moral principles so as to illuminate ethical judgments and to set standards of good character and rules of right conduct. Early in this century, however, such traditional normative ethics, concentrating on the use of moral language in making moral judgments, was newly contrasted with what was labelled as meta-ethics, focusing instead on the meaning of moral language. Most of those who engaged in the latter, called analytic philosophers, came to hold that philosophers should not be concerned with tackling practical problems. Moreover, the efficacy of moral reasoning and even the existence of moral truth were called into question by the positivist claim that the basic function of value terms, and accordingly of moral terms, is not to ascertain truth or falsity but to express emotions – a claim which was accepted by important strands of ethical thinking such as subjectivism and emotivism. Recently, however, the decline of linguistic analysis as a mode of philosophy, and the growing realization that argument does have an important role to play in ethics, made it possible for moral philosophy to comply with increasing demands for "relevance." These demands created a chain-effect that would replace a rather static general stance with a more questioning attitude towards traditional assumptions.

During the sixties and the seventies, a number of external stimuli came from different contexts. Those who were active in the various civil rights movements and against the Vietnam war looked to moral philosophy to provide them with a clear, rational basis for their struggles. Amongst other issues, most prominent was the examination and defense of the arguments for intra-human equality. Perhaps because it was not considered to be ethics, but rather political philosophy, this area of concern had escaped the past prevailing disapproval of attempts to do substantive or applied work in moral philosophy. It could thus provide an effective springboard to use in putting fresh critical arguments against the different shapes that arbitrary discrimination could take.

Over the next decade, new developments in the biological and medical sciences enormously increased our control over life and death in circumstances varying from the possibility of fertilizing human eggs outside the female body to the power of keeping comatose patients alive almost indefinitely. This gave rise to a new set of ethical issues and, consequently, to the new discipline which is now known as bioethics. While professional workers increasingly accepted that medical ethics should be seen as a matter of public concern, moral philosophers started to play a growing role as members of, or supporting staff for, the numerous committees and commissions that were set up to advise governments and parliaments on controversial topics.

Practical ethics soon became an extensive field of study. An entire set of new arguments came under scrutiny, as can easily be shown not only by the large number of scholarly books and articles that appeared, but also by the journals published in the field now. In addition to *Bioethics*, the *Journal of Medical Ethics*, and *Philosophy and Public Affairs*, these include titles ranging from the specific, like *Environmental Ethics* and the *Business and Professional Ethics Journal* to the more general *Journal of Applied Philosophy*. All this flourishing of practical ethics affected ethical theory in many ways – for example, through its discussion of the problem of our obligations to future generations, it undermined the assumption that a moral community can consist only of members who exist at the same time; and in discussing world hunger and nuclear warfare it similarly raised questions about the ways in which ethical problems can cross the boundaries of one society (Rachels 1979; De Marco and Fox 1986; Singer 1993).

As far as our present topic is concerned, we have already noticed the importance of bioethics and philosophical reflection about intra-human discrimination. It is not a coincidence that one of us, Peter Singer, who played a central role in challenging moral orthodoxy about the status of nonhuman animals, is involved both in bioethics and in issues relating to intra-human equality. It was first as a political philosopher that he argued that the principle of equal consideration of interests, which had already been defended as the best possible basis for the claim that all humans are equal, could not be confined to our species, and that to mark the bounds of its application on the grounds of characteristics other than the possession of interests – roughly, sentience – is indefensible. In saying this, he was arguing that membership of one particular species, just like membership of one particular race, is not a morally relevant characteristic. This claim was consistent with what, as a bioethicist, he would have argued a little later while criticizing the traditional sanctity-of-life doctrine – namely, that being human in the biological sense of belonging to the species *Homo sapiens* is different from, and not a sufficient condition for, being human in the philosophical sense of possessing certain characteristics like self-awareness and rationality.

While political discussion before long followed a different course, taking intra-human equality for granted and focusing on the question of how to embody it in the preferred organization of society – and we shall see below how this could happen – the bioethical debate became heated, and an important strain in it deepened its revision of the traditional theory of value. Many authors challenged humanism, that is, the doctrine that all and only human lives have an equal, absolute value (Glover 1977; Tooley 1983; Rachels 1986; Kuhse 1987). The humanistic view has two sides: an inclusive one which grants privileged moral status to all humans, and an exclusive one which grants such status only to humans. By emphasizing the moral irrelevance of species membership, and by arguing that, for example, the embryo, the fetus, or the comatose are not human in the evaluative sense, those authors undermined the inclusive side of humanism and, accordingly, the traditional notion of moral community. This naturally furthered the revision of the moral status of nonhumans which, through its criticism of the exclusive side of humanism, the ethics of animal liberation was pursuing.

These developments of philosophical reflection in applied ethics also had another result. They enabled us to look afresh at the moral implications of Darwin's theory. The easy dismissal of the idea that evolutionary theory could make a difference with respect to our treatment of animals was made possible by the shared assumption that humans and nonhumans are in wholly different moral categories. Once the ideological nature of this assumption was uncovered, it became more difficult to maintain that the human claim to a special dignity, though it had traditionally rested on a definitely non-Darwinian worldview, could safely resist the challenge of a radically different account of our place in the world. In twentieth-century ethics generally, little attention was paid to evolutionary theory because of the claim, largely accepted in modern moral philosophy, that normative conclusions cannot legitimately be derived from factual premises. But when we separate the general appeal to the gap between facts and values from the (covert) appeal to a bias in favor of our species in ethics, we can see that the general appeal to a gap between facts and values cannot serve as a basis for denying that Darwinism can have any impact on traditional morality. Evolutionary ethics, though it cannot rule out *all* possible ways of defending humanism, can, and in fact does, undermine humanism by removing its traditional supports. Moreover, at a fairly general level, it is now apparent that the acceptance of one of the tenets of Darwin's theory – namely, that there are no differences in kind, but only differences in degree, between us and the other animals – must have some impact on those views of the ethical domain that ground radical discontinuities in moral status on alleged discontinuities in the nature of human beings and other animals.

Much of our Western thinking about nonhumans has been characterized by one or other version of metaphysical dualism. The most extreme one is rather recent. Contrary to a strand of thinking traceable at least to Aristotle, in the seventeenth century René Descartes argued for a fundamental separation between ourselves and the animals, a separation reflecting the sharp distinction he drew on a more general level between thought and matter: while we have bodies and minds, animals only have bodies, and thus totally pertain to the (inferior) realm of matter. It is this absolute separation of the ontological categories we and the animals belong to that underlies the absolute dismissal of the animals from the sphere of moral concern which Descartes and his followers advocated. But Cartesianism is not the only dichotomic doctrine in the history of moral philosophy, though it is the only one that, by denying animals even consciousness, withholds from them *any* form of moral consideration. Kant's moral philosophy also makes a radical break between rational beings and the domain of mere things, which includes animals. The appeal to the allegedly exclusive possession of reason to grant differential value, and accordingly differential treatment, to human beings had already been advanced by Aquinas in the thirteenth century, and its persistence through the centuries shows that it plays a privileged role in the Western ethical tradition. The fact that both Kant and Aquinas find an indirect argument against cruelty to animals – based on the claim that those who are cruel to animals may end up being cruel to humans as well – scarcely counts against the immensity of the distance they put between humans, as rational beings, and animals. Other characteristics too have been employed to fortify the boundary of our species, among them the idea that only human beings can be free, in the sense of being detached from the natural world (Ferry 1992). At present, however, the various versions of such dualistic views can be defended only at the cost of forgetting about Darwin; and this temporary forgetfulness could (and can) go unnoticed only thanks to a presumption in favor of the infinitely superior moral worth of human beings.

Animal liberation ethics requires that animals enter the sphere of moral concern with a fundamentally equal moral status. No matter what the other characteristics of sentient beings, their interests should be counted equally with the like interests of any other beings. This points to radical changes in our attitude to, and our treatment of, nonhuman animals. Sentience is a characteristic shared by the billions of creatures which our society sees as mere means to human ends; and if we take their interests seriously, it is immediately clear that we must stop treating pigs as industrially produced food, hens as machines for turning grain into eggs, and rats as living toxicity-testing kits. Yet the gestalt switch that animal liberation ethics entails, coupled with the amount of practical changes its implementation would involve, makes the general acceptance of animal liberation ethics particularly problematic. For those who believe that humanism is irremediably flawed, however, there is one way of taking a first step towards a more enlightened ethics. This is via a long-established, well-respected notion of our moral tradition – the notion of the person.

Who is a Person?

We remarked above that modern political philosophy has taken intra-human equality for granted. This equality was normally expressed as equality between persons. Political philosophy seems to see the concept of person as unproblematic. This is not so in bioethics. Though the word "person" is, in current use, often used as if it meant the same as "human being," the terms are generally not seen as equivalent in bioethical discussions. Most authors in fact use "person" to refer in an unambiguous way to the second of the already mentioned senses of the word "human," that is, the philosophical sense of possessing certain characteristics like self-awareness and rationality; this is distinct from the biological sense of "human," meaning belonging to the species *Homo sapiens*. The relevant literature in bioethics is studded with discussions about whether the beings involved in various moral dilemmas are persons. Can fetuses or infants be considered persons? If so, at what point in their development? And are the severely mentally enfeebled or the comatose still persons?

What is it that makes these debates so heated? A distinction is often made between two uses of "person," the descriptive (also sometimes labelled as metaphysical) and the normative (or moral). On this view, to say of some being that she is a person in the descriptive sense is to convey some information about what the being is like, and this can amount to saying that she has characteristics a, b, and c; on the other hand to use the term "person" in a normative way is to use it simply to ascribe moral properties – usually some rights or duties, and frequently the right to life – to the being so denominated (Feinberg 1980). It is with reference to this normative meaning that it is so important to decide, in ethical disputes, which of the beings involved in a dilemma are persons and which are not. The question is one of moral ranking, because of the import we attach to the presence of personhood with respect to the wrongness of inflicting some specific harms, and in particular the wrongness of killing. At any rate, in this context, though it is normally emphasized that the purely normative and the purely descriptive uses of the word "person" are rather unusual, the two senses are seen as independent, and such as to grant one the possibility of choosing between them.

We think that this analysis is not wholly satisfying. True, one cannot deny that "person" is *actually* used in both senses; nor can one deny that it is totally sound to stipulate a specific way of using it starting from these premises. But this, we hold, would fail to do justice to the peculiarity of the term and its history, and thus would let some of the opportunities it offers get lost.

"Person" is a suggestive word. It comes from Latin in the form of *persona*, but it also has its corresponding term in Greek, *pròsopon*. It initially meant a mask worn by an actor in classical drama, and consequently came to refer to the character the actor performed. During the Early Roman Empire, the word was first introduced into philosophical jargon by the Stoic philosopher Epictetus, who used it to mean the role one is called to play in life. Not only the very idea of a role, but also the reference to a task to be accomplished, point towards an interpretation of the concept of person in terms of a *subject of relations* (Trendelenburg 1910).

This emphasis on relation is fundamental. Just as a role has more to do with the place a being occupies than with its nature, relation is a category which was seen, starting at least from Aristotle, as something added to, and thus accidentally and not essentially connected to, the substance of the thing. This aspect of autonomy from a definite metaphysical substratum made the concept particularly useful in, and its use was notably heightened by, the Christian theological controversies about the dogma of the Trinity, where the problem lay in expressing the relations holding between God and the Word (Christ), and between them and the Holy Ghost. After the settling of the dispute through the Council of Nicea, which stated that the Trinity is one substance and three persons, a counter-process took place, characterized by the attempt to remove from the notion of person the aspect of relation, and by the insistence on its substantiality. Hence the famous definition of person given in the sixth century by the Roman philosopher Boethius: "Person is an individual substance of rational nature." But theology had already saved the life of the concept of person: its use in connection with God had prevented it from being used so that it could refer only to human nature, or from simply becoming another term for "human being." Although this identification continued to be made in the subsequent course of philosophical reflection, its arbitrariness is shown by the fact that we can see that after we know that a given being is a human being, it remains an open question whether that being is a person.

"Person" is thus an emblematic term. It is connected with two linked key notions of premodern ethics, the notion of *role* and the notion of *relation*. To attach great importance to the roles in which people interact, and to see morality as a set of orientations for establishing and maintaining the health of relationships, are features of traditional, small-scale societies which reappear, in different ways and with a different emphasis, in much of (and not only) our cultural history (Silberbauer 1991). Homeric virtues can be identified only by identifying the basic roles of Homeric society and their specific requirements. Though Aristotle locates the ultimate human *telos* in metaphysical contemplation, in his functional concept of "man" a prominent part is played by the idea of man as a *politikon zoon*, a political animal, whose virtues are connected with a set of roles and with healthy relationships within the community or polis (MacIntyre 1981). Classical natural law, on the other hand, sees humans as created to play a part in a divinely ordained community expressing God's glory, and morality as teaching what that part is. From this perspective, then, the notion of person is conservative. But there is a sense in which one can claim the contrary. "Person" does embody two ancient notions, but it does it in a modern way. The specific requirements of the role, as well as the specific objects of the relations are not there: what is there is the abstract idea of role and relation. And this is a mark of modernity. Modern rational ethics emerges from a twofold process of abstraction: abstraction from any preconceived teleological or metaphysical framework, culminating in Henry Sidgwick's policy of keeping the nonethical commitments of moral philosophy to an absolute minimum; and abstraction in regard to the constituency of ethics, which in modern rational ethics is formed by generic individuals without distinction of sex, race, attitudes, or merits, moving in an anonymous social arena rather than standing at the center of a web of specific connections (Sidgwick 1907). It is because it is particularly well suited to this context that the notion of "person" has taken on such importance in the current philosophical debate. "Person" refers to the idea of being a locus of relations and playing a role in the ongoing drama. This makes it typically evaluative in nature. Hence to regard an entity as a person is to attribute a special kind of value to that entity. Moreover, since being a locus of relationships and playing a role is an accidental rather than an essential property of an entity, the range of application of the term can vary, thus providing a tool for moral reform.

It should now be clear why, when we initially developed the idea of what is now a book, *The Great Ape Project*, we turned to the concept of person. What we aimed at was a first attempt at overcoming the species barrier. The book is meant to build up a collective case for granting to some nonhuman animals the same basic moral status that we humans currently enjoy. Just as the best candidates for such a step are, as we shall show in more detail below, the three species which are closest to us in the evolutionary tree, chimpanzees, gorillas, and orang-utans, so the best theoretical instrument is this traditional notion of a person. Though the Declaration on Great Apes speaks in terms of admitting the other great apes into the community of equals, it is around the

concept of person that many of the arguments in the essays implicitly or
explicitly revolve.

Granted, there are differences in the interpretation of the concept of person.
To be effective, it must be given some more specific content. Its primary
meaning needs to be articulated in more detail. Historically, this has been done
in many ways. The connection with the capacity for reasoning which we have
already seen in Boethius was taken up by Aquinas ("every individual of rational
nature is called a person") and after him by a number of different authors from
different schools. But rationality seems an element that is attendant on the
more basic aspect of relation. This aspect can appear in the shape both of self-
relation (self-consciousness) and of hetero-relation (relationships with others).
Though self-relation has acquired more and more weight, gradually acquiring
supremacy, hetero-relation cannot immediately be dismissed. Apart from being
more faithful to the original meaning of the word, the latter is the only sense in
which the concept of person can be meaningfully contrasted – as it so frequently was in moral philosophy – with the concept of "thing." Since "thing"
is an older and more widespread notion than "person," the more sensible
procedure is to get going from it, and not the other way round; and the
determinative conditions of application of the concept of thing have generally
to do with passiveness and unawareness. This reading raises the question of
whether we might not ultimately move towards defining "person" in terms of
the simple possibility of relating to other beings, and consequently, if the idea
of relation is divested of any high-sounding tinsel, of mere consciousness. And
this could imply the possibility of its application to all beings with interests as
defined above.

We shall, however, leave aside this controversial question, with all its
attendant theoretical and practical problems, in order to focus on the more
pervasive and uncontroversial aspect of self-relation. This aspect begins to be
particularly prominent in the seventeenth century, when the concept of person
comes to be identified with subjective identity, that is, with the unity and
continuity of the conscious life of the self. Locke (1690: Bk 1, ch. 9, par. 29)
defines a person as "a thinking intelligent being that has reason and reflection
and can consider itself as itself, the same thinking thing, in different times and
places." Even Kant, with all his insistence on rationality, claims that it is the fact
of being able to represent to themselves their own selves that elevates persons
infinitely above all the living beings on earth (Kant 1775–80). The reference to
self-consciousness and projectivity into the future, which is now widely
accepted as a relevant factor in the concept, helps to clarify why, in contemporary bioethical debate, to say of some being that it is a person can mean not
only to attribute a kind of value to that being, but also to ascribe the right to life
to it, or to say that it is intrinsically wrong to destroy it. The idea is that to be

harmed by the loss of its future, an entity should be aware of itself as having a future (Tooley 1983; Singer 1993). (This is one, even if not the only, respect in which the notion of person is so important for the purpose of a reform of the moral status of animals.) Though until recently most authors, following the widespread trend we hinted at above, more or less covertly identified this unified stream of consciousness with the human self, the rise of applied ethics had consequences in this field too. Many moral philosophers who adopted something akin to this interpretation of person applied the term to some nonhuman selves too. The idea has also appeared under other denominations, like that of "subject of a life" (Regan 1983) or that of a being endowed with a biographical, rather than a merely biological, life (Rachels 1986). And, as we already noticed, the idea is central to *The Great Ape Project*.

The Case for the Personhood of Nonhuman Great Apes

When we sent out the Declaration, many authors responded with enthusiasm to our appeal. We ended up with thirty-four contributors from nine different countries. They include ethologists, interspecies communicators, philosophers, people working full-time for organizations concerned for animals, a lawyer, a psychologist, a biologist, two anthropologists, a physiologist, and a professor of special education. It is then no surprise that the argument emerging from this collective effort is multifarious. While Harlan Miller builds an estranging – and disquieting – philosophical parable, Steve Sapontzis criticizes the standard interpretation of person, and contrasts it with a reading that is closer to the less demanding one we associated above with mere consciousness, i.e. with the idea that to have feelings is enough to be considered a person. Barbara Noske and Raymond Corbey employ anthropological instruments to deconstruct traditional theory-laden perspectives on animals and on the other great apes in particular, the former focusing on their scientific facet, the latter from a more general point of view. The intervention of Adriaan Kortlandt can also be seen as a deconstructive operation through which the pioneer of close observation of free-living chimpanzees connects our changing images of the other great apes with major alterations in our cultural history.

The core of the book, however, revolves around the illustration of, and the drawing of moral inferences from, two intertwined elements: relatedness and similarity. The theme of relatedness is widely present in scientific essays. The shaky nature of the boundary between human beings and the other great apes is emphasized by most authors: we share 98.4 percent of our DNA with chimpanzees, and only slightly less with gorillas and orang-utans. As Robin Dunbar, professor of biological anthropology, points out, nonhuman great apes "differ only slightly more in their degree of genetic relatedness to you and me than do other populations of humans living elsewhere in the world." Jared Diamond, whose expertise ranges from physiology to ethology, goes so far as to maintain that humans do not constitute a distinct family, nor even a distinct genus, but belong in the same genus as common and pygmy chimps. Since our genus name was proposed first, and takes priority, he suggests that there are today on earth three species of the genus *Homo*: the common chimpanzee, *Homo troglodytes*; the pygmy chimpanzee, *Homo paniscus*; and the third, or human, chimpanzee, *Homo sapiens*. Relatedness is also present in Richard Dawkins's essay, in the form of an attack on the "discontinuous mind," which, dividing animals up into discontinuous species, forgets that on the evolutionary view of life there must always be intermediates, and that it is sheer luck if they are no longer here to fill the gaps that the discontinuous mind erects. These and other contributions, like the one in which James Rachels directly addresses Darwin's theory, help to erase the idea of a sharp separation between us and the other great apes by removing its traditional background. They also contribute to explaining the second main element of the book, that is, similarity.

The most evident similarity is the linguistic capacity. Language has long been considered a human prerogative – in fact, it still is, as far as it can be judged by reactions to the recent studies in inter-species communication. But we think that only prejudice can lead anyone to deny that language is being used in the Ameslan (or American sign language) interactions that occur between Francine Patterson and the gorillas Koko and Michael; between Lyn Miles and the orang-utan Chantek; and between Deborah and Roger Fouts and the community of chimpanzees associated with Washoe. Language has always been linked with important mental capacities; and certainly the great apes' acquisition and use of Ameslan does point at such capacities – in particular at the capacities for self-consciousness and for relating to others in sophisticated ways. Self-consciousness is most strikingly demonstrated by the fact that chimpanzees sometimes "think aloud," signing to themselves in appropriate ways when alone. As for the way in which chimpanzees relate to others, consider this: Washoe was looking at a magazine when her adopted son, Loulis (to whom, incidentally, she had spontaneously taught sign language), snatched the magazine and raced off out of the room. Washoe was left alone, signing "Dirty, dirty." Incidentally, Chantek also knew the sign "dirty," and was taught to use it when he needed to go to the toilet, but he sometimes used it deceptively, in order to get into the bathroom to play with the soap and washing machine; and, as Miles underlines, in order to deceive, one must be able to see the events from the other's perspective and try to negate his or her perception. Koko, who has developed a vocabulary of over 1,000 signs, recognizes herself in front of a mirror – something that is considered an important indicator of self-awareness – and also enjoys making faces at herself and examining her teeth. In addition she makes jokes (and laughs at her own jokes), and refers appropriately to past events.

We could go on indefinitely with examples like these. But one episode can perhaps convey in a more immediate way what we share with the nonhuman great apes. Geza Teleki, who spent much time in Africa studying free chimpanzees, was once sitting alone at the crest of a grassy ridge watching a sunset, when he noticed two adult males climbing toward him on opposite slopes. As they topped the crest, they saw one another and suddenly stood upright and advanced till they were face to face. Each extended his right hand to clasp and vigorously shake the other's. Then they sat down nearby and watched the sunset enfold the park.

On the basis of this evidence, it is surely indisputable that the notion of person can meaningfully be applied to the other great apes – and this is in fact what, as we have already hinted, most authors do. At this point in the argument, this seems a natural claim. All the more troubling, then, is the extent to which it clashes with the real situation of the other great apes. The other great apes are currently forced to live and die in appalling ways because they are denied the basic protection owed to persons. In a short piece about one of the hundreds of roadside zoos that exist in the United States alone, Betsy Swart portrays the fate of the intelligent, feeling, and social beings we have been describing – the same beings whose behavior has continued, for more than twenty-five years, to be "the source of astonishment, interest and pleasure" for such an acute observer as Toshisada Nishida. Konga, a chimpanzee at least 40 years old, sits with an unremovable chain on his neck, on the bare floor of his cage, extending both arms outside the bars to beg for some food. Johnny, mumbling a "Ma-Ma" which is the legacy of his past as a "show-chimp," rocks incessantly in the back of his cage. Other chimpanzees have gone totally insane from confinement: hidden from the public, they can be seen through opaque plastic screens endlessly pacing back and forth.

Yet perhaps even these miserable chimpanzees are luckier than their fellow creatures used in research. As David Cantor shows in his contribution concerning the plight of imprisoned nonhuman great apes, there are chimpanzees in laboratories who spend their entire lives alone in cages measuring 5 × 5 × 7 feet (1.6 × 1.6 × 2.1 meters). They are infected with diseases like hepatitis or viruses like HIV, and from that moment till they die are subjected to bleedings, biopsies, and laparotomies. What can this involve, not only in terms of physical suffering, but for their inner life? Like the gorillas kept in zoos or the orangutans employed in entertainment, if they were born in captivity, they *know of no other reality*. If, on the other hand, they were captured in the African forests, their mothers were probably murdered before their eyes, their family and social ties were broken, and they arrived at their final overseas destination after a voyage which killed most of their fellow-travelers. An answer to our question can come from Bimbo, a baby orang-utan rescued from his wooden crate after having been shipped upside-down from Singapore to Bangkok. Despite his curious and vivacious character, and despite the assiduous care which improved his physical condition, Bimbo had lost his will to live. He stopped eating and allowed himself to die.

For those who hold that the case for equality for chimpanzees, gorillas, and orang-utans is sound, the conclusion to draw must be political. This is the theme of our concluding essay. It is evident that the case for equality for the other great apes faces major difficulties, even if these are less dramatic than the difficulties that face the case for a more general change in the moral status of animals. Though attacked on many fronts at a theoretical level, humanism is still the ideology of our age; and considerable interests support the exploitation of the other great apes. If we add that, as has often been underscored, nonhumans lack the ability to stand up in their own defense, the picture can seem unfavorable at the very least. However, there are past and contemporary experiences to draw on. Firstly, there is the history of the abolition of the intra-human institution of slavery. In the last 200 years, human slavery has been eliminated, or virtually eliminated, from the face of the earth; along with it has gone the idea that human beings can be property. We envisage an international organization that can play for the liberation of the other great apes the role played in the past by the Anti-Slavery Society. The goal of this organization will be to bring it about that chimpanzees, gorillas, and orang-utans are removed from the category of property, both legally and morally, and are included in the category of persons. Once this goal is achieved, guardians will be needed to protect the newly sanctioned rights to life, liberty, and freedom from torture of the other great apes. This is not an obstacle: it is exactly what already happens with immature or less gifted members of our species. Finally, even the idea of protected, independent territories where nonhuman great apes could regain the dignity of an autonomous life is not without precedent, as the existence of human regions in need of external protection, the United Nations Trust Territories, shows.

We hope that this course of action will be supported by many who are involved in fields of expertise that cross the area of concern of the Great Ape Project. As scholars, they will thereby help to bridge the gap between the achievements of their disciplines and deeply rooted attitudes and paradigms. But, more important, they will follow a noble intellectual tradition of sparking change and contributing to make the world a better place in which to live.

Bibliography

Aquinas, Thomas, *Summa theologiae*, I and III. Various editions.

Aristotle, *Nicomachean ethics*. Various editions.

Boethius, *De duabus naturis et una persona Christi*. Various editions.

Cavalieri, Paola, and Singer, Peter (eds.) (1993) *The Great Ape Project: Equality beyond Humanity*. London: Fourth Estate.

DeMarco, J. P. and R. M. Fox (eds.) (1986) *New Directions in Ethics*. New York and London: Routledge.

Descartes, René, *Discourse on Method*. Various editions.

Epictetus, *The Manual* and *Discourses*. Various editions.

Feinberg, J. (1980) Abortion. In T. Regan (ed.), *Matters of Life and Death*. Philadelphia: Temple University Press.

Ferry, L. (1992) *Le nouvel ordre écologique: L'arbre, l'animal et l'homme*. Paris: Grasset.

Glover, J. (1977) *Causing Death and Saving Lives*. Harmondsworth: Penguin

Kant, Immannel (1775–80) *Lectures on Ethics and Pragmatic Anthropology*. Various editions.

Kuhse, Helga (1987) *The Sanctity of Life Doctrine in Medicine: A Critique*. Oxford: Oxford University Press.

Locke, John (1690) *Essay Concerning Human Understanding*.

MacIntyre, Alistair (1981) *After Virtue. A Study in Moral Theory*. Notre Dame, IN: University of Notre Dame Press.

Rachels, James (1979) *Moral Problems*. 3rd edn. New York: Harper & Row.

—— (1986) *The End of Life*. Oxford: Oxford University Press

—— (1990) *Created from Animals. The Moral Implications of Darwinism*. Oxford: Oxford University Press.

Regan, T. (1983) *The Case for Animal Rights*. Berkeley and Los Angeles: University of California Press.

Sidgwick, Henry (1907) *The Methods of Ethics*. 7th edn. London: Macmillan.

Silberbauer, G. (1991) Ethics in small-scale societies. In P. Singer (ed.), *A Companion to Ethics*. Oxford: Blackwell.

Singer, Peter (1990) *Animal Liberation*. 2nd edn. New York: New York Review of Books.

—— (1993) *Practical Ethics*. 2nd edn. Cambridge: Cambridge University Press.

Tooley, M. (1983) *Abortion and Infanticide*: Oxford: Oxford University Press.

Trendelenburg, A. (1910) A contribution to the history of the word "person". *Monist*, 20: 336–63.

Part Four

The Impartial Point of View

Ten

Famine, Affluence, and Morality

As I write this, in November 1971, people are dying in East Bengal from lack of food, shelter, and medical care. The suffering and death that are occurring there now are not inevitable, not unavoidable in any fatalistic sense of the term. Constant poverty, a cyclone, and a civil war have turned at least nine million people into destitute refugees; nevertheless, it is not beyond the capacity of the richer nations to give enough assistance to reduce any further suffering to very small proportions. The decisions and actions of human beings can prevent this kind of suffering. Unfortunately, human beings have not made the necessary decisions. At the individual level, people have, with very few exceptions, not responded to the situation in any significant way. Generally speaking, people have not given large sums to relief funds; they have not written to their parliamentary representatives demanding increased government assistance; they have not demonstrated in the streets, held symbolic fasts, or done anything else directed toward providing the refugees with the means to satisfy their essential needs. At the government level, no government has given the sort of massive aid that would enable the refugees to survive for more than a few days. Britain, for instance, has given rather more than most countries. It has, to date, given £14,750,000. For comparative purposes, Britain's share of the nonrecoverable development costs of the Anglo-French Concorde project is already in excess of £275,000,000, and on present estimates will reach £440,000,000.

First published in *Philosophy and Public Affairs*, 1 (1972), pp. 229–43. Copyright © The Johns Hopkins University Press. Reprinted with permission of the Johns Hopkins University Press.

The implication is that the British government values a supersonic transport more than thirty times as highly as it values the lives of the nine million refugees. Australia is another country which, on a per capita basis, is well up in the "aid to Bengal" table. Australia's aid, however, amounts to less than one-twelfth of the cost of Sydney's new opera house. The total amount given, from all sources, now stands at about £65,000,000. The estimated cost of keeping the refugees alive for one year is £464,000,000. Most of the refugees have now been in the camps for more than six months. The World Bank has said that India needs a minimum of £300,000,000 in assistance from other countries before the end of the year. It seems obvious that assistance on this scale will not be forthcoming. India will be forced to choose between letting the refugees starve or diverting funds from her own development program, which will mean that more of her own people will starve in the future.[1]

These are the essential facts about the present situation in Bengal. So far as it concerns us here, there is nothing unique about this situation except its magnitude. The Bengal emergency is just the latest and most acute of a series of major emergencies in various parts of the world, arising both from natural and from man-made causes. There are also many parts of the world in which people die from malnutrition and lack of food independent of any special emergency. I take Bengal as my example only because it is the present concern, and because the size of the problem has ensured that it has been given adequate publicity. Neither individuals nor governments can claim to be unaware of what is happening there.

What are the moral implications of a situation like this? In what follows, I shall argue that the way people in relatively affluent countries react to a situation like that in Bengal cannot be justified; indeed, the whole way we look at moral issues – our moral conceptual scheme – needs to be altered, and with it, the way of life that has come to be taken for granted in our society.

In arguing for this conclusion I will not, of course, claim to be morally neutral. I shall, however, try to argue for the moral position that I take, so that anyone who accepts certain assumptions, to be made explicit, will, I hope, accept my conclusion.

I begin with the assumption that suffering and death from lack of food, shelter, and medical care are bad. I think most people will agree about this, although one may reach the same view by different routes. I shall not argue for this view. People can hold all sorts of eccentric positions, and perhaps from some of them it would not follow that death by starvation is in itself bad. It is difficult, perhaps impossible, to refute such positions, and so for brevity I will henceforth take this assumption as accepted. Those who disagree need read no further.

My next point is this: if it is in our power to prevent something bad from happening, without thereby sacrificing anything of comparable moral importance, we ought, morally, to do it. By "without sacrificing anything of comparable moral importance" I mean without causing anything else comparably bad to happen, or doing something that is wrong in itself, or failing to promote some moral good, comparable in significance to the bad thing that we can prevent. This principle seems almost as uncontroversial as the last one. It requires us only to prevent what is bad, and not to promote what is good, and it requires this of us only when we can do it without sacrificing anything that is, from the moral point of view, comparably important. I could even, as far as the application of my argument to the Bengal emergency is concerned, qualify the point so as to make it: if it is in our power to prevent something very bad from happening, without thereby sacrificing anything morally significant, we ought, morally, to do it. An application of this principle would be as follows: if I am walking past a shallow pond and see a child drowning in it, I ought to wade in and pull the child out. This will mean getting my clothes muddy, but this is insignificant, while the death of the child would presumably be a very bad thing.

The uncontroversial appearance of the principle just stated is deceptive. If it were acted upon, even in its qualified form, our lives, our society, and our world would be fundamentally changed. For the principle takes, firstly, no account of proximity or distance. It makes no moral difference whether the person I can help is a neighbor's child ten yards from me or a Bengali whose name I shall never know, ten thousand miles away. Secondly, the principle makes no distinction between cases in which I am the only person who could possibly do anything and cases in which I am just one among millions in the same position.

I do not think I need to say much in defense of the refusal to take proximity and distance into account. The fact that a person is physically near to us, so that we have personal contact with him, may make it more likely that we *shall* assist him, but this does not show that we *ought* to help him rather than another who happens to be further away. If we accept any principle of impartiality, universalizability, equality, or whatever, we cannot discriminate against someone merely because he is far away from us (or we are far away from him). Admittedly, it is possible that we are in a better position to judge what needs to be done to help a person near to us than one far away, and perhaps also to provide the assistance we judge to be necessary. If this were the case, it would be a reason for helping those near to us first. This may once have been a justification for being more concerned with the poor in one's own town than with famine victims in India. Unfortunately for those who like to keep their moral responsibilities limited, instant communication and swift transportation have changed the situation. From the moral point of view, the development of the world into a "global village" has made an important, though still unrecognized, difference to our moral situation. Expert observers and supervisors, sent out by famine relief organizations or permanently stationed in famine-prone areas, can direct our aid to a refugee in Bengal almost as effectively as we could get it to someone in our own block. There would seem, therefore, to be no possible justification for discriminating on geographical grounds.

There may be a greater need to defend the second implication of my principle – that the fact that there are millions of other people in the same position, in respect to the Bengali refugees, as I am, does not make the situation significantly different from a situation in which I am the only person who can prevent something very bad from occurring. Again, of course, I admit that there is a psychological difference between the cases; one feels less guilty about doing nothing if one can point to others, similarly placed, who have also done nothing. Yet this can make no real difference to our moral obligations.[2] Should I consider that I am less obliged to pull the drowning child out of the pond if on looking around I see other people, no further away than I am, who have also noticed the child but are doing nothing? One has only to ask this question to see the absurdity of the view that numbers lessen obligation. It is a view that is an ideal excuse for inactivity; unfortunately most of the major evils – poverty, overpopulation, pollution – are problems in which everyone is almost equally involved.

The view that numbers do make a difference can be made plausible if stated in this way: if everyone in circumstances like mine gave £5 to the Bengal Relief Fund, there would be enough to provide food, shelter, and medical care for the refugees; there is no reason why I should give more than anyone else in the same circumstances as I am; therefore I have no obligation to give more than £5. Each premise in this argument is true, and the argument looks sound. It may convince us, unless we notice that it is based on a hypothetical premise, although the conclusion is not stated hypothetically. The argument would be sound if the conclusion were: if everyone in circumstances like mine were to give £5, I would have no obligation to give more than £5. If the conclusion were so stated, however, it would be obvious that the argument has no bearing on a situation in which it is not the case that everyone else gives £5. This, of course, is the actual situation. It is more or less certain that not everyone in circumstances like mine will give £5. So there will not be enough to provide the needed food, shelter, and medical care. Therefore by giving more than £5 I will prevent more suffering than I would if I gave just £5.

It might be thought that this argument has an absurd consequence. Since the situation appears to be that very few people are likely to give substantial amounts, it follows that I and everyone else in similar circumstances ought to give as much as possible, that is, at least up to the point at which by giving more one would begin to cause serious suffering for oneself and one's dependents – perhaps even beyond this point to the point of marginal utility, at which by giving more one would cause oneself and one's dependents as much suffering as one would prevent in Bengal. If everyone does this, however, there will be more than can be used for the benefit of the refugees, and some of the sacrifice will have been unnecessary. Thus, if everyone does what he ought to do, the result will not be as good as it would be if everyone did a little less than he ought to do, or if only some do all that they ought to do.

The paradox here arises only if we assume that the actions in question – sending money to the relief funds – are performed more or less simultaneously, and are also unexpected. For if it is to be expected that everyone is going to contribute something, then clearly each is not obliged to give as much as he would have been obliged to had others not been giving too. And if everyone is not acting more or less simultaneously, then those giving later will know how much more is needed, and will have no obligation to give more than is necessary to reach this amount. To say this is not to deny the principle that people in the same circumstances have the same obligations, but to point out that the fact that others have given, or may be expected to give, is a relevant circumstance: those giving after it has become known that many others are giving and those giving before are not in the same circumstances. So the seemingly absurd consequences of the principle I have put forward can occur only if people are in error about the actual circumstances – that is, if they think they are giving when others are not, but in fact they are giving when others are. The result of everyone doing what he really ought to do cannot be worse than the result of everyone doing less than he ought to do, although the result of everyone doing what he reasonably believes he ought to do could be.

If my argument so far has been sound, neither our distance from a preventable evil nor the number of other people who, in respect to that evil, are in the same situation as we are, lessens our obligation to mitigate or prevent that evil. I shall therefore take as established the principle I asserted earlier. As I have already said, I need to assert it only in its qualified form: if it is in our power to prevent something very bad from happening, without thereby sacrificing anything else morally significant, we ought, morally, to do it.

The outcome of this argument is that our traditional moral categories are upset. The traditional distinction between duty and charity cannot be drawn, or at least, not in the place we normally draw it. Giving money to the Bengal Relief Fund is regarded as an act of charity in our society. The bodies which collect money are known as "charities." These organizations see themselves in this way – if you send them a check, you will be thanked for your "generosity." Because giving money is regarded as an act of charity, it is not thought that there is anything wrong with not giving. The charitable man may be praised, but the man who is not charitable is not condemned. People do not feel in any way ashamed or guilty about spending money on new clothes or a new car instead of giving it to famine relief. (Indeed, the alternative does not occur to them.) This way of looking at the matter cannot be justified. When we buy new clothes not to keep ourselves warm but to look "well-dressed" we are not providing for any important need. We would not be sacrificing anything significant if we were to continue to wear our old clothes, and give the money to famine relief. By doing so, we would be preventing another person from starving. It follows from what I have said earlier that we ought to give money away, rather than spend it on clothes which we do not need to keep us warm. To do so is not charitable, or generous. Nor is it the kind of act which philosophers and theologians have called "supererogatory" – an act which it would be good to do, but not wrong not to do. On the contrary, we ought to give the money away, and it is wrong not to do so.

I am not maintaining that there are no acts which are charitable, or that there are no acts which it would be good to do but not wrong not to do. It may be possible to redraw the distinction between duty and charity in some other place. All I am arguing here is that the present way of drawing the distinction, which makes it an act of charity for a man living at the level of affluence which most people in the "developed nations" enjoy to give money to save someone else from starvation, cannot be supported. It is beyond the scope of my argument to consider whether the distinction should be redrawn or abolished altogether. There would be many other possible ways of drawing the distinction – for instance, one might decide that it is good to make other people as happy as possible, but not wrong not to do so.

Despite the limited nature of the revision in our moral conceptual scheme which I am proposing, the revision would, given the extent of both affluence and famine in the world today, have radical implications. These implications may lead to further objections, distinct from those I have already considered. I shall discuss two of these.

One objection to the position I have taken might be simply that it is too drastic a revision of our moral scheme. People do not ordinarily judge in the way I have suggested they should. Most people reserve their moral condemnation for those who violate some moral norm, such as the norm against taking another person's property. They do not condemn those who indulge in luxury instead of giving to famine relief. But given that I did not set out to present a morally neutral description of the way people make moral judgments, the way people do in fact judge has nothing to do with the validity of my conclusion. My conclusion follows from the principle which I advanced earlier, and unless that principle is rejected, or the arguments shown to be unsound, I think the conclusion must stand, however strange it appears.

It might, nevertheless, be interesting to consider why our society, and most other societies, do judge differently from the way I have suggested they should. In a well-known article, J. O. Urmson suggests that the imperatives of duty, which tell us what we must do, as distinct from what it would be good to do but not wrong not to do, function so as to prohibit behavior that is intolerable if men are to live together in society.[3] This may explain the origin and continued existence of the present division between acts of duty and acts of charity. Moral attitudes are shaped by the needs of society, and no doubt society needs people who will observe the rules that make social existence tolerable. From the point of view of a particular society, it is essential to prevent violations of norms against killing, stealing, and so on. It is quite inessential, however, to help people outside one's own society.

If this is an explanation of our common distinction between duty and supererogation, however, it is not a justification of it. The moral point of view requires us to look beyond the interests of our own society. Previously, as I have already mentioned, this may hardly have been feasible, but it is quite feasible now. From the moral point of view, the prevention of the starvation of millions of people outside our society must be considered at least as pressing as the upholding of property norms within our society.

It has been argued by some writers, among them Sidgwick and Urmson, that we need to have a basic moral code which is not too far beyond the capacities of the ordinary man, for otherwise there will be a general breakdown of compliance with the moral code. Crudely stated, this argument suggests that if we tell people that they ought to refrain from murder and give everything they do not really need to famine relief, they will do neither, whereas if we tell them that they ought to refrain from murder and that it is good to give to famine relief but not wrong not to do so, they will at least refrain from murder. The issue here is: Where should we drawn the line between conduct that is required and conduct that is good although not required, so as to get the best possible result? This would seem to be an empirical question, although a very difficult one. One objection to the Sidgwick–Urmson line of argument is that it takes insufficient account of the effect that moral standards can have on the decisions we make. Given a society in which a wealthy man who gives 5 percent of his income to famine relief is regarded as most generous, it is not surprising that a proposal that we all ought to give away half our incomes will be thought to be absurdly unrealistic. In a society which held that no man should have more than enough while others have less than they need, such a proposal might seem narrow-minded. What it is possible for a man to do and what he is likely to do are both, I think, very greatly influenced by what people around him are doing and expecting him to do. In any case, the possibility that by spreading the idea that we ought to be doing very much more than we are to relieve famine we shall bring about a general breakdown of moral behavior seems remote. If the stakes are an end to widespread starvation, it is worth the risk. Finally, it should be emphasized that these considerations are relevant only to the issue of what we should require from others, and not to what we ourselves ought to do.

The second objection to my attack on the present distinction between duty and charity is one which has from time to time been made against utilitarianism. It follows from some forms of utilitarian theory that we all ought, morally, to be working full-time to increase the balance of happiness over misery. The position I have taken here would not lead to this conclusion in all circumstances, for if there were no bad occurrences that we could prevent without sacrificing something of comparable moral importance, my argument would have no application. Given the present conditions in many parts of the world, however, it does follow from my argument that we ought, morally, to be working full-time to relieve great suffering of the sort that occurs as a result of famine or other disasters. Of course, mitigating circumstances can be adduced – for instance, that if we wear ourselves out through overwork, we shall be less effective than we would otherwise have been. Nevertheless, when all considerations of this sort have been taken into account, the conclusion remains: we ought to be preventing as much suffering as we can without sacrificing something else of comparable moral importance. This conclusion is one which we may be reluctant to face. I cannot see, though, why it should be regarded as a criticism of the position for which I have argued, rather than a criticism of our ordinary standards of behavior. Since most people are self-interested to some degree, very few of us are likely to do everything that we ought to do. It would, however, hardly be honest to take this as evidence that it is not the case that we ought to do it.

It may still be thought that my conclusions are so wildly out of line with what everyone else thinks and has always thought that there must be something wrong with the argument somewhere. In order to show that my conclusions, while certainly contrary to contemporary Western moral standards, would not have seemed so extraordinary at other times and in other places, I would like to quote a passage from a writer not normally thought of as a way-out radical, Thomas Aquinas.

> Now, according to the natural order instituted by divine providence, material goods are provided for the satisfaction of human needs. Therefore the division and appropriation of property, which proceeds from human law, must not hinder the satisfaction of man's necessity from such goods. Equally, whatever a man has

in superabundance is owed, of natural right, to the poor for their sustenance. So Ambrosius says, and it is also to be found in the *Decretum Gratiani*: "The bread which you withhold belongs to the hungry; the clothing you shut away, to the naked; and the money you bury in the earth is the redemption and freedom of the penniless."[4]

I now want to consider a number of points, more practical than philosophical, which are relevant to the application of the moral conclusion we have reached. These points challenge not the idea that we ought to be doing all we can to prevent starvation, but the idea that giving away a great deal of money is the best means to this end.

It is sometimes said that overseas aid should be a government responsibility, and that therefore one ought not to give to privately run charities. Giving privately, it is said, allows the government and the noncontributing members of society to escape their responsibilities.

This argument seems to assume that the more people there are who give to privately organized famine relief funds, the less likely it is that the government will take over full responsibility for such aid. This assumption is unsupported, and does not strike me as at all plausible. The opposite view – that if no one gives voluntarily, a government will assume that its citizens are uninterested in famine relief and would not wish to be forced into giving aid – seems more plausible. In any case, unless there were a definite probability that by refusing to give one would be helping to bring about massive government assistance, people who do refuse to make voluntary contributions are refusing to prevent a certain amount of suffering without being able to point to any tangible beneficial consequence of their refusal. So the onus of showing how their refusal will bring about government action is on those who refuse to give.

I do not, of course, want to dispute the contention that governments of affluent nations should be giving many times the amount of genuine, no-strings-attached aid that they are giving now. I agree, too, that giving privately is not enough, and that we ought to be campaigning actively for entirely new standards for both public and private contributions to famine relief. Indeed, I would sympathize with someone who thought that campaigning was more important than giving oneself, although I doubt whether preaching what one does not practice would be very effective. Unfortunately, for many people the idea that "it's the government's responsibility" is a reason for not giving which does not appear to entail any political action either.

Another, more serious reason for not giving to famine relief funds is that until there is effective population control, relieving famine merely postpones starvation. If we save the Bengal refugees now, others, perhaps the children of these refugees, will face starvation in a few years' time. In support of this, one may cite the now well-known facts about the population explosion and the relatively limited scope for expanded production.

This point, like the previous one, is an argument against relieving suffering that is happening now, because of a belief about what might happen in the future; it is unlike the previous point in that very good evidence can be adduced in support of this belief about the future. I will not go into the evidence here. I accept that the earth cannot support indefinitely a population rising at the present rate. This certainly poses a problem for anyone who thinks it important to prevent famine. Again, however, one could accept the argument without drawing the conclusion that it absolves one from any obligation to do anything to prevent famine. The conclusion that should be drawn is that the best means of preventing famine, in the long run, is population control. It would then follow from the position reached earlier that one ought to be doing all one can to promote population control (unless one held that all forms of population control were wrong in themselves, or would have significantly bad consequences). Since there are organizations working specifically for population control, one would then support them rather than more orthodox methods of preventing famine.

A third point raised by the conclusion reached earlier relates to the question of just how much we all ought to be giving away. One possibility, which has already been mentioned, is that we ought to give until we reach the level of marginal utility – that is, the level at which, by giving more, I would cause as much suffering to myself or my dependents as I would relieve by my gift. This would mean, of course, that one would reduce oneself to very near the material circumstances of a Bengali refugee. It will be recalled that earlier I put forward both a strong and a moderate version of the principle of preventing bad occurrences. The strong version, which required us to prevent bad things from happening unless in doing so we would be sacrificing something of comparable moral significance, does seem to require reducing ourselves to the level of marginal utility. I should also say that the strong version seems to me to be the correct one. I proposed the more moderate version – that we should prevent bad occurrences unless, to do so, we had to sacrifice something morally significant – only in order to show that even on this surely undeniable principle a great change in our way of life is required. On the more moderate principle, it may not follow that we ought to reduce ourselves to the level of marginal utility, for one might hold that to reduce oneself and one's family to this level is to cause something significantly bad to happen. Whether this is so I shall not discuss, since, as I have said, I can see no good reason for holding the moderate version of the principle rather than the strong version. Even if we accepted the principle only in its moderate form, however, it should be clear that we would have to give away enough to ensure that the consumer society, dependent as it is on people spending on trivia rather than giving to famine relief, would slow down and perhaps disappear entirely. There are several reasons why this would be desirable in itself. The value and necessity of economic growth are now being questioned not only by conservationists, but by economists as well.[5] There is no doubt, too, that the consumer society has had a distorting effect on the goals and purposes of its members. Yet looking at the matter purely from the point of view of overseas aid, there must be a limit to the extent to which we should deliberately slow down our economy; for it might be the case that if we gave away, say, 40 percent of our Gross National Product, we would slow down the economy so much that in absolute terms we would be giving less than if we gave 25 percent of the much larger GNP that we would have if we limited our contribution to this smaller percentage.

I mention this only as an indication of the sort of factor that one would have to take into account in working out an ideal. Since Western societies generally consider 1 percent of the GNP an acceptable level for overseas aid, the matter is entirely academic. Nor does it affect the question of how much an individual should give in a society in which very few are giving substantial amounts.

It is sometimes said, though less often now than it used to be, that philosophers have no special role to play in public affairs, since most public issues depend primarily on an assessment of facts. On questions of fact, it is said, philosophers as such have no special expertise, and so it has been possible to engage in philosophy without committing oneself to any position on major public issues. No doubt there are some issues of social policy and foreign policy about which it can truly be said that a really expert assessment of the facts is required before taking sides or acting, but the issue of famine is surely not one of these. The facts about the existence of suffering are beyond dispute. Nor, I think, is it disputed that we can do something about it, either through orthodox methods of famine relief or through population control or both. This is therefore an issue on which philosophers are competent to take a position. The issue is one which faces everyone who has more money than he needs to support himself and his dependents, or who is in a position to take some sort of political action. These categories must include practically every teacher and student of philosophy in the universities of the Western world. If philosophy is to deal with matters that are relevant to both teachers and students, this is an issue that philosophers should discuss.

Discussion, though, is not enough. What is the point of relating philosophy to public (and personal) affairs if we do not take our conclusions seriously? In this instance, taking our conclusion seriously means acting upon it. The philosopher will not find it any easier than anyone else to alter his attitudes and way of life to the extent that, if I am right, is involved in doing everything that we ought to be doing. At the very least, though, one can make a start. The philosopher who does so will have to sacrifice some of the benefits of the consumer society, but he can find compensation in the satisfaction of a way of life in which theory and practice, if not yet in harmony, are at least coming together.

Notes

1 There was also a third possibility: that India would go to war to enable the refugees to return to their lands. Since I wrote this paper, India has taken this way out. The situation is no longer that described above, but this does not affect my argument, as the next paragraph indicates.

2 In view of the special sense philosophers often give to the term, I should say that I use "obligation" simply as the abstract noun derived from "ought," so that "I have an obligation to" means no more, and no less, than "I ought to." This usage is in accordance with the definition of "ought" given by the *Shorter Oxford English Dictionary*: "the general verb to express duty or obligation." I do not think any issue of substance hangs on the way the term is used; sentences in which I use "obligation" could all be rewritten, although somewhat clumsily, as sentences in which a clause containing "ought" replaces the term "obligation."

3 J. O. Urmson, "Saints and Heroes," in *Essays in Moral Philosophy*, ed. Abraham I. Melden (Seattle and London, 1958), p. 214. For a related but significantly different view see also Henry Sidgwick, *The Methods of Ethics*, 7th edn. (London, 1907), pp. 220–1, 492–3.

4 *Summa Theologiæ*, II–II, Question 66, Article 7, in *Aquinas, Selected Political Writings*, ed. A. P. d'Entrèves, trans. J. G. Dawson (Oxford, 1948), p. 171.

5 See, for instance, John Kenneth Galbraith, *The New Industrial State* (Boston, 1967); and E. J. Mishan, *The Costs of Economic Growth* (London, 1967).

Eleven

William Godwin and the Defense of Impartialist Ethics[1]

Peter Singer, Leslie Cannold, and Helga Kuhse

Introduction

Impartialism in ethics has been said to be the common ground shared by both Kantian and utilitarian approaches to ethics. Lawrence Blum describes this common ground as follows:

> Both views identify morality with a perspective of impartiality, impersonality, objectivity and universality. Both views imply the "ubiquity of impartiality" – that our commitments and projects derive their legitimacy only by reference to this impartial perspective.[2]

During the past two decades impartialism has come under a barrage of criticism. The modern objections to impartialism can now be seen as having begun in 1970, with the publication of Iris Murdoch's *The Sovereignty of Good*, although this work did not attract much attention from mainstream philosophers at the time. A more influential critique was Bernard Williams's defense of what he called "integrity" in his contribution to *Utilitarianism For and Against*. Another line of attack was developed by Michael Stocker in a series of articles that began with "The Schizophrenia of Modern Ethical Theories." This was reinforced by Lawrence Blum's presentation of friendship as a moral phenomenon, and given some support from J. L. Mackie's defense of "self-referential

First published in *Utilitas*, 7 (1995), pp. 67–86. Reprinted with permission of Edinburgh University Press.

altruism." The publication of Carol Gilligan's *In a Different Voice* linked the issue of impartialism to debates over whether there is a distinctive feminist approach to ethics. Nel Noddings's advocacy of an "ethic of care" gave a further boost to this discussion. Thomas Nagel put the issue at the centre of his examination of ethics in *The View from Nowhere*.[3]

The various objections to impartialism contained in these works are often presented in a manner suggesting that until now philosophers have accepted impartialism without much questioning. That is not so. In this article we give an account of a debate about impartialism in ethics that took place between 1793 and 1801. We will see that in the course of that debate, many of the criticisms of impartialism being made today were raised, and in some cases answered. We have chosen to reexamine this debate not only because of its historical interest, but also because we believe that the earlier debate can help to resolve the contemporary one. If we know what paths were trodden in the past we can avoid the cul-de-sacs, and recognize the more promising paths to pursue.

Impartialism: Godwin's First Statement of his Position

William Godwin published his *Enquiry Concerning Political Justice* in 1793, at the height of the French Revolution, just a month after Louis XVI had been guillotined. The book was an immediate success, selling an astonishing number of copies for so large and abstract a work of philosophy. Godwin "blazed as a sun in the firmament of reputation; no one was more talked of, more looked up to, more sought after, and wherever liberty, truth, justice was the theme, his name was not far off."[4] *Political Justice* argues that government is tyranny, and a better society will be achieved if individuals are free to cooperate with each other in small communities, free from the coercive power of a central government. Godwin begins, however, by providing ethical foundations for the political theory that is to come. These foundations are recognizably utilitarian, although Godwin often writes of "justice" where Bentham would have written of "utility."

Godwin held that justice consists in acting so as to bring about the greatest possible benefit, viewed from an impartial perspective. As an illustration of this idea, he presented an example that was to become notorious:

> A man is of more worth than a beast, because, being possessed of higher faculties, he is capable of a more refined and genuine happiness. In the same manner the illustrious archbishop of Cambrai was of more worth than his chamber-maid, and there are few of us that would hesitate to pronounce, if his palace were in flames and the life of only one of them could be preserved, which of the two ought to be preferred.

But there is another ground of preference beside the private consideration of one of them being farther removed from the state of a mere animal. We are not connected with one or two percipient beings, but with a society, a nation, and in some sense with the whole family of mankind. Of consequence that life ought to be preferred which will be most conducive to the general good. In saving the life of Fénelon, suppose at the moment when he was conceiving the project of his immortal *Telemachus*, I should be promoting the benefit of thousands who have been cured by the perusal of it of some error, vice and consequent unhappiness. Nay, my benefit would extend farther than this, for every individual thus cured has become a better member of society and has contributed in his turn to the happiness, the information and improvement of others.

Supposing I had been myself the chamber-maid, I ought to have chosen to die rather than that Fénelon should have died. The life of Fénelon was really preferable to that of the chamber-maid. But understanding is the faculty that perceives the truth of this and similar propositions; and justice is the principle that regulates my conduct accordingly. It would have been just in the chamber-maid to have preferred the archbishop to herself. To have done otherwise would have been a breach of justice.

Supposing the chamber-maid had been my wife, my mother, or my benefactor. That would not alter the truth of the proposition. The life of Fénelon would still be more valuable than that of the chamber-maid; and justice – pure, unadulterated justice – would still have preferred that which was most valuable. Justice would have taught me to save the life of Fénelon at the expense of the other. What magic is there in the pronoun "my" to overturn the decisions of everlasting truth? My wife or my mother may be a fool or a prostitute, malicious, lying or dishonest. If they be, of what consequence is it that they are mine?[5]

Godwin was well aware that this doctrine would meet with resistance. Already in the first edition of *Political Justice* he replied to several anticipated objections. He tackles first the claim that one ought to prefer one's mother to the archbishop, because we all owe a debt of gratitude to our mothers for enduring the pains of childbearing and nourishing us in our infancy. Godwin confronts this objection head-on by denying the basis of the conventional idea that we have special obligations of reciprocity to those who have done us good. He characterizes gratitude as "a sentiment which would lead me to prefer one man to another from some other consideration than that of his superior usefulness or worth." It is therefore "no part either of justice or virtue."[6]

With equal firmness, at least in this first edition of *Political Justice*, Godwin dismisses the anticipated objection that I should have for my relatives, companions, and benefactors "an uncommon portion of my regard" because I know them, and have had personal proof of their virtues and worth; hence, this objection runs, I should judge them to be more worthy of being rescued than a stranger who may, in fact, be objectively superior to them. Godwin accepts that we often do have this kind of special concern for those we know, but describes this concern as "founded only in the present imperfection of human nature" and therefore as something that "may serve as an apology for my error, but can never turn error into truth."[7] He then goes on to draw an important philosophical distinction, one to be reiterated by later utilitarians such as Henry Sidgwick and J. J. C. Smart:[8]

> A wrong action may be done from a right disposition; in that case we condemn the action but approve the actor. If the disposition by which a man is governed have a systematical tendency to the benefit of his species, he cannot fail to obtain our esteem, however mistaken he may be in his conduct.[9]

The point of this distinction is that we may well praise someone who rescues a relative or friend whom he or she knows to be a virtuous person, thereby failing to rescue someone who, unknown to them, is a person of superior worth; but this does not show that the rescue of the relative or friend was objectively the right action.

Godwin acknowledges one further point relevant to the choice between one's mother and the archbishop. He accepts that there is something to be said "in favour of my providing in ordinary cases for my wife and children, my brothers and relations before I provide for strangers." This is, for Godwin, a consequence of the fact that property and income is distributed through a breadwinner, generally male, who passes it on to other members of his family. If all property were held in common, so that men and women, adults and children, working people and the unemployed, all had an equal claim to the necessities of life, and the community ensured that no one went without these necessities, the rule that we should provide first for our families would not apply. Even when families do rely on a breadwinner for support, Godwin adds, the rule that we should provide for our families before we concern ourselves with strangers "belongs only to ordinary cases." Where there is a "more urgent necessity," this general rule of providing for one's relatives "will be altogether impotent."[10] Thus Godwin does not see the general rule as encroaching upon impartial justice; and we must assume that the choice between Fénelon and one's mother is, for Godwin, no ordinary case.

Revisions: A Different Parent, but the Same Choice

In the third edition of *Enquiry Concerning Political Justice*, published five years after the first edition, Godwin stuck firmly by impartialism. The most striking difference in the way he treats the Fénelon example in the first and third editions is that the chamber–maid/mother has become a valet/father.[11] Historians and philosophers have postulated varied motives for the change; but the motives they propose seem to tell us as much about the assumptions of their own times as they do about Godwin himself. In 1926 Raymond Preston considered Godwin made the servant a man "perhaps to get rid of the imputation of lack of chivalry, and so to simplify the problem."[12] In 1950, D. H. Monro dismissed the change as "a sop to popular prejudice."[13] Mark Philp thinks the change may have been made to avoid a specific objection, "after all, his mother may have been pregnant with another Godwin!"[14] William St Clair, on the other hand, has attributed the sex change to the influence of Mary Wollstonecraft, the author of the foundational feminist work, *A Vindication of the Rights of Woman*, who married Godwin in 1797. The change was made, St Clair believes, "to avoid any suspicion that Godwin regarded women as intrinsicially of less value than men."[15]

Apart from changing the sex of the parent to be left to the flames, Godwin added two new paragraphs to his discussion of the Fénelon case. The first is an attempt to rebut the objection that his defense of impartiality undermines other obligations; for example, those to benefactors. Godwin insists that this is not so:

> My obligation towards my benefactor, supposing his benefit to be justly conferred, is in no sort dissolved; nor can anything authorize me to supersede it, but the requisition of a superior duty. That which ties me to my benefactor, upon these principles, is the moral worth he has displayed; and it will frequently happen that I shall be obliged to yield him the preference, because while other competitors may be of greater worth, the evidence I have of the worth of my benefactor is more complete.[16]

The problem with this passage is that everything that comes after the words "is in no sort dissolved" tends to show that here, as in the first edition, Godwin does indeed dissolve the obligation that we are conventionally regarded as having toward our benefactors – that is, the obligation of gratitude. This obligation is not usually understood as a matter of preferring those who are of the greatest moral worth, but rather, as an obligation to repay benefits conferred, irrespective of the comparative worth of the person who has conferred them. In contrast, on Godwin's view, when my duty to my benefactor conflicts with my duty to rescue a person whom I know to be of superior moral worth, impartial justice demands that I favor the person of superior moral worth. The fact that the other person is my benefactor plays no role, except to provide evidence of moral worth.

The second paragraph added to the revised edition of *Political Justice* seeks to buttress in a more general way the impartialist view that Godwin has been defending, by maintaining that only a strictly impartial stance corresponds to a truthful view of reality. Because this paragraph is important in helping us to understand the foundations of impartialism we quote it in full:

> Nothing can be less exposed to reasonable exception than these principles. If there be such a thing as virtue, it must be placed in a conformity to truth, and not to error. It cannot be virtuous, that I should esteem a man, that is, consider him as possessed of estimable qualities, when in reality he is destitute of them. It surely cannot conduce to the benefit of mankind, that each man should have a different standard of moral judgement and preference, and that the standard of all should vary from that of reality. Those who teach this, impose the deepest disgrace upon virtue. They assert in other words, that, when men cease to be deceived, when the film is removed from their eyes, and they see things as they are, they will cease to be either good or happy. Upon the system opposed to theirs, the soundest criterion of virtue is, to put ourselves in the place of an impartial spectator, of an angelic nature, suppose, beholding us from an elevated station and uninfluenced by our prejudices, conceiving what would be his estimate of the intrinsic circumstances of our neighbour, and acting accordingly.[17]

The reference to an impartial spectator in the last sentence of this paragraph echoes earlier writers like David Hume and Adam Smith.[18] It has also had more recent followers. R. M. Hare refers to this passage when, in order to explain what moral thinking at the critical level should ideally be like, he introduces the idea of an "archangel" endowed with "superhuman powers of thought, superhuman knowledge, and no human weaknesses."[19] What is most striking about the way in which Godwin argues here, however, is his claim that to be partial – for example, to save one's father in preference to Fénelon – is in some way to judge the father as more worthy or more virtuous than Fénelon. On Godwin's view, if I think I ought to save my mother and you think that you ought to save yours, we are disagreeing about who is the more virtuous or more worthy of being saved – and neither of us is accepting the reality of the situation, which is that Fénelon is more worthy than either of our mothers.

It is tempting to say that Godwin's view rests on a simple error – that my judgment that I ought to save my mother is not based on any judgment about her worth, but on the ties of affection between us, or the debt of gratitude I bear her. To make this judgment, I do not have to believe that *anyone* in such a situation ought to save *my* mother, only that *I* ought to save her. To put it in the terminology of the more modern debate, we might say that Godwin sees the issue in this way only because he takes it for granted that my reasons must be agent-neutral judgments of value. If he had allowed for the possibility of my reasons being agent-relative judgments, he would not have made the strange assumption that two people, each of whom wishes to save his or her own mother, must be disagreeing about the degree of worth possessed by their respective mothers.[20] Godwin himself was soon to allow the personal affections more scope in moral behavior; so we shall discuss the point after considering those concessions.

Godwin, Mary Wollstonecraft and the Partial Affections

In the years following the first edition of *Political Justice* Godwin and Mary Wollstonecraft met, fell in love, and – after Mary became pregnant – married. Sadly, the pregnancy ended in disaster. Less than a year after she and Godwin had first become lovers, Mary Wollstonecraft died from complications caused by the birth of their only child. Nevertheless, the relationship seems to have caused Godwin to think again about the role of the partial affections. In a memoir of his late wife, entitled *Memoirs of the Author of A Vindication of the Rights of Woman*, Godwin wrote:

> A sound morality requires that *nothing human should be regarded by us as indifferent*; but it is impossible we should not feel the strongest interest for those persons whom we know most intimately, and whose welfare and sympathies are united to our own. True wisdom will recommend to us individual attachments; for with them our minds are more thoroughly maintained in activity and life than they can be under the privation of them, and it is better that man should be a living being, than a stock or a stone. True virtue will sanction this recommendation; since it is the object of virtue to produce happiness; and since the man who lives in the midst of domestic relations will have many opportunities of conferring pleasure, minute in the detail, yet not trivial in the amount, without interfering with the purposes of general benevolence. Nay, by kindling his sensibility, and harmonizing his soul, they may be expected, if he is endowed with a liberal and manly spirit, to render him more prompt in the service of strangers and the public.[21]

We can hardly avoid the impression that it was Godwin's own sensibilities which were happily kindled by his life "in the midst of domestic relations." But is this passage consistent with his treatment of the Fénelon case in *Political Justice*? By the end of this essay, we shall have an answer to this question.

Godwin's next major work was *St. Leon*, a novel. Its theme may well have surprised readers of *Political Justice*, for it is enthusiastic in its praise of partial affections, and especially those relating to love and marriage. In his preface, Godwin anticipated the question to which this would give rise:

> Some readers of my graver productions will perhaps, in perusing these little volumes, accuse me of inconsistency, the affections and charities of private life being every where in this publication a topic of the warmest eulogium, while in the Enquiry Concerning Political Justice they seemed to be treated with no great degree of indulgence and favour.[22]

In explanation, Godwin said that he had been anxious for an opportunity to modify some of the earlier chapters of *Political Justice* so as to make it conform with the sentiments of the present work. He hastened to add that he saw no cause "to make any change respecting the principle of justice, or anything else fundamental to the system there delivered." In order to show how these "jarring principles" can be reconciled, he includes in the preface the entire passage from the *Memoirs*, quoted earlier. His point is one made often in the contemporary debate about the partial affections; that the partial affections themselves have an impartial justification in view of the greater overall happiness that they produce.

Samuel Parr's Criticisms

On Easter Tuesday, 1800, Dr Samuel Parr, a well-known liberal clergyman, preached a sermon which was a sustained critique of what he called "universal philanthropy" or sometimes "universal benevolence." His audience would have had little difficulty in recognizing it as an attack on Godwin's impartialist ethic.[23] The sermon, with added notes that multiplied its length sevenfold, was published in 1801 under the title *A Spital Sermon*.[24]

As the text for his sermon, Parr takes an injunction from Paul's epistle to the Galatians: "As we have, therefore, opportunity, let us do good unto all men, especially unto them who are of the household of faith."[25] It is a text that begins by suggesting something similar to Godwin's concern with doing good to all, but then, by giving preference to those of one's own religion, departs from the standards of Godwinian impartiality. Parr's sermon starts by juxtaposing this text with "the new doctrine of universal philanthropy." As a Christian, he acknowledges and approves of benevolence, understood as:

> a disposition to wish, and, as opportunity may occur, to desire and do good, rather than harm, to those with whom we are quite unconnected.

But he immediately adds:

> I approve of it as a capacity sometimes to receive uneasiness from their pains, and satisfaction from their joys; but an uneasiness and a satisfaction far *less* frequent,

less intense, less permanent than the uneasiness and satisfaction which we feel for those around us, and by which we are stimulated to act, as we feel in their behalf.[26]

Parr argues against impartialism in ethics on the grounds that it takes an unrealistic view of human nature, and hence demands something that human beings cannot, in general and most of the time, give: "the moral obligations of men", he writes, "cannot be stretched beyond their physical powers."[27] Our real desires, our lasting and strongest passions, are not for the good of our species as a whole, but, at best, for the good of those who are close to us.

Contemporary philosophers have often made similar points. J. L. Mackie rejects "moralities of universal concern" because, he says, they deny "a quite ineradicable part of human nature." Even when we are being benevolent, Mackie says, we are not acting from universal concern, but rather in accordance with what he calls "self-referential altruism – concern for others, but for others who have some special connection with oneself; children, parents, friends, workmates, neighbours in the literal, not the metaphorically extended, sense."[28] Similarly, in the course of advocating an ethic based on caring for others, Nel Noddings writes:

> [W]e cannot care for everyone. Caring itself is reduced to mere talk about caring when we attempt to do so. We must acknowledge, then, that an ethic of caring implies a limit on our obligation.
>
> Our obligation is limited and delimited by relation. We are never free, in the human domain, to abandon our preparedness to care; but practically, if we are meeting those in our inner circles adequately as ones-caring and receiving those linked to our inner circles by formal chains of relation, we shall limit the calls upon our obligation quite naturally...I am not obliged to care for starving children in Africa, because there is no way for this caring to be completed in the other unless I abandon the caring to which I am obligated.[29]

After asserting that it is unrealistic to ask human beings to put the good of the species as a whole ahead of the good of those to whom we are close, Parr goes on to argue that even if this somehow were possible, it would not be desirable. The argument is worth quoting at length in order to display Parr's style:

> And thus we may ask, if the elements which give life and vigour to the moral world should be dissolved – if the mother could forget the child that "hanged from her breasts" – if the friend "with whom we took sweet counsel together" should forsake us, when we are compelled to beg our daily bread – if they, to whose succour we ran on the first sight of their distress, and poured "wine and

oil into their bleeding wounds", should ponder, ere they stretch forth their hands
to rescue us from wretchedness, and pause, lest peradventure some other human
being might be found a little more virtuous, and a little more miserable than
ourselves – if the tears of the widow and the cries of the orphan should be
disregarded, till their conduct had passed the ordeal of some rigid principle, or it
may be too, of some untoward prejudice, in those before whom they lie prostrate
– if they who have trodden the same soil with ourselves, spoken the same
language, followed the same customs, enjoyed the same rights, obeyed the
same laws, bowed before the same altar, should be no more endeared to us
than other men, whose kindness we have *never* experienced, whose faces we
have never seen, whose voices we have never heard – if all these things were
done under the pretence of some obligation, which stern, inflexible justice lays
upon us, to be extreme in marking what is done amiss, and to weigh every action
of man, every motive to act, every consequence of acting, in the balance which
every individual may set up within his own bosom for adjusting in every case the
direct and most efficacious means to promote the general good – what would
become of society, which parental affection, which friendship, which gratitude,
which compassion, which patriotism do not uphold? how changed would be the
scenes around us? how blunted the edge of all our finer affections? how scanty
the sum of our happiness? how multiplied and embittered the sources of our
woe?[30]

Parr goes on to suggest that the modern reformers may have a greater
influence "in furnishing their disciples with pleas for the neglect of their
ordinary duties than in stimulating their endeavours for those which are
extraordinary and perhaps ideal." In summary, Parr says, universal philanthropy
tends "to debase the dignity and weaken the efficacy of those particular
affections, for which we have daily and hourly occasion in the events of real
life," and he fears that instead of producing good that is "*visible* and *useful*,
though *limited*," these ideas will lead to nothing but "the ease of speculation
and the pride of dogmatism."[31] Parr's point was memorably encapsulated in
Charles Dickens's portrayal of Mrs Jellyby, who "could see nothing nearer than
Africa," neglecting her own children so that she could better care for those in
foreign lands.[32]

If Charles Dickens can be cited on Parr's side, however, it is appropriate to
mention on the other side Charlotte Perkins Gilman, a prominent early
twentieth-century American feminist. Gilman's short story "The Unnatural
Mother" considers the actions of Esther Greenwood, a young and unconven-
tional mother, who notices that a dam above the village in which she lives is
about to burst. She runs past her own house, in which her baby is asleep, in
order to rouse the village and send word to two other villages further down the
valley. She then loses her own life, trying to go back for her baby (which

miraculously survives). The story concludes with the following exchange between two older village women and the daughter of one of them:

> "Well, now, Mother," said Maria Amelia Briggs. "It does seem to me that she did her duty. You know yourself that if she hadn't given warnin' all three of the villages would 'a been cleaned out – a matter of fifteen hundred people. And if she'd stopped to lug that child, she couldn't have got here in time. Don't you believe she was thinkin' of those mill hands' children?"
>
> "Maria 'Melia, I'm ashamed of you!" said old Mis' Briggs. "But you ain't married and ain't a mother. A mother's duty is to her own child! She neglected her own to look after other folks' – the Lord never gave her them other children to care for!"
>
> "Yes," said Miss Jacobs, "and here's her child, a burden on the town! She was an unnatural mother!"[33]

In his sermon Parr does not mention Godwin by name. In the notes attached to the published version, however, Parr presents Godwin's case of a forced choice between Fénelon and one's father, and goes on to quote, with his own emphasis, the words we have already quoted above: "What *magic* is there in the pronoun '*my*' that should justify us in overturning the decisions of impartial truth. My brother or my father may be a fool, or a profligate, malicious, lying or dishonest. If they be, of what consequence is it that they are mine?" After quoting this passage, Parr comments:

> Probably, if the appeal were made to the common sense and common experience of mankind, the circumstance, that they are mine, would, even in the case supposed by our philosopher, be of great consequence. But, what if a father were neither a fool nor a profligate, would it *then* be of consequence that he was mine? Would the remembrance of his relation to me be no cause of endearment, no incitement to acts of beneficence towards him?...The pronoun my, I believe, will always be found to have great weight, both in the sentiments and the duties of mankind.[34]

Parr then refers the reader to a passage from Aristotle's *Politics*, already quoted in the text of the sermon. The passage is interesting, both for its direct relevance to Godwin's denial of the magic of "my," and because it takes us back to an even earlier impartiality debate: that between Plato and Aristotle. Plato, in the *Republic*, urged that many things should be held in common among the guardians, including wives and children. In the best-ordered state, he said, as many people as possible would use the words "mine" and "not mine" of the same things. In this kind of society, the whole community would regard the gain or loss of any individual as a gain or loss to itself.[35] To this

Aristotle responds (we here quote slightly more of the passage than Parr quoted, and in a more recent translation):

> But in a state having wives and children in common, the fraternal spirit will wear thin; no father will readily say "my son," nor any son "my father." As the sweetness of a little wine mingled with a great deal of water is imperceptible after the mixture, so, in a community such as that recommended by Plato, the very idea of relationship implied by these names will vanish; there will be no reason why a father should care about his so-called son, or vice versa, or a brother about his brother. The two factors which principally inspire concern and affection – that a thing is one's own, and that it is the keystone of one's hopes and fears – cannot exist in this sort of community.[36]

The quotation adds the weight of Aristotle's authority to Parr's argument, previously quoted, that the insistence on impartiality has the effect of debasing the particular affections. But since Aristotle is a philosopher renowned for his common sense, it is also support for Parr's contention that, in finding significance in particular relationships, rather than the general good, he is in accordance with the common experience of human beings.

Godwin's Defense

Godwin replied to Parr in 1801, in an eighty-page essay entitled *Thoughts Occasioned by the Perusal of Dr Parr's Spital Sermon.*[37] He begins by reminding the reader of the points he had already made, prior to Parr's sermon, in the preface to *St. Leon*, objecting, in other words, to Parr's venomous attack on a position on which "certain essential modifications" have already been made. The modification is not, he maintains, in what he thinks we ought or ought not to do, for in *Political Justice* he recognized that justice requires "our talents, our understanding, our strength and our time," and since we can often most effectively use our time in ensuring the happiness of those close to us, this is what justice tells us to do. The modification of his theory consists in his saying not only that I ought, "in ordinary cases, to provide for my wife and children, my brothers and relations, before I provide for strangers," but that this "should arise from the operation of those private and domestic affections, by which through all the ages of the world the conduct of mankind has been excited and directed."[38]

Godwin then develops his own view of virtuous character. Virtue consists, he says, in acting in accordance with "regulated affections." The affections of parents, relatives, lovers, and friends, as well as "the love of our country," are all admirable and should serve to motivate our everyday life; but these affections, he says, are liable to be followed further than they should be:

> I must be attentive to the welfare of my child; because I can...be conferring pleasure and benefit on him, when I cannot be directly employed in conferring benefit on others. I best understand his character and his wants...I do not require that, when a man is employed in benefiting his child, be should constantly recollect the abstract principle of utility, but I do maintain that his actions in prosecuting that benefit are no further virtuous than in proportion as they square with that principle.

So the father who will "rather consent that millions should perish, than that [a] miserable minion of his dotage should suffer a moment's displeasure" is not to be regarded with approbation. Such a father may be acting from affection for his child, but his affection surpasses the limits justifiable in terms of an impartial ethic. Godwin takes the same view of patriotism: love of one's country and one's compatriots is desirable, up to a point, but it exceeds that point when, for example, it becomes the kind of patriotism that "vents itself in uttering hisses, and perhaps casting stones at the unprotected foreigner as he passes along our streets." Impartial justice or utility remains for Godwin the ultimate criterion of what we ought to do.[39]

Modern partialists question whether these "regulated affections" are really affections at all. Michael Stocker finds a kind of "schizophrenia" in the view that what we value or justify may be at odds with our motives in this way. He imagines that during a long stay in hospital, you are regularly visited by a friend, Smith. You feel that he is a real friend for taking so much trouble to make these cheering visits, and you warm to him as a result. If, however, you discover that he comes essentially because he thinks that it is his duty, perhaps because by doing so he will maximize utility, then something has gone wrong. As Stocker puts it, "love, friendship, affection, fellow feeling, and community all require that the other person be an essential part of what is valued. The person – not merely the person's general values nor even the person-qua-producer-or-possessor-of-general-values – must be valued."[40]

But the position Stocker criticizes differs from Godwin's in an important way. Godwin explicitly denies that we should love our children *because* that is the way to maximize pleasure; rather he says that because the love parents naturally have for their children is an important source of pleasure, we may follow the promptings of these natural inclinations – at least up to the point at which they plainly go beyond what is for the greater good of all. Similarly, he would not say that we should visit sick friends in hospital *because* doing so maximizes pleasure, but rather that because friendship is a source of pleasure, we may visit our sick friends, rather than simply the sick person most in need of cheering up. The impartial perspective provides, for Godwin, a boundary on our partial passions; but not an unreasonably constraining one.

In this respect Godwin's view anticipates a point made with greater precision by Sidgwick:

> the doctrine that Universal Happiness is the ultimate *standard* must not be taken to imply that Universal Benevolence is the only right or always the best *motive* of action. For, as we have observed, it is not necessary that the end which gives the criterion of rightness should always be the end at which we consciously aim; and if experience shows that the general happiness will be more satisfactorily obtained if men frequently act from other motives than pure universal philanthropy, it is obvious that these other motives are reasonably to be preferred on Utilitarian principles.[41]

Peter Railton takes a similar view. He distinguishes between two husbands, John and Juan. Each loves his wife and is attentive to her needs, but John's account of why he does so is couched in terms of the fact that a world in which people take special care of the ones they love is a better world than one in which they do not, while Juan speaks directly of his love for his wife, recognizing at the same time that this kind of love can fit within an impartial moral framework. In Railton's terminology, John is a "subjective consequentialist." In his daily life, John consciously aims at the overall good. Juan, on the other hand, is a "sophisticated consequentialist." He is a person who "has a standing commitment to leading an objectively consequentialist life [that is, a life that, of those available to the agent, brings about the best outcomes] but who need not set special stock in any particular form of decision making and therefore does not necessarily seek to lead a subjectively consequentialist life."[42] Godwin seems to have been advocating sophisticated consequentialism.

Next Godwin turns to Parr's comments on Fénelon. First, repeating a point he already made in *Political Justice*, Godwin separates the objective rightness of an action from its blameworthiness. Few will be disposed to blame me if I save my father. Nor should they be so disposed, because we are "accustomed, and rightly accustomed, to consider every man in the aggregate" and saving one's father in such a manner would demonstrate that at least I "have *my heart in the right place.*" This is a way of saying that the filial affection I have displayed is "pregnant with a thousand good and commendable actions," and hence praiseworthy. But then Godwin goes beyond the question of praise and blame, and makes a point relevant to the objective rightness of the action itself. This is whether "I should act upon the utility of the case separately taken, or should refuse to proceed in violation of a habit, which is fraught with a series of successive utilities."[43] Here Godwin appears to be contemplating a departure from the straightforward act-utilitarianism that led him to so uncompromising a position in the Fénelon case. In suggesting that we ought to give weight to the fact that we are breaking a habit or rule that has the best consequences in most cases, Godwin is anticipating the modern distinction between act-and rule-utilitarianism, or as it has more recently become in the work of R. M. Hare, between critical and intuitive levels of moral reasoning.[44]

Godwin then attempts to meet Parr's concern that the choice between saving one's father or Fénelon is a choice that pits "the effort of passion" against "cool, phlegmatic arithmetical calculation." This objection to anything smacking of mathematical calculation finds a modern echo in Carol Gilligan's account of the "different voice" that women use when talking about ethical questions. In Gilligan's words, the men interviewed by Lawrence Kohlberg see the moral dilemmas with which they are presented as "a math problem with humans"; in contrast the women to whom Gilligan spoke view these same moral dilemmas as narratives of relationships that extend over time.[45] To Parr's attempt to present the choice as one between passion and cool calculation, Godwin responds:

> No great and honourable deed can be achieved but from passion. If I save the life of Fénelon, unprompted to do so by an ardent love of the wondrous excellence of the man, and a sublime eagerness to achieve and secure the welfare and improvement of a million, I am a monster..[46]

So Godwin is for passion, in the cause of utility. He concludes his discussion of the Fénelon example by saying that it was a mistake for him to use Fénelon as an example of the person to be saved, because the benefits that come from the writing of books are too remote to take hold of our imagination.

An Assessment

What are we to make of Godwin's revised position, after his defense of it against Parr? Commenting on the modifications Godwin had made to his position on impartiality in the third edition of *Political Justice* and in *St. Leon*, Parr at one point reports a remark he has heard, that "after the surrender of so many outworks, the citadel itself is scarcely tenable."[47] This is the nub of the current debate between partialism and impartialism over the place of personal relationships in ethics. Partialists have argued that impartialist theories cannot recognize the good of personal relationships such as friendship; impartialists have risen to the attack, suggesting various ways in which their theory can take account of such goods. Sometimes, however, one cannot avoid the feeling that too many essential characteristics of impartialism have indeed been surrendered in order to blunt the attacks on the position; and as a result what remains intact is no longer recognizably impartialist.[48]

On the tenability of the citadel, Godwin himself is of regrettably little assistance, because in his reply he takes his "citadel" to be not the principle of impartial justice, but rather his belief in "the progressive nature of man." He then goes on to show that this belief is not rendered untenable by his change of mind about the domestic affections.[49] This is an odd response, given that Parr's remark occurs in the context of a discussion of Godwin's view of impartial justice. Most likely, however, if Godwin had taken Parr to be referring to the "citadel" of impartiality, his response would have been to argue that this citadel too is no less impregnable given his new views about the domestic affections. D. H. Monro plausibly interprets Godwin not merely as accepting the domestic affections, but as relying on them as the basis for a broader passion. Godwin believes, as Monro notes, that we can appreciate the suffering of humanity as a whole only because we have learnt to do so by understanding the suffering of particular individuals. Thus Godwin, according to Monro:

> did not want to advocate a bloodless reason that turned its back on the human affections. There should be no conflict between the greatest happiness principle and the affections. We should not stifle them in trying to follow the tight-lipped axioms of morality, general rules in which we see only from a distance. The point is rather that we should have as vivid an apprehension of the sufferings of the rest of humanity as of our dearest friends. So far from wishing to sacrifice emotion to reason, Godwin wants reason to be charged with emotion.[50]

Yet whether the conflict is between reason and passion, or between an impartial passion to put an end to suffering in general, as against a partial passion to help a particular friend, a doubt must remain. We are being pulled in opposite directions. How can an ethical theory defend impartiality, and not deny, at some level, the partiality we must feel for our spouse, our children, our lovers or close friends? The answer is that, *at some level*, it cannot. This creates an insoluble problem for single-level impartialist theories: that is, not only for theories which (as Blum put it in the quotation with which this paper began) derive the legitimacy of our commitments and projects by reference to an impartialist perspective, but also for theories which hold that those projects and commitments should actually be impartialist through and through. An example of such a theory would be a form of act utilitarianism that required each individual act to be aimed directly at maximizing good, impartially conceived. Perhaps such a theory lies behind Godwin's initially unqualified insistence that when it comes to a choice between Fénelon and your mother, you must rescue Fénelon. As his views developed, however, he edged towards a recognizably two-level version of utilitarianism. We shall conclude by focusing on such a view, because it offers the best prospect of defending impartialism against the objections we have been considering.

Our feelings for our spouses, children, lovers, or close friends have their roots deep in our human nature. We have evolved as mammals living in small and relatively stable social groups. This means that we are concerned to protect our kin, and liable to form long-lasting reciprocal relationships with others who are not related to us. While we cannot draw ethical conclusions directly from the fact that these partial affections are natural to us, it should not come as a surprise to us that any successful set of rules or principles for everyday living is likely to reflect, and build upon, these aspects of our nature. To do anything else would be to cut too deeply against the grain. Since utilitarians want an ethic that brings about good consequences when applied by real human beings, utilitarians should give broad support to systems of rules or principles that are suited for human beings as they are, or at least as there is some hope that they may become in the foreseeable future.

But we are also reasoning beings. We can, to quote the subtitle of one of Godwin's novels, see "things as they are."[51] This means that we can see that others suffer as our mothers, fathers, and friends suffer; and we can see that the parents and friends of other people mean just as much to them as our parents and friends mean to us. So we can think and make practical judgments from a standpoint that has this insight built into its foundations and into the meanings of the words we use when we are making judgments from this standpoint. So the tension between partialism and impartialism is real. It is part of our nature, and should not be condemned as "schizophrenia" or thought of as an aspect only of particular moral theories. The tension cannot be entirely resolved, unless we either jettison our personal relationships, or, more probably, refuse to see things as they are, and focus only on our own personal concerns and relationships, forgetting that the personal concerns and relationships of others matter just as much to them as our own do to us.

In this situation, a solution along the lines indicated by Godwin in his later reflections on the Fénelon case is likely to be the best we can do: that is, we accept the partial affections, recognizing that even from an impartial perspective, we do better to follow them and seek to reinforce them, at least up to a point. We therefore foster "habits," or intuitive ways of reaching moral decisions, that are consistent with such "regulated affections." To do so, we may praise the person who acts on the basis of such affections, even if in some very unusual cases we recognize that a different act would have been better from the perspective of the critically thinking "impartial spectator of an angelic nature." Put in more modern terminology, we can often give agent-neutral reasons for praising those who act on agent-relative grounds. In the end it is from an agent-neutral standpoint that we determine whether an action was right; but it is a mistake to focus always on the rightness of individual actions, rather than on the habits or intuitive ways of thinking that can be expected, over a lifetime, to do the most good. Here virtue theory should be given its due, for objecting to the exclusive focus on the rightness of actions, and instead directing our attention to the question of what kind of character a good person has. Nevertheless at least one theory that is impartialist in the sense defined in the first paragraph of this article still stands: two-level consequentialism. This is the position defended by Godwin after his relationship with Mary Wollstonecraft had brought home to him the importance of personal affections; it is also the view held by Hare and Railton. It is, admittedly, a muted impartialism. It does not require us to be impartialist in our everyday life. For that reason, it cannot strictly be said to require us to save Fénelon rather than our mother or father. To be the kind of person who could do this, we would have to give up too much else that is of value. Nevertheless when attention is focused only on the choice that the rescuer must make, this form of consequentialism may hold that it would be best if Fénelon were saved.

We may find it discouraging that most modern criticism of impartialism simply repeats points to which Godwin had already replied nearly 200 years ago. As we have seen, in Godwin's reply to Parr and other critics, we can find answers to many of the objections made to impartialism in the past two decades. That moral philosophy repeatedly goes over the same ground is scarcely a good omen for the future of the subject. But there is a more positive way of looking at the fact that the debate seems a perennial, or at least a recurrent, one. Perhaps both impartialism and partialism are ineliminable elements of ethics. Philosophers tend to give too much weight first to one, and then to the other. This in turn supports the idea that the only tenable position is one that recognizes the importance of both elements.

Notes

1 The research on which this essay is based was supported by a grant from the Australian Research Council. We thank Justin Oakley for helpful comments.
2 Lawrence Blum, "Iris Murdoch and the Domain of the Moral," *Philosophical Studies*, I (1986), p. 344. Blum notes that the term "impartialism" derives from Stephen Darwall's *Impartial Reason* (Ithaca, NY, 1983), although Darwall applies it only to Kantianism.
3 See Iris Murdoch, *The Sovereignty of Good* (London, 1970); Bernard Williams, "A Critique of Utilitarianism," *Utilitarianism For and Against*, ed. J. J. C. Smart and

Bernard Williams (Cambridge, 1973); Michael Stocker, "The Schizophrenia of Modern Ethical Theories," *Journal of Philosophy*, lxxvi (1976), pp. 453–66; Lawrence Blum, *Friendship, Altruism and Morality* (London, 1980); J. L. Mackie, *Ethics: Inventing Right and Wrong* (Harmondsworth, 1977), p. 132; Carol Gilligan, *In a Different Voice: Psychological Theory and Women's Development* (Cambridge, MA), 1982; Nel Noddings, *Caring: A Feminine Approach to Ethics and Moral Education* (Berkeley and Los Angeles, 1986); Tom Nagel, *The View from Nowhere* (New York, 1986). The importance of Murdoch's work for the contemporary debate is emphasized by Blum in the work referred to in note 2 above.

4   William Hazlitt, *The Spirit of the Age* (1825) (Oxford, 1954), pp. 19–20, as cited by William St Clair, *The Godwins and the Shelleys: The Biography of a Family* (London, 1989), p. 91.

5   William Godwin, *An Enquiry Concerning Political Justice and its Influence on General Virtue and Happiness* [1793], ed. and abr. Raymond Preston (New York, 1926), pp. 41–2. Henceforth this work will be referred to simply as *Political Justice*. (We refrain from commenting here on Godwin's reason for holding "a man" to be of more worth than "a beast.")

6   *Political Justice*, p. 43.

7   Ibid.

8   Henry Sidgwick, *The Methods of Ethics*, 7th edn. (London, 1907), pp. 428–9; J. J. C. Smart, "An outline of a system of utilitarian ethics," in *Utilitarianism For and Against*, Smart and Williams, pp. 53–6.

9   *Political Justice*, p. 52; see also p. 44.

10   Ibid., pp. 44–5.

11   William Godwin, *Enquiry Concerning Political Justice: With selections from Godwin's other writings*, ed. K. Codell Carter (Oxford, 1971), p. 71.

12   Raymond Preston, in his Introduction to *Political Justice*, p. xxx.

13   D. H. Munro, "Archbishop Fénelon versus My Mother," *Australasian Journal of Philosophy*, xxviii (1950), p. 154.

14   Mark Philp, *Godwin's Political Justice* (London, 1986), p. 209.

15   St Clair, *The Godwins and the Shelleys*, p. 175.

16   *Political Justice*, ed. K. Codell Carter, pp. 72–3.

17   Ibid., p. 72.

18   See David Hume, *An Enquiry Concerning the Principles of Morals*, *British Moralists 1650–1800*, ed. D. D. Raphael, 2 vols. (Oxford, 1969) i. 86, and Adam Smith, *The Theory of Moral Sentiments*, i. 226.

19   R. M. Hare, *Moral Thinking* (Oxford, 1981), pp. 44–5.

20   For the terminology of "agent-neutral" and "agent-relative" see Derek Parfit, *Reasons and Persons* (Oxford, 1984), p. 143; for further discussion see Nagel, *The View from Nowhere*, pp. 152ff.

21   William Godwin, *Memoirs of the Author of a Vindication of the Rights of Woman*, 2nd edn., ch. 6, p. 90, quoted in William Godwin, *Thoughts Occasioned by the Perusal of Dr Parr's Spital Sermon* (1801), reprinted in *Uncollected Writings (1785–1822) by William Godwin*, ed. J. Marken and B. Pollin (Florida, 1968), pp. 314–15. As K.

Codell Carter notes (*Political Justice*, p. 320 n. 2) the passage italicized in the original is from Terence (*Heautontimorumenos*, I. 77), and is usually translated as "nothing human is alien to me." Godwin's argument for the importance of "individual attachments" is reminiscent of Aristotle's discussion of the need for friendship in his *Nicomachean Ethics*, Bk. IX, § 9.

22 William Godwin, *St. Leon: A Tale of the Sixteenth Century*, p. viii, quoted in William Godwin, *Thoughts Occasioned by the Perusal of Dr Parr's Spital Sermon*, pp. 314–15.

23 For details on the life of Samuel Parr, see Warren Derry, *Dr Parr: A Portrait of the Whig Dr Johnson* (Oxford, 1966).

24 Samuel Parr, *A Spital Sermon preached at Christ Church upon Easter Tuesday, April 15, 1800, to which are added notes*, London, 1801. Henceforth cited as *A Spital Sermon*.

25 *Galatians* 6: 10.

26 *A Spital Sermon*, p. 6.

27 Ibid., p. 4.

28 Mackie, *Ethics*, p. 132. Mackie takes the useful term "self-referential altruism" from C. D. Broad, but without giving a source, and we have been unable to find the reference.

29 Noddings, *Caring*, p. 86; for a related passage see also p. 112.

30 *A Spital Sermon*, pp. 9–10.

31 Ibid., pp. 10–11.

32 Charles Dickens, *Bleak House* (1853, London), ch. 4. (We owe this reference to Christina Hoff Sommers: "Filial Morality," in *Women and Moral Theory*, ed. Eva Feder Kittay and Diana T. Meyers (Totowa, NJ, 1987), p. 72.)

33 Charlotte Perkins Gilman, "The Unnatural Mother," *The Charlotte Perkins Gilman Reader*, ed. Ann J. Lane (New York, 1980), p. 65; first published in *The Forerunner* (November 1916), pp. 281–5. We thank Erin McKenna for drawing our attention to this story.

34 *A Spital Sermon*, pp. 33–4.

35 Plato, *The Republic*, trans. Desmond Lee, 2nd edn. (Harmondsworth, 1974), p. 247 (462c–e).

36 Aristotle, *Politics*, Bk. II, 1262b; ed. and trans. John Warrington (London, 1959), p. 33.

37 Godwin, *Thoughts Occasioned by the Perusal of Dr Parr's Spital Sermon*, in *Uncollected Writings*. Henceforth cited as *Thoughts*, with the first set of page numbers referring to those in the original, and the second set, preceded by "M," to the Marken and Pollin edition.

38 *Thoughts*, pp. 27–8 (M 316–17).

39 Ibid., pp. 32–4 (M 321–3). Godwin's argument that I am entitled to give more attention to my child because "I best understand his character and his wants" can be found later in Sidgwick, *The Methods of Ethics*, pp. 432–4, and in Frank Jackson, "Decision-Theoretic Consequentialism and the Nearest and Dearest Objection," *Ethics*, ci (1991), 461–82; see especially 474–5.

40 Stocker, "The Schizophrenia of Modern Ethical Theories," p. 459; the example of Smith's visit is on p. 462.

41 Sidgwick, *The Methods of Ethics*, p. 413. In "Utilitarian Morality and the Personal Point of View," *Journal of Philosophy*, lxxxiii (1986), pp. 417–38, at p. 421 n. 13, David Brink employs this distinction in his defense of utilitarianism, meets objections to it, and provides references to several other statements of the same point. The earliest of these – Joseph Butler's *Fifteen Sermons* (see Sermon XII, § iv, par. 31) – precedes Godwin, having been first published in 1726. See also Jackson, "Decision-Theoretic Consequentialism," pp. 465ff.

42 Peter Railton, "Alienation, Consequentialism and the Demands of Morality," *Philosophy and Public Affairs*, xiii (1984), p. 153. The example of John is to be found on p. 135, and of Juan on p. 150.

43 *Thoughts*, p. 41 (M 330).

44 For a selection of key articles in the modern debate on act- and rule-utilitarianism, see *Contemporary Utilitarianism*, ed. Michael Bayles (New York, 1968), or *Consequentialism*, ed. Philip Pettit (Aldershot, 1993), Pt. IV. See also David Lyons, *Forms and Limits of Utilitarianism* (Oxford, 1965), and Hare, *Moral Thinking*. Godwin was not, however, the first to point to the distinction between judging on the basis of the utility of each act, and judging on the basis of conformity to a rule or habit that is itself productive of utility. For a discussion of earlier comments along similar lines by David Hume and Richard Price, see Jonathan Harrison, "Utilitarianism, Universalisation and Our Duty to Be Just," *Proceedings of the Aristotelian Society*, liii (1952–3), pp. 105–34; reprinted in *Contemporary Utilitarianism*, Bayles.

45 Gilligan, *In a Different Voice*, p. 28.

46 *Thoughts*, p. 41 (M 330).

47 *A Spital Sermon*, p. 52.

48 That view could, for example, be taken of Samuel Scheffler's attempt to reconcile consequentialism and partiality in *The Rejection of Consequentialism* (Oxford, 1982), or of Peter Railton's "sophisticated consequentialism," defended in his "Alienation, Consequentialism, and the Demands of Morality." For recent discussion of the issue of consequentialism and personal relationships, see Neera Kapur Badhwar, "Why it is wrong to be always guided by the best: consequentialism and friendship," *Ethics*, 101 (1991), pp. 483–504; see also *Friendship: A Philosophical Reader*, ed. Neera Kapur Badhwar (Ithaca, NY, 1993), especially the editor's introduction at pp. 28–32.

49 *Thoughts*, p. 46 (M 336).

50 Monro, "Archbishop Fénelon," p. 171; also in D. H. Monro, *Godwin's Moral Philosophy* (London, 1953), p. 33.

51 The novel is *Caleb Williams, or Things as they are*; the significance of its subtitle is pointed out by Monro, "Archbishop Fénelon," p. 167.

Part Five

Unsanctifying Human Life

Twelve

The Moral Status of the Embryo

Helga Kuhse and Peter Singer

A living human embryo comes into existence as soon as a human egg and sperm have joined together. If the embryo is then implanted into the mother, it cannot be objected that the embryo has been denied any respect that might be due to it, for it has been placed into the environment that gives it the greatest possible chance of survival. But what if more eggs have been fertilized than can be reimplanted? What is to be done with them? Should they be frozen? But what if the couple who provided the egg and sperm do not wish to have the excess embryos reimplanted into the woman? (Perhaps the first embryo developed successfully, and they do not want any more children.) And what if, while not wishing to use the embryo themselves, the couple also do not like the idea of their genetic material being used by another couple? Should the embryos then be kept frozen for ever? What point would there be in that? Or can these excess embryos simply be tipped down the sink?

Many people find such questions bewildering. Seeing no way of answering them, they throw up their hands and say, "It's all up to the individual's subjective judgment." Our aim is to show that there is a rational answer to these questions, which should carry conviction with everyone who accepts one very widely held premise: that it is not wrong to destroy either the egg or the sperm before they have united.

First published in *Test-Tube Babies: A Guide to Moral Questions, Present Techniques, and Future Possibilities*, ed. William A. W. Walters and Peter Singer (Melbourne: Oxford University Press, 1982), pp. 57–63.

On the basis of this premise we shall argue that there is no moral obligation to preserve the life of the embryo. Our argument applies specifically to the very early kind of embryo produced by the IVF program. In other words, we are talking about an embryo that has developed for only some hours or at the most a day or two. It will only have divided a few times, into two, four, eight, or sixteen cells. (Technically, this is known as a zygote, but we shall continue to refer to it by the more widely known term "embryo.") At this stage, of course, the embryo has no brain, or even a nervous system. (Even the brain of a tadpole has more than 5,000 cells.) The embryo could not possibly feel anything or be conscious in any way. Therefore, what we shall argue about this kind of embryo has no *necessary* application to an embryo at a later stage of development, for example, at a stage of development at which it does have a brain, and could feel pain.

The Premise

Our argument begins from the premise that it is not wrong to destroy either the egg or the sperm – the gametes, as they are collectively known – before they have united. We do not know of anyone who seriously asserts that the moral status of the egg and sperm before fertilization is such that it is wrong to destroy them. For instance, if a man is asked to produce a specimen of semen so that it can be tested to see if he is fertile, no one objects to the semen being tipped out once the test is complete. And after all, in our normal lives eggs and sperm are constantly being wasted. Every normal female between puberty and menopause wastes an egg each month that she does not become pregnant; and after puberty every normal male wastes millions of sperm in sexual intercourse in which contraceptives are used, or in which the woman is not fertile; and the same applies when he masturbates or has a nocturnal emission. Does anyone regard all of this as a terrible tragedy? Not to our knowledge; and so we do not think the premise of our argument is likely to be challenged.

We shall consider some imaginary stories. They do not describe any actual occurrences or even probable ones. We are using them to illustrate a moral point.

First Story

Doctors working on an IVF program have obtained a fertile egg from a patient and some semen from the patient's husband. They are just about to drop the semen into the glass dish containing the egg, when the doctor in charge of the patient calls to say that he has discovered that she has a medical condition which makes pregnancy impossible. The egg could be fertilized and returned to the womb, but implantation would not occur. The embryo would die and be expelled during the woman's next monthly cycle. There is therefore no point in proceeding to fertilize the egg. So the egg and semen are tipped, separately, down the sink.

In accordance with our premise, as far as the moral status of the egg or the sperm before they have united is concerned, nothing wrong has been done.

Second Story

Everything happens exactly as in the first story, except that the doctor in charge of the patient calls with the bad news just *after* the egg and sperm have been placed in the glass dish and fertilization has already taken place. The couple are asked if they are prepared to consent to the newly created embryo being frozen to be implanted into someone else, but they are adamant that they do not want their genetic material to become someone else's child. Nor is there any prospect of the woman's condition ever changing, so there is no point in freezing the embryo in the hope of reimplanting it in her at a later date. The couple ask that the embryo be disposed of as soon as possible.

If the embryo has a special moral status that makes it wrong to destroy it, it would be wrong to comply with the couple's request. What, then, *should* be done with the embryo?

How plausible is the belief that it was not wrong to dispose of the egg and sperm separately but would be wrong to dispose of them after they have united? For those who believe that there is a real distinction between the two stories, here is a third story, not to be taken too seriously, but intended to bring out the peculiarity of that belief.

Third Story

This story begins just as the first one does. The doctor's call comes before the egg and sperm have been united, and so they are tipped, separately, down the sink. But as luck would have it, the sink is blocked by a surgical dressing. As a result, the egg has not actually gone down the drainpipe before the semen is thrown on top of it. A nurse is about to clear the blockage and flush them both away when a thought occurs to her: perhaps the egg has been fertilized by the semen that was thrown on top of it! If that has happened, or if there is even a significant chance of that having happened, those who believe that the embryo has a special moral status which makes it wrong to destroy it must now believe that it would be wrong to clear the blockage; instead the egg must now be rescued from the sink, checked to see if fertilization has occurred, and if it has, efforts should presumably be made to keep it alive.

On what grounds could one try to defend the view that the coming together of the egg and sperm makes such a crucial difference to the way in which they ought to be treated? We shall consider three possible grounds which have been put forward.

The Claim that a Human Life Exists from Conception

The claim that a human life exists from the moment of conception is often used as an argument against abortion. We are not here considering the issue of abortion but rather the moral status of the embryo. Nevertheless, the claim is relevant to our topic, because it is often assumed that once it is acknowledged that a human life exists from the moment of conception, it will also have to be conceded that from the moment of conception the embryo has the same basic right to life as normal human beings after birth.

To assess the claim that a human life exists from conception, it is necessary to distinguish two possible senses of the term "human being." One sense is strictly biological: a human being is a member of the species *Homo sapiens*. The other is more restricted: a human being is a being possessing, at least at a minimal level, the capacities distinctive of our species which include consciousness, the ability to be aware of one's surroundings, to be able to relate to others, perhaps even rationality and self-consciousness.

When opponents of abortion say that the embryo is a living human being from conception onwards, all they can possibly mean is that the embryo is a living member of the species *Homo sapiens*. This is all that can be established as a scientific fact. But is this also the sense in which every "human being" has a right to life? We think not. To claim that every human being has a right to life solely because it is biologically a member of the species *Homo sapiens* is to make species membership the basis of rights. This is as indefensible as making race membership the basis of rights. It is the form of prejudice one of us has elsewhere referred to as "speciesism," a prejudice in favor of members of one's own species, simply because they are members of one's own species. The logic of this prejudice runs parallel to the logic of the racist who is prejudiced in favor of members of his race simply because they are members of his race. If we are to attribute rights on morally defensible grounds, we must base them on some morally relevant characteristic of the beings to whom we attribute rights. Examples of such morally relevant characteristics would be consciousness, autonomy, rationality, and so on, but not race or species.

Hence, although it may be possible to claim with strict literal accuracy that a human life exists from conception, it is not possible to claim that a human life exists from conception in the sense of a being which possesses, even at the most minimal level, the capacities distinctive of most human beings. Yet it is on the possession of these capacities that the attribution of a right to life, or of any other special moral status, must be based.

The Claim from the Potential of the Embryo

It may be admitted that the embryo consisting of no more than sixteen cells cannot be said to be entitled to any special moral status because of any characteristics it actually possesses. It is, once again, far inferior to a tadpole in respect of all characteristics that could be regarded as morally relevant. But what of its potential? Unlike a tadpole, it has the potential to develop into a normal human being, with a high degree of rationality, self-consciousness, autonomy, and so on. Can this potential justify the belief that the embryo is entitled to a special moral status?

We believe it cannot, for the following reason. Everything that can be said about the potential of the embryo can also be said about the potential of the egg and sperm. The egg and sperm, if united, also have the potential to develop into a normal human being, with a high degree of rationality, self-consciousness, autonomy, and so on. On the basis of our premise that the egg and sperm separately have no special moral status, it seems impossible to use the potential of the embryo as a ground for giving it special moral status.

It is, of course, true that something may go wrong. The egg may be surrounded by semen, and yet not be fertilized. But it is also true that something may go wrong with the development of the embryo. It may fail to implant. It may implant but spontaneously abort. And so on. There is a possibility of something going wrong at every stage, from the production of egg and sperm right through to the time at which there is a rational and self-conscious being. That there is one more stage that the egg and sperm must go through, compared to the embryo, can scarcely make a decisive difference.

The Uniqueness of the Embryo

Some will concede that there is a sense in which both the embryo and the egg and sperm, taken separately, have the same potential, namely the potential to develop into a mature human being. Yet, they will want to say, there is a difference between these two forms of potential. As long as the egg and sperm are separate, the genetic nature of the individual human being that may come to exist is still to be determined. We have no way of telling which of the hundreds of thousands of sperm in a drop of semen will fertilize the egg. The unique genetic constitution of the embryo, on the other hand, has been determined for all time.

Can this difference provide a reason for giving the embryo higher status than the egg and sperm? Surely not, for the difference still does not show that the embryo has a different potential from the egg and sperm. The egg and sperm have the potential to develop into a mature human being. There are no genetically indeterminate human beings, and every genetically determinate human being is unique, with the exception of identical twins, triplets, and so on. Thus, the uniqueness of the embryo is nothing *additional* to its potential for becoming human. Why should our inability to tell which sperm will fertilize the egg make such a difference? If we were better able to predict which sperm would fertilize the egg, would we then say that the egg and sperm were now entitled to the same moral status as the embryo?

If it is uniqueness as such that we are talking about, and not the potential to develop into a mature human being, we should also remember that it is not only human beings who are genetically unique. Each individual chimpanzee is genetically unique too; so is each individual pig, and each individual rat, and each individual sparrow. Does that entitle them to special moral status? (Is it less evil to kill one of a pair of identical twins than it is to kill one of a pair of fraternal twins?)

Finally, if uniqueness is thought to be a basis for special moral status, what will happen when advances in the technique of cloning make it possible for each human cell to become an embryo? An embryo that is developed from the nucleus of a human cell in this manner would not be unique. Any other embryo developed in the same manner from a cell taken from the same person would be genetically identical to it. Would this mean that a cloned embryo would not have the moral status of a normal embryo? This seems an absurd conclusion; certainly it is one that cuts against all the other arguments we have been considering, for a cloned embryo is as much a living human being, and as much a potentially rational and self-conscious being, as a normal embryo.

Since none of these three grounds suffice to support a sharp distinction between the moral status of the embryo and that of the egg and sperm, we are left with just three possibilities: we must find another plausible reason for making this distinction, or we must abandon our initial premise, which was that the egg and sperm are not entitled to a special moral status which would make it wrong to destroy them, or we must hold that the embryo in its very earliest stage of life is also not entitled to a special moral status which would make it wrong to destroy it. We can find no other plausible reason for making the distinction. Our premise still seems well grounded. Hence we conclude that the newly created embryo is not entitled to a special moral status which makes it wrong to destroy it.

Our conclusion is contrary to the views of many theologians...On the other hand it does not seem to be at odds with the views of our community as a whole. There appears to be little or no opposition to the use of intrauterine devices, or IUDs, as a means of preventing pregnancy. There is evidence that these devices often work not strictly as contraceptives, that is, not by preventing conception but by ensuring that any egg that is fertilized will fail to implant in the womb. The fertilized egg, or embryo, is then expelled from the womb and dies. If the embryo, from its earliest stages, were entitled to a special moral status which makes it wrong to kill it, the use of IUDs would be a serious violation of that special moral status.

We are not claiming that two wrongs make a right. We have argued that the embryo in its earliest stages does not have a special moral status that makes it wrong to kill it. Hence we do not think that it is wrong to use an IUD, or to discard any excess embryos produced by IVF techniques. We have mentioned IUDs only to make the point that anyone who objects to the disposal of excess embryos produced in the course of attempts at IVF should also, to be consistent, object just as strongly to the use of an IUD. Anyone who calls for a ban on the use of IVF because it may lead to the discarding of human embryos will be on very weak ground unless he or she also calls for a ban on the use of IUDs.

The view we have argued for justifies the common-sense reaction which we believe most readers will have had to the three stories we told earlier. If you felt that it would be absurd to hold that the medical staff are under a moral obligation to try to rescue the egg that may have been accidentally fertilized in the blocked sink, you were right. Similarly, whether the doctor's call came a minute before the egg and sperm were to be united, or a minute afterwards, makes no crucial difference. In none of these cases has a being come into existence which is capable of feeling or experiencing anything at all. In none of these cases is there a being that has a right to life.

Thirteen

Individuals, Humans, and Persons: The Issue of Moral Status

Helga Kuhse and Peter Singer

Some well-known arguments against nontherapeutic embryo research rest on the premise that fertilization marks the beginning of "genetically new human life organized as a distinct entity oriented towards further development,"[1] and the additional premise that it is wrong to destroy such life, either because of what it currently is, or because of what it has the potential to become. This type of argument, put forward in the majority report of the Australian Senate Select Committee on the Human Experimentation Bill 1985,[2] can also be found in the Vatican's *Instruction on Respect for Human Life*.[3]

We believe there are good reasons for rejecting this type of argument. In Section I of this chapter we outline the reasons why we should reject the view that a zygote or early human embryo is a distinct human individual;[4] in Section II, we argue against the common view that an early embryo has a right to life because it is an innocent human being; in Section III, we put the argument that experimentation on early human embryos is no harder to justify than various other reproductive choices; and finally, in Section IV, we shall sketch a positive account of how we should think about embryo research.

First published in *Embryo Experimentation*, ed. Peter Singer, Helga Kuhse, Stephen Buckle, Karen Dawson, and Pascal Kasimba (Cambridge: Cambridge University Press, 1990), pp. 65–75. Reprinted with permission of Cambridge University Press.

I

It is often assumed that the answer to the question: "When does a particular human life begin?" will also provide the answer to the question of how that life ought, morally, to be treated. We shall, however, set the moral question aside for the moment and instead focus on some prior issues that must be faced by anyone who wants to claim that fertilization marks the time when a particular human life or "I" began to exist.[5]

What this claim amounts to is that the newly fertilized egg, the early embryo and I are, in some sense of the term, the same individual. Now, in one very obvious sense, the zygote that gave rise to me and I, the adult, are not the same individual – the former is a unicellular being totally devoid of consciousness, whereas I am a conscious being consisting of many millions of cells. So the claim that the zygote and I are the same individual must rely on a different sense of "individual." And so it does.

It is usually thought that the zygote and I are the same individual in one or both of the following two senses: first, that there is a genetic continuity between the zygote and me (we share the same genetic code); and, second, that there is what, for want of a better term, one might call "numerical continuity" between us (we are the same single thing). In other words, the zygote does not just have the potential to produce an as-yet-unidentifiable individual, rather the zygote is, from the first moment of its existence, already a particular individual – Tom, or Dick, or Harry. But, as we shall see, this view, which we shall call the "identity thesis," faces some very serious problems. For, contrary to what is often believed, recent scientific findings do not support the view that fertilization marks the event when a particular, identifiable individual begins to exist.

It is true that the life of the fertilized ovum is a genetically new life in the sense that it is neither genetically nor numerically continuous with the life of the egg or the sperm before fertilization. Before fertilization, there were two genetically distinct entities, the egg and the sperm; now there is only one entity, the fertilized egg or zygote, with a new and unique genetic code. It is also true that the zygote will – other things being equal – develop into an embryo, fetus, and baby with the same genetic code.

But, as we shall see, things are not always equal and some serious problems are raised for supporters of the identity thesis.

Here are two scenarios of what might happen during early human development.

In the first scenario, a man and a woman have intercourse, fertilization takes place, and a genetically new zygote, let's call it Tom, is formed. Tom has a specific genetic identity – a genetic blueprint – that will be repeated in every cell once the first cell begins to split, first into two, then into four cells, and so on. On day 8, however, the group of cells which is Tom divides into two separate identical cell groups. These two separate cell groups continue to develop and, some nine months later, identical twins are born. Now, which one, if either of them, is Tom? There are no obvious grounds for thinking of one of the twins as Tom and the other as Not-Tom; the twinning process is quite symmetrical and both twins have the same genetic blueprint as the original Tom. But to suggest that both of them are Tom does, of course, conflict with numerical continuity: there was one zygote and now there are two babies.

People have thought in various ways about this: for example, that when the original cell split, Tom ceased to exist and that two new individuals, Dick and Harry, came into existence. But if that were conceded then it would, of course, no longer be true that the existence of the babies Dick and Harry began at fertilization: their existence did not begin until eight days *after* fertilization. Moreover (and we shall come back to this in a moment) if Tom died on day 8, how is it that he left no earthly remains?

Now consider the second scenario. A man and a woman have intercourse and fertilization takes place. But this time, two eggs are fertilized and two zygotes come into existence – Mary and Jane. The zygotes begin to divide, first into two, then into four cells, and so on. But, then, on day 6, the two embryos combine, forming what is known as a chimera, and continue to develop as a single organism, which will eventually become a baby. Now, who is the baby – Mary or Jane, both Mary and Jane, or somebody else – Nancy?

In one plausible sense of the term, there is genetic continuity between Mary, Jane, and the baby. Because the baby is a chimera, she carries the unique genetic code of both Mary and Jane. Some of the millions of cells that make up her body contain the genetic code of Mary, others the genetic code of Jane. So in that sense the baby would seem to be both Mary and Jane. But in terms of numerical continuity, this poses a problem. There is now only one individual where there were formerly two. Does this mean that Mary or Jane, or both of them, have ceased to exist? But to suggest that one of them has ceased to exist poses the problem of explaining why one and not the other should have ceased to exist. Moreover, to say that anyone has ceased to exist will put one in the difficult position (already encountered in the previous example of Tom) of having to explain how it can be that a human individual has ceased to exist when nothing has been lost or has perished – in other words, when there has been a death but there is no corpse.

We could sketch other scenarios to show further complexities, but enough has been said to demonstrate that even before the advent of new reproductive technologies serious problems were raised for the "identity thesis." As we shall see, these problems have been compounded by new scientific findings.

It is now believed that early embryonic cells are totipotent; that is, that, contrary to the "identity thesis," an early human embryo is not one particular individual, but rather has the potential to become one or more different individuals. Up to the eight-cell stage, each single embryonic cell is a distinct entity in the sense that there is no fusion between the individual cells; rather, the embryo is a loose collection of distinct cells, held together by the zona pellucida, the outer membrane of the egg. Animal studies on four-cell embryos indicate that each one of these cells has the potential to produce at least one fetus or baby.

Take a human embryo consisting of four cells. On the assumption that this embryo is a particular human individual, we shall call it Adam. Because each of Adam's four cells is totipotent, any three cells could be removed from the zona pellucida and the remaining cell would still have the potential to develop into a perfect fetus or baby. Now, it might be thought that this baby is Adam, the same baby that would have resulted had all four cells continued to develop jointly. But this poses a problem because we could have left any one of the other three cells in the zona pellucida, each with the potential to develop into a baby. The same baby – Adam? Things are not made any easier by the recognition that the three "surplus" cells, each placed into an empty zona pellucida, would also have the potential to develop into babies. We now have four distinct human individuals with the potential to develop into four babies. Because it does not make good sense to identify any one particular individual as Adam, let's call them Bill, Charles, David, and Eddy.

This example shows that there are not only problems regarding individual identity, but also closely related problems regarding the early embryo's potential to produce one or more human individuals. In the above example, the zygote had the potential to produce either one individual, Adam, or four individuals – Bill, Charles, David, and Eddy. But this is not where its potential ends. Had we waited until the embryo had cleaved one more time in its petri dish, there would have been not four, but eight, totipotent cells – that is, eight distinct individual entities oriented towards further development and hence eight potential babies: Fred, Graeme, Harry, Ivan, and so on. Moreover, since these individual cells also have the potential to recombine to form, say, just one or two distinct individuals, fertilization cannot be regarded as the beginning of a particular human life.

. Those who want to object to embryo experimentation because it destroys a particular or identifiable human life would be on much safer ground were they to argue that a particular human life begins not at fertilization but at around day 14 after fertilization. By that time, totipotency has been lost, and the development of the primitive streak precludes the embryo from becoming two or more different individuals through twinning. Once the primitive streak has formed, it would thus be much easier to argue that it is Adam, Bill, or Charles that is developing, or all three of them, but as distinct individuals.

II

Next we want to raise the moral question that we set aside at the beginning of this chapter. Let us assume that we have settled the issue of when a particular individual's life begins – and for the moment it doesn't matter whether this happens at around day 14 or at fertilization. All that we need to assume for our present purposes is that there is such a marker event, that we have identified it, and that the entity we are talking about has crossed this particular developmental hurdle.

Now what is it about the new human entity that could raise moral questions about destructive embryo experimentation? Many people believe that it is wrong to use human embryos in research because these embryos are human beings, and all human beings have a right to life. The syllogism goes like this:

Every human being has a right to life.
A human embryo is a human being.
Therefore the human embryo has a right to life.

In case anyone is worrying about issues like capital punishment, or killing in self-defense, we should perhaps add that the term "innocent" is here and henceforth assumed whenever we are talking of human beings and their rights.

The standard argument has a standard response: to accept the first premise – that all human beings have a right to life – but to deny the second premise, that the human embryo is a human being. This standard response, however, runs into difficulties, because the embryo is clearly a being, of some sort, and it can't possibly be of any other species than *Homo sapiens*. Thus it seems to follow that it must be a human being.

Questioning the First Premise

So the standard argument for attributing a right to life to the embryo can withstand the standard response. It is not easy to challenge directly the claim that the embryo is a human being. What the standard argument cannot withstand, however, is a more critical examination of its first premise: that every human being has a right to life. At first glance, this seems the stronger premise. Do we really want to deny that every (innocent) human being has a right to life? Are we about to condone murder? No wonder it is on the second premise that most of the fire has been directed. But the surprising vulnerability of the first premise becomes apparent as soon as we cease to take "Every human being has a right to life" as an unquestionable moral axiom, and instead inquire into the moral basis for our particular objection to killing human beings.

By "our particular objection to killing human beings," we mean the objection we have to killing human beings, over and above any objection we have to killing other living beings, such as pigs and cows and dogs and cats, and even trees and lettuces. Why do we think killing human beings is so much more serious than killing these other beings?

The obvious answer is that human beings are different from other animals, and the greater seriousness of killing them is a result of these differences. But which of the many differences between humans and other animals justify such a distinction? Again, the obvious response is that the morally relevant differences are those based on our superior mental powers – our self-awareness, our rationality, our moral sense, our autonomy, or some combination of these. They are the kinds of thing, we are inclined to say, which make us "uniquely human." To be more precise, they are the kinds of thing which make us persons.

That the particular objection to killing human beings rests on such qualities is very plausible. To take the most extreme of the differences between living things, consider a person who is enjoying life, is part of a network of relationships with other people, is looking forward to what tomorrow may bring, and is freely choosing the course her or his life will take for the years to come. Now think about a lettuce, which, we can safely assume, knows and feels nothing at all. One would have to be quite mad, or morally blind, or warped, not to see that killing the person is far more serious than killing the lettuce.

We shall postpone asking which mental qualities make it more morally serious to kill a person than to kill a lettuce. For our immediate purposes, we will merely note that the plausibility of the assertion that human beings have a right to life depends on the fact that human beings generally possess mental qualities that other living beings do not possess. So should we accept the premise that every human being has a right to life? We may do so, but only if we bear in mind that by "human being" here we refer to those beings who have the mental qualities which generally distinguish members of our species from members of other species.

If this is the sense in which we can accept the first premise, however, what of the second premise? It is immediately clear that in the sense of the term "human being" which is required to make the first premise acceptable, the second premise is false. The embryo, especially the early embryo, is obviously not a being with the mental qualities that generally distinguish members of our species from members of other species. The early embryo has no brain, no nervous system. It is reasonable to assume that, so far as its mental life goes, it has no more awareness than a lettuce.

It is still true that the human embryo is a member of the species *Homo sapiens*. That is why it is difficult to deny that the human embryo is a human being. But we can now see that this is not the sense of "human being" needed to make the standard argument work. A valid argument cannot equivocate on the meanings of its central terms. If the first premise is true when "human" means "a being with certain mental qualities" and the second premise is true when "human" means "member of the species *Homo sapiens*," the argument is based on a slide between the two meanings, and is invalid.

Can the argument be rescued? It obviously can't be rescued by claiming that the embryo is a being with the requisite mental qualities. That might be arguable only for some later stage of the development of the fetus. If the second premise cannot be reconciled with the first, then, can the first perhaps be defended in a form which makes it compatible with the second? Can it be argued that human beings have a right to life, not because of any moral qualities they may possess, but because they – unlike pigs, cows, dogs, or lettuces – are members of the species *Homo sapiens*?

This is a desperate move. Those who make it find themselves having to defend the claim that species membership is in itself morally relevant to the wrongness of killing a being. But why should that be so? If we are considering whether it is wrong to destroy something, surely we must look at its actual characteristics, not just the species to which it belongs. If visitors from other planets turn out to be sensitive, thinking, planning beings, who form deep and lasting relationships just like we do, would it be acceptable to kill them simply because they are not members of our species? What if we substituted "race" for "species" in the question? If we reject the claim that membership of a particular race is in itself morally relevant to the wrongness of killing a being, it is not easy to see how we could accept the same claim when based on species membership. The fact that other races, like our own, can feel, think, and plan for the future is not relevant to this question, for we are considering membership in a particular group – whether race or species – as the sole basis for determining the wrongness of killing members of one group or another. It seems clear that neither race nor species can, in itself, provide any justifiable basis for such a distinction.

So the standard argument fails. It does so not because the embryo is not a human being, but because the sense in which the embryo is a human being is not the sense in which we should accept that every human being has a right to life.

III

We have now seen the inadequacies of arguing that the human zygote or early embryo is a distinct human individual, and that destructive embryo experimentation is wrong because the zygote or embryo is a member of the human species. But there are other reasons why one might consider embryo experimentation wrong. Since the early embryo, devoid of a nervous system or a brain, can experience neither pain or pleasure, nor any of the things occurring in the world, the most important thing about it is that it is a potential baby or person, a person just like us. In other words, when we destroy an early human embryo in research, a potential baby or person will now not exist.

Why is this fact morally significant? One plausible answer is provided by R. M. Hare when he appeals, in a well-known article on abortion, to a type of formal argument, captured in the ancient Christian and pre-Christian Golden Rule, which has been the basis of almost all theories of moral reasoning: that we should do to others as we wish them to do to us.[6] In other words, given that we are glad that nobody destroyed us when we were embryos, we should, other things being equal, not destroy an embryo that would have a life like us.

It might seem that the Golden Rule applied to embryo experimentation would impose on us an extremely conservative position, for it would seem to rule out the destruction of all but the most seriously abnormal zygote or embryo. But before we too readily embrace that conclusion, we should also note something already pointed out by Hare in the abortion context: when you are glad that you exist, you do not confine this gladness to gladness that you were not aborted when an embryo or fetus. Rather, you are also glad that you were brought into existence in the first place – that your parents had intercourse without contraception when they did.[7]

Let us apply this sort of thinking to our present context – that of the IVF embryo – and assume that, at some time between the beginning of the process of fertilization and the formation of the primitive streak, the existence of an identifiable individual began. Let us also assume that you developed from that individual. Now, it will immediately become apparent that regardless of what event marked the beginning of your life as an identifiable entity, none of the other events that preceded it were any less important for your present existence. Just as you would not have existed had a scientist performed a destructive experiment on the embryo from which you developed when it was fourteen days old, so you would not have existed had she or he performed it on the zygote when it was one day old. Similarly, you would not have existed had your mother's egg with your father's sperm already inside it been destroyed just before syngamy had occurred, or just after that event. Nor, we should hasten to add, would you have existed had the scientist, instead of using one particular egg, used another egg or had a different sperm fertilized the egg, and so on.

The upshot is that the marker event for the beginning of a human individual, on whose identification so much time and energy is being expended, is of no importance so far as the existence of a particular person is concerned. If it is the existence of a particular person that is relevant – a Tom, a Dick, or a Harry – who would treasure his life in much the same way as we do, then it does not matter whether his existence was thwarted before or after fertilization, or the formation of the primitive streak, had occurred.

We should also note that there are numerous ways in which the existence of particular individuals can be thwarted. A totipotent IVF embryo, for example, is not, as we saw, one particular individual, but rather an entity with the potential to become one or more different individuals, because each cell is a distinct entity with the potential for further development. What are we doing, then, when we refrain from separating the cells, leaving all four or eight of them together? And what are we doing when we extract and destroy a single cell for gene-typing of the embryo? We believe we should, in consistency, say that we are depriving a number of human individuals of their chance of existence.

This is one important point. The other important point is this: our reproductive choices almost invariably constitute an explicit or implicit choice between different individuals. We said a moment ago that had the scientist who assisted your imaginary IVF conception used a different sperm or a different egg, you would not have existed, and the same thing applies, of course, to other scenarios in natural reproduction as well. But – and this is the morally important point – seeing that your parents wanted to raise a child of their own, it is likely that another child would have been born. While this person would not have been you, it would have been a person just like you in the morally relevant sense that she or he would now, presumably, be just as glad to exist as you are glad to exist.

But if our reproductive choices typically constitute a choice between different individuals, then the destruction of early human embryos – particularly if it makes possible improved IVF techniques and, therefore, the existence of IVF children who would not otherwise have existed – is no harder to justify than many of our other reproductive choices: for example, when and with whom to have intercourse, without contraception, to have the two or three children we are going to have.

IV

We have now seen that some of the most common objections to destructive experimentation on early human embryos are seriously flawed. But when, in its development from zygote to baby, does the embryo acquire any rights or interests? We believe the minimal characteristic needed to give the embryo a claim to consideration is sentience, or the capacity to feel pleasure or pain. Until that point is reached, the embryo does not have any interests and, like other nonsentient organisms (a human egg, for example), cannot be harmed – in a morally relevant sense – by anything we do. We can, of course, damage the embryo in such a way as to cause harm to the sentient being it will become, if it lives, but if it never becomes a sentient being, the embryo has not been harmed, because its total lack of awareness means that it has never had any interests at all.

The fact that the early embryo has no interests is also relevant to a distinction embodied in the *Infertility (Medical Procedures) Act 1984 (Vic.)* between "spare" embryos left over from infertility treatments (which may be used in experimentation), and the creation of embryos especially for research (which is prohibited).[8] The report of the Waller Committee, on which the legislation is based, speaks of such a creation as using a human being as a means rather than as an end.[9] This is a principle of Kantian ethics that makes some sense when applied to rational, autonomous beings – or perhaps even, though more controversially, when applied to sentient beings who, though not rational or autonomous, may have ends of their own. There is no basis at all, however, for applying it to a totally nonsentient embryo, which can have no ends of its own.

Finally, we point to a curious consequence of restrictive legislation on embryo research. In sharp contrast to the human embryo at this early stage of its existence, nonhuman animals such as primates, dogs, rabbits, guinea pigs, rats, and mice, clearly can feel pain, and thus are often harmed by what is done to them in the course of scientific research. We have already suggested that the species of a being is not, in itself, relevant to its ethical status. Why, then, is it considered acceptable to poison conscious rabbits in order to test the safety of drugs and household chemicals, but not considered acceptable to carry out tests on totally nonsentient human embryos? It is only when an embryo reaches the stage at which it may be capable of feeling pain that we need to control the experimentation which can be done with it. At this point the embryo ranks, morally, with those nonhuman animals we have mentioned. These animals have often been unjustifiably made to suffer in scientific research. We should have stringent controls over research to ensure that this cannot happen to embryos, just as we should have stringent controls to ensure that it cannot happen to animals.

At what point, then, does the embryo develop a capacity to feel pain? Though we are not experts in this field, from our reading of the literature, we would say that it cannot possibly be earlier than 6 weeks, and it may well be as late as 18 or 20 weeks.[10] While we think we should err on the side of caution, it seems to us that the 14-day limit suggested by both the Waller and Warnock committees is too conservative.[11] There is no doubt that the embryo is not sentient for some time after this date. Even if we were to be very, very cautious in erring on the safe side, a 28-day limit would provide sufficient protection against the possibility of an embryo suffering during experimentation.

Notes

1   Senate Select Committee on the Human Embryo Experimentation Bill 1985, *Human Embryo Experimentation in Australia* (Senator Michael Tate, chairman), (Canberra: AGPS, 1986), p. 13.

2   Ibid.

3   Congregation for the Doctrine of the Faith, *Instruction on Respect for Human Life in its Origin and on the Dignity of Procreation – Replies to Certain Questions of the Day* (Vatican City, 1987).

4   Section I of this chapter was inspired by Michael Coughlan's: "'From the Moment of Conception...': The Vatican Instruction on Artificial Procreation Techniques," *Bioethics*, II, 3 (July 1988).

5   For a more detailed discussion of this issue, see Norman Ford, *When did I begin?* (Cambridge: Cambridge University Press, 1988).

6   R. M. Hare, "Abortion and the golden rule," *Philosophy and Public Affairs*, 4 (1975), pp. 201–22.

7   Ibid, p. 212.

8   *Infertility (Medical Procedures) Act 1984* (Vic.).

9   Committee to Consider the Social, Ethical and Legal Issues Arising from In Vitro Fertilization, *Report on the Disposition of Embryos Produced by In Vitro Fertilization* (Prof. Louis Waller, chairman), (Melbourne: Victorian Government Printer, 1984), para. 3.27.

10 For an expert opinion on when a fetus may begin to be capable of feeling pain, see the report of the British Government's Advisory Group on Fetal Research, *The Use of Foetuses and Foetal Material for Research* (Sir John Peel, chairman), (London: HMSO, 1972). A clear summary of some relevant scientific evidence, with further references, can be found in M. Tooley, *Abortion and Infanticide* (Oxford: Clarendon Press, 1983), pp. 347–407.

11 Waller, *Report*, para. 3.29; and *Report of the Committee of Inquiry into Human Fertilization and Embryology* (Mary Warnock, chair), (London: HMSO, 1984), pars. 11.19–11.22.

Fourteen

IVF Technology and the Argument from Potential

Peter Singer and Karen Dawson

I

In many respects the current debate about embryo experimentation resembles the older debate about abortion. Although one central argument *for* abortion – the claim that a woman has the right to control her own body – is not directly applicable in the newer context, the argument *against* embryo experimentation remains essentially the same as the argument against abortion. This argument has two forms, one relying on the claim that from the moment of fertilization the embryo is entitled to protection because it *is* a human being, and the other asserting instead that the embryo is entitled to protection because from the moment of fertilization it is a *potential* human being.[1]

The first form of this argument will not concern us here;[2] our focus is on the argument from potential. Those who use this argument against embryo experimentation frequently describe the potential of the early *in vitro* embryo in terms identical with those used in the context of the abortion debate to describe the potential of the early embryo inside the female body. Teresa Iglesias, for example, writes: "We know that a new human individual organism with the internal potential to develop into an adult, given nurture, comes into existence as a result of the process of fertilization at conception."[3] But can the familiar claims about the potential of the embryo in the uterus be applied to the

First published in *Philosophy and Public Affairs*, 17 (1988), pp. 87–104. Copyright © The Johns Hopkins University Press. Reprinted with permission of the Johns Hopkins University Press.

embryo in culture in the laboratory? Or does the new technology lead to an embryo with a different potential from that of embryos made in the old way? Asking this question leads us to probe the meaning of the term "potential." This probing will raise doubts about whether it is meaningful to talk of the potential of an entity independently of the context in which that entity exists and independently of the probability that that entity will develop in a specific way. In particular, we will argue that while the notion of potential may be relatively clear in the context of a naturally occurring process such as the development of an embryo inside a female body, this notion becomes far more problematic when it is extended to a laboratory situation, in which *everything* depends on our knowledge and skills, and on what we decide to do. This line of argument will lead us to the conclusion that there is no coherent notion of potential which allows the argument from potential to be applied to embryos in laboratories in the way those who invoke the argument are seeking to apply it.

We begin by considering how recent developments in reproductive technology force us to revise some previously universal truths about embryos. Before Robert Edwards began the research which was to lead to the IVF (*in vitro* fertilization) procedure, no one had observed a viable human embryo prior to the stage at which it implants in the wall of the uterus. In the normal process of reproduction inside the body, the embryo, or "pre-embryo" as it is now sometimes called, remains unattached for the first seven to fourteen days. As long as such embryos existed only inside the woman's body, there was no way of observing them during that period. The very existence of the embryo could not be established until after implantation.

Under these circumstances, once the existence of an embryo was known, that embryo had a good chance of becoming a person, unless its development was deliberately interrupted. The probability that such an embryo would become a person was therefore very much greater than the probability that an egg in a fertile woman would unite with sperm from that woman's partner and lead to a child. It was also considerably greater than the chance that an as yet unimplanted embryo would become a child.

There was also, in those pre-IVF days, a further important difference between any embryo, whether implanted or not, and the egg and sperm. Whereas the embryo inside the female body has some definite chance (we shall consider later how great a chance) of developing into a child *unless* a deliberate human act interrupts its growth, the egg and sperm can develop into a child *only* if there *is* a deliberate human act. So in the one case, all that is needed for the embryo to have a prospect of realizing its potential is for those involved to refrain from stopping it; in the other case, they have to carry out a positive act. The development of the embryo inside the female body can therefore be seen as a mere unfolding of a potential that is inherent in it. The development of the separated egg and sperm is more difficult to regard in this way, because no further development will take place unless the couple have sexual intercourse or use artificial insemination. (This is, to be sure, an over-simplification, for it takes no account of the positive acts involved in childbirth; but it is close enough for our purposes.)

Now consider what has happened as a result of the success of IVF. The procedure involves removing one or more eggs from a woman's ovary, placing them in culture medium in a glass dish, and then adding sperm to the culture. In the more proficient laboratories, this leads to fertilization in about 80 percent of the eggs thus treated. The embryo can then be kept in culture for two to three days, while it grows and divides into two, four, and then eight cells. At about this stage, if the embryo is to have any prospect of developing into a child, it must be transferred to a woman's uterus. Although the transfer itself is a simple procedure, it is after the transfer that things are most likely to go wrong: for reasons which are not fully understood, with even the most successful IVF teams the probability that a given embryo which has been transferred to the uterus will actually implant there and lead to a continuing pregnancy is always less than 20 percent, and generally no more than 10 percent.[4] (Figures quoted for pregnancies per transfer procedure may be higher, but this is because it is common to transfer more than one embryo; for our purposes the important figure is the probability that any given embryo will result in a child.) We should also note that if the embryo is allowed to continue to grow in culture much beyond the eight-cell stage, it is less likely to implant when transferred. Embryos can be grown in the laboratory to the later blastocyst stage, when the cells are arranged as a hollow sphere and those which will form the embryo proper have become distinct from those which will form the extraembryonic membranes, that is, the chorion and the amnion. The blastocyst may then develop further, to the point at which it consists of hundreds of cells. No pregnancies, however, have resulted from embryos transferred at so late a stage of development. Nor, as yet, is there any prospect of keeping embryos alive and developing *in vitro* until they become viable infants. So although Edwards has reported keeping an embryo alive in culture for nine days,[5] with our present state of knowledge, such an embryo has zero probability of becoming a person.

In summary, then, before the advent of IVF, it would have been true to say of any normal human embryo known to us that, unless it was deliberately interfered with, it would most likely develop into a person. The process of IVF, however, leads to the creation of embryos which cannot develop into a person unless there is some deliberate human act (the transfer to the uterus) and which even then, in the best of circumstances, will most likely *not* develop into a person.

The upshot of all this is that IVF has reduced the difference between what can be said about the embryo and what can be said about the egg and sperm, considered jointly. Before IVF, any normal human embryo known to us had a far greater chance of becoming a child than any egg and sperm prior to fertilization. But with IVF, there is a much more modest difference in the probability that a child will result from a two-cell embryo in a glass dish and the probability that a child will result from an egg and some sperm in a glass dish. To be specific, if we assume that the laboratory's fertilization rate is 80 percent and its rate of pregnancy per embryo transferred is 10 percent, then the probability that a child will result from a given embryo is 10 percent, and the probability that a child will result from an egg which has been placed in a culture medium to which sperm has been added is 8 percent.

II

It has occasionally been suggested that there is no difference between the potential of the embryo, on the one hand, and the potential of the egg and sperm when still separate, but considered jointly, on the other hand.[6] But there has been little analysis of the notion of potential in the context of the *in vitro* embryo, and the suggestions made have not succeeded in dispelling the intuitive idea that there is a major difference between the potential of the embryo and the potential of the pair of gametes. To provide this analysis, we must ask what we mean when we refer to the embryo as a potential person.

An obvious place to begin our search for the meaning of this claim is the dictionary definition of the word "potential." The *Oxford English Dictionary* offers several meanings of the term, of which the following seems to be the most relevant to our present concerns: "Possible as opposed to actual; existing *in posse* or in a latent or undeveloped state, capable of coming into being or action; latent." Following the dictionary definition, it would seem that *at the least* we must mean that it is *possible* for the embryo to become a person. Possibility is a necessary condition for potentiality (whether it is also a sufficient condition is not something we need consider here). But what sort of possibility?

Philosophers commonly distinguish between logical possibility and physical possibility. It is logically possible, but physically impossible, for the authors of this paper to jump over the Empire State Building. It is both logically and physically possible for us to jump over a brick. It is not logically possible for anyone to be a biological parent without having any children.

Since something is logically impossible only if its assertion involves a contradiction, it is not logically impossible for a human blastocyst in a laboratory to develop into a person. But then, it is not logically impossible for a human egg to develop into a person either – parthenogenesis happens often in some species, and no logical contradiction is involved in imagining it happening in our species. So those who claim that the human embryo is a potential person, whereas the human egg is not, cannot appeal to the mere fact that it is logically possible for the embryo to become a person.

The sense of "possibility" that lies behind these claims that the embryo, but not the egg, is a potential person must, therefore, be real, physical possibility. We must, however, further refine the relevant sense of physical possibility. Does it refer to what is physically possible given the present state of our knowledge and technology? In that case, the eight-cell embryo in the laboratory may be a potential person, but a late-stage blastocyst in the laboratory, consisting of hundreds of cells, cannot be a potential person; we know that if we attempt to transfer such a blastocyst, it will simply be discharged from the uterus without implanting. This yields the result that two blastocysts, to all appearances identical in their internal properties, have entirely different potentials: one, because it has resulted from natural intercourse and has implanted in the uterus, is a potential person, while the other one is not because it is in a laboratory culture.

Such a result is counterintuitive, for it means that while the eight-cell embryo in the laboratory is a potential human being, the embryo loses that status simply by continuing to develop in the laboratory. But perhaps we could come to accept such a view. There are analogous situations in which we would also say that a being has lost the potential it once had. Imagine, for instance, a doctor monitoring a risky pregnancy. The doctor might observe a healthy fetus at one stage during the pregnancy, and say: "Yes, we have a potential person there." Gradually, however, the condition of the fetus may deteriorate to such an extent that it is evident that it will die before reaching the point at which a caesarean delivery could offer any hope of producing a viable infant. The doctor might then say that the potential for personhood has been lost.

This account of potentiality may appear to confuse potential with probability. So far, however, we have been doing no more than exploring a *minimum* necessary condition, suggested by the dictionary definition, for X to have the potential to become Y. That minimum condition is that it be *possible* for X to become Y. Once we accept that it is a present physical possibility, and not logical possibility, that is meant here, we cannot disregard the differences between the eight-cell embryo in the laboratory and those blastocysts which consist of hundreds of cells. These differences do mean that, given our present state of knowledge and technology, it is possible for the former to become a person, but quite impossible, in the relevant physical sense, for the blastocyst just described to become a person. If physical possibility in our present state of knowledge and technology is a necessary condition for potentiality, it follows that the blastocyst in the laboratory is not a potential person.

Given the implications of this view, it might be said that the relevant sense of "physically possible" should *not* refer to the present state of our knowledge and technology. If we should one day discover how to induce late blastocysts to implant, or if we should perfect laboratory development to such an extent that embryos can develop into infants without ever being transferred to a woman – the process known as ectogenesis – then late blastocysts in laboratories will be able to become people. Perhaps this is all the "possibility" that is needed for an embryo to be a potential person.

This may indeed be the sense of "possibility" which lies behind a proper attribution of potential; but it cannot help those who wish to distinguish the potential of the embryo from that of the egg alone. For if it is true that we may one day discover how to induce late blastocysts to implant, it is also true that we may one day discover how to induce parthenogenetic development in the human egg. (Scientists putting human eggs in culture media for IVF have reported seeing, on rare occasions, the beginnings of parthenogenetic development.)[7] So the same sense of "possibility" which would allow the late embryo to be a potential person would also allow every human egg to be a potential person.

At one stage in the development of reproductive technology – roughly from 1983 until 1985 – it might have been argued that the late blastocyst had a genuine possibility of becoming a person in a way that the egg did not. In 1983, human embryos were first successfully preserved by freezing, in a manner which made it possible for them to continue normal development after thawing. Until 1985, however, there was no known way of freezing human eggs which did not cause them damage so severe as to make continued development impossible. A blastocyst could therefore have been frozen to await discovery either of a technique for implanting it successfully in a uterus or of the means of developing it to viability in an artificial womb. A human egg could not have been frozen to await the development of a means of inducing parthenogenesis. Since 1985, however, it has been possible to freeze eggs as well as embryos. So if the combination of freezing and the possibility of future discoveries means that a laboratory blastocyst is a potential person, the same combination must now mean that an unfertilized egg in a laboratory is also a potential person.

Unraveling the notion of potential is leading us in an unexpected direction, and one which will not be welcomed by those who oppose experimentation on human embryos while permitting experimentation on human eggs.[8] The problem, however, is not with the analysis we have proposed, but with the attempt to develop a notion of potential which supports the idea that there is a sharp distinction between the potential of the embryo and that of either the separate egg or the egg and sperm when separate but considered jointly. Is there any way in which the notion can be restored to something more suitable to those purposes?

In a discussion of parthenogenesis, Warren Quinn suggests that in this situation the environmental agent producing parthenogenetic development can be treated as a prefertilization entity that is incorporated into the "zygote" at the onset of development.[9] In this way, he seeks to preserve the view that even if parthenogenesis occurs, the egg alone is not a potential person; it becomes a potential person only when parthenogenetic development has been triggered. But Quinn's suggestion does not succeed in marking a distinction between the egg and the embryo. For the embryo also needs a specific environment if it is to develop; and if the particular environment which leads to parthenogenesis is allowed to count as an entity for the purposes of denying potential to the egg on its own outside that environment, then the particular environment which leads to development of the embryo must also be allowed to count as an entity, and we should deny potential to the embryo on its own outside that environment.

One might try to defend Quinn's analysis by claiming that the embryo has an *inherent* potential to develop into a person, whereas the egg needs an *external* trigger if it is to develop. At first glance, this appears promising; but on closer scrutiny the promise evaporates. Both the egg and the embryo have an internal genetic code which can, in the right environment, lead to the development of a human being. True, in the embryo the forty-six chromosomes are already present, whereas in the egg the twenty-three chromosomes which are present will need to duplicate themselves to form the forty-six chromosomes necessary for further development. But in neither case does additional genetic information have to be supplied from an external source. In both cases, on the other hand, a great deal else does have to come from outside. In the case of the embryo in the uterus, this includes all the nutrients needed for growth; and of course in the case of the embryo in the laboratory, it also includes skilled human intervention to transfer the embryo to a uterus. In the case of the egg, skilled human intervention would also be required to induce parthenogenetic development. The difference seems to be one of degree rather than of kind.

It might be said that the induction of parthenogenesis marks a more radical change than that caused by the provision of nutrients because it marks the beginning of a new individual, and that in this respect parthenogenesis and fertilization are alike, while the subsequent stages of growth and development have a different, and lesser, significance. But why should we regard the egg after parthenogenesis as a different individual from the egg before parthenogenesis?

The following reason can be offered: before either fertilization or partheno-genesis, the egg could develop into any number of different people, because it could be fertilized by any number of different sperm or develop parthenogen-etically. After fertilization or parthenogenesis, the developing embryo can become only one person. (Because of the possibility of twinning this is not strictly true, but the contrast between an indefinite range of possibilities and a very limited range of possibilities remains.)

In our view the fact that the embryo, but not the egg, has a uniquely determined potential does not suffice to show that the embryo is a different individual from the egg, or that it, but not the egg, is a potential person. Consider the analogy of a block of marble, rough-hewn from the quarry. In the hands of Michelangelo, it is a potential David, or a Moses, or a Pietà. Later, when the sculptor has chiseled it into the rough outline of a standing youthful figure, it can only become a David. Certainly, by working the marble in this way, Michelangelo has taken its development a stage further. The stage is significant because now the marble has the potential to become only one kind of sculpture (though of course there is still scope for great variation in many important details). Yet the marble is continuous in space and time with the original block. It is not a different piece of marble. That original block, we can now see, had the potential to be a David all along, and the fact that at an earlier stage it could also have become something else does not count against the claim that, even then, it was a potential David. Similarly, fertilization or parthenogenesis takes the development of the egg a stage further, but the potential of the egg is retained. The resulting embryo now has the potential to become only one kind of person (though here too there is still scope for great variation in many important details).[10] Yet the egg had the potential to become this person all along, just as it had the potential to become, in different circumstances, any one of a wide range of other people. Potentiality is one thing; uniqueness is something quite different.

Although we have used the possibility of parthenogenetic development as a means of illustrating some of the problems of attempts to separate the potential of the late blastocyst from the potential of the human egg, our general analysis of the notion of potential does not rely on this. We could equally well have returned to the simpler case of the egg and sperm together in their culture medium prior to the occurrence of fertilization. For all the senses of "possibil-ity" that we have considered, it is no less possible for the egg and sperm in the laboratory to develop into a person than it is for the laboratory embryo, also in its culture medium, to develop into a person. One could even say the same about the egg alone, treating the presence of sperm as part of the environment necessary for further development, just as the presence of nutrients is necessary for the further development of the embryo.

A more promising approach to distinguishing the potential of the embryo from the potential of the egg and sperm in their culture medium is to acknowledge openly a link between potential and probability, by relating potential not to the bare *possibility* of the embryo's becoming a person, but rather to the *probability* that this will happen. This has the inevitable result that potential ceases to be an all-or-nothing matter, and becomes a matter of degree. Traditional defenders of the right to life of the embryo have been reluctant to introduce degrees of potential into the debate, because once the notion is accepted, it seems undeniable that the early embryo is less a potential person than the later embryo or the fetus. This could easily be understood as leading to the conclusion that the prohibition against destroying the early embryo is less stringent than the prohibition against destroying the later embryo or fetus. Nevertheless, some defenders of the argument from potential have invoked probability and degrees of potential. Among those who have spoken most openly of probability are the Roman Catholic theologian John Noonan and the philosopher Werner Pluhar. As Noonan puts it:

> As life itself is a matter of probabilities, as most moral reasoning is an estimate of probabilities, so it seems in accord with the structure of reality and the nature of moral thought to found a moral judgment on the change in probabilities at conception. . . . Would the argument be different if only one out of ten children conceived came to term? Of course this argument would be different. This argument is an appeal to probabilities that actually exist, not to any and all states of affairs which may be imagined. . . . If a spermatozoon is destroyed, one destroys a being which had a chance of far less than 1 in 200 million of developing into a reasoning being, possessed of the genetic code, a heart and other organs, and capable of pain. If a fetus is destroyed, one destroys a being already possessed of the genetic code, organs and sensitivity to pain, and one which had an 80 percent chance of developing further into a baby outside the womb who, in time, would reason.[11]

Pluhar is almost as explicit:

> if we allow a mere potential for simple consciousness to give rise to a prima facie right to life, then it seems that we must accord a similar right to the staggering number of gamete pairs that likewise have some such potential. . . . Clearly, however, the gamete pair's potential is vastly lower than that of the insentient fetus: even given absence of interference plus at most a modest amount of assistance, the probability of a given gamete pair's producing the individual that it has some potential to produce is so vanishingly small as to be totally negligible in practice.[12]

If, following Noonan and Pluhar, we take the probability that an embryo will become a reasoning being (or, in Pluhar's case, become sentient) as relevant to the potential of the embryo to become a person, it must follow that the potential of the laboratory embryo currently diminishes after the eight-cell stage, when the probability that the transferred embryo will result in a pregnancy begins to decline; and by the late blastocyst stage, on this view, the laboratory embryo has no potential at all. This may well be an implication which opponents of embryo experimentation are happy to accept; they may say that this loss of the potential to become a person is one reason why it is wrong to keep human embryos alive in laboratories, or perhaps even why it is wrong to create them *in vitro* at all.

Accepting that there are degrees of potential associated with probability does, however, have other consequences which are less likely to be congenial to opponents of embryo experimentation. For on this view, contrary to what Noonan and Pluhar claim, the distinction between the potential of the embryo in culture and the potential of the gametes in the laboratory before fertilization becomes a difference of degree, and not a marked difference at that. Fertilization is, as we have seen, one of the relatively reliable steps in the *in vitro* fertilization procedure, with success rates commonly around 80 percent. Thus if we base degrees of potential on the probability that a person will ultimately result from an embryo, we cannot treat as crucially significant the line between the stage at which we have a set of gametes and the stage at which we have an embryo. At least so far as potential is concerned, the division between the stage at which we have an embryo in the laboratory and the stage at which we have an embryo implanted in the uterus is much more significant. Insofar as the argument from potential is important to the morality of experimenting on or disposing of an entity, we cannot support the prohibition of experimenting on or disposing of embryos while remaining unconcerned about how eggs and sperm are treated.

There are two possible replies to this argument. The first claims that to speak of the potential of the egg and sperm while they are still separate is nonsense, because they are two discrete entities, and hence cannot have a single potential. The second reply is Noonan's; it asserts that the distinction between embryo and gametes does mark a sharp distinction in probability, because the probability that an embryo will become a child is very great, whereas the probability that any *one* sperm will participate in fertilization is 1 in 200 million. We will consider these replies in turn.

The first reply fails because there is no reason why an entity with potential must consist of a single object, rather than of two or more discrete objects. There is, for instance, nothing problematic about the statement (made, let us assume, shortly before the battle of El Alamein) "Montgomery's army has the potential to defeat Rommel's army."[13] Yet Montgomery's army consisted of thousands of discrete individuals, spread over many miles of desert. We can even speak of the potential of entities which are spread across the entire planet – as Noah might have spoken of the potential of the raindrops falling all over the world to cause a great flood. So why should there be any problem about speaking of the potential of a set of gametes in a glass dish?

Noonan's reply faces several problems. One has been raised by Mark Strasser.[14] Why, Strasser asks, does Noonan focus on the probability that a given single sperm will participate in fertilization, and not on the probability of fertilization by any one of the sperm? This would, of course, provide a very different result: in the case of a normally fertile woman who has sexual intercourse without contraception during that part of her cycle when she is most likely to be fertile, the probability that fertilization will occur and result in a child is not greatly different from the probability that the newly fertilized egg will result in a child – certainly not different by the orders of magnitude Noonan suggests. Similarly, Noonan does not discuss the probability that the *egg*, rather than the sperm, will participate in fertilization. This also would give a very different result.

Even if Noonan can provide an answer to Strasser's objection, his position has, like other claims about the potential of embryos, become much more difficult to maintain in the light of new knowledge and new developments in reproductive technology. The initial difficulty is that Noonan's figures for embryo survival even in the uterus are no longer regarded as accurate. At the time Noonan wrote, the estimate of pregnancy loss was based on clinically recognized or stable, ongoing pregnancies. These pregnancies are about six to eight weeks after fertilization – embryonic heartbeat is detectable, menses has ceased, and enzyme assays will give reliable results indicating pregnancy. Currently such pregnancies are associated with a 15 percent loss through spontaneous abortion.[15] Though the total pregnancy wastage rate remains largely unknown, recent technical advances allowing earlier recognition of pregnancy suggest that this figure is an underestimate of total loss and represents an oversimplification of the real situation.[16] Estimates of the natural wastage at various stages of pregnancy can now be taken into account, and they provide startlingly different figures from those supplied by Noonan. If pregnancy is diagnosed before implantation (within fourteen days of fertilization) the estimated chance of a birth resulting is 25 to 30 percent.[17] After implantation this chance increases initially to between 40 and 60 percent,[18] and it is not until six weeks' gestation that the chance of birth occurring increases to between 85 and 90 percent.[19]

Noonan claimed that his argument is "an appeal to probabilities that actually exist, not to any and all states of affairs which may be imagined." We have now seen that the real probabilities are very different from what Noonan believed them to be. Once we substitute the real probabilities, Noonan's argument no longer supports the moment of fertilization as the time at which the embryo gains a significantly different moral status. Indeed, if we were to require an 80 percent probability of further development into a baby – the figure used in the passage from Noonan quoted above – we would have to wait until about six weeks after fertilization before the embryo would have the significance Noonan wants to claim for it. If, on the other hand, we simply look for the moment at which the chance of birth resulting becomes close to or better than 50 percent, that time would seem to be around the moment of implantation.

To cope with the development of IVF, some readjustment of the parts of Noonan's argument pertinent to gametes is also necessary. Most importantly, the figures for embryo survival are very different when we consider the laboratory embryo rather than the embryo implanted in a uterus; an embryo survival rate of 10 percent would be relatively optimistic, even in a proficient laboratory. In addition, Noonan estimates the probability that any one sperm will participate in fertilization as 1 in 200 million, based on the number of sperm in a male ejaculate. In IVF, however, only about 50,000 sperm are used to fertilize an egg, increasing greatly the chances that any one sperm will fertilize the egg.[20]

Perhaps Noonan's claim that there is a sharp difference between the embryo and the sperm, based on the probability of proceeding to the next stage of development, could survive these changes in the figures. The relevant figure for the embryo *in vitro* is now 1 in 10, and for the sperm participating in *in vitro* fertilization, about 1 in 50,000. This is still a very marked difference. The difference virtually disappears, however, if we focus on the egg rather than the sperm, or if, as Strasser suggests, we consider the prospects of a birth resulting not from a *given* sperm, but from *any* of the sperm in the seminal fluid.

In any case, the argument faces still one more difficulty. Scientists are at present on the brink of trying out a new means of overcoming male infertility caused by a low sperm count or sperm which is insufficiently motile. The egg will be removed and cultured as in the normal *in vitro* procedure, but instead of adding a drop of seminal fluid containing about 50,000 sperm, a single sperm will be microinjected under the outer membrane of the egg. This procedure has already been carried out with human gametes, although no attempt has been made to produce a pregnancy from the resulting zygote.[21] Problems may arise in the use of the technique to overcome male infertility, but assuming that it is successful, the unique genetic blueprint of the individual-to-be will be determined before fertilization; it will, to be precise, be determined at the moment when the single sperm has been selected for microinjection. So if we compare the probability that the embryo will become a person with the probability that the egg, together with the single sperm about to be micro-injected into the egg, will become a person, we will be unable to find any sharp distinction between the two. Even the genetic blueprint will have been determined in both cases.

III

An Australian Senate Select Committee has recently discussed the question of the potential of the embryo in the context of human embryo experimentation. Its report, *Human Embryo Experimentation in Australia*, consists of a majority report signed by the chairman, Senator Michael Tate, with four other senators, and a dissenting report signed by two senators.[22] The majority report seems to take the notion of the potential of the laboratory embryo as unproblematic, stating that it works from the premise that "the embryo may be properly described as genetic-ally new human life organized as a distinct entity oriented towards further development."[23] The majority clearly did not regard the egg in a similar light, for whereas they recommended the prohibition of destructive experimentation on human embryos, they made no such recommendation regarding experimen-tation on human eggs. They also made recommendations designed to reduce the incidence of embryo freezing, in view of the high risk of mortality for frozen embryos, encouraging instead the development and use of egg freezing.[24]

The dissenting report from Senators Rosemary Crowley and Olive Zakharov took a radically different view of potential:

> Any object or thing has an infinite number of possible future courses. For a non-sentient or inanimate thing, e.g. a rock, the particular future outcome that actually happens is determined by forces outside of itself. An embryo is like a rock in this respect – it cannot make decisions for itself. Its future is decided by others. It has potential only in virtue of decisions by others about it. If there is a clearly defined responsible party or parties their decisions determine the embryo's potential and that becomes the embryo's potential.[25]

This is a bold departure from the conventional view of potential, although it is not a great distance from the view that the potential of an entity to become a person is related to the probability that the entity will become a person. But Crowley and Zakharov have noticed something that is overlooked by straight-forward attempts to identify potentiality with probability, and that is the role of human decision.

As we noticed earlier, whereas the embryo inside the female body has some definite chance of developing into a child unless a deliberate human act interrupts its growth, the egg and sperm can develop into a child only if there is a deliberate human act; *and in this respect the IVF embryo in the laboratory is like the egg and sperm, and not like the embryo in the human body.*

Lurking in the background of discussions of the potential of the embryo is the idea that there is a "natural" course of events, governed by the "inherent" potential of the embryo, or as the majority report of the Senate committee might have put it, resulting from the "organization of the embryo as an entity oriented towards further development." For if it were not for this notion of a "natural" course of events, why would the Senate committee not have noticed that the human egg is also "genetically new human life organized as a distinct entity oriented towards further development"? After all, the egg is human, not from any other animal, and it is also alive, not dead. Moreover, what the egg needs to continue its development is a sperm, just as what the embryo needs is a suitable environment, nutrients, and so on. Neither can develop without an external element, and both can develop with the right external element.[26] If we set aside the idea that the embryo will develop "naturally" as opposed to the egg, which will develop only if a sperm is placed in proximity to it, what difference in terms of "orientation towards further development" remains?

We have seen, however, that this notion of "natural" development – development not requiring the assistance of a deliberate human act – has no application to the IVF embryo. Hence those who wish to use the potential of the IVF embryo as a ground for protecting it cannot appeal to this notion of natural development; and for this reason, they find themselves in difficulty in explaining why the embryo in the laboratory has a potential greatly different from that of either the egg alone or the egg and sperm considered jointly. Crowley and Zakharov are correct to point to the crucial role played by human decision in determining the future of the embryo, and to focus, as they do in their dissenting report, on the question of who should have the responsibility of making this decision. (They conclude that it should be the woman or the gamete donors.)

The view of Crowley and Zakharov that an embryo has potential only in virtue of decisions by others about it amounts to the rejection of our common notion of potential, for it makes potential relative to the wishes and acts of human decision makers. Such a rejection of the common notion is strongly supported by the difficulties we have found with it in examining a range of arguments which invoke the potential of the embryo as a reason for according it a special moral status, different from that of the egg or of the egg and sperm when separate but considered jointly. Whether these arguments succeed in establishing that in the normal reproductive situation the embryo has a potential different from that of the egg and sperm is a question we have left open. But even if these arguments are applicable to the normal situation, they cannot validly be applied to *in vitro* embryos and eggs and sperm. The new reproduct-ive technology makes it necessary for us to think again about how our established views about the potential of the human embryo should be applied to the embryo in a laboratory.

Notes

1   This work was supported by a National Health and Medical Research Council of Australia Special Initiative Grant to Professor J. Swan, Dr. M. Brumby, Dr. H. Kuhse, and Professor L. Waller. We thank all four for their helpful comments, and we thank also Michaelis Michael, whose unpublished paper on the argument from potential spurred us to clarify our own ideas, as well as the editors of *Philosophy and Public Affairs*, who forced us to confront additional objections to our argument.
    For examples of the popular arguments against embryo experimentation, see *Test-Tube Babies*, ed. William Walters and Peter Singer (Melbourne: Oxford University Press, 1982), ch. 4.

2   One of us has discussed the argument previously: see Peter Singer, *Practical Ethics* (Cambridge: Cambridge University Press, 1979; 2nd edn., 1993), ch. 6.

3   Teresa Iglesias, "*In Vitro* Fertilization: The Major Issues," *Journal of Medical Ethics*, 10 (1984), pp. 32–7.

4   For these figures, see Ian Johnston, "IVF: The Australian Experience," a paper presented at the Royal College of Gynaecologists and Obstetricians Study Group on AID and IVF, November 1984, reprinted in *Hansard*, Commonwealth of Australia, Senate, Select Committee on the Human Embryo Experimentation Bill, 1985, report of hearings of 26 February 1986 (Canberra: Commonwealth Government Printer, 1986), pp. 560–87.

5   Robert Edwards and Patrick Steptoe, *A Matter of Life* (London: Sphere, 1981), p. 146.

6   See, for example, Helga Kuhse and Peter Singer, "The Moral Status of the Embryo," in *Test-Tube Babies*, ed. Walters and Singer, pp. 56–63 (see pp. 181–7 in this book), and John Robertson, "Extracorporeal Embryos and the Abortion Debate," *Journal of Contemporary Health Law and Policy*, 2 (1986), p. 63.

7   R. Edwards, and also A. Trounson, "Discussion on the Growth of Human Embryos *in Vitro*," in *Human Conception in Vitro*, ed. R. Edwards and J. Purdy (London: Academic Press, 1982), pp. 219–33.

8   As was recommended by the Victorian Government's Committee to Consider the Social, Ethical, and Legal Issues Arising from *In Vitro* Fertilization, chaired by Professor Louis Waller. See the committee's *Report on the Disposition of Embryos Produced by In Vitro Fertilization* (Melbourne: Victorian Government Printing Office, August 1984). The subsequent Victorian legislation, the Infertility (Medical Procedures) Act of 1984, sec. 6, incorporates these recommendations by tightly restricting embryo experimentation while explicitly exempting experimentation on human ova.

9   Warren Quinn, "Abortion: Identity and Loss," *Philosophy and Public Affairs*, 13 (1984), p. 28.

10 On the range still possible after fertilization, see Karen Dawson, "Fertilisation and Moral Status: A Scientific Perspective," *Journal of Medical Ethics*, 13 (1987), pp. 173–8.

11 John T. Noonan, Jr., "An Almost Absolute Value in History," in *The Morality of Abortion*, ed. J. T. Noonan, Jr. (Cambridge, MA: Harvard University Press, 1970), pp. 56–7.

12 Werner Pluhar, "Abortion and Simple Consciousness," *Journal of Philosophy*, 74 (1977), p. 167.

13 The example is taken from a letter by Brian Scarlett (*Journal of Medical Ethics*, 10 (1984), pp. 217–18) arguing, in a different context, against the views of Peter Singer and Helga Kuhse on the potential of the embryo.

14 Mark Strasser, "Noonan on Contraception and Abortion," *Bioethics*, I (1987), pp. 199–205.

15 J. Grudzinskas and A. Nysenbaum, "Failure of Human Pregnancy after Implantation," *Annals of the New York Academy of Science*, 442 (1985), pp. 39–44.

16 Ibid.

17 C. Roberts and C. Lowe, "Where Have All the Conceptions Gone?" *Lancet* (1975), 1:498–9.

18 J. Muller et al., "Fetal Loss after Implantation," *Lancet* (1980), 2:554–6.

19 D. Braunstein, "Chorionicgonadotrophin (HCG) and HCG-like Substances in Human Tissue and Bacteria," in *Pregnancy Proteins: Biology, Chemistry and Clinical Application*, ed. J. Grudzinskas et al. (London: Academic Press, 1982), pp. 39–49.

20 M. Mahadevan and G. Baker, "Assessment and Preparation of Semen for *In Vitro* Fertilization," in *Clinical In Vitro Fertilization*, ed. C. Wood and A. Trounson (New York: Springer, 1984), pp. 99–116.

21 Personal communication from Dr. Ismail Kola, Centre for Early Human Development, Monash University.

22 Senate Select Committee on the Human Embryo Experimentation Bill, *Human Embryo Experimentation in Australia* (Canberra: Australian Government Publishing Service, 1986).

23 Ibid., para. 3.27.

24 Ibid., para. 5.13.

25 Ibid., para. D20.

26 This point parallels that made in our earlier discussion of Quinn.

Fifteen

Unsanctifying Human Life

As a preface to the substantive part of this chapter, I offer a comment on the nature of medical ethics which may clarify my approach.

The professional philosopher with an interest in ethics, and in particular what might be called "applied moral philosophy," may well discuss with his students and colleagues the moral problems that doctors encounter in the course of their practice. Since the professional philosopher is specially trained to think about these issues and has all the time he requires at his disposal to do so, one might think that the philosopher would be able to give considerable assistance to the doctor, whose training and time are devoted to medicine rather than moral philosophy. Yet with few exceptions, this is not the case. Doctors discuss their ethical dilemmas in the medical journals and philosophers keep to the philosophical journals; the footnotes in each case remain within the circle of the author's colleagues.

All this is not just a matter of the old academic failure to look at work outside one's own discipline. Anyone who reads both philosophical and medical journals containing discussions of problems in medical ethics can hardly avoid noticing that there is a more fundamental gap between the discussions than the fact that they appear in different kinds of journals. There is also a difference in the presuppositions employed and the problems discussed.

For example, in recent issues of philosophical journals we can find articles in which it is argued, quite seriously and on plausible grounds, that a normal,

First published in *Ethical Issues Relating to Life and Death*, ed. John Ladd (New York and Oxford: Oxford University Press, 1979), pp. 41–61.

healthy human infant has no right to life and that it is, in this respect, in the same position as a fetus.[1] Doctors, on the other hand, are so far from even considering this position that they regard as serious ethical dilemmas such questions as, What should be done with a patient certain never to recover consciousness? or, Are parents to be given the option of deciding how far a doctor should go in using all available techniques to save the life of a hopelessly retarded infant with, in addition, a congenital heart defect?[2]

There are a number of reasons why the ethical concerns of philosophers and practicing physicians should be so far apart. One important reason is the different ways in which they are affected by the law. The busy doctor, who would rather be doing medicine than philosophy, turns to ethical questions only when they actually confront him. He tends not to raise questions which he would never face in practice, since he has enough problems without thinking up hypothetical ones. So if some course of action is straightforwardly illegal – for instance, the direct killing of a retarded infant – then most doctors are not even going to consider whether this course of action might be morally justifiable. When the law is clear, it resolves the doctor's ethical problem for him. So long as the doctor obeys the law, he can hardly be blamed for the outcome, because he can regard himself as purely a medical man, a technician whose business it is to carry out policy but not to set it; if he goes against the law, however, he risks criminal proceedings and disqualification from practice. No wonder that most medical ethics is concerned with cases on which the law fails to give any clear guide – cases like those involving the use of extraordinary means to save life.

The philosopher, of course, is in a quite different position. Untroubled by such mundane issues as what the law allows, he turns his attention to cases which invoke basic moral principles. If real cases do not serve this purpose, he is free to make up hypothetical ones. So he follows the argument wherever it leads him, and if it leads him to the view that infanticide is often justifiable, well, this conclusion is not likely to cause him, personally, any problems.

Now one can certainly sympathize with the doctor who confines his attention to those cases that he *has* to deal with, and regards the moral philosopher as an irresponsible theorizer. Nevertheless, the resulting limited scope of much of the work by medical people in medical ethics has had, I think, a harmful effect on the conclusions reached even within those areas that have received close attention. While we may agree that in general a doctor ought to obey the law, there has been a tendency to lose sight of the difference between this view and the idea that the law, and the conventional moral standards it embodies, is an indisputable starting point for further ethical debate. Because in practice a doctor can not challenge the law when it is clear and straightforward, the moral standards behind the law also do not often get challenged; if these conventional moral standards are in fact dubious, however, then conclusions which presuppose them are also likely to be dubious.

My purpose in what follows is to challenge one of these conventional moral doctrines: the doctrine of the sanctity of human life. I know that in taking this approach I run the risk of being regarded as yet another philosopher far removed from the world of real people. I shall try to guard against this danger by discussing some current, widely accepted medical practices. My strategy will be to bring together two distinct areas of medicine that are normally discussed only in quite separate moral contexts, and to show thereby that current attitudes in medical ethics are either plainly inconsistent or else guilty of a crude form of discrimination that is no more defensible than racial discrimination. In this way I want to force those involved in medicine to reconsider the foundations of the decisions they make. Foundations that give rise to the kind of inconsistency or discrimination that I am referring to are in urgent need of reconsideration; and the core of the problem, I believe, is the doctrine of the sanctity of human life.

People often say that life is sacred. They almost never mean what they say. They do not mean, as their words seem to imply, that *all* life is sacred. If they did, killing a pig or even pulling up a cabbage would be as contrary to their doctrine as infanticide. So when in the context of medical ethics people talk of the sanctity of life, it is the sanctity of *human* life that they really mean. It is this doctrine that I shall be discussing from now on.

In discussing the doctrine of the sanctity of human life, I shall not take the term "sanctity" in any specifically religious sense. Although I think that the doctrine does have a religious origin, and I shall say more about this shortly, it is now part of a broadly secular ethic, and it is as part of this secular ethic that it is most influential today. Not all those who talk about "the sanctity of life" are religious, and of those that are religious, in many cases their affirmation of the sanctity of life is independent of their religious views. In the secular context in which problems of medical ethics are usually discussed today, those who talk of the sanctity of human life are trying to say essentially that human life has some very special value; and a crucial implication of this assertion is the idea that there is a radical difference between the value of a human life and the value of the life of some other animal – a difference not merely of degree, but of quality or kind.

It is this idea, the idea that *human* life as such has unique value, that I shall criticize. Before I do so, however, I want to demonstrate how deep-seated and pervasive this idea of the unique value of human life is and how far this idea is sometimes taken in our own society and within the field of medicine. To demonstrate this, I offer two instances from different areas of medicine.

First, as an example of the value attributed to human life, a summary of a case history from Anthony Shaw's recent article, "Dilemmas of 'Informed Consent' in Children":

> A baby was born with Down's syndrome (mongolism), intestinal obstruction, and a congenital heart condition. The mother, believing that the retarded infant would be impossible for her to care for adequately, refused to consent to surgery to remove the intestinal obstruction. Without surgery, of course, the baby would soon die. Thereupon a local child-welfare agency, invoking a state child-abuse statute, obtained a court order directing that surgery be performed. After a complicated course of surgery and thousands of dollars worth of medical care, the infant was returned to her mother. In addition to her mental retardation, the baby's physical growth and development remained markedly retarded because of her severe cardiac disease. A follow-up enquiry eighteen months after the baby's birth revealed that the mother felt more than ever that she had been done an injustice.[3]

This case shows how much some people are prepared to do in order to ensure that a human infant lives, irrespective of the actual or potential mental capacities of the infant, its physical condition, or the wishes of the mother.

While some doctors are struggling to preserve life in cases of this sort, others are using their medical training in another way: they design and carry out experiments on nonhuman animals. I will give an example of the kind of work that is quite frequently done because its nature is not as well known as it ought to be. This particular experiment was carried out at the University of Michigan Medical School and funded by the National Research Council and the US Public Health Service. The description which follows is drawn from the researchers' own account, which they published in the journal *Psychopharmocologia:*

> The researchers confined sixty-four monkeys in small cubicles. These monkeys were then given unlimited access to a variety of drugs through tubes implanted in their arms. They could control the intake by pressing a lever. In some cases, after the monkeys had become addicted, supplies were abruptly cut off. Of the monkeys that had become addicted to morphine, three were "observed to die in convulsions" while others found dead in the morning were "presumed to have died in convulsions." Monkeys that had taken large amounts of cocaine inflicted severe wounds upon themselves, including biting off their fingers and toes, before dying convulsive deaths. Amphetamines caused one monkey to "pluck all of the hair off his arms and abdomen." In general, the experimenters found that "The manifestations of toxicity ... were similar to the well-known toxicities of these drugs in man." They noted that experiments on animals with addictive drugs had been going on in their laboratory for "the last 20 years."[4]

I know that it is not pleasant to think about experiments of this nature; but since they are a real part of medicine, they should not be ignored. In fact this experiment is by no means exceptional and is perhaps no worse than the routine testing of new drugs, foodstuffs, and cosmetics, which results in the poisoning of millions of animals annually in the United States.[5] Nor, for that matter, is the case of the mongoloid infant exceptional, apart from the fact that it was necessary to invoke the law; more commonly, the doctors would have obtained the mother's signature, though how often that signature implies genuine "informed consent" is another matter.

The question that arises from consideration of these two kinds of case is simply this: Can it be right to make great efforts to save the life of a mongoloid human infant when the mother does not want the infant to live, and at the same time can it not be wrong to kill, slowly and painfully, a number of monkeys?

One obvious defence of the addiction experiment that might be offered is that by means of such experiments, results are obtained which lead to the elimination of more suffering than is caused by the experiments themselves. Certainly in the experiment I described, no startling new discoveries were made, and any connection with the alleviation of suffering seems very tenuous. However, this defense is irrelevant to the comparison I am drawing between the way we treat humans and other animals. We would not forcibly addict mongoloid infants to drugs and then allow them to die in convulsions even if we did believe that useful knowledge could thus be obtained. Why do we think it wrong to treat members of our own species in the same way that we treat other species?

Can it ever be right to treat one kind of being in a way that we would not treat another kind? Of course it can, if the beings differ in relevant respects. Which respects are relevant will depend on the treatment in question. We could defend a decision to teach young members of our own species to read, without making the same effort on behalf of young dogs, on the grounds that the two kinds of being differ in their capacity to benefit from these efforts. This difference is obviously relevant to the particular proposal. On the other hand, anyone who proposed teaching some humans to read but not others, on the grounds that people whose racial origin is different from his own should not be encouraged to read, would be discriminating on an arbitrary basis since race as such has nothing to do with the extent to which a person can benefit from being able to read.

Now what is the position when we compare severely and irreparably retarded human infants with nonhuman animals like pigs and dogs, monkeys and apes? I think we are forced to conclude that in at least some cases the human infant does not possess any characteristics or capacities that are not also possessed, to an equal or higher degree, by many nonhuman animals. This is true of such capacities as the capacity to feel pain, to act intentionally, to solve problems, and to communicate with and relate to other beings; and it is also true of such characteristics as self-awareness, a sense of one's own existence over time, concern for other beings, and curiosity.[6] In all these respects adult members of the species I have mentioned equal or surpass many retarded infant members of our own species; moreover some of these nonhumans surpass anything that some human infants might eventually achieve even with intensive care and assistance. (In case anyone should be uncertain about this, it should be noted that chimpanzees have now been taught to communicate by means of American Sign Language, the standard language used by deaf people in this country, and have mastered vocabularies of well over a hundred signs, including signs which indicate that they possess both self-awareness and the idea of time.)[7]

So when we decide to treat one being – the severely and irreparably retarded infant – in one way, and the other being – the pig or monkey – in another way, there seems to be no difference between the two that we can appeal to in defense of our discrimination. There is, of course, the fact that one being is, biologically, a member of our own species, while the others are members of other species. This difference, however, cannot justify different treatment, except perhaps in very special circumstances; for it is precisely the kind of arbitrary difference that the most crude and overt kind of racist tries to use to justify racial discrimination. Just as a person's race is in itself nearly always irrelevant to the question of how that person should be treated, so a being's species is in itself nearly always irrelevant. If we are prepared to discriminate against a being simply because it is not a member of our own species, although it has capacities equal or superior to those of a member of our own species, how can we object to the racist discriminating against those who are not of his own race, although they have capacities equal or superior to those of members of his own race?

I said a moment ago that a difference of species cannot justify different treatment except perhaps in very special circumstances. It may be worth mentioning the circumstances I have in mind. If we discovered a new drug which we thought could be a very powerful aid in the treatment of serious diseases, we might feel that it should be tested in some way before being used on normal humans, in order to see if it had dangerous side-effects. Assuming that there was no reliable way of testing it except on a living, sentient creature, should we test it on a severely and irreparably retarded human infant, or on some other animal, like a monkey? Here, if the capacities of the beings are equal, I think we might be justified in saying that the biological species of the being was relevant. Since many drugs affect different species in unpredictably different ways, we would probably achieve our goal sooner by testing the drug on the retarded member of our own species than on the monkey; this would mean that we would have to use fewer subjects for our experiment and so inflict less suffering all told. This seems to be a reasonable ground for preferring to use the human infant, rather than the monkey, if we have already decided to test the drug on one or the other. So discrimination on the basis of species, in the rare cases in which it is justified, seems to go *against* our present practices rather than in favor of them. (Even here we would not really be discriminating on the basis of species *as such*, but rather using the species of the being as an indication of further possible unknown differences between them.)

The doctrine of the sanctity of human life, as it is normally understood, has at its core a discrimination on the basis of species and nothing else. Those who espouse the doctrine make no distinction, in their opposition to killing, between normal humans who have developed to a point at which they surpass anything that other animals can achieve, or humans in a condition of hopeless senility, or human fetuses, or infant humans, or severely brain-damaged humans. Yet those who use the sanctity of life doctrine as a ground for opposition to killing any human beings show little or no concern over the vast amount of quite unnecessary killing of nonhuman animals that goes on in our society, despite the fact that many of these other animals equal or surpass humans (except for normal humans beyond the age of infancy) on any test that I can imagine to be relevant, in all the categories I have just mentioned. It is significant to note, too, that even if we allow the relevance of a being's potential (and I agree with Michael Tooley that there are serious objections to so doing),[8] there are still human beings – the hopelessly senile and the irreparably brain-damaged – whose life is allegedly sacrosanct, who cannot be distinguished from other animals in respect of their potential.

A doctrine which went by the name of "the sanctity of human life" would not necessarily have to be a speciesist doctrine. The term "human" is not strictly a biological term and, as Tooley has pointed out, it is a mistake to assume that "human being" refers to precisely the same beings as are designated by the biological idea of "member of the species *Homo sapiens*." "Human," according to the *Oxford English Dictionary*, means "of, belonging to, or characteristic of man"; or in a slightly different sense, "having or showing the qualities or attributes proper to or distinctive of man." If the advocates of the "sanctity of human life" doctrine were to take this definition seriously, they would find their views radically transformed. According to the definition, whether we class a being as "human" will depend on what qualities or attributes we think characteristic of, proper to, or distinctive of man (and I assume that by "man," the dictionary here means men and women, mankind as a whole). So we would then have to try to draw up a list of these qualities or attributes –

something which some writers in the field have already tried to do.[9] This list would probably include some or all of the capacities and characteristics that I mentioned earlier, when comparing retarded infants and monkeys, but to decide which properties were necessary and which sufficient would be difficult. Let us say, though, just to take an example, that we decide that what is characteristic or distinctive of men and women is a capacity of self-awareness or self-consciousness. Then we will not count severely retarded infants as human beings even though they are clearly members of *Homo sapiens*; at the same time we might decide, after examining the abilities displayed by apes, dolphins, and perhaps some other mammals, to count these beings as human beings.

In any case, if we follow the dictionary definition of "human," one point seems certain no matter what criteria we eventually select as distinctive of men and women: severely and irreparably retarded *Homo sapiens* infants would be in the same category as a great many members of other species. This seems true, anyway, so long as we stay within the secular context that I have been assuming throughout this discussion. If we allow appeals to religious doctrines, based on special revelations, other conclusions might be possible – a point on which I shall say a little more later.

Is the only problem with the doctrine of the sanctity of human life, then, a misconception about the boundaries of "human"? Is it just that the advocates of this doctrine have got hold of a biological notion of what it is to be human instead of a notion that defines the term as the dictionary suggests it should be defined, with regard to characteristics distinctive of our species?

We could, perhaps, try to save the doctrine by modifying it in this way (and it would be no small modification). I chose my two contrasting examples of medical practice to show how far from this kind of position our present attitudes are. The suggested modification of the doctrine would place lethal experiments on the more developed nonhuman animals in the same category as experiments on severely retarded members of our own species. Similarly if, as Jonathan Swift once suggested, human infants, boiled, roasted, or fricasseed, make a tasty dish, then we would have to choose between ceasing to rear animals like pigs and cattle for food, and admitting that there is no moral objection to fattening retarded infants for the table. Clearly, this is not a position that many present advocates of the sanctity of human life would be prepared to embrace. In fact, it is so far from what present advocates of the doctrine mean that it would be downright misleading to continue to use the same name for the doctrine. Whatever the proper or dictionary meaning of the word, "human" is now, in popular usage, too closely identified with "member of the species *Homo sapiens*" for us to apply it to chimpanzees or deny it to retarded infants. I myself, in this paper, have used and for reasons of convenience shall continue to use the word in its popular, rather than dictionary, sense.

A further difficult question which conditions any attempt to redraw the boundaries of the "human" community is: where do we place normal embryonic or infant members of our species who have the potential, given normal development, to satisfy the criteria for membership but do not satisfy them at present? Judged by the characteristics they actually possess, and excluding for the moment such indirect factors as the concerns of parents or others, an infant *Homo sapiens* aged six months would seem to be much less of a "human" than an adult chimpanzee; and if we consider a one-month-old infant, it compares unfavorably with those adult members of other species – pigs, cattle, sheep, rats, chickens, and mice – that we destroy by the million in our slaughterhouses and laboratories. Does the potential of these infants make a difference to the wrongness of killing them?

It is impossible for me to discuss this question adequately here, so I will only point out that if we believe it is the potential of the infant that makes it wrong to kill it, we seem to be committed to the view that abortion, however soon after conception it may take place, is as seriously wrong as infanticide. Moreover, it is not easy to see on what grounds mere potential could give rise to a right to life, unless we valued what it was that the being had the potential to become – in this case a rational, self-conscious being. Now while we may think that a rational, self-conscious being has a right to life, relatively few of us, I think, value the existence of rational self-conscious beings in the sense that the more of them there are, the better we think it is. If we did value the existence of rational self-conscious beings in this way, we would be opposed to contraception, as well as abortion and infanticide, and even to abstinence or celibacy. But most of us think that there are enough rational, self-conscious beings around already – in which case I find it hard to see why we should place great moral weight on every potentially rational, self-conscious being realizing its potential. For further discussion of this important topic, though, I must refer you to the articles by Tooley and Warren that I have already mentioned.

Assuming that we can settle the criteria for being "human" in the strict sense, and can settle this problem about potentially "human" beings, would this mean that we had settled the question of which lives are sacred and which beings it is justifiable to kill for rather trivial reasons? Unfortunately, even then we would not have solved all our problems for there is no necessary connection between what is characteristic of, or distinctive of, mankind, and what it is that makes it wrong to kill a being. Proponents of the doctrine of the sanctity of human life, even after revising their definition of "human" so that it refers to characteristics distinctive of our species, need to *argue* for the view that the lives of all and only humans, so defined, are sacred. To believe that this connection was automatic and followed immediately without further argument would only be a slightly more sophisticated form of speciesism than the crude biological basis of discrimination discussed earlier. While we might, in the end, decide that all and only those beings whose lives were sacred were those that possessed the characteristics distinctive of mankind, this would be a moral decision that could not be deduced simply from the definition of "human." We might, on reflection, decide the other way – for instance, we might hold that no sentient being should be killed if the probability is that its life will contain a favorable balance of pleasure or happiness over pain and suffering.

Although I have been unable to make up my own mind about the necessary criteria for a right to life – and I leave this question open in the hope that others will be able to help me decide – it is clear that we shall have to change our attitudes about killing so as to obliterate the sharp distinction that we currently make between beings that are members of our own species and beings that are not. How shall we do this?

There are three possibilities:

1 While holding constant our attitudes to members of other species, we change our attitudes to members of our own species so that we consider it legitimate to kill retarded human infants in painful ways for experimental purposes even when no immediately useful knowledge is likely to be derived from these experiments; and in addition we give up any moral objections we may have to rearing and killing these infants for food.

2 While holding constant our attitudes to members of our own species, we change our attitudes to members of other species so that we consider it wrong to kill them because we like the taste of their flesh or for experimental purposes even when the experiment would result in immediately useful knowledge; moreover we refuse to kill them even when they are suffering severe pain from some incurable disease and are a burden to those who must look after them.

3 We change our attitudes to both humans and nonhumans so that they come together at some point in between the present extremes.

None of these three positions makes an arbitrary discrimination on the basis of species, and all are consistent. So we cannot decide between them on these grounds; accordingly, while I am quite certain that our present attitudes are wrong, I am a little more tentative about which of these possibilities is right. Still, if we look at what each implies, I think we can see that the third possibility has much in its favor – not surprisingly, in view of its median position. Thus, I doubt that anyone could seriously advocate performing an experiment like that I described earlier on retarded infants of our own species; nor do I think that many of us could treat retarded infants as if they were purely means towards our gastronomic ends. I think that we can only carry on these practices with regard to other species because we have a huge prejudice in favor of the interests of our own species and a corresponding tendency to neglect the interests of other species. If I am right about this, we are not likely to transfer this prejudice to members of our own species. White racist slave-owners, if forced to stop discriminating, would be unlikely to start enslaving their fellow whites.

As for the second possibility, while I advocate a very radical change in our attitudes toward other species, I do not think this change should go so far as to imply that we should eliminate all mercy-killing or attempt to keep alive an animal which can only live in misery.

So we have to change our attitudes in both directions. We have to bring nonhumans within the sphere of our moral concern and cease to treat them purely as means to our ends. At the same time, once we realize that the fact that severely and irreparably retarded infants are members of the species *Homo sapiens* is not in itself relevant to how we should treat them, we should be ready to reconsider current practices which cause suffering to all concerned and benefit nobody. As an example of such a practice, I shall consider, very briefly, the practice of allowing these infants to die by withholding treatment.

It quite often happens that a severely and irreparably retarded infant has, in addition to its retardation, a condition which unless treated will cause it to die in some foreseeable period – perhaps a day, perhaps a few months or a year. The condition may be one which doctors could, and in the case of a normal infant certainly would, cure; but sometimes, when the infant is severely and irreparably retarded, the doctor in charge will withhold this treatment and allow the infant to die. In general, we can only guess at how often this occurs but a recent investigation of the Yale-New Haven special care nursery showed that over a $2\frac{1}{2}$ year period, 43 deaths, or 14 percent of all deaths in the nursery, were related to withholding treatment. The decision to withhold treatment at this nursery was in each case made by parents and physicians together on the basis that there was little or no chance for a meaningful life for the infant.[10] The investigators, Duff and Campbell, cautiously endorse this practice, and within the alternatives legally available to the doctors, it does seem to be the best that they can do; but if it is justifiable to withhold available forms of treatment knowing that this will result in the death of the infant, what possible grounds can there be for refusing to kill the infant painlessly?

The idea that there is a significant moral distinction between an act and an omission, between killing and letting die, has already been attacked by philosophers.[11] I accept their arguments and have nothing new to add to them, except for the reflection that we would never consider allowing a horse or dog to die in agony if it could be killed painlessly. Once we see that the case of a dying horse is really quite parallel to the case of a dying infant, we may be more ready to drop the distinction between killing and letting die in the case of the infant too.

This is by no means an academic issue. Enormous, and in my view utterly needless, suffering is caused by our present attitudes. Take, for example, the condition known as spina bifida, in which the infant is born with its spinal cord exposed. Three out of every thousand babies have this condition, which adds up to a large number of babies. Although treatment is possible, with the more severe cases even immediate surgery and vigorous treatment will not result in successful rehabilitation. The children will grow up severely handicapped, both mentally and physically, and they will probably die in their teens. The burden on the family can easily be imagined, and it is doubtful if the child's life is a benefit for him. But what is the alternative to surgery, under present medical ethics?

If surgery is not performed, the spina bifida baby will die – but not immediately. Some of them, perhaps a third, will last more than three months and a few will survive for several years. One writer has described their condition in the following terms:

> Virtually all will be paralysed from the waist down, and incontinent because of damage to their exposed nerves. Four out of five of these survivors will get hydrocephalus; their heads will swell out, some until they are too heavy to hold up. Severely retarded, often spastic and blind, they will spend their childhood in institutions that most of us do not care to think about, let alone visit. By adolescence virtually all will be dead.[12]

This kind of life is the alternative that parents must face if they hesitate to consent to surgery. It is a horrible, immoral choice to offer anyone, let alone parents immediately after the birth of their child. The obvious alternative to trying to bring up a severely retarded and handicapped child – a swift, painless death for the infant – is not available because the law enforces the idea that the infant's life is sacred and cannot be directly terminated.

This, then, is one way in which our treatment of severely and irreparably retarded infants needs to be brought closer to our better form of treatment of members of other species.

I said at the beginning of this paper that the moral philosopher and the doctor with an interest in medical ethics have different concerns, at least partly because of their different positions vis-à-vis the law. No doubt this applies to the practice of allowing infants to die while refusing to kill them. The law prohibits killing, but gives no clear directive about letting die; so doctors do what they can to relieve suffering within the boundaries of the law. For this, of course, they are to be commended; but there are indications that a policy which should be defended only in terms of making the best of a bad legal situation is also being thought of as embodying a significant moral distinction. Doctors can be heard sagely quoting Arthur Clough's lines: "Thou shalt not kill, but needst not strive officiously to keep alive," as if these lines were a piece of ancient wisdom – they seem to be unaware that the lines were written to satirize the moral position in support of which they are being quoted.[13] More seriously, the House of Delegates of the American Medical Association recently adopted a policy statement condemning "the intentional termination of the life of one human being by another" as "contrary to that for which the medical profession stands," although the same statement went on to allow the "cessation of the employment of extraordinary means to preserve the life of the body."[14] But what is the cessation of any form of life-sustaining treatment if it is not the intentional termination of the life of one human being by another? And what exactly is it for which the medical profession stands that allows it to kill millions of sentient nonhuman beings while prohibiting it from releasing from suffering an infant *Homo sapiens* with a lower potential for a meaningful life? While doctors may have to obey the law, they do not have to defend it.

I have suggested some ways in which, once we eliminate speciesist bias from our moral views, we might bring our attitudes to human and nonhuman animals closer together. I am well aware that I have not given any precise suggestions about when it is justifiable to kill either a retarded infant or a nonhuman animal. I have not made up my mind on this problem, but hope that others will offer suggestions.

In the remainder of this chapter, I shall look at the doctrine of the sanctity of human life from a perspective rather different from that which I have used up to now. Instead of producing arguments against the doctrine, I shall comment briefly on its historical origins. My motive for so doing is not, of course, the belief that normative consequences follow logically from historical facts. That belief is mistaken. To refute a doctrine it is necessary to produce sound arguments against it. Unfortunately, when a doctrine is very deeply embedded in people's moral institutions, it is sometimes necessary to do more than refute the doctrine in order to convince people that it is false. If one produces apparently valid objections to the doctrine but does no more, one is liable to be met by a reply rather like that which Moore used when he said that he was more certain of the existence of his hands than he could possibly be of the validity of any argument that purported to show that he could not know that his hands existed. In moral philosophy too people will say that they are more certain of the wrongness of killing human infants and the rightness of killing monkeys and pigs than they are of the validity of any arguments to the contrary. Instead of jettisoning their intuitions they will seek desperately for any foothold, however slender, from which they can support their intuitions.

So the following historical excursion is intended to be a kind of softening-up operation on your intuitions, to persuade you that the doctrine of the sanctity of human life is a legacy of attitudes and beliefs that were once widespread, but which few people would now try to defend.

The doctrine of the sanctity of all human life, and the seriousness with which the killing of any member of our species is regarded, mark off the Christian ethical and cultural tradition from almost all others. Of course there have been cultures which regard all life, or at least all sentient life, as sacred and which prohibit the taking of the life of *Homo sapiens*; and there have been other cultures which are as careless of the life of nonhuman animals as the Christian tradition, without being as scrupulous of the lives of all human beings; but the Christian tradition is distinctive for the sharpness of the line it draws between all beings that are members of our species and all other beings.

That very many different societies have seen no moral objection to abortion and infanticide is, I think, well-known. Even if we restrict our attention to infanticide, the list is almost endless. Westermarck's *Origin and Development of the Moral Ideas* has twenty pages chronicling the practice in societies which range geographically from the South Sea Islands over every continent to Greenland, and vary in habits and culture from nomadic Australian aborigines to the sophisticated city-dwellers of ancient Greece or mandarin China. In some of these cultures infanticide is not merely permitted, it is, in certain circumstances, morally obligatory. The use of either exposure or the direct killing of the new-born infant as a means of population control is not unusual, and in many societies the killing of deformed or sickly infants is obligatory. In other cultures where infanticide is not obligatory, it may still be performed without any sense of guilt or wrongdoing.[15]

It is, of course, possible to disregard accounts of the morals of so-called "primitive" societies by taking the line that we have advanced as far beyond these cultures in morals as we have in technology. Sometimes there is a certain amount of truth in this view. It is perhaps less easy to feel comfortable about the certainty of our own intuitions when we find them at variance with the views of cultures for whose moral sense we have considerable respect. I am thinking primarily of ancient Greece. Everyone knows that the Spartans exposed deformed or weak infants, but then no one cares much for Spartan morality anyway. Less often commented on is the fact that both Plato, in the *Republic*, and Aristotle, in his *Politics*, propose that the state command the killing of deformed infants.[16] In making these recommendations, Plato and Aristotle were merely endorsing the legislative codes said to have been drawn up by the renowned law-givers Lycurgus and Solon.

In Roman times, too, we find a moralist like Seneca, whose humanitarian outlook has survived the centuries, advocating infanticide for the sick and deformed.[17] Up to this time, this was thought of as a natural and humane solution, obviously preferable to the alternative of a miserable life for both parents and children. We find nothing resembling the doctrine that the lives of all born of human parents are sacred in the pre-Christian literature.

There can be no doubt that the change in European attitudes to abortion and infanticide is a product of the coming of Christianity. What is especially important to note about this change, for the purposes of the present discussion, is that the change had a special theological motivation in the new religion; that is to say, the change occurred not because of some general broadening of people's moral concern that was part of a more enlightened moral outlook, but because of the Christian doctrine that all born of human parents have immortal souls and are destined for an eternity of bliss or for everlasting torment. This central belief of the new religion placed a yawning gulf between *Homo sapiens* and all other species, so far as the significance of their lives was concerned. To kill a human being was an act of fearful significance, since it consigned him or her to an eternal fate. Moreover this idea was coupled with another doctrine that made abortion and infanticide still more terrible. As the sixth-century Saint Fulgentius says in his treatise *De Fide:*

> It is to be believed beyond doubt that not only men who are come to the use of reason, but infants, whether they die in their mother's womb or after they are born, without baptism in the name of the Father, Son and Holy Ghost, are punished with everlasting punishment in eternal fire, because although they have no actual sin of their own, they carry along with them the condemnation of original sin from their first conception and birth.[18]

This was the orthodox view of the Latin Church. The unborn fetus, from the moment it acquired its soul, was destined to rise again on the day of judgment and face its Judge. If its responsibility for the sin of Adam had not been removed by baptism, it was doomed to hell for ever. No wonder that while previously abortion and infanticide had been looked upon as not crimes at all, or if crimes, then far less serious than the murder of an adult, after the coming of Christianity they were often thought of as worse than ordinary murder. Nor was this doctrine merely current among scholarly theologians. It was embodied in various early Christian laws. The Lex Bajuwariorum, one of the medieval Germanic codes, expressly provides for a daily compensation for children killed in the womb, on account of the daily suffering of those children in hell; and other codes provide for distinctively cruel modes of execution for mothers who kill their infants.[19] As W. E. H. Lecky puts it in his classic *History*

of European Morals: "That which appealed so powerfully to the compassion of
the early and medieval Christians, in the fate of the murdered infants, was not
that they died, but that they commonly died unbaptised."[20]

Over the centuries of Christian domination of European thought, the moral
ideas based on these doctrines took a firm hold. They became part of the basic
moral beliefs of most Europeans. They were not seriously challenged until the
eighteenth century, when rationalist thinkers started to question various religious dogmas. Then Bentham, among others, pointed out that the law's
treatment of infanticide ignored the differences between this act and ordinary
murder. He referred to the killing of an infant by an unmarried mother as

> what is improperly called the death of an infant, who has ceased to be, before
> knowing what existence is, – a result of a nature not to give the slightest
> inquietude to the most timid imagination; and which can cause no regrets but
> to the very person who, through a sentiment of shame and pity, has refused to
> prolong a life begun under auspices of misery.[21]

The challenge to theological doctrines that gave rise to the doctrine of the
sanctity of human life has, by and large, succeeded. The challenge to the
moral attitudes themselves has made slower progress. Laws against abortion
have been substantially weakened or abolished in many countries, but a doctor
may still be charged with murder if he kills an infant, no matter how retarded.
My brief historical survey suggests that the intuitions which lie behind these
laws are not insights of self-evident moral truths, but the historically condi-
tioned product of doctrines about immortality, original sin, and damnation
which hardly anyone now accepts; doctrines so obnoxious, in fact, that if
anyone did accept them, we should be inclined to discount any other moral
views he held. Although advocates of the doctrine of the sanctity of human
life now frequently try to give their position some secular justification, there
can be no possible justification for making the boundary of sanctity run parallel
with the boundary of our own species, unless we invoke some belief about
immortal souls.

Before I finish I should mention one major objection, practical rather than
theoretical, to my proposal that we reject the idea of the sanctity of human life.
People are liable to say that while the doctrine may be based on an arbitrary and
unjustifiable distinction between our own species and other species, this
distinction still serves a useful purpose. Once we abandon the idea, this
objection runs, we have embarked on a slippery slope that may lead to a loss
of respect for the lives of ordinary people and eventually to an increase in crime
or to the selective killing of racial minorities or political undesirables. So the
idea of the sanctity of human life is worth preserving because the distinction it

makes, even if inaccurate at some points, is close enough to a defensible distinction to be worth preserving.

There is no evidence that taking the lives of members of our own species under certain special circumstances will have any kind of contagious effect on our attitudes to killing in other circumstances. Historical evidence suggests the contrary. Ancient Greeks, as we have seen, regularly killed or exposed infants, but appear to have been at least as scrupulous about taking the lives of their fellow-citizens as medieval Christians or modern Americans. In Eskimo societies it was the custom for a man to kill his elderly parents, but to murder a normal, healthy adult was virtually unknown.[22] White colonists in Australia would shoot Aborigines for sport, as their descendents now shoot kangaroos, with no discernible effect on the seriousness with which the killing of a white man was regarded. If we can separate such basically similar beings as Aborigines and Europeans into distinct moral categories without transferring our attitudes from one group to the other, there is surely not going to be much difficulty in marking off severely and irreparably retarded infants from normal human beings. Moreover, anyone who thinks that there is a risk of bad consequences if we abandon the doctrine of the sanctity of human life must still balance this possibility against the tangible harm to which the doctrine now gives rise: harm both to infants whose misery is needlessly prolonged, and to nonhumans whose interests are ignored.

Notes

1   See Michael Tooley, "Abortion and Infanticide," *Philosophy and Public Affairs*, 2 no. 1 (1972); a similar conclusion seems to be implied by Mary Anne Warren, "The Moral and Legal Status of Abortion," *The Monist*, 57 no. 1 (1975).
2   See Henry K. Beecher, "Ethical Problems Created by the Hopelessly Unconscious Patient," *New England Journal of Medicine*, 278 no. 26 (1968); Anthony Shaw, "Dilemmas of 'Informed Consent' in Children," *New England Journal of Medicine*, 289 no. 17 (1973).
3   Ibid.
4   G. Deneau, T. Yanagita, and M. Seevers, "Self-Administration of Psychoactive Substances by the Monkey," *Psychopharmocologia*, 16 (1969), pp. 30–48.
5   See Richard Ryder, *Victims of Science* (London: Davis-Poynter, 1975).
6   This list is a compound of the main indicators of "humanhood" or "personhood" suggested by Mary Anne Warren, "The Moral and Legal Status of Abortion," and Joseph Fletcher, "Indicators of Humanhood: A Tentative Profile of Man," *Hastings Center Report* (Institute of Society, Ethics and the Life Sciences, Hastings-on-Hudson, NY) 2 no. 5 (1972).
7   For an early report, see R. A. Gardner and B. T. Gardner, "Teaching Sign Language to a Chimpanzee," *Science*, 165 (1969); and for a more recent informal

summary of progress in this area see the report by Peter Jenkins, *The Guardian* (London) (10 July, 1973), p. 16, reprinted in T. Regan and P. Singer (eds.), *Animal Rights and Human Obligations* (Englewood Cliffs, NJ: Prentice-Hall, 1976).

8   Michael Tooley, "Abortion and Infanticide."

9   See note 6.

10 R. S. Duff and A. G. M. Campbell, "Moral and Ethical Dilemmas in the Special Care Nursery," *New England Journal of Medicine*, 289 no. 17 (1973).

11 See Jonathan Bennett, "Whatever the Consequences," *Analysis*, 26 (1966); Tooley, and "Abortion and Infanticide," and chapters 7 and 8 of *Ethical Issues Relating to Life and Death*, ed. John Ladd (New York and Oxford: Oxford University Press, 1979); for a contrary view, see chapter 2 of Ladd's book.

12 Gerald Leach, *The Biocrats* (Harmondsworth: Penguin, 1972), p. 197.

13 I owe this point to Jonathan Glover. See his *Causing Death and Saving Lives* (Harmondsworth: Penguin, 1977), ch. 7.

14 *New York Times*, 5 Dec. 1973.

15 Edward Westermarck, *The Origin and Development of Moral Ideas*, vol. 1 (London: Macmillan, 1924), pp. 394–413.

16 Aristotle, *Politics* 7.1335^b; Plato, *Republic* 5.460.

17 Seneca, *De Ira* 1.15 (referred to by Westermarck, *Moral Ideas*, p. 419).

18 St. Fulgentius, *De Fide* 27 (quoted by Westermarck, pp. 416–17).

19 W. E. H. Lecky, *History of European Morals*, vol. 2 (London: Longmans, 1892), p. 23 n.

20 Ibid., p. 23. John T. Noonan has argued (in *The Morality of Abortion: Legal and Historical Perspective* (Cambridge, MA: Harvard University Press, 1970)) that Christian opposition to abortion and infanticide did not depend on narrow theological doctrines, but on the spirit of the scriptural injunction to love our neighbor as ourself. So Noonan says, "The fetus as human was a neighbor; his life had parity with our own" (p. 58). But if we do not take account of theological doctrines, how can it be explained why, for the Christian, *any* human, including a fetus, is my neighbor, while a horse or a dog is not my neighbor, even though they resemble me more closely than the fetus in important characteristics like sentience and self-awareness, and I have more contact with them and am able to relate to them in a much more neighborly manner? Once this question is asked the influence of theological doctrines becomes apparent.

21 Jeremy Bentham, *Theory of Legislation*, pp. 264f. (quoted by Westermarck, *Moral Ideas*, p. 413 n).

22 For the practice of killing elderly parents and other forms of euthanasia among the Eskimo, see the sources cited by Westermarck, *Moral Ideas*, p. 387, n. 1 and p. 392, n. 1–3; for the rarity of homicide outside such special circumstances and the severe condemnation with which it is regarded among the same people, see Westermarck, *Moral Ideas*, pp. 329; 330; 331, n. 2; 334.

Sixteen

Should All Seriously Disabled Infants Live?

Helga Kuhse and Peter Singer

Modern medical technology has given us the means to sustain the lives of many seriously ill or handicapped young children who, only a decade or two ago, would have died soon after birth because the means were not available to keep them alive. But should we always try to preserve every child's life by all available means, or are there times when a young child should be allowed, or helped, to die because she is seriously ill or handicapped?

It is frequently claimed that all human beings, including handicapped new-born infants, have a "right to life" and that it is morally wrong to base life and death decisions in the practice of medicine on the quality or kind of life in question. In this article, we shall dispute that claim and argue that quality and kind of life constitute a proper basis for medical decision-making for seriously ill or handicapped young children.

To begin, let us consider the following case. It is described by Fred M. Frohock, a professor of political science, in his recent book *Special Care*, written after he had spent four months as an observer in a modern neonatal intensive care unit of an unnamed American hospital (Frohock 1986).

Parts of this chapter are drawn from the authors' book, *Should the Baby Live? The Problem of Handicapped Infants* (Oxford: Oxford University Press, 1985) and from an article "For Sometimes Letting – and Helping – Die," *Law, Medicine, and Health Care*, 14 (1986), pp. 149–54. The article was written as part of a larger study on "Life and Death Choices for Defective Newborns," supported by the Australian Research Grants Scheme. We wish to thank the ARGS for thier support.

First published in this form in *Children, Parents, and Politics*, ed. Geoffrey Scarre (Cambridge: Cambridge University Press, 1989), pp. 168–81. Reprinted with permission of Cambridge University Press.

Stephanie Christopher. On March 8, Stephanie Christopher was born prematurely after only 30 weeks' gestation. Her main problem, however, was not her prematurity but rather a congenital disorder, epidermolysis bullosa. This disorder causes widespread and constant blistering of the skin. Lesions occur both on the outer surface of the body and on skin within the body, such as the mouth and esophagus. Secondary growth retardation and severe anemia are part of the syndrome.

Whilst the disease can take different forms, the prognosis is grave and many of those afflicted with it succumb to it within the first two years of life. In those who survive, the lesions may clear and they can frequently expect a satisfactory quality of life. Stephanie was put on a regime of antibiotics and had to be kept in isolation (since the major cause of death in these children is infection). She also needed an operation to clear two intestinal obstructions.

Stephanie lived for two months. During these two months, she endured much. Despite the operation to clear the intestinal obstructions, Stephanie was unable to take sufficient nourishment orally and had to be fed intravenously. But fluid oozed out through her damaged skin, and there were imbalances in hydration and nutrition. There were difficulties in suctioning Stephanie and in inserting tubes because her internal skin, like her external skin, would slough off. She was repeatedly described as a "burns victim" – a burns victim who was burning up every day. Swathed in vaseline-soaked bandages, Stephanie was given oxygen through a mask placed close to her face, morphine to ease the pain, and another drug, narcan, to counter the effects of too much morphine.

Despite the administration of large doses of morphine, Stephanie did, however, still experience discomfort and pain. On April 8, four weeks after Stephanie's birth, Frohock recorded the following observations in his journal:

> [Stephanie] is breathing rapidly, her face a few inches away from the oxygen mask. She looks like an accident victim – tired, even worn out, from some disaster that has struck her. . . .
>
> Stephanie is crying as the gauze is removed. Her left leg is bloody, her foot scraped raw over the ankle and on top. Her right leg looks better except for a large lesion with a scab under the area of the knee. Some of the gauzes are soaked with blood. Her hands are also bloody. . . . (Frohock 1986, p. 118)

There was also constantly blood in Stephanie's stools and urine.

And, ten days later, on April 18, Frohock writes:

> The oxygen mask still blows into her face. She is crying, moving restlessly. Her legs and arms are wrapped in vaseline gauze. . . . Her body is slick with sweat and vaseline. This is pure suffering. Is there any point to it? (Frohock, 1986, p. 133)

Doctors continued to give antibiotics and oxygen to Stephanie. Also, a decision had been made that Stephanie would be stimulated manually should she stop breathing, but that there would be no resuscitation attempts should her heart stop. This happened on May 11, and Stephanie died.

Should we always try to prolong every infant's life by all possible means, or should we sometimes allow an infant to die because – even if we might be able to sustain her life – we cannot give her an acceptable quality of life?

Sanctity of Life or Quality of Life?

People often say that every human life is equally inviolable and valuable – has "sanctity" – and that we must not base medical decision-making on the quality or kind of life in question. This view has traditionally been taken by the Roman Catholic Church and, was recently reiterated by Pope John Paul during his visit to Australia:

> The Church . . . never ceases to proclaim the sacredness of all human life. . . . Nothing should be done which is against life in the reality of a concrete individual, no matter how weak, or defenceless, no matter how undeveloped or advanced. (Pirrie 1986a)

The Protestant theologian Paul Ramsey, too, affirms the "sanctity" of all human life:

> [T]here is no reason for saying that [six months in the life of a baby born with the invariably fatal Tay Sachs disease] are a life span of lesser worth to God than living seventy years before the onset of irreversible degeneration. . . . All our days and years are of equal worth whatever the consequence; death is no more a tragedy at one time than at another time. (Ramsey 1978, p. 191)

The view that all human life is equally valuable and inviolable is deeply rooted in many people's pre-reflective thinking and is enshrined in Anglo-American law. As a Melbourne [Australia] Supreme Court Judge, Mr. Justice Vincent, recently put it when ordering medical treatment for a baby suffering from spina bifida:

> The law does not permit decisions to be made concerning the quality of life nor any assessment of the value of any human being. . . . No parent, no doctor, no court has any power to determine that the life of any child, however disabled the child may be, will be deliberately taken from them. (Pirrie 1986b)

Those who take the view that all human life, irrespective of its quality or kind, has sanctity would seem to have solved the difficult question of how to treat seriously ill or handicapped young children; there is no decision to be made – every child, even one like Stephanie Christopher, has to be kept alive no less vigorously than would any other child. Thus, if antibiotics, oxygen, intravenous feeding, and resuscitation are commonly used in the modern hospital setting, then it is wrong to withhold these life-sustaining means from an infant just because she is handicapped, or experiences a poor quality of life. But few people, if any, ultimately take the view that all human life is equally valuable and inviolable to its logical conclusion. While their judgments that some readily available and effective life-sustaining means may sometimes be withheld or withdrawn may not explicitly refer to quality-of-life considerations, such considerations are nonetheless implicit in their judgments.

As we saw, Paul Ramsey is an advocate of the "sanctity-of-life" view. He holds that "all our days and years are of equal worth" and urges that we avoid quality-of-life judgments because they violate the equality of human life (Ramsey 1978, p. 191). And yet, when discussing the case of permanently comatose Karen Ann Quinlan, Ramsey quite clearly makes a quality-of-life judgment: he suggests that life-sustaining treatment may be withdrawn in this case because "it will affect... the patient's condition in no significant respect except to prolong dying" (Ramsey 1976, p. 16). But to say that treatment which would prolong life may be withdrawn *because it does not affect the patient's condition* (Karen's comatose state), is to make an implicit quality-of-life judgment; it is to suggest that treatment may be withdrawn not because it will no longer sustain the patient's life, nor because the patient is "dying," but rather because it will sustain only a particular *kind* of life – permanently comatose human life (Kuhse 1987, ch. 4).

Implicit quality-of-life judgments are also inherent in the distinction between ordinary and extraordinary means of treatment, traditionally employed in Catholic moral theology. The Jesuit theologian Gerald Kelly has provided the now classical definition of what constitutes "extraordinary treatment." Extraordinary means – those that need not be used to sustain life – are "all medicines, treatments and operations which cannot be obtained without excessive expense, pain or inconvenience or which, if used, would not offer a reasonable hope of benefit" (Kelly 1958, p. 129).

But how do we determine whether a treatment is excessively expensive, painful, or inconvenient, or whether it offers a reasonable hope of benefit? The answer to that question depends largely, and frequently exclusively, on the patient's quality of life with or after treatment. Even the Roman Catholic Church acknowledges this implicitly; in its *Declaration on Euthanasia* (Sacred Congregation for the Doctrine of the Faith 1980, p. 10) it is suggested that it might be better to replace the term "extraordinary means" by the term "disproportionate means." But what is "disproportionate" will of course vary with the patient's medical condition and with the quality and quantity of life available to her after treatment. A resuscitation attempt, for example, might be "disproportionate" because it would extend an already burdensome life like Stephanie's by only a short period. On the other hand, if a patient were to gain another year, or ten, of normal life, then the same procedure would not be "disproportionate."

Leonard Weber, a Catholic theologian, has considered the question of when we should attempt to resuscitate seriously disabled infants. Weber rejects the view that such decisions should accommodate quality-of-life considerations. Rather, he says, such decisions should be based on the question of whether resuscitation constitutes an ordinary or an extraordinary means. Resuscitation would be extraordinary, or non-obligatory, in the following case:

> If, for example, the oxygen supply to the brain has been stopped and the opportunity to resuscitate only comes when it is probable that extensive damage has already been done to the brain, it should be considered an extraordinary means to attempt to restore normal blood circulation, no matter how common the procedure. (Weber 1976, pp. 92–3)

In other words, no matter how common a procedure might be, it should be considered "extraordinary" or non-obligatory when it will extend a life that is seriously impaired or damaged. But this means, of course, that Weber – like the other writers we cited before him – is making a quality-of-life judgment.

In short, quality-of-life judgments are ubiquitous – and properly so. For the view that all human lives, irrespective of their quality or kind, are equally valuable and inviolable would, if applied consistently, have the grotesque consequence that life would have to be prolonged even in a situation where the patient would not benefit from such efforts or would be harmed by them.

One example would be the extension of an infant's life in a situation where that infant – either because it is born without a brain or has suffered severe brain damage after birth – will never be able to have conscious experiences. While such an infant will not experience pain or suffering, neither will it experience pleasure or joy – or any of the things that make life valuable. Its life would be like a dreamless sleep. Would it be of value to the infant to have its life prolonged? We think not, for the infant cannot be benefited by anything we do.

In this case, life would be of *no* value to the infant. But there are also situations where life can be of disvalue. Stephanie's life is, in our view, a case in point. Considering Stephanie's life solely from her point of view – disregarding entirely what those who watched her suffering went through, and the cost of her medical care – it would have been better if she had died shortly after her birth. Most of her life was wrought with pain and suffering, and even if she did experience some moments of pleasure or well-being, these moments could hardly have compensated her for what she endured.

Looking back over Stephanie's life now that it is over, this judgment seems undeniable, but could one argue that at the time it was in Stephanie's interests that vigorous efforts were made to keep her alive? After all, even if her chances were slim, Stephanie *might* have survived and experienced a worthwhile life. Was it therefore in her interest to endure what had to be endured? In answering that question, the fact that we are dealing with infants, rather than with older children or adults, is relevant.

Infants and Persons

Asking himself how to weigh the interests of Stephanie, Fred Frohock reflects on the distinction between competent adult patients and young children:

> The quality and future of Stephanie's life are problems for everyone who comes into contact with her. No one knows how to weigh her interests in deciding whether to continue or stop her therapy.... She is alive. Her neurological functions are intact.... Yet her pain and bleak prospects might lead a rational adult to say, "Enough" – and choose death. Stephanie cannot make this choice, nor affirm its opposite – life – as a choice. Whoever decides for her will have to make very fine decisions on benefits versus burdens, and perhaps even examine quality-of-life conditions in general, for Stephanie can have no thoughts on whether her particular life is worth living. (Frohock 1986, p. 82)

One important difference between infants and competent adult patients is thus that competent patients can express choices and act on them in a way in which infants cannot. However, Frohock's reflection that "Stephanie can have no thoughts on whether her particular life is worth living" also points to a more fundamental difference between infants and older patients: Infants and older patients have different *kinds* of life.

Before Stephanie Christopher was born, her mother had already given birth to one other child suffering from epidermolysis bullosa. That child had lived for six weeks. To avoid the birth of another child afflicted with the disease, Ms. Christopher underwent prenatal diagnosis during the sixth month of the pregnancy that was to determine whether the child she was now carrying would suffer from this devastating disease. If the tests had been positive, she would presumably have had an abortion. The tests were inconclusive, however, and Ms. Christopher decided to continue the pregnancy. Stephanie was born a little later, when her mother was 30 weeks pregnant.

In making abortions for conditions such as epidermolysis bullosa, spina bifida, and many other handicapping afflictions available to women who want them, we are distinguishing, in our practices, between different *kinds* of life – the lives of fetuses and the lives of more mature human beings; and we draw from this the practical conclusion that different kinds of human life may be treated differently. Whereas many people would agree that fetal life may (at least sometimes) be terminated in the practice of medicine, few people would think it right for doctors to terminate the lives of competent mature patients against these patients' wishes, even if these patients were suffering from conditions that otherwise serve as grounds for abortion.

Is such a distinction between different kinds of human life – adult life and fetal life – defensible? We believe it is. But we also believe that, as far as questions regarding the prolongation or termination of life are concerned, new-born infants are in most morally relevant respects more like fetuses than like older children or adults.

The validity of this assertion depends on the answer to a prior question: When, and why, are certain actions such as the taking of life directly wrong? The philosopher Michael Tooley has discussed that question – in the context of abortion and infanticide – more systematically than anyone else (Tooley 1983). Employing the language of rights, he suggests that for a being to have a right to something, it must have an interest in it, and, to have an interest in continuing to exist, a being must be a "continuing self" – that is, a being which has at some time had the concept of itself as existing over time. Beings who are not "continuing selves" do not have a right to life and it is not directly wrong to take their lives (Tooley 1983, ch. 5). We believe Tooley's argument is basically sound, and shall use the term "person" to refer to those beings who are capable of seeing themselves as continuing selves – that is, as self-aware beings existing over time.

This, then, is the morally relevant difference between fetuses and infants on the one hand, and more mature human beings on the other: Normal adults and children, but not fetuses and infants, are persons; that is, they are self-aware and purposeful beings with a sense of the past and the future. They can see their lives as a continuing process, they can identify with what has happened to them in the past, and they have hopes and plans for the future. For this reason we can say that in normal circumstances they value, or want, their own continued existence, and that life is in their interest. The same does not apply to fetuses or new-born infants. Neither a fetus nor an infant has the conceptual wherewithal to contemplate a future and to want, or value, that future. This is, perhaps, what Fred Frohock had in mind when he wrote that Stephanie, in distinction from an adult, "can have no thoughts on whether her particular life is worth living."

But if an infant cannot value, or want, its own continued existence, then the loss of life for a new-born infant must be less significant than the loss of life for an older child or adult who wants to go on living. This conclusion has, as we shall see, far-reaching consequences for our treatment of seriously ill or handicapped infants.

Infants, Interests, and Potential Persons

We have suggested that the death of a new-born infant or a fetus does not have the same moral significance as the death of an older child or adult because the infant is not a continuing self, capable of valuing its own continued existence. But, someone might object, there are many infants – and this includes many seriously ill or handicapped infants – who have the potential to become persons and of one day valuing their own lives in much the same way as we, who are already persons, value our lives. What makes the death of an infant so tragic in terms of this objection is that there never will be a person leading a worthwhile life. That an infant is not yet a person scarcely matters when we consider such a loss.

But frequently there can be a future person only if we inflict considerable pain and suffering on an infant. Can we justify this suffering? Many people believe the answer is "yes." Pointing to the successful survivors of neonatal intensive care, they will say that it was in the infants' interests to undergo the treatment. Based on this view, many people believe that the guiding principles for decision-making ought to be "the best interests of the infant." Life-sustaining treatment should be given to an infant if its life, with or after treatment, is likely to contain more benefits than burdens. While this view has an obvious appeal, there are a number of reasons why we should not accept it. The most important reasons have to do with the special status of infants.

Obviously, there is a tight connection between the interests a being has and the rightness or wrongness of our actions towards that being. But what *are* the interests of a new-born infant? Infants are not continuing selves and hence have no interest in their own continued existence. They do have other interests though – momentary interests that merely require the presence of a conscious or sentient being, not the self-awareness of a person.

Infants are sentient beings. As such, they can experience pain and discomfort and be cold and hungry. They therefore have an interest in not experiencing pain and discomfort and in being warm and well fed. But here an objection is sometimes put forth. Doctors and others sometimes say that any pain experienced by infants is less significant than the pain experienced by persons, because infants cannot remember, anticipate, or fear pain (McIntosh 1986). We regard the view that infants cannot remember or anticipate pain as entirely plausible, for if, as we have argued, infants are not continuing selves, lacking a sense of the past and the future, then it follows that they can neither remember past experiences nor anticipate future ones – be these painful or pleasant ones. But does it also follow from an infant's inability to remember or anticipate pain that its momentary painful experiences do not count as much as the moment-ary painful experiences of a person? We do not think so. While a person's ability to anticipate and remember pain gives rise to some additional consider-ations, such considerations do not justify giving the actual experience of pain on a moment-by-moment basis a different weight in an infant and a person. If this is correct, then it follows that the moments of pain experienced by an infant must, other things being equal, be given the same moral weight as similar moments of pain experienced by a person.

Those who argue that medical decision-making for seriously ill or handi-capped infants should be based on "the best interests of the infant" may not dispute that an infant's experience of pain and suffering should count. But this suffering, so the argument frequently goes, may well be outweighed by future benefits. Those who take this view – the prestigious American President's Commission for the Study of Ethical Problems in Medicine and Biomedical and Behavioral Research, for example, in its report *Deciding to Forgo Life-Sustaining Treatment* (President's Commission 1983) – do not just look at the momentary interests of the infant (to be free from pain, warm, comfortable, and so on); they look much further ahead, to the whole future interests of the child or person into whom the infant may develop. In other words, they are asking: Will this future life in its totality contain more benefits than harms for this person?

If the issue is put like this, there will be many instances where the potential for a worthwhile life would seem to justify the infliction of some considerable suffering on an infant. There is, however, a fundamental problem in seeing life five or fifty years hence, no matter how good a life it may be, as in the interest of *this infant* now. There is, of course, a physical continuity between the infant and the later person. The former develops into the latter. Because of this, they may be said to be the same physical organism, despite the great changes that will have taken place. But there is no mental continuity, and in this crucial sense *we* are not, and never were, infants, fetuses, or embryos. Our lives as *persons* – as self-aware and purposeful beings with a sense of the past and the future – did not begin until some time after birth, when we ceased to be beings with momentary interests and became "continuing selves."

This undermines the claim that the existence of a person, glad to be alive, shows that a decision to continue treatment was "in the best interests of the infant." The infant, while still an infant, had no interest in becoming the child and adult. Its interests were much more limited than that: not to be in pain, to be warm and comfortable, and so on. If an infant has a reasonable prospect of intact survival, but in the meanwhile must experience prolonged pain and suffering, we may be keeping the infant alive not in accordance with, but *despite* the best interests of the infant. While such a decision may sometimes be justified because, among other things, it makes possible an enjoyable and worthwhile life for a child or adult, it is a mistake to assume that it can be justified by appealing to the best interests of the infant. The infant cannot be compensated for its suffering by the benefits bestowed on a potential future person. These benefits are, as it were, bestowed on someone else.

The issue of how much pain and suffering we may justifiably inflict on an infant in our attempts to keep it alive has recently been raised in a particularly stark manner in the context of infants born prematurely, at the margin of viability (Scanlon 1985; Rovner 1986). In some cases, doctors will not give anesthetics or analgesics for invasive treatments – including major surgery – because these would put an additional strain on the infant's immature system, thereby threatening the infant's survival. While Dr. Willis McGill, chief of anesthesiology at the Children's Hospital National Medical Center in Washington, DC, agrees that an anesthetic should be given whenever possible for procedures that are painful and of significant duration, he none the less implies that there will be situations where such an anesthetic will not be administered because he tries to ensure that the patient is in the best possible condition, and, as he puts it, "It doesn't do any good to have a dead patient who doesn't feel pain" (Rovner 1986, p. 7).

One mother recently told of her horror when she discovered, almost inadvertently, that her premature son, Jeffrey – born after 26 weeks' gestation and weighing less than two pounds – was awake throughout a major operation at the Children's Hospital National Medical Center. The operation included chest incisions and prying his ribs apart. The infant was paralyzed with Pavulon, a curare-type drug that left him unable to move, but totally conscious. He died six weeks after the surgery (Rovner 1986, p. 7; Scanlon 1985).

We have not recounted this case, nor that of Stephanie, to arouse horror, but rather to raise an important question that has, from our viewpoint, so far received insufficient discussion: How much suffering may we justifiably inflict on an infant who has but short-term desires and interests – an infant who cannot yet value its own continued existence? Because such painful life-sustaining procedures are never in the infant's best interest even though they may be in the interest of the person whom the infant might become, we believe that there will be some cases where the suffering of the infant – unavoidable if it is to be kept alive – may in itself be sufficient reason to forgo the treatment. The situations of Stephanie and of Jeffrey may have been two such instances.

The mental discontinuity between infants and persons is one reason why we cannot justify painful treatment by simply pointing to the possible existence of a person who, five or twenty years from now, will be glad to be alive. There is, however, another reason as well. For if the argument is that it would be *wrong* to let an infant die because this would result in there never being a person leading a worthwhile life, then the same argument would lead to the condemnation not only of abortion but also of nonconception. In both cases, a person who might have existed will not exist. And from the future person's perspective, it makes but little difference whether her existence was thwarted through nonconception, abortion, or through being allowed to die in early infancy.

In Whose Interests?

So far we have sketched the philosophical difficulties that lurk behind the idea that decision-making should be based on "the best interests of the infant." These difficulties are one reason why we think this approach is misguided. There is, however, another – more straightforward – reason: many other factors should be taken into account – including the interests of the parents and of any children they already have.

There is no reason to assume that the momentary interests of the infant, or the interests of the person who the ill or handicapped infant might become, should automatically outweigh all these other interests. The birth of a severely handicapped infant can dramatically change the lives of the parents and siblings. It is, for example, often pointed out that the survival of a handicapped child is also the creation of a handicapped family (Simms 1983, p. 18). While that judgment may be too severe in some cases, in others it is the simple truth. To disregard these other interests altogether is incompatible with the principle of equal consideration of the interests of all those affected by our decisions – and such a principle is fundamental to ethics (Singer 1979, ch. 2).

When speaking about equal consideration of interests, there is also one other interest which we have not, so far, mentioned: the interests of the "next child in the queue." One of the more firmly established findings about families with a disabled child is that they are less likely than other families to have a further child (Kew 1975, p. 52). Shouldn't we take the interests of that child into account – the interests of the child who will not be born if the seriously ill or handicapped child survives?

The argument that we should take the "next child" into account has been well put by R. M. Hare (1976). Discussing the question of whether to abort a fetus known to have a handicap, Hare asks us to suppose that a couple have planned to have two children. During the second pregnancy it is found that the fetus has a serious handicap. If the handicapped fetus lives, the couple will not have any more children. If the fetus is aborted, the couple will seek to have a second child. There is a high probability that this second child will be normal. In this situation, Hare argues, we should consider not only the interests of the child now in the womb, but also the interests of the possible child who is likely to live if, and only if, the fetus dies.

The same sort of reasoning can be applied after a seriously ill or handicapped child is born. Should we exclude the "next child" from our deliberations on whether to treat a handicapped infant? We think we should not – at least not if we believe that treatment is justified in terms of the interests of the future child or person. There is, of course, another reason as well: the pain and suffering that will sometimes have to be inflicted in our efforts to achieve the survival of a sick or handicapped infant.

Conclusion

We have argued that we should not always try to preserve every infant's life by all available means because quality and kind of life constitute a proper basis for life and death decisions in the practice of medicine. What we have not yet discussed is *how* an infant should die when it has been decided that its life should no longer be sustained.

It is frequently thought that a morally relevant distinction exists between "doing something" that results in death, and merely "doing nothing" that also results in death – or between killing a patient and allowing a patient to die. Thus it is often thought that letting die is sometimes permissible in the practice of medicine but killing is not. Depending on this distinction, doctors will frequently not act to preserve the life of a child – as they did, for example, when they decided that Stephanie should not be resuscitated should her heart fail – but not take active steps to end the infant's life. While we can understand that it may sometimes be psychologically easier for doctors to decide not to resuscitate an infant than to administer a lethal dose of a drug, there is no intrinsic moral – and arguably no legal – difference between bringing about an infant's death by an omission or an action. If all other factors, such as intention, motivation, and outcome are the same, then killing an infant and allowing it to die are morally equivalent (Kuhse 1984).

Does this mean that it is morally irrelevant whether an infant's life is ended actively or passively? We do not think so. Once the decision has been made that an infant should be allowed to die, it will often be better to hasten death than to stand by and wait until "nature" takes her often cruel course. Would it not have been better if Stephanie's life had ended sooner than it did, if those responsible for her care had at least spared her the suffering she endured between the time it had been decided that her life should not be prolonged by resuscitation and the time when her heart finally failed? We believe the answer is a resounding "Yes."

References

Frohock, Fred M. (1986). *Special Care – Medical Decisions at the Beginning of Life* (Chicago and London: University of Chicago Press).

Hare, R. M. (1976). "Survival of the Weakest," in *Moral Problems in Medicine*, ed. S. Gorovitz et al. (Englewood Cliffs, NJ: Prentice-Hall), pp. 364–9.

Kelly, G. (1958). *Medico-Moral Problems* (St. Louis, MO: The Catholic Hospital Association of the United States).

Kew, S. (1975). *Handicap and Family Crisis* (London: Pitman).

Kuhse, H. (1984). "A Modern Myth. That Letting Die is not the Intentional Causation of Death: some reflections on the trial and acquittal of Dr. Leonard Arthur," *Journal of Applied Philosophy*, 1, pp. 21–38.

—— (1987). *The Sanctity-of-Life Doctrine in Medicine* (Oxford: Oxford University Press).

McIntosh, P. (1986). "Doctors seek pain relief for patients who can't say how much it hurts," *The Age* (Melbourne), September 22.

Pirrie, M. (1986a). "Pontiff appeals for IVF Morality," *The Age* (Melbourne), November 29.

—— (1986b). "Judge: baby should live," *The Age* (Melbourne), July 3.

President's Commission for the Study of Ethical Problems in Medicine and Biomedical and Behavioral Research (1983). *Deciding to Forgo Life-Sustaining Treatment* (Washington: US Government Printing Office).

Ramsey, P. (1976). "Prolonged Dying: Not Medically Indicated," *Hastings Center Report*, 6, pp. 14–17.

—— (1978). *Ethics at the Edges of Life* (New Haven and London: Yale University Press).

Rovner, S. (1986). "Surgery Without Anesthesia: Can Preemies Feel Pain?" *Washington Post*, August 13.

Sacred Congregation for the Doctrine of the Faith (1980). *Declaration on Euthanasia* (Vatican City).

Scanlon, J. W. (1985). "Barbarism," *Prenatal Press*, 9 no. 7, pp. 103–4.

Simms, M. (1983). "Severely Handicapped Infants," *New Humanist*, 98 no. 2, pp. 1–8.

Singer, P. (1979). *Practical Ethics* (Cambridge: Cambridge University Press).

Tooley, M. (1983). *Abortion and Infanticide* (Oxford: Oxford University Press).

Weber, L. (1976). *Who Shall Live?* (New York: Paulist Press).

Seventeen

Is the Sanctity of Life Ethic Terminally Ill?

I Introduction

It is surely no secret to anyone that I have for a long time been a critic of the traditional sanctity of life ethic. So if I say that I believe that, after ruling our thoughts and our decisions about life and death for nearly two thousand years, the traditional sanctity of life ethic is at the point of collapse, some of you may think this is mere wishful thinking on my part. Consider, however, the following three signs of this impending collapse, which have taken place – coincidentally but perhaps appropriately enough – during the past two years in which I have had the honor of holding the office of President of the International Association of Bioethics.

- On February 4, 1993, in deciding the fate of a young man named Anthony Bland, Britain's highest court threw out many centuries of traditional law and medical ethics regarding the value of human life and the lawfulness of intentionally ending it.
- On November 30, 1993, the Netherlands parliament finally put into law the guidelines under which Dutch doctors have for some years been openly giving lethal injections to patients who suffer unbearably without hope of improvement, and who ask to be helped to die.

First published in *Bioethics*, 9 (1995), pp. 327–43. Reprinted with permission of Blackwell Publishers.

● On May 2, 1994, twelve Michigan jurors acquitted Dr. Jack Kevorkian of a charge of assisting Thomas Hyde to commit suicide. Their refusal to convict Kevorkian was a major victory for the cause of physician-assisted suicide, for it is hard to imagine a clearer case of assisting suicide than this one. Kevorkian freely admitted supplying the carbon monoxide gas, tubing and a mask to Hyde, who had then used them to end a life made unbearable by the rapidly progressing nerve disorder ALS.

These three events are the surface tremors resulting from major shifts deep in the bedrock of Western ethics. We are going through a period of transition in our attitude to the sanctity of human life. Such transitions cause confusion and division. Many factors are involved in this shift, but I shall focus on ways in which our growing technical capacity to keep human beings alive has brought out some implications of the sanctity of life ethic that – once we are forced to face them squarely – we cannot accept. This will lead me to suggest a way forward.

II   Revolution by Stealth: the Redefinition of Death

The acceptance of brain death – that is, the permanent loss of all brain function – as a criterion of death has been widely regarded as one of the great achievements of bioethics. It is one of the few issues on which there has been virtual consensus; and it has made an important difference in the way we treat people whose brains have ceased to function. This change in the definition of death has meant that warm, breathing, pulsating human beings are not given further medical support. If their relatives consent (or in some countries, as long as they have not registered a refusal of consent), their hearts and other organs can be cut out of their bodies and given to strangers. The change in our conception of death that excluded these human beings from the moral community was among the first in a series of dramatic changes in our view of life and death. Yet, in sharp contrast to other changes in this area, it met with virtually no opposition. How did this happen?

Everyone knows that the story of our modern definition of death begins with "The Ad Hoc Committee of the Harvard Medical School to Examine the Definition of Brain Death." What is not so well known is the link between the work of this committee and Dr. Christiaan Barnard's famous first transplantation of a human heart, in December 1967. Even before Barnard's sensational operation, Henry Beecher, chairman of a Harvard University committee that oversaw the ethics of experimentation on human beings, had written to Robert Ebert, Dean of the Harvard Medical School, suggesting that the Committee should consider some new questions. He had, he told the Dean, been speaking with Dr. Joseph Murray, a surgeon at Massachusetts General Hospital and a pioneer in kidney transplantation. "Both Dr Murray and I," Beecher wrote, "think the time has come for a further consideration of the definition of death. Every major hospital has patients stacked up waiting for suitable donors."[1] Ebert did not respond immediately; but within a month of the news of the South African heart transplant, he set up, under Beecher's chairmanship, the group that was soon to become known as the Harvard Brain Death Committee.

The committee was made up mostly of members of the medical profession – ten of them, supplemented by a lawyer, an historian, and a theologian. It did its work rapidly, and published its report in the *Journal of the American Medical Association* in August 1968. The report was soon recognized as an authoritative document, and its criteria for the determination of death were adopted rapidly and widely, not only in the United States but, with some modification of the technical details, in most countries of the world. The report began with a remarkably clear statement of what the committee was doing and why it needed to be done:

> Our primary purpose is to define irreversible coma as a new criterion for death. There are two reasons why there is a need for a definition: (1) Improvements in resuscitative and supportive measures have led to increased efforts to save those who are desperately injured. Sometimes these efforts have only a partial success so that the result is an individual whose heart continues to beat but whose brain is irreversibly damaged. The burden is great on patients who suffer permanent loss of intellect, on their families, on the hospitals, and on those in need of hospital beds already occupied by these comatose patients. (2) Obsolete criteria for the definition of death can lead to controversy in obtaining organs for transplantation.

To a reader familiar with bioethics in the 1990s, there are two striking aspects of this opening paragraph. The first is that the Harvard Committee does not even attempt to argue that there is a need for a new definition of death because hospitals have a lot of patients in their wards who are really dead, but are being kept attached to respirators because the law does not recognize them as dead. Instead, with unusual frankness, the committee said that a new definition was needed because irreversibly comatose patients were a great burden, not only on themselves (why to be in an irreversible coma is a burden to the patient, the Committee did not say), but also to their families, hospitals, and patients waiting for beds. And then there was the problem of "controversy" about obtaining organs for transplantation.

In fact, frank as the statement seems, in presenting its concern about this controversy, the Committee was still not being entirely candid. An earlier draft had been more open in stating that one reason for changing the definition of death was the "great need for tissues and organs of, among others, the patient whose cerebrum has been hopelessly destroyed, in order to restore those who are salvageable." When this draft was sent to Ebert, he advised Beecher to tone it down it because of its "unfortunate" connotation "that you wish to redefine death in order to make viable organs more readily available to persons requiring transplants."[2] The Harvard Brain Death Committee took Ebert's advice: it was doubtless more politic not to put things so bluntly. But Beecher himself made no secret of his own views. He was later to say, in an address to the American Association for the Advancement of Science:

> There is indeed a life-saving potential in the new definition, for, when accepted, it will lead to greater availability than formerly of essential organs in viable condition, for transplantation, and thus countless lives now inevitably lost will be saved ...[3]

The second striking aspect of the Harvard Committee's report is that it keeps referring to "irreversible coma" as the condition that it wishes to define as death. The committee also speaks of "permanent loss of intellect" and even says "we suggest that responsible medical opinion is ready to adopt new criteria for pronouncing death to have occurred in an individual sustaining irreversible coma as a result of permanent brain damage." Now "irreversible coma as a result of permanent brain damage" is by no means identical with the death of the whole brain. Permanent damage to the parts of the brain responsible for consciousness can also mean that a patient is in a "persistent vegetative state," a condition in which the brain stem and the central nervous system continue to function, but consciousness has been irreversibly lost. Even today, no legal system regards those in a persistent vegetative state as dead.

Admittedly, the Harvard Committee report does go on to say, immediately following the paragraph quoted above: "*we are concerned here only with those comatose individuals who have no discernible central nervous system activity.*" But the reasons given by the Committee for redefining death – the great burden on the patients, their families, the hospitals, and the community, as well as the waste of organs needed for transplantation – apply in every respect to *all* those who are irreversibly comatose, not only to those whose entire brain is dead. So it is worth asking: why did the Committee limit its concern to those with no brain activity at all? One reason could be that there was at the time no reliable way of telling whether a coma was irreversible, unless the brain damage was so severe that there was no brain activity at all. Another could be that people whose whole brain is dead will stop breathing after they are taken off a respirator, and so will soon be dead by anyone's standard. People in a persistent vegetative

state, on the other hand, may continue to breathe without mechanical assistance. To call for the undertakers to bury a "dead" patient who is still breathing
would be a bit too much for anyone to swallow.

We all know that the redefinition of death proposed by the Harvard Brain
Death Committee triumphed. By 1981, when the United States President's
Commission for the Study of Ethical Problems in Medicine examined the
issue, it could write of "the emergence of a medical consensus" around criteria
very like those proposed by the Harvard Committee.[4] Already, people whose
brains had irreversibly ceased to function were considered legally dead in at
least fifteen countries, and in more than half of the states of the United States.
In some countries, including Britain, Parliament had not even been involved in
the change: the medical profession had simply adopted a new set of criteria on
the basis of which doctors certified a patient dead.[5] This was truly a revolution
without opposition.

The redefinition of death in terms of brain death went through so smoothly
because it did not harm the brain-dead patients and it benefited everyone else:
the families of brain-dead patients, the hospitals, the transplant surgeons, people
needing transplants, people who worried that they might one day need a
transplant, people who feared that they might one day be kept on a respirator
after their brain had died, taxpayers, and the government. The general public
understood that if the brain has been destroyed, there can be no recovery of
consciousness, and so there is no point in maintaining the body. Defining such
people as dead was a convenient way around the problems of making their
organs available for transplantation, and withdrawing treatment from them.

But does this way round the problems really work? On one level, it does. By
the early 1990s, as Sweden and Denmark, the last European nations to cling to
the traditional standard, adopted brain-death definitions of death, this verdict
appeared to be confirmed. Among developed nations, only Japan was still
holding out. But do people really think of the brain-dead as *dead*? The Harvard
Brain Death Committee itself couldn't quite swallow the implications of what
it was recommending. As we have seen, it described patients whose brains have
ceased to function as in an "irreversible coma" and said that being kept on a
respirator was a burden to them. Dead people are not in a coma, they are dead,
and nothing can be a burden to them any more.

Perhaps the lapses in the thinking of the Harvard Committee can be
pardoned because the concept of brain death was then so new. But twenty-
five years later, little has changed. Only last year the *Miami Herald* ran a story
headlined "Brain-Dead Woman Kept Alive in Hopes She'll Bear Child"; while
after the same woman did bear her child, the *San Francisco Chronicle* reported:
"Brain-Dead Woman Gives Birth, then Dies." Nor can we blame this entirely
on the lamentable ignorance of the popular press. A study of doctors and nurses

who work with brain-dead patients at hospitals in Cleveland, Ohio, showed that one in three of them thought that people whose brains had died could be classified as dead because they were "irreversibly dying" or because they had an "unacceptable quality of life."[6]

Why do both journalists and members of the health-care professions talk in a way that denies that brain death is really death? One possible explanation is that even though people know that the brain-dead are dead, it is just too difficult for them to abandon obsolete ways of thinking about death. Another possible explanation is that people have enough common sense to see that the brain-dead are not really dead. I favor this second explanation. The brain-death criterion of death is nothing other than a convenient fiction. It was proposed and accepted because it makes it possible for us to salvage organs that would otherwise be wasted, and to withdraw medical treatment when it is doing no good. On this basis, it might seem that, despite some fundamental weaknesses, the survival prospects of the concept of brain death are good. But there are two reasons why our present understanding of brain death is not stable. Advances in medical knowledge and technology are the driving factors.

To understand the first problem with the present concept of brain death, we have to recall that brain death is generally defined as the irreversible cessation of all functions of the brain.[7] In accordance with this definition, a standard set of tests are used by doctors to establish that all functions of the brain have irreversibly ceased. These tests are broadly in line with those recommended in 1968 by the Harvard Brain Death Committee, but they have been further refined and updated over the years in various countries. In the past ten years, however, as doctors have sought ways of managing brain-dead patients, so that their organs (or in some cases, their pregnancies) could be sustained for a longer time, it has become apparent that even when the usual tests show that brain death has occurred, *some brain functions continue*. We think of the brain primarily as concerned with processing information through the senses and the nervous system, but the brain has other functions as well. One of these is to supply various hormones that help to regulate several bodily functions. We now know that some of these hormones continue to be supplied by the brains of most patients who, by the standard tests, are brain-dead. Moreover, when brain-dead patients are cut open in order to remove organs, their blood pressure may rise and their heartbeat quicken. These reactions mean that the brain is still carrying out some of its functions, regulating the responses of the body in various ways. As a result, the legal definition of brain death, and current medical practice in certifying brain-dead people as dead, have come apart.[8]

It would be possible to bring medical practice into line with the current definition of death in terms of the irreversible cessation of *all* brain function. Doctors would then have to test for all brain functions, including hormonal functions, before declaring someone dead. This would mean that some people who are now declared brain-dead would be considered alive, and therefore would have to continue to be supported on a respirator, at significant cost, both financially and in terms of the extended distress of the family. Since the tests are expensive to carry out and time-consuming in themselves, continued support would be necessary during the period in which they are carried out, even if in the end the results showed that the person had no brain function at all. In addition, during this period, the person's organs would deteriorate, and may therefore not be usable for transplantation. What gains would there be to balance against these serious disadvantages? From the perspective of an adherent of the sanctity of life ethic, of course, the gain is that we are no longer killing people by cutting out their hearts while they are still alive. If one really believed that the quality of a human life makes no difference to the wrongness of ending that life, this would end the discussion. There would be no ethical alternative. But it would still be true that not a single person who was kept longer on a respirator because of the need to test for hormonal brain functioning would ever return to consciousness.

So if it is life with consciousness, rather than life itself, that we value, then bringing medical practice into line with the definition of death does not seem a good idea. It would be better to bring the definition of brain death into line with current medical practice. But once we move away from the idea of brain death as the irreversible cessation of *all* brain functioning, what are we to put in its place? Which functions of the brain will we take as marking the difference between life and death, and why?

The most plausible answer is that the brain functions that really matter are those related to consciousness. On this view, what we really care about – and ought to care about – is *the person* rather than the body. Accordingly, it is the permanent cessation of function of the cerebral cortex, not of the whole brain, that should be taken as the criterion of death. Several reasons could be offered to justify this step. First, although the Harvard Brain Death Committee specified that its recommendations applied only to those who have "no discernible central nervous system activity," the arguments it put forward for its redefinition of death applied in every respect to patients who are permanently without any awareness, whether or not they have some brainstem function. This seems to have been no accident, for it reflected the view of the Committee's chairman, Henry Beecher, who in his address to the American Association for the Advancement of Science, from which I have already quoted, said that what is essential to human nature is:

> . . . the individual's personality, his conscious life, his uniqueness, his capacity for remembering, judging, reasoning, acting, enjoying, worrying, and so on . . .[9]

As I have already said, when the Harvard Committee issued its report, the irreversible destruction of the parts of the brain associated with consciousness could not reliably be diagnosed if the brainstem was alive. Since then, however, the technology for obtaining images of soft tissues within the body has made enormous progress. Hence a major stumbling block to the acceptance of a higher brain definition of death has already been greatly diminished in its scope, and will soon disappear altogether.

Now that medical certainty on the irreversibility of loss of higher brain functions can be established in at least some cases, the inherent logic of pushing the definition of death one step further has already led, in the United States, to one Supreme Court judge suggesting that the law could consider a person who has irreversibly lost consciousness to be no longer alive. Here is Mr Justice Stevens, giving his judgment in the case of Nancy Cruzan, a woman who had been unconscious for eight years and whose guardians sought court permission to withdraw tube feeding of food and fluids so that she could die:

> But for patients like Nancy Cruzan, who have no consciousness and no chance of recovery, there is a serious question as to whether the mere persistence of their bodies is "life," as that word is commonly understood . . . The State's unflagging determination to perpetuate Nancy Cruzan's physical existence is comprehensible only as an effort to define life's meaning, not as an attempt to preserve its sanctity . . . In any event, absent some theological abstraction, the idea of life is not conceived separately from the idea of a living person.[10]

Admittedly, this was a dissenting judgment; the majority decided the case on narrow constitutional grounds that are not relevant to our concerns here, and what Stevens said has not become part of the law of the United States. Nevertheless, dissenting judgments are often a way of floating an idea that is "in the air" and may become part of the majority view in a later decision. As medical opinion increasingly comes to accept that we can reliably establish when consciousness has been irreversibly lost, the pressure will become more intense for medical practice to move to a definition of death based on the death of the higher brain.

Yet there is a very fundamental flaw in the idea of moving to a higher brain definition of death. If, as we have seen, people already have difficulty in accepting that a warm body with a beating heart on a respirator is really dead, how much more difficult would it be to bury a "corpse" that is still breathing while the lid of the coffin is nailed down? That is simply an absurdity. Something has gone wrong. But what?

In my view, the trouble began with the move to brain death. The Harvard Brain Death Committee was faced with two serious problems. Patients in an utterly hopeless condition were attached to respirators, and no one dared to turn them off; and organs that could be used to save lives were rendered useless by the delays caused by waiting for the circulation of the blood in potential donors to stop. The committee tried to solve both these problems by the bold expedient of classifying as dead those whose brains had ceased to have any discernible activity. The consequences of the redefinition of death were so evidently desirable that it met with scarcely any opposition, and was accepted almost universally. Nevertheless, it was unsound from the start. Solving problems by redefinition rarely works, and this case was no exception. We need to begin again, with a different approach to the original problems, one which will break out of the intellectual straitjacket of the traditional belief that all human life is of equal value. Until last year, it seemed difficult to imagine how a different approach could ever be accepted. But last year Britain's highest court took a major step toward just such a new approach.

III   Revolution by the Law Lords: the case of Anthony Bland

The revolution in British law regarding the sanctity of human life grew out of the tragedy at Hillsborough Football Stadium in Sheffield, in April 1989. Liverpool was playing Nottingham Forest in an FA Cup semifinal. As the match started, thousands of supporters were still trying to get into the ground. A fatal crush occurred against some fencing that had been erected to stop fans getting onto the playing field. Before order could be restored and the pressure relieved, 95 people had died in the worst disaster in British sporting history. Tony Bland, a 17-year-old Liverpool fan, was not killed, but his lungs were crushed by the pressure of the crowd around him, and his brain was deprived of oxygen. Taken to hospital, it was found that only his brainstem had survived. His cortex had been destroyed. Here is how Lord Justice Hoffmann was later to describe his condition:

> Since April 15 1989 Anthony Bland has been in persistent vegetative state. He lies in Airedale General Hospital in Keighley, fed liquid food by a pump through a tube passing through his nose and down the back of his throat into the stomach. His bladder is emptied through a catheter inserted through his penis, which from time to time has caused infections requiring dressing and antibiotic treatment. His stiffened joints have caused his limbs to be rigidly contracted so that his arms are tightly flexed across his chest and his legs unnaturally contorted. Reflex movements in the throat cause him to vomit and dribble. Of all this, and the presence of members of his family who take turns to visit him, Anthony Bland

has no consciousness at all. The parts of his brain which provided him with consciousness have turned to fluid. The darkness and oblivion which descended at Hillsborough will never depart. His body is alive, but he has no life in the sense that even the most pitifully handicapped but conscious human being has a life. But the advances of modern medicine permit him to be kept in this state for years, even perhaps for decades.[11]

Whatever the advances of modern medicine might permit, neither Tony Bland's family nor his doctors could see any benefit, to him or to anyone else, in keeping him alive for decades. In Britain, as in many other countries, when everyone is in agreement in these situations it is quite common for the doctors simply to withdraw artificial feeding. The patient then dies within a week or two. In this case, however, the coroner in Sheffield was inquiring into the deaths caused by the Hillsborough disaster, and Dr. Howe decided that he should notify the coroner of what he was intending to do. The coroner, while agreeing that Bland's continued existence could well be seen as entirely pointless, warned Dr. Howe that he was running the risk of criminal charges – possibly even a charge of murder – if he intentionally ended Bland's life.

After the coroner's warning, the administrator of the hospital in which Bland was a patient applied to the Family Division of the High Court for declarations that the hospital might lawfully discontinue all life-sustaining treatment, including ventilation, and the provision of food and water by artificial means, and discontinue all medical treatment to Bland "except for the sole purpose of enabling Anthony Bland to end his life and to die peacefully with the greatest dignity and the least distress."

At the Family Division hearing a public law officer called the Official Solicitor was appointed guardian for Bland for the purposes of the hearing. The Official Solicitor did not deny that Bland had no awareness at all, and could never recover, but he nevertheless opposed what Dr. Howe was planning to do, arguing that, legally, it was murder. Sir Stephen Brown, President of the Family Division, did not accept this view, and he made the requested declarations to the effect that all treatment might lawfully be stopped. The Official Solicitor appealed, but Brown's decision was upheld by the Court of Appeal. The Official Solicitor then appealed again, thus bringing the case before the House of Lords.

We can best appreciate the significance of what the House of Lords did in the case of Tony Bland by looking at what the United States Supreme Court would not do in the similar case of Nancy Cruzan. Like Bland, Cruzan was in a persistent vegetative state, without hope of recovery. Her parents went to court to get permission to remove her feeding tube. The Missouri Supreme Court refused, saying that since Nancy Cruzan was not competent to refuse life-sustaining treatment herself, and the state has an interest in preserving life, the court could only give permission for the withdrawal of life-sustaining treatment if there were clear and convincing evidence that this was what Cruzan would have wanted. No such evidence had been presented to the court. On appeal, the United States Supreme Court upheld this judgment, ruling that the state of Missouri had a right to require clear and convincing evidence that Cruzan would have wanted to be allowed to die, before permitting doctors to take that step. (By a curious coincidence, that evidence was produced in court shortly after the Supreme Court decision, and Cruzan was allowed to die.)

The essential point here is that in America the courts have so far taken it for granted that life-support must be continued, *unless* there is evidence indicating that the patient would not have wished to be kept alive in the circumstances in which she now is. In contrast, the British courts were quite untroubled by the absence of any information about what Bland's wishes might have been. As Sir Thomas Bingham, Master of the Rolls of the Court of Appeal, said in delivering his judgment:

> At no time before the disaster did Mr Bland give any indication of his wishes should he find himself in such a condition. It is not a topic most adolescents address.[12]

But the British courts did not therefore conclude that Bland must be treated until he died of old age. Instead, the British judges asked a different question: what is in the best interests of the patient?[13] In answer, they referred to the unanimous medical opinion that Bland was not aware of anything, and that there was no prospect of any improvement in his condition. Hence the treatment that was sustaining Bland's life brought him, as Sir Stephen Brown put it in the initial judgment in the case, "no therapeutical, medical, or other benefit."[14] In essence, the British courts held that when a patient is incapable of consenting to medical treatment, doctors are under no legal duty to continue treatment that does not benefit a patient. In addition, the judges agreed that the mere continuation of biological life is not, in the absence of any awareness or any hope of ever again becoming aware, a benefit to the patient.

On one level, the British approach is straightforward common sense. But it is common sense that breaks new legal ground. To see this, consider the following quotation from John Keown:

> Traditional medical ethics...never asks whether the patient's *life* is worthwhile, for the notion of a worthless life is as alien to the Hippocratic tradition as it is to English criminal law, both of which subscribe to the principle of the sanctity of human life which holds that, because all lives are intrinsically valuable, it is always wrong intentionally to kill an innocent human being.[15]

As a statement of traditional medical ethics and traditional English criminal law, this is right. The significance of the *Bland* decision is that it openly embraces the previously alien idea of a worthless life. Sir Thomas Bingham, for example, said:

> Looking at the matter as objectively as I can, and doing my best to look at the matter through Mr Bland's eyes and not my own, I cannot conceive what benefit his continued existence could be thought to give him...[16]

When the case came before the House of Lords, their lordships took the same view. Lord Keith of Kinkel discussed the difficulties of making a value judgment about the life of a "permanently insensate" being, and concluded cautiously that:

> It is, however, perhaps permissible to say that to an individual with no cognitive capacity whatever, and no prospect of ever recovering any such capacity in this world, it must be a matter of complete indifference whether he lives or dies.[17]

In a similar vein, Lord Mustill concluded that to withdraw life-support is not only legally but also ethically justified, "since the continued treatment of Anthony Bland can no longer serve to maintain that combination of manifold characteristics which we call a personality."[18]

There can therefore be no doubt that with the decision in the Bland case, British law has abandoned the idea that life itself is a benefit to the person living it, irrespective of its quality. But that is not all that their lordships did in deciding Tony Bland's fate. The second novel aspect of their decision is that it was as plain as anything can be that the proposal to discontinue tube feeding was *intended* to bring about Bland's death. A majority of the judges in the House of Lords referred to the administrator's intention in very direct terms. Lord Browne-Wilkinson said:

> What is proposed in the present case is to adopt a course with the intention of bringing about Anthony Bland's death...the whole purpose of stopping artificial feeding is to bring about the death of Anthony Bland.[19]

Lord Mustill was equally explicit:

> the proposed conduct has the aim for...humane reasons of terminating the life of Anthony Bland by withholding from him the basic necessities of life.[20]

This marks a sharp contrast to what for many years was considered the definitive view of what a doctor may permissibly intend. Traditionally the law had held that while a doctor may knowingly do something that has the effect of shortening life, this must always be a mere side-effect of an action with a different purpose, for example, relieving pain. As Justice (later Lord) Devlin said in the celebrated trial of Dr John Bodkin Adams:

> . . . it remains the fact, and it remains the law, that no doctor, nor any man, no more in the case of the dying than of the healthy, has the right deliberately to cut the thread of human life.[21]

In rewriting the law of murder regarding the question of intention, the British law lords have shown a clarity and forthrightness that should serve as a model to many others who try to muddle through difficult questions by having a little bit of both sides. There is no talk here of ordinary and extraordinary means of treatment, nor of what is directly intended and what is merely foreseen. Instead the judges declared that Bland's doctors were entitled to take a course of action that had Bland's death as its "whole purpose"; and they made this declaration on the basis of a judgment that prolonging Bland's life did not benefit him.

Granted, this very clarity forces on us a further question: does the decision allow doctors to kill their patients? On the basis of what we have seen so far, this conclusion seems inescapable. Their lordships, however, did not think they were legalizing euthanasia. They drew a distinction between ending life by actively doing something, and ending life by not providing treatment needed to sustain life. That distinction has long been discussed by philosophers and bioethicists, who debate whether it can make good sense to accept passive euthanasia while rejecting active euthanasia. In the *Bland* case, it is significant that while the Law Lords insist that in distinguishing between acts and omissions they are merely applying the law as it stands, they explicitly recognize that at this point law and ethics have come apart, and something needs to be done about it. Lord Browne-Wilkinson, for example, expressed the hope that Parliament would review the law. He then ended his judgment by admitting that he could not provide a moral basis for the legal decision he had reached! Lord Mustill was just as frank and even more uncomfortable about the state of the law, saying that the judgment, in which he had shared, "may only emphasize the distortions of a legal structure which is already both morally and intellectually misshapen."[22]

The Law Lords' problem was that they had inherited a legal framework that allowed them some room to maneuver, but not a great deal. Within that framework, they did what they could to reach a sensible decision in the case of Anthony Bland, and to point the law in a new direction that other judges could follow. In doing so, they recognized the moral incoherence of the position they were taking, but found themselves unable to do anything about it, beyond drawing the problem to the attention of Parliament. They could hardly have done more to show clearly the need for a new approach to life-and-death decisions.

IV   Conclusion

What is the link between the problems we face in regard to the concept of brain death, and the decision reached by their lordships in the case of Tony Bland? The link becomes clearer once we distinguish between three separate questions, often muddled in discussions of brain death and related issues:

1   When does a human being die?
2   When is it permissible for doctors intentionally to end the life of a patient?
3   When is it permissible to remove organs such as the heart from a human being for the purpose of transplantation to another human being?

Before 1968, in accordance with the traditional concept of death, the answer to the first question would have been: when the circulation of the blood stops permanently, with the consequent cessation of breathing, of a pulse, and so on.[23] The answer to the second question would then have been very simple: never. And the answer to the third question would have been equally plain: when the human being is dead.

The acceptance of the concept of brain death enabled us to hold constant the straightforward answers to questions two and three, while making what was presented as no more than a scientific updating of a concept of death rendered obsolete by technological advances in medicine. Thus no ethical question appeared to be at issue, but suddenly hearts could be removed from, and machines turned off, on a whole new group of human beings.

The *Bland* decision says nothing about questions 1 and 3, but dramatically changes the answer that British law gives to question 2. The simple "never" now becomes "when the patient's continued life is of no benefit to her": and if we ask when a patient's life is of no benefit to her, the answer is: "when the patient is irreversibly unconscious." If we accept this as a sound answer to question 2, however, we may well wish to give the same answer to question 3. Why not, after all? And if we now have answered both question 2 and question 3 by reference not to the death of the patient, but to the impossibility of the patient regaining consciousness, then question 1 suddenly becomes much less relevant to the concerns that the Harvard Brain Death Committee was trying to address. We could therefore abandon the redefinition of death that it pioneered, with all the problems that have now arisen for the brain death criterion. Nor would we feel any pressure to move a step further, to defining death in terms of the death of the higher brain, or cerebral cortex. Instead, we could, without causing any problems in the procurement of organs or the withdrawal of life-support, go back to the traditional conception of death in terms of the irreversible cessation of the circulation of the blood.[24]

Notes

1   Henry Beecher to Robert Ebert, 30 October 1967. The letter is in the Henry Beecher manuscripts at the Francis A. Countway Library of Medicine, Harvard University, and is noted by David Rothman, *Strangers at the Bedside* (New York: Basic Books, 1991), pp. 160–1.

2   The first draft and Ebert's comment on it are both quoted by Rothman, *Strangers at the Bedside*, pp. 162–4. The documents are in the Beecher Manuscript collection.

3   Henry Beecher, "The New Definition of Death, Some Opposing Viewpoints," *International Journal of Clinical Pharmacology*, 5 (1971), pp. 120–1 (italics in original).

4   President's Commission for the Study of Ethical Problems in Medicine, *Defining Death: A Report on the Medical, Legal and Ethical Issues in the Determination of Death* Washington, DC: US Government Printing Office, 1981, pp. 24, 25.

5   *Defining Death*, pp. 67, 72.

6   Stuart Youngner et al., "'Brain Death' and Organ Retrieval: A Cross-sectional Survey of Knowledge and Concepts Among Health Professionals," *Journal of the American Medical Association*, 261 (1990), p. 2209.

7   See, for example, the United States Uniform Determination of Death Act. Note that the Harvard Committee had referred to the absence of central nervous system "activity" rather than function. The use of the term "function" rather than "activity" makes the definition of brain death more permissive, because, as the United States President's Commission recognized (*Defining Death*, p. 74), electrical and metabolic activity may continue in cells or groups of cells after the organ has ceased to function. The Commission did not think that the continuation of this activity should prevent a declaration of death.

8   Robert Truog, "Rethinking brain death," in K. Sanders and B. Moore (eds.), *Anencephalics, Infants, and Brain Death Treatment Options and the Issue of Organ Donation* (Law Reform Commission of Victoria, Melbourne, 1991), pp. 62–74; Amir Halevy and Baruch Brody, "Brain Death: Reconciling Definitions, Criteria and Tests," *Annals of Internal Medicine*, 119:6 (1993), pp. 519–25; Robert Veatch, "The Impending Collapse of the Whole-Brain Definition of Death," *Hastings Center Report*, 23:4 (1993), pp. 18–24.

9   Henry Beecher, "The New Definition of Death: Some Opposing Views," unpublished paper presented at the meeting of the American Association for the Advancement of Science, December 1970, p. 4, quoted from Robert Veatch, *Death, Dying, and the Biological Revolution*, New Haven: Yale University Press, 1976, p. 39.

10　*Cruzan v. Director, Missouri Department of Health* (1990) 110 S. Ct. pp. 2886–7.

11　*Airedale N.H.S. Trust v. Bland (C.A)* (19 February 1993) 2 Weekly Law Reports, p. 350.

12　Ibid., p. 333; the passage was quoted again by Lord Goff of Chieveley in his judgment in the House of Lords, p. 364.

13　Ibid., pp. 374, 386.

14　Ibid., p. 331.

15　John Keown, "Courting Euthanasia? Tony Bland and the Law Lords", *Ethics & Medicine*, 9:3 (1993) p. 36.

16　*Airedale N.H.S. Trust v. Bland*, p. 339.

17　Ibid., p. 361.

18　Ibid., p. 400.

19　Ibid., p. 383.

20　Ibid., p. 388.

21　*R. v. Adams* (1959), quoted by Derek Morgan, "Letting babies die legally," *Institute of Medical Ethics Bulletin* (May 1989), p. 13. See also Patrick Devlin, *Easing the Passing: The Trial of Dr John Bodkin Adams* (London: Faber and Faber, 1986), pp. 171, 209.

22　*Airedale N.H.S. Trust v. Bland*, pp. 388–9.

23　For a statement of the traditional definition, see, for example, *Blacks Law Dictionary*, 4th edn. (London: West, 1968).

24　This address incorporates material subsequently published in my book *Rethinking Life and Death* (Melbourne: Text, 1994; New York: St. Martin's Press, 1995).

Part Six

Choosing Between Lives

Eighteen

Allocating Health Care Resources and the Problem of the Value of Life

Helga Kuhse and Peter Singer

Each year hundreds, if not thousands, of new medical technologies enter the health care system – from drugs to therapeutic and diagnostic devices to such dramatic procedures as the transplantation of donor organs and artificial hearts. They may make the difference between a patient's living or dying. But they also raise some very profound ethical questions regarding the value of life. These questions arise not only at the level of individual patients and their doctors, but also at the level of governments and health care policy-makers, who must decide what technologies to employ when a society cannot afford them all.

We shall begin by discussing some of these issues as they arise at the individual or patient/doctor level; we shall then take a brief look at resource allocation questions on a social level; and, finally, we shall raise the issue of how we might maximize our chances of having a long and healthy life.

I

On the individual patient/doctor level, the most common question is whether a particular medical treatment should or should not be given to a particular patient. This question might arise because there is a shortage of resources – where, say, two patients need artificial respiration but only one respirator is

First published in *Death and the Value of Life*, ed. David Cockburn (*Trivium*, 27, 1992), pp. 7–23. Reprinted with permission of Trivium Publications.

available. We shall, however, not discuss the issue of resource rationing – or triage – at the doctor/patient level. We believe – although space does not allow us to argue for it here – that it would be inappropriate for doctors to take on the role of triage masters. The traditional role of doctors has been to act in their patients' best interests; they would be ill-suited to act as "gate-keepers" for society's limited resources. If hard choices have to be made, these ought to be made by society as a whole.[1]

But the question of whether a particular medical treatment should be administered to a particular patient also arises when there is no shortage of resources. This is probably the most common situation facing patients and doctors, and the one we assume for the first part of our subsequent discussion. Here we shall focus on the most momentous of these treatment decisions: those concerning life and death. Should aggressive attempts always be made to prolong every patient's life, or are there times when a readily available life-sustaining means should not be employed and the patient allowed to die? Whilst we might readily agree that doctors should normally do everything they can to prolong their patients' lives, should they, for example, also resuscitate the patient suffering from an inoperable and painful cancer so that she may have another week or two of life; and should they do everything possible to sustain the life of a patient who is permanently comatose, even though she will never again have any conscious experiences?

These questions bring us quickly to a fundamental ethical and philosophical issue – that of the value of life. Is human life intrinsically valuable, that is, valuable in itself, irrespective of its quality? Or is it valuable only when it has a certain quality and is of value to the person whose life it is? We believe (and we have argued for this elsewhere) that *human* life is not the only life that has value. The lives of other conscious or self-conscious creatures – rats, cats, dogs, whales, pigs, and, if there be any, Martians – have value too. Moreover, we also believe that life is *not* an intrinsic good, not a good in itself, but rather a precondition for other goods or values, such as the existence of pleasurable states of consciousness, the satisfaction of preferences and desires, and so on.[2]

Karen Ann Quinlan

Take the well-known case of Karen Ann Quinlan, the New Jersey woman who, in 1975, was diagnosed as irreversibly comatose. Until her death in 1985, Karen Quinlan's life was sustained by various medical means and she lived for another ten years. But did these additional ten years of life have any value? We think not. Karen Quinlan did not benefit from having her life prolonged: she had no conscious awareness of the extra years of life – for to be permanently comatose is, from the subjective point of view, the same as being dead.[3]

Abe Perlmutter

Similar questions about the value of life are raised by the case of Abe Perlmutter. In 1977, 73-year-old Abe Perlmutter was diagnosed as suffering from motor neuron disease, a progressively debilitating illness for which there is no cure. By May 1978 he was almost totally incapacitated and was sustained by a mechanical respirator, attached to a hole in his trachea.

As his condition became increasingly unbearable, Abe Perlmutter tried repeatedly to disconnect the respirator. He was thwarted each time by an automatic alarm which summoned nurses, who turned the machine back on. Finally, hospital personnel resorted to strapping his arms to his bed.

Abe Perlmutter filed a complaint with the Broward County Court in Florida, asking that he be given the right to determine whether or not to continue life-sustaining treatment. The judge paid a bedside visit to Abe Perlmutter to determine whether he was competent and understood that he would die if the tube connecting him to the respirator was removed. Abe Perlmutter indicated that he did understand. "Death," he whispered, "can't be any worse than what I'm going through now." The judge granted Abe Perlmutter's request and the Florida Supreme Court, to which the case was appealed, upheld that decision.

On October 4, 1978, Abe Perlmutter called his family to his bedside. His son unplugged the respirator and Abe Perlmutter removed the tube from his throat. He died forty hours later.[4]

These cases illustrate in a rough and ready way why we believe that life is not intrinsically valuable. Before life can have any value, there must be the capacity for conscious experience (this capacity was, of course, absent in the case of Karen Ann Quinlan); and these conscious experiences must be of a certain kind: they must be of value to the person whose life it is (Abe Perlmutter, for example, did not think that his severely truncated life had any value). We could also put this another way and say that it was not in Karen Ann Quinlan's and Abe Perlmutter's interests to have their lives prolonged.

There is thus a close connection between the value of life and the interests or desires of individual persons. Life may be in a person's interest, or it may not – depending on what the life is like.

But when is life – or death – in a person's best interests? The concept of "interests" is a difficult one but the following account will be adequate for our purposes. All patients capable of experiencing pleasant or unpleasant states of consciousness – and this includes newly born infants, patients who are senile, and many severely mentally retarded patients – have an interest in well-being, that is, in freedom from pain or suffering, restoration of functioning, and so on. But in addition to that, normal adult or competent patients also have an interest in self-determination – in controlling and shaping their lives and in acting as autonomous or self-determining moral agents. In other words, we are suggesting that there are two main values to which human life gives rise: pleasurable states of consciousness or well-being; and the value of liberty or self-determining action.[5]

What implications does this have for life and death decisions in medicine? In the case of incompetent patients an answer is relatively easy to find. Because there is only one value – well-being – incompetent patients should, other things being equal, have their lives prolonged if continued existence is of value or benefit to them. They should be allowed to die if their future existence is likely to hold more burdens than benefits. Of course, it will not always be easy to determine in practice when life or death is in such a patient's best interests. But in many cases, the answer will be fairly clear. Thus, focus on a Down's syndrome infant's future well-being will not in itself be a sufficient reason for withholding a simple life-saving operation to remove an intestinal obstruction. Whilst Down's syndrome is associated with mental retardation, it is not a painful condition and the child can, provided it is well cared for, expect to live a happy – albeit somewhat truncated – life. The case is different when an infant is born with a disease or disability that makes it likely that the child's life will contain little but pain and suffering. Here such conditions as Tay Sachs disease and epidermolysis bullosa come to mind. The latter is a painful blistering disease which, in its severe manifestations, makes it unlikely that an infant will survive for long. What is more, there is little to compensate such a child for the pain and suffering it must endure during its short life. These children cannot enjoy loving physical contact with their parents or those who look after them – for any handling is likely to damage their fragile skin and cause additional pain.[6]

But what about competent patients – patients like Abe Perlmutter or, to give another example, an elderly patient in her sixties who does not want to live in an incapacitated state and refuses to have her gangrenous leg amputated, knowing that she will die as a consequence? How do we balance her well-being against her decision not to have the life-saving surgery? At the very heart of medical decision-making there is thus a tension. It has its source in the choice between respecting the freedom and liberty of competent patients and securing their well-being.[7] How is this tension to be resolved?

John Stuart Mill's famous essay *On Liberty*, written more than a century ago, is still an excellent starting point for reflection on that issue.[8] Mill urged that the only legitimate basis on which the individual may be coerced is to protect others; the individual's own good, whether physical or mental, is not sufficient warrant.

Whilst we might not want to apply this principle too rigidly in all areas of life, we believe it ought to be the determining one in the practice of medicine where life and death decisions for seriously ill or incapacitated patients are at issue. Competent patients ought to be able to choose whether to have or refuse any treatment – including life-sustaining treatment. Because different patients value life, health, pain, or disability differently, they will also make different life and death decisions. These choices ought to be respected. To keep somebody alive who has a considered and enduring wish to die is to do that person great harm, just as it is to do great harm to allow to die someone who wants to go on living.

One thing is clear; resources spent on keeping patients alive for whom life no longer holds any value are ill spent, not only because these resources could have done some good in other areas of medicine, but also because such actions are not compatible with respect for the patient's liberty or autonomy, or, if the patient is incompetent, with her well-being.

Before we conclude this section, one final point needs to be raised: *how* patients should die if life-sustaining treatment is discontinued.

Many people draw a moral distinction between "doing something" that results in death and merely "doing nothing" that also results in death, or between killing a patient and allowing her to die. Those who subscribe to that distinction usually think that allowing to die is sometimes permissible, while killing – or helping to die – is not. We do not believe that there is an intrinsic moral distinction between killing and letting die. If all other morally relevant factors, such as motivation and outcome, are the same, then there is no morally relevant difference between the two.[9] This does not mean, though, that it is irrelevant whether a patient is killed or allowed to die. To the extent that being allowed to die can often be a drawn-out and distressing process (for example, it took Abe Perlmutter forty hours to die after the respirator was disconnected), we think that there will be circumstances where patients should not only be allowed to die, but should be *helped* to die – for example, when a competent patient requests active euthanasia, or when much suffering would be involved for a patient who cannot request active euthanasia for herself.

Now we turn from the perspective of the individual patient and doctor to that of policy-makers or administrators who must decide how to allocate resources between different areas of medicine.

II

But why, someone might ask, do problems of resource allocation in health care arise? Part of the answer is that there are problems because many new, and often expensive, medical technologies have been developed that were simply not available a decade or two ago. We need to think here only of such diagnostic procedures as CAT scans or nuclear magnetic resonance imaging, of large-scale testing programs for breast or cervical cancers, or of therapies such as organ transplants, *in vitro* fertilization, total parenteral nutrition, neonatal intensive care for extremely premature infants weighing as little as 500 grams, and so on. The other part of the answer is that medicine's successes in saving many lives that would have been lost in earlier times have led to changes in disease patterns and related demographic changes. For example, there are now many more older people than there were even in the 1950s; and older people are generally more likely to suffer from chronic diseases and disabilities requiring medical treatment than younger ones. The following figures come from the United States, but similar trends can be found in many other developed countries as well. In 1950, 12.3 million (8.1 percent of the population) were older than 65 years. It is now projected that the number of persons older than 65 years will be 31.8 million (12.2 percent of the population) by the year 2000 – an increase of 157 percent in fifty years. But the longer people live, the more likely they are to develop chronic diseases and disabilities, with the consequence that there is a continually increasing demand for health care.[10]

Pressures on resources also come from the other end of life. It is now possible to keep alive infants born after a gestation period of only 24 or 25 weeks, and weighing as little as 500 grams. But, again, such lives have a price. A recent Australian study has conservatively estimated that if neonatal intensive care were offered to all premature infants weighing 500 grams or more, this would on average cost $A50,000 per life saved.[11] Costs for individual infants may far exceed this amount. In the USA, where health care costs are considerably higher than in Australia, an individual premature infant may incur costs in excess of $US500,000 – without this huge expenditure being any guarantee that the infant will survive, or survive without serious handicap. Can we afford all the health care that all people might need or want? Can we afford to save or prolong every life that might be prolonged?

People will often say "Life is infinitely valuable" or "Expense is no consideration when a life is at stake." But we live in a world of limited resources and in such a world absolutes can have no place. Australia is currently spending some 8 percent of its GNP on health care,[12] and the 1980 US figure was 11 percent.[13] If we were to double or treble these amounts, many more lives could be saved – but these lives would have a price: every dollar spent on health care is a dollar that cannot be spent on something else that we value – better and safer roads, national parks, overseas aid, education, the arts, defense, and so on. In demanding both lower taxes and upper limits on health insurance premiums, people are indicating that they value other goods and services more than an ever-increasing supply of health care. This means that there will always be some health care needs that will not be met, some lives that will not be saved. Thus we need to find some way of deciding how best to allocate our health care dollars: how many dollars should we allocate to, say, neonatal intensive care for extremely premature infants, how many dollars to the treatment of end-stage renal disease, and how many dollars to the treatment of such crippling diseases as arthritis and osteoporosis?

It is sometimes suggested that these questions are unanswerable and that the distribution of health care resources should be left to the market. Just as the market decides who gets other goods and services, so the market should decide who gets such health care goods and services as kidney dialysis, a new heart, or neonatal intensive care. Most developed societies believe, however, that the poor and those unable to care for themselves should not die for want of treatment. They allocate public funds to ensure that at least some basic level of health care is available to the poor. This means that even if the market were allowed to prevail in some areas of health care, we would still need to find some way of deciding how best to allocate our public funds – how to get the most value for each dollar spent.

Cost-effectiveness analysis is an attempt to provide such an evaluation of health care. It requires the identification and quantification of costs, and offers a means of comparing the value we are getting for our dollars in different medical programs. But an important assumption underlies cost-effectiveness analysis: the assumption that the lives of the young are worth more than the lives of the old, and that it is, other things being equal, always better to save a young person rather than an older one. (Whilst we restrict our discussion to cost-effectiveness analysis, much of what we have to say about cost-effectiveness analysis is, however, also applicable to another widely used method of evaluating the efficacy of health care spending, cost-benefit analysis.)[14]

In the present section, we shall give one major reason why we regard these assumptions as problematical and why we think that it is not always better to save a very young patient in preference to an older one; in the third and final section of the paper, we shall once again raise the question of age and argue that some non-objectionable discrimination against the aged will maximize everyone's chances of leading a long and healthy life.

How, then, does cost-effectiveness analysis attempt to measure the efficacy of health care programs? The first problem is to define the benefit in terms of which efficacy is to be measured. Traditionally, in life-endangering situations, that benefit has been easy to find. A treatment is more effective, or gives us more value for our money, if – for a given cost – it saves more lives than another program or treatment.

But to speak of benefits simply in terms of "lives saved" is clearly not enough. Surely, when we want to evaluate a treatment's efficacy, we are interested not only in whether a treatment can "save a life," but also for *how long* it can save a life, and what the *quality* of that life will be like. Thus, whilst a longer life is normally preferable to a shorter one, the cases of Karen Ann Quinlan and Abe Perlmutter illustrate that this may not always be the case.

An increasingly prominent way of measuring the effectiveness of health care programs has recently been developed. It combines length of survival with an attempt to measure the quality of the additional life years gained: the *quality-adjusted life year* or *QALY*.

The QALY was developed by Alan Williams, a well-known British health economist. He describes it in the following way:

> The essence of a QALY is that it takes a year of healthy life expectancy to be worth 1, but regards a year of unhealthy life expectancy as worth less than 1. Its precise value is lower the worse the quality of life of the unhealthy person (which is what the "quality adjusted" bit is all about). If being dead is worth zero, it is, in principle, possible for a QALY to be negative, i.e., for the quality of someone's life to be judged worse than being dead.

> The general idea is that a beneficial health care activity is one that generates a positive amount of QALYs, and that an efficient health care activity is one where the cost per QALY is as low as it can be. A high-priority health care activity is one where the cost-per-QALY is low, and a low-priority activity is one where cost-per-QALY is high.[15]

The essential idea of a quality-adjusted life year is thus simple. If you believe that a year of life with a particular condition – say, end-stage renal failure requiring dialysis – is worth only half as much as a year of normal life, it would attract a QALY value of 0.5 – or, to put it another way, it would indicate that you would be willing to give up two years of life on a kidney machine for one year of normal life.

A life without consciousness – like that of Karen Ann Quinlan – would attract no QALYs at all – for (as we argued earlier) to be permanently comatose is from the patient's point of view the same as being dead; and being dead, of course, rates as zero on Alan Williams' scale of effectiveness.

A life like Abe Perlmutter's, on the other hand, might attract a negative QALY rating. Abe Perlmutter at least preferred death to continued life in an increasingly debilitated condition, and it is reasonable to suppose that many other people would have similar preferences.

But there are two main ways in which QALYs can be used.

Firstly, they can be used to decide which one of two alternative therapies is more efficacious in treating a particular medical condition. Let us assume that a new method of treating end-stage renal failure has been developed which produces more QALYs than other conventional methods. Clearly, in such a situation it would be desirable to adopt the new method – both from the individual's point of view and also from the vantage point of a society trying to cope with limited health care resources.

We regard this way of applying QALYs as relatively unproblematical. It is the second way of applying QALYs that raises concerns. QALYs could also be used to decide not whether particular patients would be better served by, say, our hypothetical new method of treating end-stage kidney disease than by one of the traditional methods, but rather to decide which treatments (and, by implication, categories of patients) should have priority in the allocation of health care resources. It is here that the systematic age bias of QALYs emerges.

Let us assume that we cannot afford all treatments for all people. Which treatments should we select? QALYs would offer us an initially persuasive and attractive way of choosing between health care programs. They would allow us to rank all programs and treatments in terms of the QALYs they produce, thus enabling us to make what appears to be a rational choice. Those treatments and programs that produce most QALYs will be funded first, then those that produce slightly less, and so on, until all our funds are exhausted. Whilst this would leave some programs unfunded, the unfunded programs would be the least efficient ones in terms of the QALYs that they produce. This would seem a reasonable policy to adopt.

Before we too readily embrace QALYs as the solution to our allocation problems, however, we need to reflect a little further. Suppose that we wanted to compare the efficacy of neonatal intensive care for premature infants with that of other medical procedures. In a well-known study, researchers from McMaster University in Ontario, Canada have investigated the cost of neonatal intensive care. This study found that with infants weighing from 500 to 999 grams, the cost of neonatal intensive care per quality-adjusted life year gained was $22,400 (expressed in 1978 Canadian dollars).[16] One of Australia's leading neonatologists has compared the results of this study with those of other studies of medical practices. The comparison shows that neonatal intensive care for these very small babies costs more, per QALY gained, than antepartum anti-D therapy, or thyroid screening, or treatment for both severe and mild hypertension; but it costs less than coronary artery bypass surgery, or continuous ambulatory peritoneal dialysis, or hospital hemodialysis.[17] Does this mean that we should necessarily choose neonatal intensive care in preference to coronary artery bypass surgery or dialysis? We think not. Our reasons have to do with differences in the interests of these two groups of patients, and with the special status of newly born infants.

Most of the potential recipients of dialysis or coronary bypass surgery are elderly patients; all of the potential recipients of neonatal intensive care are very young infants. This difference in the ages of the two groups of patients explains, of course, why saving an infant will – for the same amount of dollars spent – produce more QALYs than saving an older patient.[18]

But it is not only a difference in age which separates these two groups of patients; there is also a difference in interests, and it is this difference in interests which makes a comparison of the programs in terms of QALYs inappropriate.

Because premature infants, unlike older patients, are not self-determining moral agents, their interests are necessarily limited to their well-being (freedom from pain, being warm and well-fed, and so on); the typical recipients of coronory bypass surgery and kidney dialysis, on the other hand, have interests that go far beyond well-being. As we argued in section I, competent patients do not only have an interest in well-being, but also in liberty and in acting as self-determining autonomous moral agents. There is, however, another cluster of related and morally relevant differences between infants and older patients as well. Infants, because they have but simple and short-term interests, cannot desire their own continued existence, they cannot value their own lives in the way in which older patients do; they have no hopes and plans for the future, and they are quite unaware of the prospect of death. Thus, as far as their present capacities and interests are concerned, premature infants are much more like fetuses or some nonhuman animals than like normal adults. In other words, the life of an infant does not have the same value as the life of an older person. But if this is correct, then it must also be correct that QALYs cannot readily be employed to help us choose between health-care programs for very young children on the one hand and health-care programs for older patients on the other.

III

Despite these obvious difficulties, however, we believe that QALYs, or a close analogue of them, are an indispensable tool in helping us to decide between health care programs for groups of patients who share the same interests. Here, too, QALYs will favor the young. But is it always morally indefensible to have a medical policy that favours younger patients over older ones – a policy, say, that favours a 20-year-old patient over a 65-year-old patient – when both have the same interests, value their own life, and desire their continued existence? Take the practice of the British National Health Service of not providing renal dialysis to those aged 65 and more.[19] Can such discrimination on the basis of age ever be justified?

For the purposes of our reflections, let us assume that kidney transplants are just as medically effective for those aged 65 and more as they are for younger patients. We need to make this assumption so that age is not simply a guide to medical suitability for a treatment. An analysis based on quality-adjusted life years would favor the younger patient. Should we reject it, just as we rejected QALYs as an appropriate tool for evaluating neonatal intensive care?

Some people believe that discrimination against the aged can be justified. After all, so the argument might go, aged people have had their life and if substantial medical resources are required to keep them alive, it might be better if these resources were spent on younger members of society. As the Governor of Colorado, Richard D. Lamm, put it in a widely publicized statement in March 1984: the aged may have a "duty to die."

This point was already made in 1975 by Dr. Donald Gould, when he wrote in the *New Statesman*:

> In the name of justice, as well as efficiency, we have got to adopt new methods of medical accounting. One such assesses the relative importance of threats to health in terms of the loss of life-years they cause. Calculations are based on the assumption that all who survive their first perilous year ought then to live to the age of 70 (any extra years are a bonus). In Denmark, for example, there are 50,000 deaths a year, but only 20,000 among citizens in the 1–70 bracket. These are the ones that count. The annual number of life-years lost in this group totals 264,000. Of these, 80,000 are lost because of accidents and suicides, 40,000 because of coronary heart disease, and 20,000 are due to lung disease. On the basis of these figures, a large proportion of the "health" budget ought to be spent on preventing accidents and suicides and a lesser but still substantial amount on attempting to prevent and cure heart and lung disease. Much less would be spent on cancer, which is predominantly a disease of the latter half of life, and which therefore contributes relatively little to the total sum of life-years lost. . . . No money at all would be available for trying to prolong the life of a sick old man of 82.[20]

If such a scheme would achieve a larger total number of QALYs, should we adopt it, or are there good reasons for resisting its introduction?

The British philosopher John Harris discusses the question of age discrimination in his book *The Value of Life*.[21] Harris argues that "ageism" (i.e. discrimination against the aged) is generally wrong because all those of us who want to go on living, no matter how old we are, have something that is of equal value to each one of us: the rest of our life. So long as we don't know when we will die, the "rest of our life" is of indefinite duration – regardless of whether we are 20 or 65 years old. Thus, the "rest of our life" is all any one of us can ever have and it would be invidious to give preference to a 20-year-old over a 30-year-old, or a 30-year-old over a 65-year-old.

Harris's argument is thus that there is something wrong about preferring a younger person to an older one if both value their lives and desire to live the rest of their lives. It would be wrong, Harris says, to frustrate a person's desire to live merely because another individual who has exactly the same desire happens to have a longer statistical life expectancy.

But there is also another argument, Harris points out, which might pull us in a different direction. Whilst one might agree that the anti-ageist argument has some plausibility when we have to choose between, say, saving a 20-year-old and saving a 25-year-old, it becomes much less plausible when we have to choose between saving a 25-year-old and a 65- or even 85-year-old patient. Is it proper for a person who has had a "fair innings" to want more when somebody younger, who has not been as fortunate in getting so far, will lose out as a consequence?

We believe that the notion of a "fair innings" – traditionally thought of in terms of three score years plus ten – points us in the right direction. In a situation of scarcity, where an individual doctor would be forced to choose between two of her patients, it would seem morally appropriate to opt for the younger person if one but not both can be saved.

But should we also allow such discrimination on the basis of age on a social level, that is, should we adopt health-care policies that will favor those who have not yet had a "fair innings"? We believe the answer is a cautious "yes."

Suppose we were rational, self-interest-maximizing individuals, choosing a method of allocating medical resources from a position in which we are forced to choose impartially because we don't know our own medical conditions, genetic predispositions, environmental conditions, and, the focus of our present discussion, our age. Let us assume that we must, from behind such a "veil of ignorance,"[22] choose one of the following two schemes for the society in which we live:[23]

SCHEME *A* has some similarities with the British National Health Service and permits no one over the age of 65 or 70 to get certain high-cost life-extending technologies, such as dialysis, bypass operations, or angioplasty. Because rationing by age will greatly reduce the utilization of each technology, funds will become available for the further development of these services, and the possible development of other services.

SCHEME *B* rejects rationing on the basis of age. With medical suitability and need being the only selection criteria, it can develop just one such service – e.g. dialysis – making it available to anyone who needs it; or it can develop several technologies and ration them by, say, lottery.

Which scheme should we rationally choose if we wanted to maximize our chances of having as long and healthy a life as possible? As rational and prudent individuals (who, it will be remembered, do not know whether they will be old or young, or sick or healthy), we would most likely choose Scheme A. Scheme A would entail that certain expensive life-extending technologies would not be available to people who have reached a certain age, but through this self-imposed restriction, we would be able to maximize our chances of gaining most in terms of QALYs.

The restriction of expensive life-extending services to the aged would allow the expansion of life-saving services to the young and would also provide other health and social support services which could greatly improve the *quality* of the lives for the aged. Whilst it is true that we increase our chances of shortening our life in old age because of this restriction, we might also reason that this risk is well worth taking. At a time when we have had a "fair innings," many of us will prefer quality of life to quantity.

This imaginative exercise shows, we believe, that some rationing of health-care services to the aged can be justified. Such rationing need not be discriminatory in a morally objectionable sense. Viewed from a social perspective over time, discrimination on the basis of age in the provision of life-sustaining technology is fundamentally different from other objectionable forms of discrimination, such as racism and sexism. Racism and sexism discriminate on the basis of irrelevant characteristics, and cannot be justified from an impartial point of view. When length of life is at stake, however, preference for those who have longer to live or who have not had a "fair innings" can be justified from an impartial perspective. We were all young once and, as long as life is of value to us, hope to get old. This means that we would not be choosing unfairly if, because we consider the *whole* of our lives, we choose to restrict some treatments on the basis of age. Viewed timelessly, such a policy is in *everyone's* interest.

It is important to note the qualification we have made – "when length of life is at stake." Discrimination against the elderly *is* just as indefensible as racism or sexism when it means that the interests of the young are treated more favorably than the *similar* interests of the old. For example, it is just as bad for an elderly person to have to live through a year of chronic pain as it is for a young person to have to live through such a year; just as bad for an elderly person to have to put up with preventable limited mobility for six months as it would be for a younger person; and so on. Since it is a fundamental principle of morality or justice that like interests be treated alike, a morally defensible health care policy would have to ensure that there is no discrimination against the elderly when such things as pain, suffering, handicaps, and discomforts are at issue.

It is important to draw out one of the implications of this. Death will not always come swiftly when life-sustaining treatment is denied and the patient may experience a slow and distressing decline – as might, for example, be the case when a patient suffers renal failure and dialysis is not provided. This means that a society which rations life-sustaining treatment to some of its members must still divert adequate funds into palliative and other care for these dying patients. It would also mean that such a society will have to consider seriously the question of active euthanasia. Whilst numerous groups and individuals are already demanding active voluntary euthanasia as a right, it will be much harder to ignore the possible demands of those who are denied life-sustaining treatment as a matter of public policy and suffer as a consequence.[24]

These are not pleasant scenarios to contemplate and it would be nice if rationing could be avoided. But this does not appear to be an option open to us. Implicit rationing is already taking place in many countries and is likely to become more prevalent and more visible.[25] As one respected American analyst recently put it: "Of all the resource-shortage crises this nation is expected to confront in the future, the problem is likely to be most acute and problematic in medicine . . . the future is likely to be filled with accounts of persons who have been refused treatment."[26]

It is high time, then, that we gave some serious thought to policies that will allow us to allocate our limited resources on a rational basis. The present approach will not do – at least, not if the comment of the chief executive of a major Australian hospital is an indication of what generally happens in the area of resource allocation. Asked at a conference which touched on resource allocation how hospitals justified their requests for funds, he replied that it was just a case of "pigs in the trough – get your snouts in first, and spread your elbows wide to keep your neighbors from getting what is yours."[27]

Let us draw our conclusions together. In the first part of our paper, we argued that human life has no intrinsic value but gives rise to two values: well-being and the value of liberty or self-determining action. We argued that doctors should, whenever possible, maximize these values. This may include active euthanasia, and we accepted this implication. We also suggested that doctors should not be forced into a position where they are rationing health care for their own patients. But health care must somehow be rationed. This, then, must be the task of health-care administrators and duly elected governments. In section II, we said that in order to be able to evaluate and compare different health-care programs, we have to use techniques like cost-effectiveness analyses which allow us to measure, in terms of the value of life gained, the effectiveness of different treatments and programs. This brought us to the notion of a quality-adjusted life year, or QALY. But QALYs tend to favor the young. We have questioned whether this is appropriate when all things are not equal – as they are not when we compare the life of a newborn infant with the life of an older person. But when everything is equal, and length of life itself is at stake, then – we said in section III of our paper – we consider it legitimate to favor the young – provided, once again, that those who die because they are denied life-sustaining treatment receive adequate palliative and other care, which may have to include active euthanasia.

Notes

1 Norman G. Levinsky, "The Doctor's Master," *New England Journal of Medicine*, 311 (1984), pp. 1573–5.

2 See, for example, Peter Singer, *Practical Ethics* (Cambridge: Cambridge University Press, 1979); Helga Kuhse, *The Sanctity-of-Life Doctrine in Medicine: A Critique* (Oxford: Clarendon Press, 1987).

3 *In the Matter of Karen Quinlan, an Alleged Incompetent*, 70 N.J., Supreme Court of New Jersey, argued Jan. 26, 1976.

4 See, for example, Mary Voboril, *Miami Herald*, July 1, 1978 (as cited by Margaret Pabst Battin, "Euthanasia," in D. VanDeWeer and T. Regan (eds.), *Health Care Ethics* (Philadelphia: Temple University Press, 1987), p. 60.

5 See also President's Commission for the Study of Ethical Problems in Medicine and Biomedical and Behavioral Research: *Deciding to Forgo Life-Sustaining Treatment: Ethical, Medical, and Legal Issues in Treatment Decisions* (Washington, DC: Government Printing Office, 1983).

6 For an account of the short life of "Stephanie," a baby afflicted with epidermolysis bullosa, see F. Frohock, *Special Care: Medical Decisions at the Beginning of Life* (Chicago: University of Chicago Press, 1986); see also pp. 233–5 in this volume.

7 See note 5.

8 John Stuart Mill, *On Liberty* (London: J. M. Dent & Sons, 1960).

9 See note 5.

10 See, for example, Roger W. Evans, "Health Care Technology and the Inevitability of Resource Allocation and Rationing Decisions," Parts I and II, *Journal of the American Medical Association*, 249 (1983), pp. 2047–53 and 2208–19.

11 J. Beveridge, "The cost of caring for very low birthweight infants in relation to other health needs," in *The Very Low Birthweight Infant: Medical, Ethical, Social, Legal and Economic Considerations* (abstracts of a conference held at the University of Sydney, Westmead Centre, 1985).

12 J. Richardson, "Economic Assessment of Medical Technology: Problems and Solutions." Paper presented to the Workshop of Technologies and Health Care, Australian National University, 1985, p. 1.

13 Congress of the United States, Office of Technology Assessment, *Life-Sustaining Technologies and the Elderly* (Washington, DC: Government Printing Office, 1987), p. 65.

14 On the inherent age bias in these analyses, see also J. Avorn, "Benefit and Cost Analysis in Geriatric Care – Turning Age Discrimination into Health Policy," *New England Journal of Medicine*, 310 (1984), pp. 1294–301.

15 Alan Williams, "The Value of QALYs," *Health and Social Services Journal* (July 1985), p. 3.

16 M. H. Boyle, G. W. Torrance, J. P. Sinclair, and S. P. Horwood, "Economic Evaluation of Neonatal Intensive Care of Very-Low-Birth-Weight Infants," *New England Journal of Medicine*, 308 (1983), pp. 1330–7.

17 Y. V. H. Yu, "The Case for Neonatal Intensive Care," *Medical Journal of Australia*, 142 (1985), p. 154.

18 For a more detailed discussion of this, see Helga Kuhse and Peter Singer, *Should the Baby Live? The Problem of Handicapped Infants* (Oxford: Oxford University Press, 1985).

19 A. Caplan, "What are the Morals of our Treatment of Renal Failure," in L. J. Hodges (ed.) *Social Responsibility: Journalism, Law and Medicine* (Washington, DC: 1980), pp. 32–50.

20 We owe this quotation to Jonathan Glover, *Causing Death and Saving Lives* (Harmondsworth: Penguin Books, 1977), pp. 220–1.

21 John Harris, *The Value of Life* (Routledge & Kegan Paul, 1985).

22 This is the notion developed by John Rawls in his influential book *A Theory of Justice* (Cambridge, MA: Harvard University Press, 1971), where people in the "original position" must choose from behind a "veil of ignorance" the social institutions and patterns of distribution for their society.

23 These Schemes come from Normal Daniels, "Am I my parent's keeper?" in the Report of the President's Commission for the Study of Ethical Problems in Medicine and Biomedical and Behavioral Research: *Securing Access to Health Care: The Ethical Implications of Differences in the Availability of Health Services* (Washington, DC: Government Printing Office, 1983), vol. 2, pp. 265–91.

24 See also Margaret P. Battin, "Age Rationing and the Just Distribution of Health Care: Is There a Duty to Die?", *Ethics*, 97 (1987), pp. 317–40.

25 We are thinking here of long waiting lists for hip replacements in Victoria/ Melbourne, of nonmedically indicated age ceilings for organ transplants, and so on.

26 Roger W. Evans, "Health Care Technology," p. 2217.

27 As cited by Peter Singer, "A Report from Australia – Which Babies are too Expensive to Treat?" *Bioethics*, 1 (1987), pp. 275–83.

Nineteen

Double Jeopardy and the Use of QALYs in Health Care Allocation

Peter Singer, John McKie, Helga Kuhse, and Jeff Richardson

We can all agree that when we spend money from the public purse on health care, we should try to get value for money. But there the agreement stops. What *is* value for money in health care? The outcomes of health care expenditure are so diverse that we need a common standard by which to compare them. The most promising common standard, many believe, is the Quality Adjusted Life-Year, or QALY. In essence, this standard says that the value we get from spending money on health care can be measured in terms of the number of years of life gained, as long as we provide an appropriate rate of discount for periods in which, as a result of ill-health or disability, the quality of life is poor. Several techniques have been used to establish the appropriate rate of discount. The most direct of these, the time trade-off, asks people how long a period of life in the given health condition they would be prepared to trade for one year of normal health. For example, they may say that for one year in normal health, they would give up two years bedridden. Then the appropriate rate of discount for being bedridden is 0.5, because that is the rate of quality adjustment at which a gain of two life-years when bedridden equals a gain of one year in normal health.[1]

There are, however, several objections to the use of the QALY as a way of measuring the value gained by a given unit of health care expenditure. This article deals with one of them: that for those who are unfortunate enough to have a permanent disability or illness, the use of the QALY as a measure of

First published in the *Journal of Medical Ethics*, 21 (1995), pp. 144–50. Reprinted with permission of BMJ Publishing Group.

value gained by health care puts them at an additional disadvantage. The first appearance of this argument in the discussion of QALYs is, as far as we are aware, in an article by John Harris, and we follow him by referring to it as "double jeopardy."[2] In rejecting the Oregon plan for rationing health care, the United States Secretary for Health and Human Services used a form of the double jeopardy objection.[3]

Here is the way Harris puts the double jeopardy argument:

> QALYs dictate that because an individual is unfortunate, because she has once become a victim of disaster, we are required to visit upon her a second and perhaps graver misfortune. The first disaster leaves her with a poor quality of life and QALYs then require that in virtue of this she be ruled out as a candidate for life-saving treatment, or at best, that she be given little or no chance of benefiting from what little amelioration her condition admits of.[4]

What is sound, and what is unsound, in this objection?

1   Ameliorating the Victim's Condition

Harris says that if treatment is allocated on the basis of gaining the most QALYs per dollar, then "at best" the victim of an earlier disaster will have little or no chance of benefiting from treatment that could ameliorate her condition. Is this right?

Imagine that Karen is the victim of a disaster – to be precise, she has been injured in a car accident that has left her a paraplegic. She is confined to a wheelchair and has persistent, often severe, back pain. Let us assume that the QALY scale rates two years of life in this condition as worth one year of life in good health. Hence Karen's quality-of-life score is 0.5. Given her age and general health, her life expectancy is another forty years. Thus the number of QALYs that her life would be expected to contain, if her condition remains unchanged, is 20. Now let us assume that a treatment is available for Karen's back pain. She will still be a paraplegic, and need to use a wheelchair, but the pain will go entirely. Her quality-of-life score will rise from 0.5 to 0.75. The treatment will not change her life-expectancy. Hence the expected QALYs in her life will rise from 20 to 30.

Another woman, Lisa, was also injured in a car accident, but it can scarcely be called a disaster. If Lisa has no treatment, beyond the initial first aid she has already received, she will be left with a limp, but she will not have any pain from the injury. This gives her, we shall say, a quality-of-life score of 0.95. Her life expectancy is, like Karen's, forty years, so if her condition remains unchanged, she has an expectation of 38 QALYs. There is, however, a treatment that will eliminate the limp, returning her quality-of-life score to 1.00, and bringing her post-treatment QALY score to 40.

For simplicity, let us suppose that Karen's and Lisa's operations cost the same, $10,000 each. Is it true that allocating our health dollars so as to produce the largest number of QALYs per dollar will always give Karen – the victim of the disaster that has left her permanently a paraplegic – less chance of treatment than Lisa, who has suffered a relatively minor injury? Obviously not. The $10,000 we spend on Karen brings a net gain of 10 QALYs, in other words we have to spend $1,000 for each QALY gained. On the other hand the $10,000 we spend on Lisa returns us only 2 QALYs, at a cost of $5,000 per QALY. So if we spend our health care budget in order to maximize QALYs, we will prefer operations like those that Karen needs to operations like those that Lisa needs; there is no problem of double jeopardy here.

What the example shows is that where amelioration of a disabling or painful condition is possible, a policy of maximizing QALYs does not systematically disadvantage a person with a severe disability or illness. The reason for this is simple enough: what is important, from the point of view of using our health care resources effectively, is not the health status of the person at any one point in time (whether that is before the treatment or after the treatment) but rather the *change* in a person's health status brought about by medical intervention.[5] The principle of QALY maximization requires directing resources to those groups of patients where the greatest QALY gains can be expected, and this is not necessarily the patients who will have the highest QALY levels at the end of the treatment.

We have not yet, however, tackled the double jeopardy argument on its strongest ground.

2   Saving the Victim's Life

Now let us consider another couple, Michele and Nina, who have also had accidents, and suffered injuries identical to those suffered by Karen and Lisa, respectively, with one important difference: there is no treatment that can help either Michelle or Nina. For the rest of her life, Michelle must expect to be confined to a wheelchair, with persistent, and often severe, back pain; and Nina will walk with a limp for as long as she lives. Initially, it seems that this is likely to be forty years in each case; but then each of them is afflicted by a heart condition that, without treatment, will rapidly prove fatal. A heart transplant offers the only hope, at a cost of $100,000. What are the QALY implications of providing heart transplants to Michelle and Nina?

For simplicity, let us assume that without the transplant, each will die immediately, and with the transplant, each will live for forty years. Remember, however, that each year of Michelle's wheelchair-bound life is rated at only 0.5 QALYs, whereas Nina's rates 0.95 percent. So with the transplant, Michelle will have 20 QALYs and Nina 38. If the operation is given to Michelle each QALY gained will have cost $5,000, whereas if it is given to Nina, the cost per QALY gained will be only $2,632. If those in charge of the hospital budget were to ration heart transplants on the basis of these figures, Nina might receive a transplant whereas Michelle might miss out. Here indeed is a solid basis for Harris's assertion of double jeopardy: because Michelle was once a victim of an accident that left her with a much reduced quality of life, now it seems she is to be visited with a still greater misfortune. She will not receive the treatment she needs to have a chance of continuing to live.

It is easy enough to see what is going on here. As the case of Karen and Lisa made clear, the QALY approach does not take notice of an individual's quality of life *per se*, but it is sensitive to the incremental QALY gain which a treatment makes. In the case of Michelle and Nina, the gain is composed of two factors: the additional length of life, and the quality of this life. The former is the same for everyone in the two examples, but the latter is very different. Since one year of Michelle's life is equivalent to only half a year of life in full health, whereas the same length of time for Nina equals very nearly a full year in normal health, the QALY approach counts the gain made by the operation as much greater in the case of Nina than in the case of Michelle.

We accept, then, that there is some kind of double jeopardy in these circumstances. Intuitively, this seems unfair. But this intuition needs, at least, some scrutiny. If our resources are limited and we cannot save every life that could be saved by some form of health care, is it really unfair to give a lower priority to saving the lives of those with incurable conditions that significantly reduce their quality of life?

As a step towards an answer to this question, consider a final example. Two other patients, Otto and Richard, have not been in any accidents, but they have heart conditions just like those of Michelle and Nina. Without transplants they will soon die, with transplants they will be able to continue to live their lives in full health. But Otto also has an entirely separate incurable medical condition that – while it causes him no problems now – will suddenly flare up and end his life. Because of this, his life expectancy is only twenty years, whereas Richard's is almost twice this – to be precise, thirty-eight years.

In QALY terms, the Michelle/Nina pair of patients and the Otto/Richard pair are identical, and if heart transplants were being rationed on the basis of QALYs, preference would in each case be given to the second member of the pair. For those who count only QALYs, it makes no difference whether the smaller number of QALYs gained comes from a lower quality of life, or from a shorter expected lifespan. What about those who oppose the use of QALYs as a basis of allocation of health care? Does it make a difference to them whether QALYs disadvantage a person with a lower quality of life, or with a shorter expected lifespan?

Consistently with his general objection to QALYs, Harris would appear to hold that it is wrong to give preference to someone like Nina over someone like Michelle, and also wrong to give preference to someone like Richard over someone like Otto. In both cases, Harris thinks we should focus on the patients' desire to go on living, rather than the number of QALYs gained. Considering a case in which more QALYs can be gained by giving a life-saving treatment to one person, who with the treatment has a long life expectancy, rather than to six, who even with treatment have only a short life expectancy, he writes:

> If each of the seven *wants* to go on living for as long as he or she can, if each values the prospective term of remission available, then to choose between them on the basis of life-years (quality adjusted or not) is in this case to give no value to the lives of six people.[6]

And in a subsequent article Harris says:

> I believe that the value of life can only sensibly be taken to be that value that those alive place on their lives. Consequently, if you and I are of different ages but we both want to live, then it is unfair to prefer your life to mine simply because you are three months younger.[7]

The final sentence of the second passage invokes an example that makes it difficult to disagree with Harris's claim. But he is making it too easy for himself. If he wants to stand by the claim that the value of life is nothing else but the value that those alive place on their lives, he would have also to object to giving the treatment to Otto rather than Richard if they both wanted very much to live, even if the heart transplant could offer Otto only a year or two, while it still offered Richard thirty-eight years (and, we assume, everything else about Otto and Richard is the same – it is not the case that Otto needs the time to finish his literary masterpiece, or carry through his promising research into a method of achieving perpetual peace). Indeed, it isn't clear what basis Harris would have for giving the treatment to Richard rather than Otto, even if the latter would have only a month, or a week, to live. No doubt Harris would want to say that there is a threshold below which his argument is not valid – but if both Richard and Otto want to live, it is difficult to see how such a threshold could be defended, consistently with the general position Harris takes.

More Troubling

Although Harris objects to QALYs because they favor those who will live longer as well as because they favor those who have a better quality of life, some may think that the latter case is more troubling. But what about a case in which the difference in quality of life is as dramatic as was the difference in life expectancy in the version of the case of Otto and Richard that we have just considered? Suppose that Michelle's accident has made her a quadriplegic, and she finds her existence in this condition tolerable, but very much inferior to life before her accident. In fact, she says – and means it – that she would gladly give up ten years of life as a quadriplegic for a single year in normal health. This makes her QALY score 0.1. She has a life expectancy of forty years. If Nina, who has a similar life expectancy and a near-normal quality of life, needs a life-saving operation, would it be wrong to give her priority?

Some may say that it would be. But such intuitions should not be accepted uncritically. What could incline us to accept QALY verdicts when the difference in life expectancy is responsible for the difference in QALY outcomes, but not when the outcome is determined by differences in quality of life? We might be more confident that a difference in life expectancy is an objective measure of something, whereas we are suspicious of attempts to put cardinal values on people's quality of life. In other words, we know that two years are twice as long as one year, but we lack conviction that a year of life in normal health really is as good as two years of life scored as 0.5. We may know that that is exactly what the figures mean, if the scoring is done correctly, but we may reasonably doubt whether, in practice, anyone can possibly get such calculations right.

Another ground for doubts about giving preference to Nina takes us into more fundamental ethical questions. This is the view that because Michelle has suffered more from her accident than Nina, it is only fair to redress the balance by now conferring a benefit on her rather than on Nina. On the QALY approach this regard for past suffering is not relevant. The QALY approach is wholly forward-looking. All that matters is putting resources where they will achieve the greatest future QALY gain. In contrast, those who argue from a basis of desert or compensatory justice hold that people should not have to endure more than their "fair share" of human suffering, and we should do what we can to smooth out great differences in the amount people suffer.

This position is supported by Kappel and Sandøe, who distinguish between two different views concerning the span of time within which it is proper to compare the QALY gains and losses of different people:

The life-time view sees equality as something that concerns a whole life-time. To value the lives of two persons equally we should aim at distributing resources so that each in his life viewed as a whole will have his fundamental interests fulfilled to the same degree as the other person.

The present time view sees equality as something that concerns the present moment. To value the lives of two persons equally we should at any time aim at distributing resources so that they get their actual fundamental interests fulfilled to the same degree.[8]

Kappel and Sandøe support the life-time view. According to this view, since Michelle has had greater suffering as a result of the accident than Nina, then, other things being equal, she is more deserving (though perhaps not overridingly more deserving) of treatment which will improve her subsequent quality of life. To treat people equally we should distribute resources so that each person's fundamental interests are fulfilled to the same degree, including their ongoing interest in enjoying good health. (Note that the greater the time interval between the original accident and the need for life-saving treatment, the stronger this argument is. If Michelle has already had to endure many years of suffering as a result of her injuries, the case for compensatory preferential treatment is strong; if, however, both Michelle and Nina are still in hospital, just recovering from their injuries, when the need for life-saving treatment arises, the case will be weak.)

In support of the view that a person who has suffered more in the past should get priority in the competition for scarce resources, other things being equal, Kappel and Sandøe point out the appropriateness in other contexts of compensating people for ills which have befallen them. For example, we all think it fair if someone who works extra hours under sufferance, because their special skills are needed, is compensated in the form of extra payment or some extra time off – "even if, when the time comes for him to be compensated, he is no worse off than other people who are not given extra money or extra time off."[9]

But there are problems with appealing in this way to past suffering in the allocation of health care resources. For example, it is an implication of the life-time view defended by Kappel and Sandøe that someone who is now suffering moderate or mild pain should have a higher priority for treatment than someone who is now suffering intense pain if the former person has suffered more in the past (provided that person's past suffering is greater than the anticipated suffering of the latter person, should he or she fail to receive treatment). In other words, it is an implication of the life-time view that, under certain circumstances, someone presently suffering less should be helped in preference to someone presently suffering more. As Kappel and Sandøe acknowledge, "this seems counterintuitive."

Kappel and Sandøe are not deterred by this criticism. They suggest that the intuition in favor of helping the person who is presently suffering more may reflect the fact that moderate and mild pain are comparatively tolerable without treatment, whereas intense pain must be treated unless the person is going to suffer badly. In support of this they suggest that if the difference in degree of suffering is lessened we are more inclined to favor the person suffering least (if they have suffered more in the past). "Imagine that both persons suffer from intense pain but the pain of the first patient is just slightly more intense than the pain of the other patient. In that case it seems more reasonable to treat the person that earlier suffered the most pain."[9]

Timeless View

However, in giving credence to the intuition that when the difference in degree of suffering is slight it is more reasonable to treat the person who earlier suffered the most pain, Kappel and Sandøe could be accused of begging the question. To the extent that the purpose of health care is to lessen pain and suffering, and to the extent that nothing humanly possible can be done to lessen past pain and suffering, it would seem more reasonable to treat the person who is presently suffering more, since at least this person's suffering can be lessened. Nothing can be done about past suffering, whereas (often) something can be done about present and future suffering. This does not imply a lack of sympathy, nor a callous attitude toward past suffering. With the passage of time, present suffering becomes past suffering. Therefore the best way (indeed the only way) to reduce past suffering, as viewed from the future, is to minimize present and future suffering. So if we take a timeless view, this is where our efforts should be directed.

The view we have just been considering is an argument for compensatory justice. This is one strand of the double jeopardy objection, but the double jeopardy objection can also, as we have already seen, be put in a purer form, based simply on the claim that it is unfair that those who are the victims of one disaster should for that reason be put at a further disadvantage by resource allocation decisions. On this view QALYs give the wrong answer, not because they ignore past suffering, but simply because they discriminate against those who are now disabled or living a life of poor quality. John Broome, for instance, points out that the aim of doing the most good may tell us to give lower priority to a disabled person, and then says flatly: "However, we know this is unfair."[10] Although Broome then goes on to argue that in some cases, this unfairness may be outweighed by a gain in the good achieved, we do not find it self-evident that it would be unfair to give lower priority to the disabled person.

In order to discuss this claim that double jeopardy is simply unfair, let us assume that we have a suitable measure of the value that continued life holds for the person whose life is at stake. This value may be identical to what is now measured by QALYs, or it may be a measure of strength of preference, or it may be something else altogether. For simplicity, we shall refer to it as a person's "interest in continued life." If two people both have an interest in continued life, and we cannot offer life-saving treatment to both of them, we have the choice of offering it to neither, or using some method of selecting one of them. Offering it to neither would mean that both patients would die; if we use a method of selecting between the patients, this could be one that relies on chance, or one that employs a principle of selection. In this situation, what course of action is ethically justifiable?

Veil of Ignorance

There are many possible ways of deciding that a social arrangement is ethical or just. Two well-known examples are Kant's Categorical Imperative, which requires us to act only on maxims that we can will to be universal laws, and the utilitarian proposal that each is to count for one and none for more than one.[11] Both suggest some form of impartiality; and John Rawls has drawn on this tradition by suggesting that we can decide whether social arrangements are just by asking if they would be agreed to by rational egoists choosing from behind a veil of ignorance.[12] The idea of the veil of ignorance is that it forces an impartial choice by preventing people knowing whether they will be advantaged or disadvantaged by the proposed arrangement. So, in this case, we imagine people choosing a basis for allocating health care without knowing whether, at some point in their lives, they will be in need of health care to prolong their lives; we imagine also that they do not know whether, if this happens, they will be among those whose interest in continued life is low, or among those whose interest is high.

How would two rational egoists choose if they were faced with a situation in which they each needed life-saving treatment, and each had an interest in continued life, but there was enough life-saving treatment for only one?

Obviously each would choose the treatment for him- or herself, if he or she could; but suppose they had to make the choice behind a veil of ignorance, in which they knew the details of the two patients' conditions, but did not know which patient they were? They would certainly not choose the option of giving the treatment to neither patient. For this would mean that they would certainly die. In comparison with that prospect, tossing a coin would at least give them a 50 percent chance of survival, and so would be preferable. But a random method would in turn seem less attractive than a method of selection that gives preference to the person with a stronger interest in continuing to live. For those choosing the basis for allocating health care will know that, if they choose a random method of selection in order to avoid discrimination in situations when a treatment cannot be given to everyone, then some with a higher interest in continued life will not receive such treatment. To maximize the satisfaction of their own interests, rational egoists would have to choose a system that gives preference to saving life when it is most in the interests of the person whose life is saved. This means that if QALYs were an accurate way of measuring when life is most in one's interests, then rational egoists would choose to allocate in accordance with QALYs. But they cannot do this without building double jeopardy into their principles of distribution. Thus by one widely accepted, and undoubtedly impartial, way of deciding on the justice of principles of distribution, double jeopardy is not a sign of injustice or unfairness.

The previous argument assumes that the rational egoist is faced with a life-and-death decision. A similar argument also applies to a case in which two people, at present equally disadvantaged, could each be given treatment that would improve their quality of life, but in one case, this would bring the patient back to full health, whereas in the other case, perhaps because of an unrelated preexisting disability, the treatment would result in a lower quality of life. Let us also assume that both patients have a similar life expectancy, and this is unaffected by the treatment. In this situation, since both patients started out from a similar level, the patient who can be brought to full health will gain more from the treatment. Assuming that everything else is equal, the calculation has been carried out properly and the treatment can be given to only one patient, a rational egoist choosing from behind a veil of ignorance would choose to give the treatment to the patient who will gain more from it.

This argument from the hypothetical consent of rational egoists is, in our view, an adequate response to the double jeopardy objection, since that objection is based on the assumption that QALYs are unjust or unfair because they lead to double jeopardy. The argument is, however, not new, and Harris has already considered and rejected it. Before concluding, we shall respond to what Harris has said about hypothetical consent as a defence of QALYs.[13] Harris makes three points. The first, citing Ronald Dworkin, is that hypothetical agreement does not provide an independent argument for the fairness of the arrangement that would be agreed to, because:

> . . . you use the device of a hypothetical agreement to make a point that might have been made without that device, which is that the solution recommended is so obviously fair and sensible that only someone with an immediate contrary interest could disagree.[14]

That is true, by and large, although we would add to the last clause, after the words "someone with an immediate contrary interest," "or someone who has fixed ideas about what constitutes 'unjust discrimination' and has not reflected adequately on the implications of these ideas." For while the device of a hypothetical agreement is certainly just an expository device, it can reveal aspects of a situation that were not well understood beforehand.

Harris then argues that even if arrangements are chosen behind a veil of ignorance, that does not ensure they are just or impartial. He offers the example of people choosing a slave-owning society, gambling on being a member of the large number of slave-owners who enjoy living luxurious lives, rather than one of the small number of wretched slaves. But it is difficult to know what to make of this example, because it is not clear if Harris is talking about a world rather like our own, or one in which human nature is quite different from what it is now. If the gamble is really one that well-informed rational egoists would make, then either the number of slaves must be very small indeed, or their lives not so wretched after all – for in the real world, who would think the difference between being the slave of a slave-owner and a citizen of a slave-owning society was so great as to be worth even a one-in-ten chance of ending up as a slave? Moreover, in the real world, a ratio of one slave to every ten free people would certainly not be enough to make the lives of the slave-owners wonderfully luxurious. Of course, some will impatiently wave aside such petty calculations. Slavery is unjust, and we know that much better than we know how many slaves it takes to create luxurious lives for their masters. Indeed we do, but that is because in the real world, those who support slavery know very well that they are the masters and not the slaves; if there were any uncertainty at all about this, they would not support it. In other words: if we change the nature of human beings enough to make it plausible that rational egoists would choose to allow slavery without knowing if they were to be slaves or masters, then yes, slavery might be just. But as long as human beings stay roughly as they are, rational egoists behind a veil of ignorance would not choose to allow slavery.

Finally, Harris points out that Rawls himself holds that rational egoists behind a veil of ignorance would choose two specific principles of justice, and the second of these principles is that inequalities in wealth and resources are justifiable only insofar as they operate to the advantage of the worst-off members of society. This second principle is, of course, incompatible with the idea of distribution in a way that maximizes QALYs. Harris therefore says that if it could be shown that the device of choice behind a veil of ignorance leads to the reverse of Rawls's second principle of justice, this would discredit the plausibility of the device itself. Here, however, we disagree. There have long been good grounds for thinking that in *A Theory of Justice* Rawls "cooked the books" in order to derive from his hypothetical device the principles that he believed squared with our considered moral judgments about justice.[15] In his own later work Rawls has effectively conceded this point, for he has shifted away from defending the two principles of justice in terms of their derivation from a choice made by rational egoists under conditions of ignorance, and instead has focused on the "fundamental ideas viewed as latent in the public political culture of a democratic society."[16] If we are right in concluding that rational egoists behind the veil of ignorance would opt for a QALY-based method of allocating health care resources, and if this is incompatible with the principles of justice Rawls claims to have derived from the hypothetical choices of rational egoists, then this discredits Rawls's derivation of the two principles of justice, rather than the device of hypothetical choice itself.

Overall Utility

One final point. We have rejected the claim that QALYs are unjust or unfair because they lead to double jeopardy. This does not necessarily mean that we think that health care should always be distributed so as to produce the largest possible number of health-related QALYs. There is more to overall utility than health-related QALYs, and it is plausible to suppose that tilting the balance of health care towards the more disadvantaged members of society will reinforce feelings of concern and sympathy, and lead to a more compassionate society. This in turn may be a society with more community feeling and therefore one that provides a higher level of general welfare than a less compassionate society.

In a recent survey of the attitudes of Australians to the distribution of health care, we found that many respondents were ready to depart from QALY maximization in order to avoid expressing a priority for the treatment of some patients over others, and this may also be explained by a concern for the effects that a direct maximization approach has on the kind of society we are. For example, when asked whether, among patients who are suffering equally, some priority should be given to those who will be helped most from treatment, only about half (53 percent) of those answering favored doing so; the remainder thought that those who could become a little better should have the same priority as those who could become much better. Even more striking responses were received to a hypothetical choice between patients who can be helped at low cost and those who are equally ill, but can only be helped at high cost. Overwhelmingly (81 percent), respondents favored equal treatment irrespective of cost, except when the costs are extremely high. Even when presented with a hypothetical example showing that giving priority to low-cost patients would allow more patients to be treated overall, most respondents did not choose to maximize health benefits.[17]

It is at least possible that Australians (and no doubt some other nationals as well) consider it important to act in ways that go beyond abstract justice or fairness, instead tilting the balance so that it favors those who would otherwise feel themselves arbitrarily disadvantaged. On these grounds, we could understand a preference for avoiding double jeopardy, even though double jeopardy is not in itself unjust or unfair.

Acknowledgement

The authors thank the Australian National Health and Medical Research Council which has supported this research through a Public Health Research Project Grant to Dr. H. Kuhse and Professor P. Singer.

References and Notes

1 G. W. Torrance, "Measurement of health state utilities for economic appraisal: review," *Journal of Health Economics*, 5 (1986), pp. 1–30. If we discount for future life-years, a small additional adjustment of the calculation would be needed. For simplicity, in this article we disregard the issue of discounting.
2 J. Harris, "QALYfying the value of human life," *Journal of Medical Ethics*, 13 (1987), pp. 117–23.
3 N. Daniels, "Rationing fairly: programmatic considerations," *Bioethics*, 7 (1993), p. 227. Daniels is citing a press release by Louis Sullivan of the Health and Human Services Press Office which was issued on August 3, 1992.
4 Harris, "QALYfying," p. 120.
5 D. C. Hadorn, "The Oregon priority-setting exercise: quality of life and public policy," *Hastings Center Report* 21: 3 (1991), supplement pp. 11–16.

6   Harris, "QALYfying," p. 118.

7   J. Harris, "More and better justice," in J. M. Bell and S. Mendus (eds.), *Philosophy and Medical Welfare* (Cambridge: Cambridge University Press, 1988), p. 3.

8   K. Kappel and P. Sandøe, "QALYs, age and fairness," *Bioethics*, 6 (1992), pp. 297–316.

9   Ibid., p. 315.

10 J. Broome, "Fairness versus doing the most good," *Hastings Center Report*, 24: 4 (1994), pp. 36–9. See also J. Broome, "Fairness," *Proceedings of the Aristotelian Society*, 91 (1990), pp. 87–102.

11 I. Kant, "The foundations of the metaphysics of morals," in *The Philosophy of Immanuel Kant*. This was first published in 1785. We refer to p. 80 of the edition translated by L. W. Beck and published in 1949 by the University of Chicago Press. The utilitarian dictum is attributed to Jeremy Bentham by John Stuart Mill in *Utilitarianism*, which was first published in 1863. We refer to p. 58 of the edition published in 1960 by J. M. Dent, London.

12 J. Rawls, *A Theory of Justice* (Oxford: Oxford University Press, 1972), ch 1.

13 Harris, "More and better justice," pp. 88–90.

14 R. Dworkin, *Taking Rights Seriously* (London: Duckworth, 1977), p. 151.

15 B. Barry, *The Liberal Theory of Justice* (Oxford: Clarendon Press, 1973), ch 9.

16 J. Rawls, "The priority of right and ideas of the good," *Philosophy and Public Affairs*, 17 (1988), p. 252. See also, J. Rawls, *Political Liberalism* (New York: Columbia University Press, 1993).

17 E. Nord, J. Richardson, A. Street, H. Kuhse, and P. Singer, "Maximizing health benefits versus egalitarianism: an Australian survey of health issues," *Social Science and Medicine*, 41 (1995), pp. 1429–37.

Part Seven

How We Should Live

Twenty

A Vegetarian Philosophy

Over the next twenty years eating meat could follow smoking into disrepute. Like smoking, the heavily meat-based diet followed by most people in affluent countries has been shown to cause cancer and heart disease. On top of that, the BSE scare hurt the beef industry, not only because of the risk of contracting the disease itself, but because consumers learned that today's cattle eat abattoir byproducts.

While cattle in developing countries are more likely to eat grass, the grassland is often felled rainforest, taken after tribal people have been pushed off their land. The destruction of the rainforest carries implications for global warming that threaten the lives of millions of people farming low-lying land in regions like Bangladesh and Egypt. Pollution of streams and ground water by toxic animal wastes is another major problem for the meat industry. And the animal movement is convincing growing numbers of people that our treatment of animals is grounded on a prejudice against taking seriously the interests of beings who are not members of our species. No wonder that the number of vegetarians and near-vegetarians continues to grow.

Issues around eating meat were highlighted in 1997 by the longest trial in British legal history. *McDonald's Corporation and McDonald's Restaurants Limited* v. *Steel and Morris*, better known as the "McLibel" trial, ran for 313 days and heard 180 witnesses. In suing McDonald's, Helen Steel and David Morris, two

First published in *Consuming Passions: Food in the Age of Anxiety*, ed. Sian Griffiths and Jennifer Wallace (Manchester: Manchester University Press, 1998), pp. 71–80. Reprinted with permission of Manchester University Press.

activists involved with the London Greenpeace organization, put on trial the way in which its fast food products are produced, packaged, advertised, and sold, as well as their nutritional value, the environmental impact of producing them, and the treatment of the animals whose flesh and eggs are made into that food.

Admittedly, even if McDonald's had lost on every point, producers of animal products by organic farming methods could justifiably have claimed that the decision was irrelevant to what they were doing. So the trial was not a test of the morality of eating meat. But for the majority of consumers, whether they eat at McDonald's, at a rival fast food chain, or just pick up their meat at a supermarket with an eye more to its cost than to the manner in which it is produced, the morality of the meat they are eating was on trial.

The case provided a remarkable opportunity for weighing up evidence for and against modern agribusiness methods. The leaflet "What's Wrong with McDonald's" that provoked the defamation suit had a row of McDonald's arches along the top of each page. Two of these arches bore the words "McMurder" and "McTorture." One section below was headed "In what way are McDonald's responsible for torture and murder?" The leaflet answered the question as follows:

> The menu at McDonald's is based on meat. They sell millions of burgers every day in 35 countries throughout the world. This means the constant slaughter, day by day, of animals born and bred solely to be turned into McDonald's products. Some of them – especially chickens and pigs – spend their lives in the entirely artificial conditions of huge factory farms, with no access to air or sunshine and no freedom of movement. Their deaths are bloody and barbaric.

McDonald's claimed that the leaflet meant that the company was responsible for the inhumane torture and murder of cattle, chickens, and pigs, and that this was defamatory. In considering this claim, Mr. Justice Bell based his judgment on what he took to be attitudes that were generally accepted in Britain. Thus for the epithet "McTorture" to be justified, he held, it would not be enough for Steel and Morris to show that animals were under stress or suffered some pain or discomfort:

> Merely containing, handling and transporting an animal may cause it stress; and taking it to slaughter certainly may do so. But I do not believe that the ordinary reasonable person believes any of these things to be cruel, provided that the necessary stress or discomfort or even pain is kept to a reasonably acceptable level. That ordinary person may know little about the detail of farming and slaughtering methods but he must find a certain amount of stress, discomfort, or even pain acceptable and not to be criticized as cruel.

By the end of the trial, however, Mr. Justice Bell found that the stress, discomfort, and pain inflicted on some animals amounted to more than this acceptable level, and hence did constitute a "cruel practice" for which McDonald's was "culpably responsible." Chickens, laying hens, and sows, he said, kept in individual stalls suffered from "severe restriction of movement" which "is cruel." He also found a number of other cruel practices in the production of chickens, including the restricted diet fed to breeding birds, which leaves them permanently hungry, the injuries inflicted on chickens by catchers stuffing 600 birds an hour into crates to take them to slaughter, and the failure of the stunning apparatus to ensure that all birds are stunned before they have their throats cut. Judging by entirely conventional moral standards, Mr. Justice Bell held these practices to be cruel, and McDonald's to be culpably responsible for them.

It was not libelous to describe McDonald's as "McTorture," because the charge was substantially true. What follows from this judgment about the morality of buying and eating intensively raised chickens, pig products that come from the offspring of sows kept in stalls, or eggs laid by hens kept in battery cages? Surely that, too, must be wrong?

This claim has been challenged. At a conference dinner some years ago I found myself sitting opposite a Buddhist philosopher from Thailand. As we helped ourselves to the lavish buffet, I avoided the various forms of meat on offer, but the Thai philosopher did not. When I asked him how he reconciled the dinner he had chosen with the first precept of Buddhism, which tells us to avoid harming sentient beings, he told me that in the Buddhist tradition it is wrong to eat meat only if you have reason to believe that the animal was killed specially for you. The meat he had taken, however, was not from animals killed specially for him; the animals would have died anyway, even if he were a strict vegetarian, or had not been in that city at all. Hence, by eating it, he was not harming any animals.

I was unable to persuade my dinner companion that this defense of meat eating was better suited to a time when a peasant family might kill an animal especially to have something to put in the begging bowl of a wandering monk than it is to our own era. The flaw in the defence is the disregard of the link between the meat I eat today and the future killing of animals. Granted, the chicken lying in the supermarket freezer today would have died even if I had never existed; but the fact that I take the chicken from the freezer, and ignore the tofu on a nearby shelf, has something to do with the number of chickens, or blocks of tofu, the supermarket will order next week, and thus contributes, in a small way, to the future growth or decline of the chicken and tofu industries. That is what the laws of supply and demand are all about.

Some defenders of a variant of the ancient Buddhist line may still want to argue that one chicken fewer sold makes no perceptible difference to the chicken producers, and therefore there can be nothing wrong with buying chicken. The division of moral responsibility in a situation of this kind does raise some interesting issues, but it is a fallacy to argue that a person can do wrong only by making a perceptible harm. The Oxford philosopher Jonathan Glover has explored the implications of this refusal to accept the divisibility of responsibility in an entertaining article called "It makes no difference whether or not I do it" (*Proceedings of the Aristotelian Society*, 1975).

Glover imagines that in a village, 100 people are about to eat lunch. Each has a bowl containing 100 beans. Suddenly, 100 hungry bandits swoop on the village. Each bandit takes the contents of the bowl of one villager, eats it, and gallops off. Next week, the bandits plan to do it again, but one of their number is afflicted by doubts about whether it is right to steal from the poor. These doubts are set to rest by another of their number who proposes that each bandit, instead of eating the entire contents of the bowl of one villager, should take one bean from every villager's bowl. Since the loss of one bean cannot make a perceptible difference to any villager, no bandit will have harmed anyone. The bandits follow this plan, each taking a solitary bean from 100 bowls. The villagers are just as hungry as they were the previous week, but the bandits can all sleep well on their full stomachs, knowing that none of them has harmed anyone.

Glover's example shows the absurdity of denying that we are each responsible for a share of the harms we collectively cause, even if each of us makes no perceptible difference. McDonald's has a far bigger impact on the practices of the chicken, egg, and pig industries than any individual consumer; but McDonald's itself would be powerless if no one ate at its restaurants. Collectively, all consumers of animal products are responsible for the existence of the cruel practices involved in producing them. In the absence of special circumstances, a portion of this responsibility must be attributed back to each purchaser.

Without in any way departing from a conventional moral attitude towards animals, then, we have reached the conclusion that eating intensively produced chicken, battery eggs, and some pig products is wrong. This is, of course, well short of an argument for vegetarianism. Mr. Justice Bell found "cruel practices" only in these areas of McDonald's food production. But he did not find that McDonald's beef is "cruelty-free." He did not consider that question, because he drew a distinction between McDonald's responsibility for practices in the beef and dairy industries, and those in the chicken, egg, and pig industries. McDonald's chickens, eggs, and pig products are supplied by a relatively small number of very large producers, over whose practices the corporation could quite easily have a major influence. On the other hand, McDonald's beef and dairy requirements came from a very large number of producers, in respect of whose methods, Mr. Justice Bell held, "there was no evidence from which I could infer that [McDonald's] would have any effective influence, should it try to exert it." Whatever one may think of that view – it seems highly implausible to me – the judge, in accepting it, decided not to address the evidence presented to him of cruelty in the raising of cattle, so that no conclusions either way can be drawn.

This does not mean that the trial itself had nothing to say about animal suffering in general. McDonald's called as a witness Mr. David Walker, Chief Executive of one of their major United Kingdom suppliers, McKey Food Services Ltd. In cross-examination, Helen Steel asked Walker whether it was true that, "as the result of the meat industry, the suffering of animals is inevitable?" Walker replied: "The answer to that must be 'yes'."

Walker's admission raises a serious question about the ethics of the meat industry: how much suffering are we justified in inflicting on animals in order to turn them into meat, or to use their eggs or milk? To answer this question we need to depart from Mr. Justice Bell's presuppositions and ask whether conventional moral views about animals are defensible. The prevailing Western ethic is still essentially pre-Darwinian. It shows this even in the language it uses, which, by contrasting "humans" and "animals," denies that humans are animals.

The twin roots of the Western ethic lie in Aristotle's idea that the world is a hierarchy in which the less rational exist in order to serve the more rational, and in the Judeo-Christian teaching that humans have "dominion" over animals, and a God-given right to make use of them. Whether or not people still believe that humans alone are made "in the image of God," most do think of animals as distinctly "lower creatures." The assumption is that human beings are infinitely superior in moral status to all forms of animal life, and that they are in some way meant to serve our ends. With the exception of concerns about endangered species – which are not really concerns about the interests of individual animals at all – the general view is that if our interests conflict with theirs, it is always the interests of the animals that have to give way.

Since the rise of the modern animal liberation movement in the 1970s, this view has been under attack. Animal liberationists question the right of our species to assume that our interests must always prevail. They want to extend the basic moral ideas of equality and rights beyond the species barrier. If, they ask, we reject racist or hierarchical ideas about human beings, and instead insist on the equality of all humans, what is it that entitles us to put nonhuman beings outside that sphere of equality?

Obviously, this view does not mean that animals should have equal rights to vote, or to free speech. The kind of equality which animal liberationists want to extend to animals is equal consideration of interests. The basic right that animals should have is the right to equal consideration. If an animal feels pain, the pain matters as much as it does when a human feels pain – if the pain hurts just as much, and will last just as long, and will not have further bad consequences for the human that it does not have for the nonhuman animal. Pain is pain, whatever the species of being that experiences it.

The principle of equal consideration of interests does not imply that it is as wrong to kill a chicken as it is to kill a normal human being. The interest that beings have in continuing to live will depend on the capacities that they have. In what ways can they enjoy their lives? Do they know that they have a life to lead? Are they aware that they exist over time, have a past, and could have a future? Do they have desires to do things in the future, which they will not be able to do if they are killed? All these questions are relevant to the wrongness of killing. What is not relevant, according to the principle of equal consideration of interests, is the species to which the being belongs. Species membership may be an indication of the capacities a being has, but it is the capacities themselves, not the species membership, that is ethically significant.

The principle of equal consideration of interests is not absolutist and does not require vegetarianism in all possible circumstances. A person shipwrecked on a desert island may be justified in eating meat to survive. A little more relevant to most of us is the claim made on behalf of organic farmers, that there are ways of rearing animals that fully respect their interests throughout their lives. If the animals do have good lives, and do not have sufficient self-awareness to have desires for the future, it could be argued that killing them painlessly for food would not be wrong. The issue is a complex one, leading into some of the most baffling questions in ethics. Is it wrong to kill animals because it deprives them of the future life they would have enjoyed, even if they know nothing of it? Perhaps it is; but what if we can then replace that animal with another, who will have as good a life? "If all the world were Jewish, there would be no pigs at all," Leslie Stephen once argued in an attempt to refute vegetarians. But can we justify ending the life of one animal by conferring benefits on an as yet nonexistent animal?

These questions are philosophically intriguing, but of minor practical significance. We must not lose sight of the larger picture. The case for vegetarianism is at its strongest when we see it as a moral protest against our use of animals as mere things, to be exploited for our convenience in whatever way makes them most cheaply available to us. Only the tiniest fraction of the tens of billions of farm animals slaughtered for food each year – the figure for the United States alone is nine billion – were treated during their lives in ways that respected their interests. Questions about the wrongness of killing in itself are not relevant to the moral issue of eating meat or eggs from factory-farmed animals, as most people in developed countries do. Even when animals are roaming freely over large areas, as sheep and cattle do in Australia, operations like hot-iron branding, castration, and dehorning are carried out without any regard for the animals' capacity to suffer. The same is true of handling and transport prior to slaughter. In the light of these facts, the issue to focus on is not whether there are some circumstances in which it could be right to eat meat, but on what we can do to avoid contributing to this immense amount of animal suffering.

The answer is to boycott all meat and eggs produced by large-scale commercial methods of animal production, and encourage others to do the same. Consideration for the interests of animals alone is enough justification for this response, but the case is further strengthened by the environmental problems that the meat industry causes. Although Mr. Justice Bell found that the allegations directed at McDonald's regarding its contribution to the destruction of rainforests were not true, the meat industry as a whole can take little comfort from that, because Bell accepted evidence that cattle-ranching, particularly in Brazil, had contributed to the clearing of vast areas of rainforest. The problem for David Morris and Helen Steel was that they did not persuade the judge that the meat used by McDonald's came from these regions. So the meat industry as a whole remains culpable for the loss of rainforest, and all the consequences of that, from global warming to the deaths of indigenous people fighting to defend their way of life.

Environmentalists are increasingly recognizing that the choice of what we eat is an environmental issue. Animals raised in sheds or on feedlots eat grains or soy beans, and they use most of the food value of these products simply in order to maintain basic functions and develop unpalatable parts of the body like bones and skin. To convert eight or nine kilos of grain protein into a single kilo of animal protein wastes land, energy, and water. On a crowded planet with a growing human population, that is a luxury that we are becoming increasingly unable to afford.

Intensive animal production is a heavy user of fossil fuels and a major source of pollution of both air and water. It releases large quantities of methane and other greenhouse gases into the atmosphere. We are risking unpredictable changes to the climate of our planet – which means, ultimately, the lives of billions of people, not to mention the extinction of untold thousands of species of plants and animals unable to cope with changing conditions – for the sake of more hamburgers.

A diet heavy on animal products, catered for by intensive animal production, is a disaster for animals, the environment, and the health of those who eat it. The scale of the disaster will be multiplied many times over if the trend for other countries to copy Western diets and methods of production continues. It is already happening in the more successful economies of East Asia, and it seems bound to spread further as the sphere of prosperity widens. One billion Chinese, eating a Western diet produced by intensive farming methods, would dwarf the contribution to global warming and pollution now made by the agribusiness industries of the entire European Community.

There is an urgent need for a concerted effort to halt the spread of our disastrous diet. This will require an interdisciplinary effort, bringing together the best scientific studies from experts in nutrition, public health, and environmental science, along with philosophers working on the ethical issues involved in our treatment of animals and the environment. One sign that this kind of work may be getting under way is the establishment of the Center for a Livable Future, under the direction of Dr. Robert Lawrence, of the School of Public Health at Johns Hopkins University in Baltimore. The center's aim is not more research into the harmful effects of a diet that is already high in animal products – there is already ample evidence of that – but rather to find ways of changing people's attitudes so that they do not want this diet.

University teachers of philosophy should be playing a role in bringing about this change. Food must be seen as one of the most profound ethical issues we face. When we consider how much attention is paid in ethics courses to issues that students rarely (if ever) confront (for example, euthanasia), it is extraordinary how we neglect the ethics of an issue that we face three times a day. Of course, the question of the ethics of our treatment of our animals is now a part of many ethics courses and that makes a welcome contrast with the situation that prevailed until about twenty years ago. But the ethics of what we eat brings in other considerations as well, and it should be the subject of a more focused discussion.

In the end, the example that we in the developed Western nations set to the rest of the world will probably be more influential than anything we tell them. For that reason it is important that we start thinking about the ethics of our diet. Challenging our students with some of the issues outlined above is a good place to begin.

Further Reading

Eisnitz, Gail, *Slaughterhouse* (Amherst, NY: Prometheus, 1997).
Johnson, Andrew, *Factory Farming* (Oxford: Blackwell, 1991).
Rifkin, Jeremy, *Beyond Beef* (New York: Dutton, 1992).
Singer, Peter, *Animal Liberation*, 2nd ed. (London: Pimlico, 1995).
Vidal, John, *McLibel – Burger Culture on Trial* (London: Macmillan, 1997).
Wynne-Tyson, Jon, *Food for a Future* (Wellingborough: Thorsons, 1988).

A Recipe

This recipe is vegan, very simple, nutritious, and tasty. It's also eaten by hundreds of millions of people every day.

Dal

1 cup red lentils
3 cups water
1 onion, chopped
2 cloves garlic, crushed
2 tbsp. oil
1 400 g tin of tomatoes or equivalent chopped fresh tomatoes
1 stick cinnamon
bay leaf
1 tsp. medium curry powder or to taste
50 g. creamed coconut or half cup coconut milk (optional)
Juice of one lemon (optional)
Salt to taste.

In a deep frying pan, heat the oil and fry the onion and garlic until translucent. Add the lentils and fry them for a minute or two, then add the water, bay leaf, cinnamon stick, and curry powder. Stir, bring to the boil, then let simmer for twenty minutes, adding a little more water from time to time if it gets dry. Add the can of tomatoes, and simmer another ten minutes. By now the lentils should be very soft. Add the creamed coconut or coconut milk, lemon juice, and salt to taste. Remove cinnamon stick and bay leaf before serving.

The final product should flow freely – add more water if it is too stodgy. It is usually served over rice, with some lime pickle and mango chutney. Sliced banana is another good accompaniment, and so too are poppadams.

Twenty-one

Environmental Values

Introduction

A river tumbles through steep wooded valleys and rocky gorges toward the sea. The state hydroelectricity commission sees the falling water as untapped energy. Building a dam across one of the gorges would provide three years of employment for a thousand people, and longer-term employment for twenty or thirty. The dam would store enough water to ensure that the state could economically meet its energy needs for the next decade. This would encourage the establishment of energy-intensive industry in the state, thus further contributing to employment and economic growth.

The rough terrain of the river valley makes it accessible only to the reasonably fit, but it is nevertheless a favored spot for bushwalking. The river itself attracts the more daring whitewater rafters. Deep in the sheltered valleys are stands of Huon pine, thousands of years old. The valleys and gorges are home to many birds and animals, including an endangered species of marsupial mouse found in only one other place in Australia. There may be other rare plants and animals as well, but no one knows, for scientists have yet to investigate the region fully.

Should the dam be built? This is one example of a situation in which we must choose between very different sets of values. The description is clearly reminiscent of the controversy over the proposed dam on the Franklin River,

First published in *The Environmental Challenge*, ed. Ian Marsh (Melbourne: Longman Cheshire, 1991), pp. 3–24.

in Tasmania's southwest, although I have not tried to make it exact, and it should be treated as a hypothetical case. Many other examples would have posed the choice between values equally well: logging virgin forests; building a paper mill that will release pollutants into coastal waters; or opening a new mine on the edge of a national park. A different set of examples would raise related, but slightly different, issues: banning the use of CFCs to prevent the depletion of the ozone layer; restricting the use of fossil fuels in an attempt to slow the greenhouse effect; mining uranium, where the issue is not the potential damage to the area around the mine, but the hazards of nuclear fuel. My aim in this chapter is to explore the values that underlie debates about these decisions, and the example I have presented can serve as a point of reference to these debates. I shall focus particularly on the values at issue in controversies about the preservation of wilderness, not only because in Australia these have been the most highly publicized and most heated environmental controversies, but also because here the fundamentally different values of the two parties are most apparent. On controversies like water pollution and the control of greenhouse gases, the difference in values tends to be obscured by scientific debates on what is really happening, what the costs are, and what measures will be effective. When we are talking about flooding a river valley, the choice before us is starkly clear.

In general terms, we can say that those who favor building the dam are valuing employment and a higher per capita income for the state above the preservation of wilderness, of plants and animals (both common ones and members of an endangered species) and of opportunities for outdoor recreational activities. Some fundamental questions of philosophy lie behind this difference of values. In what follows, I shall assume that the values we hold may properly be subjected to rational scrutiny and criticism: they are not simply matters of taste, about which argument is futile.[1] Before we begin to scrutinize the values of those who would have the dam built and those who would not, however, let us briefly investigate the origins of modern attitudes toward the natural world.

The Western Tradition

When Europeans came to Australia, they brought with them attitudes to the natural environment that were a legacy of more than 2,000 years of Western civilization. These attitudes ruled with very little challenge until the rise of the environmental movement in the 1970s, and it could be argued that they are still the predominant force in decisions about the environment.

Western attitudes to nature grew out of a blend of those of the Hebrew people, as represented in the early books of the Bible, and the philosophy of ancient Greece, particularly that of Aristotle. In contrast to some other ancient traditions, for example, those of India, both the Hebrew and the Greek traditions made human beings the center of the moral universe; indeed not merely the center, but very often the entirety of the morally significant features of this world.

The biblical story of creation makes very clear the Hebrew view of the special place of human beings in the divine plan:

> And God said, Let us make man in our image, after our likeness: and let them have dominion over the fish of the sea, and over the fowl of the air, and over the cattle, and over all the earth, and over every creeping thing that creepeth upon the earth.
>
> So God created man in his own image, in the image of God created he him; male and female created he them.
>
> And God blessed them, and God said unto them, Be fruitful, and multiply, and replenish the earth, and subdue it; and have dominion over the fish of the sea and over the fowl of the air, and over every living thing that moveth upon the earth.[2]

Today Christians debate the meaning of this grant of "dominion"; and those concerned about the environment claim that it should be regarded not as a license to humanity to do as they will with other living things, but rather as a directive to look after them, on God's behalf, and be answerable to God for the way in which they are treated.[3] There is, however, little justification in the text itself for such an interpretation; and given the example God set when he drowned almost every animal on earth in order to punish Noah for his wickedness, it is no wonder that people should think the flooding of a single river valley is nothing worth worrying about. After the flood there is a repetition of the grant of dominion in more ominous language:

> And the fear of you and the dread of you shall be upon every beast of the earth, and upon every fowl of the air, upon all that moveth upon the earth, and upon all the fishes of the sea; into your hand are they delivered.[4]

The implication is clear: to act in a way that causes fear and dread to everything that moves on the earth is not improper; it is, in fact, in accordance with a God-given decree.

The most influential early Christian thinkers had no doubts about how human dominion was to be understood. "Doth God care for oxen?" asked Paul, in the course of a discussion of an Old Testament command to rest one's ox on the sabbath, but it was only a rhetorical question – he took it for granted that the answer must be negative, and the command was to be explained in terms of some benefit to humans.[5] Augustine shared this line of thought; referring to stories in the New Testament in which Jesus destroyed a fig tree and caused a herd of pigs to drown, Augustine explained these puzzling incidents as intended to teach us that "to refrain from the killing of animals and the destroying of plants is the height of superstition."[6]

When Christianity prevailed in the Roman Empire, it also absorbed elements of the ancient Greek attitude to the natural world. The Greek influence was entrenched in Christian philosophy by the greatest of the medieval scholastics, Thomas Aquinas, whose life work was the melding of Christian theology with the thought of Aristotle. Aristotle regarded nature as a hierarchy in which those with less reasoning ability exist for the sake of those with more:

> Plants exist for the sake of animals, and brute beasts for the sake of man – domestic animals for his use and food, wild ones (or at any rate most of them) for food and other accessories of life, such as clothing and various tools.
>
> Since nature makes nothing purposeless or in vain, it is undeniably true that she has made all animals for the sake of man.[7]

In his own major work, the *Summa Theologiae*, Aquinas followed this passage from Aristotle almost word for word, adding that the position accords with God's command, as given in Genesis. In his classification of sins, Aquinas has room only for sins against God, ourselves, or our neighbor. There is no possibility of sinning against nonhuman animals, or against the natural world.[8]

This was the thinking of mainstream Christianity for at least its first eighteen centuries. There were gentler spirits certainly, like Basil, John Chrysostom, and Francis of Assisi, but for most of Christian history they have had no significant impact on the dominant tradition.[9] It is therefore worth emphasizing the major features of this dominant Western tradition, because these features can serve as a point of comparison when we discuss different views of the natural environment.

According to the dominant Western tradition, the natural world exists for the benefit of human beings. God gave human beings dominion over the natural world, and God does not care how we treat it. Human beings are the only morally important members of this world. Nature itself is of no intrinsic value, and the destruction of plants and animals cannot be sinful, unless by this destruction we harm human beings.

Harsh as this tradition is, it does not rule out concern for the preservation of nature, as long as that concern can be related to human well-being. Often, of course, it can be. We could, entirely within the limits of the dominant Western tradition, oppose the mining of uranium on the grounds that nuclear fuel, whether in bombs or power stations, is so hazardous to human life that the uranium is better left in the ground. Similarly, many arguments against pollution, the use of gases harmful to the ozone layer, the burning of fossil fuels, and the destruction of forests, could be couched in terms of the harm to human health and welfare from the pollutants, or the changes to the climate that may occur as a result of the use of fossil fuels and the loss of forest. Since human beings need an environment in which they can thrive, the preservation of such an environment can be a value within a human-centered moral framework.

From the standpoint of a form of civilization based on growing crops and grazing animals, wilderness may seem to be a wasteland, a useless area that needs clearing in order to render it productive and valuable. There was a time when villages surrounded by farmland seemed like oases of cultivation among the deserts of forest or rough mountain slopes. Now, however, a different metaphor is more appropriate: the remnants of true wilderness left to us are like islands amid a sea of human activity that threatens to engulf them. This gives wilderness a scarcity value that provides the basis for a strong argument for preservation, even within the terms of a human-centered ethic. That argument becomes much stronger still when we take a long-term view. To this immensely important aspect of environmental values we shall now turn.

Valuing the Future

A virgin forest is the product of all the millions of years that have passed since the beginning of our planet. If it is cut down, another forest may grow up, but the continuity has been broken. The disruption in the natural life cycles of the plants and animals means that the forest will never again be as it would have been, had it not been cut. The gains made from cutting the forest – employment, profits for business, export earnings, and cheaper cardboard and paper for packaging – are short-term. Once the forest is cut or drowned, however, the link with the past is gone forever. That is something that may be regretted by every generation that succeeds us on this planet. True wilderness now has a high value because it is already scarce. In future, and considering the world as a whole, it is bound to become scarcer still. It is for that reason that environmentalists are right to speak of wilderness as a "world heritage." It is something that we have inherited from our ancestors, and that we must preserve for our descendents, if they are to have it at all.

In contrast to many more stable, tradition-oriented human societies, our modern political and cultural ethos has great difficulty in recognizing long-term values. It is notorious that politicians rarely look beyond the next election; but even if they do, they will find their economic advisors telling them that anything to be gained in the future should be discounted to such a degree as to make it easy to disregard the long-term future altogether. Economists have been taught to apply a discount rate to all future goods. In other words, a million dollars in twenty years is not worth a million dollars today, even when we allow for inflation. Economists will discount the value of the million dollars by a certain percentage, usually corresponding to the real long-term interest rates. This makes economic sense, because if I had a thousand dollars today I could invest it so that it would be worth more, in real terms, in twenty years. But the use of a discount rate means that values gained a hundred years hence rank very low in comparison to values gained today and values gained a thousand years in the future scarcely count at all. This is not because of any uncertainty about whether there will be human beings or other sentient creatures inhabiting this planet at this time, but merely because of the cumulative effect of the rate of return on money invested now. From the standpoint of the priceless and timeless values we can gain from the wilderness, however, applying a discount rate gives us the wrong answer. There are some things that, once lost, no amount of money can regain. Thus to justify the destruction of an ancient forest on the grounds that it will earn us substantial export income is problematic, even if we could invest that income and increase its value from year to year; for no matter how much we increased its value, it could never buy back the link with the past represented by the forest.

This argument does not show that there can be no justification for cutting any virgin forests, but it does mean that any such justification must take full account of the value of the forests to the generations to come in the more remote future, as well as in the more immediate future. This value will obviously be related to the particular scenic or biological significance of the forest; but as the proportion of true wilderness on the earth dwindles, every part of it becomes significant, because the opportunities for experiencing wilderness become scarce, and the likelihood of a reasonable selection of the major forms of wilderness being preserved is reduced. Moreover, it is not only the people who visit wilderness who gain from its presence. Popular support for wilderness preservation is far broader than could be the case if only those who visited were in favor of preserving it. It seems that people like to "know that it is there" even if they never see it except on their television sets.

Can we be sure that future generations will appreciate wilderness? Perhaps they will be happier sitting in air-conditioned shopping malls, playing computer games more sophisticated than any we can imagine. That is possible, but there are several reasons why we should not give this possibility too much weight. Firstly, the trend has been in the opposite direction: the appreciation of wilderness has never been higher than it is today, especially among those nations that have overcome the problems of poverty and hunger and have relatively little wilderness left. Wilderness is valued as something of immense beauty, as a reservoir of scientific knowledge still to be gained, for the unique recreational opportunities that it provides, and because many people just like to know that something natural is still there, relatively untouched by modern civilization. If, as we all hope, future generations are able to provide for the basic needs of most people, we can expect that, for centuries to come, they too will value wilderness for the same reasons that we value it.

Secondly, arguments for preservation based on the beauty of wilderness are sometimes treated as if they were of little weight because they are "merely aesthetic." That is a mistake. We go to great lengths to preserve the artistic treasures of earlier human civilizations. It is difficult to imagine any economic gain that we would be prepared to accept as adequate compensation for the destruction of the paintings in the Louvre, for instance. How should we compare the aesthetic value of a wild river valley or a virgin forest with that of the paintings in the Louvre? Here, perhaps, judgment does become inescapably subjective, so I shall report my own experiences. I have looked at the paintings in the Louvre, and in many of the other great galleries of Europe and the USA. I think I have a reasonable sense of appreciation of the fine arts, yet I have not had, in any museum, experiences that have filled my aesthetic senses in the way that I experience when I walk in a natural setting, and pause to survey the view from a rocky peak overlooking a forested valley, or sit by a stream tumbling over moss-covered boulders set amongst tall green tree-ferns. I do not think that I am alone in this. For many people, wilderness is the source of the greatest feelings of aesthetic appreciation; even nonreligious people tend to describe it in terms of a spiritual experience.

It may nevertheless be true that this appreciation of nature may not be shared by people living a century or two hence. But if wilderness can be the source of such deep joy and satisfaction, that would be a great loss. Moreover, whether future generations value wilderness is up to us; it is, at least, something we can influence. By our preservation of areas of wilderness, we provide an opportunity for generations to come, and by the books and films we produce, we create a culture that can be handed on to our children and their children. If we feel that a walk in the forest, with senses attuned to the appreciation of such an experience, is a more deeply rewarding way to spend a day than playing computer games, or if we feel that to carry one's food and shelter in a backpack for a week while hiking through an unspoilt natural environment will do more to develop character than watching television for an equivalent period, then we ought to encourage future generations to have a feeling for nature; if they end up preferring computer games, we shall have failed.

Finally, if we preserve intact the amount of wilderness that exists now, future generations will at least be able to have the choice of getting up from their computer games and going to see a world that has not been created by human beings. They may like to know that some parts of the world in which they are living are much as they were before we humans developed our fearsome powers of destruction. At present, there are still both wilderness and non-wilderness areas. If we destroy the wilderness, that choice is gone forever. Just as we will spend large sums to preserve cities like Venice, even though future generations conceivably may not be interested in such architectural treasures, so we should preserve wilderness even though it is possible that future generations will care little for it. Thus we will not wrong future generations, as we have been wronged by members of past generations whose thoughtless actions have deprived us of so many possibilities, like the chance of glimpsing the thylacine when walking through Tasmanian forests. We must take care not to inflict equally irreparable losses on the generations to follow us.

Thus a human-centered ethic can be the basis of powerful arguments for what we may call "environmental values." Even from the perspective of such an ethic, economic growth based on the exploitation of irreplaceable resources can be seen as something that brings gains to the present generation, and possibly the next generation or two, at a price that will be paid by every generation to come. The price to be paid by future human beings is too high. But should we limit ourselves to a human-centered ethic? We now need to consider more fundamental challenges to this traditional Western approach to environmental issues.

Is there Value beyond the Human Species?

Although some debates about significant environmental issues can be conducted by appealing only to the long-term interests of our own species, in any serious exploration of environmental values a central issue will be whether there is anything of intrinsic value beyond human beings. To explore this question we first need to understand the notion of "intrinsic value." Something is of intrinsic value if it is good or desirable in itself; the contrast is with instrumental value, that is, value as a means to some other end or purpose. Our own happiness, for example, is of intrinsic value, at least to most of us, in that we desire it for its own sake. Money, on the other hand, is only of instrumental value to us. We want it because of the things we can buy with it, but if we were marooned on a desert island, we would not want it (whereas happiness would be just as important to us on a desert island as anywhere else).

Now consider again for a moment the issue of damming the river described at the beginning of this chapter. Should the decision be made on the basis of human interests alone? If we say that it should, we shall balance the economic benefits for Tasmanians of building the dam against the loss for bushwalkers, scientists, and others, now and in the future, who value the preservation of the river in its natural state. We have already seen that because this calculation includes an indefinite number of future generations, the loss of the wild river is a much greater cost than we might at first imagine. Even so, if we are justified in arguing that the decision whether to dam the river should be made on the basis of values that include, but are not limited to, the interests of human beings, we may have much more to set against the economic benefits for Tasmanians of building the dam. We may take into account the interests of the animals who will die if the valley is drowned; we may give weight to the fact that a species may be lost, that trees that have stood for thousands of years will die, and that an entire local ecosystem will be destroyed; and we may give the preservation of the animals, the species, the trees, and the ecosystems a weight that is independent of the interests of human beings – whether economic, recreational, or scientific – in their preservation.

Here we have a fundamental moral disagreement: a disagreement about what kinds of beings ought to be considered in our moral deliberations. Many people think that once we reach a disagreement of this kind, argument must cease. As I have already briefly indicated, I am more optimistic about the scope of rational argument in ethics. In ethics, even at a fundamental level, there are arguments that should convince any rational person. Take, as an example, a view held by one of the founders of the Western ethical tradition: Aristotle's notorious justification of slavery. Aristotle thought that captured barbarians were "living instruments" – that is, human beings who were not of intrinsic value, but who existed in order to serve some higher end. That end was the welfare of their Greek captors or owners. He justified this view by arguing that barbarians were less rational than Greeks and, in the hierarchy of nature, the purpose of the less rational is to serve the more rational.[10]

No one now accepts Aristotle's defence of slavery. We reject it for a variety of reasons. We would reject his assumption that non-Greeks are less rational than Greeks, although given the cultural achievements of the different groups at the time, that was by no means an absurd assumption to make. More importantly, from the moral point of view, we reject the idea that the less rational exist in order to serve the more rational. Instead we hold that all humans are equal. We regard racism and slavery based on racism as wrong because they fail to give equal consideration to the interests of all human beings. This would be true whatever the level of rationality or civilization of the slave, and therefore Aristotle's appeal to the higher rationality of the Greeks would not have justified the enslavement of non-Greeks, even if it had been true. Members of the "barbarian" tribes can feel pain, as Greeks can; they can be joyful or miserable, as Greeks can; they can suffer from separation from their families and friends, as Greeks can. To brush aside these needs so that Greeks could satisfy much more minor needs of their own was a great wrong and a blot on Greek civilization. This is something that we would expect all reasonable people to accept, as long as they can view the question from an impartial perspective, and are not improperly influenced by having a personal interest in the continued existence of slavery.

Now let us return to the question of the moral status of those who are not humans. We shall consider, first, nonhuman animals. In keeping with the dominant Western tradition, many people still hold that all the nonhuman natural world has value only or predominantly insofar as it benefits human beings. A powerful objection to the dominant Western tradition turns against this tradition an extended version of the objection just made against Aristotle's justification of slavery. Many nonhuman animals are also capable of feeling pain, as humans are; they can certainly be miserable, and perhaps in some cases their lives could also be described as joyful; and members of many mammalian species can suffer from separation from their family group. Is it not therefore a blot on human civilization that we brush aside these needs of nonhuman animals to satisfy minor needs of our own?

Pain is pain, and the extent to which it is intrinsically bad depends on factors like its duration and intensity, not on the species of the being who experiences it. Hence there is no justifiable basis for drawing the boundary of value around our own species. To do so is to give preference to the interests of members of one's own species, simply because they are members of one's own species. This is speciesism, a moral failing that is parallel to racism, because it attempts to put a morally crucial divide in a place that is not justified on any basis other than a preference for "us" over "them." To put it another way, if we are prepared to defend practices based on disregarding the interests of members of other species because they are not members of our own group, how are we to object to those who wish to disregard the interests of members of other races because they are also not members of our own group? I shall not here go further into this argument, because I have developed it elsewhere at some length.[11] The argument shows that the dominant Western tradition is untenable, at least in regard to creatures capable of suffering.

Rejecting the dominant Western tradition in this way makes a radical difference to the value basis on which we should consider environmental policy. Into the calculations about damming the river must now go the interests of all the nonhuman animals who live in the area that will be flooded. A few may be able to move to a neighboring area that is suitable, but wilderness is not full of suitable niches awaiting an occupant; if there is territory that can sustain a native animal, it is most likely already occupied. Thus most of them will die: either they will be drowned, or they will starve.

Neither drowning nor starvation is an easy way to die, and the suffering involved in these deaths should, as we have seen, be given no less weight than we would give to an equivalent amount of suffering experienced by human beings. That, in itself, may be enough to swing the balance against building the dam. What of the fact that the animals will die, apart from the suffering that will occur in the course of dying? Are we also to weigh the deaths of nonhuman animals as equivalent to the deaths of a similar number of human beings? If so, it would seem that almost no development of any area can be justified; even industrial wastelands provide habitat for rodents who will die if the land is built upon. But the argument presented above does not require us to regard the death of a nonhuman animal as morally equivalent to the death of a human being, since humans are capable of foresight and forward planning in ways that nonhuman animals are not. This is surely relevant to the seriousness of death which, in the case of a human being capable of planning for the future, will thwart these plans, and which thus causes a loss that is different in kind from the loss that death causes to beings incapable even of understanding that they exist over time and have a future. It is also entirely legitimate to take into account the greater sense of loss that humans feel when people close to them die; whether nonhuman animals will feel a sense of loss at the death of another animal will depend on the social habits of the species, but in most cases it is unlikely to be as prolonged, and perhaps not as deep, as the grief that humans feel. These differences between causing death to human beings and to nonhuman animals do not mean that the death of a nonhuman animal should be treated as being of no account. On the contrary, death still inflicts a loss on the animal – the loss of all its future existence, and the experiences that that future life would have contained. When a proposed dam would flood a valley and kill thousands, perhaps millions, of sentient creatures, these deaths should be given great importance in any assessment of the costs and benefits of building the dam.

Let us summarize the conclusions reached so far. We have seen that the dominant Western tradition would restrict environmental values to human interests; but this tradition is based on an indefensible prejudice in favor of the interests of our own species. We share our planet with members of other species who are also capable of feeling pain, of suffering, and of having their lives go well or badly. We are justified in regarding their experiences as having the same kind of value as our own similar experiences. The infliction of suffering on other sentient creatures should be given as much weight as we would give to the infliction of suffering on human beings. The deaths of nonhuman animals, considered independently from the suffering that often accompanies death, should also count, although not as much as the deaths of human beings.

Is there Value beyond Sentient Beings?

Reverence for life

The position we have now reached extends the ethic of the dominant Western tradition, but in other respects is recognizably of the same type. It draws the boundary of moral consideration around all sentient creatures, but leaves other living things outside that boundary. This means that if a valley is to be flooded, we should give weight to the interests of human beings, both present and future, and to the interests of the wallabies, possums, marsupial mice, and birds living there; but the drowning of the ancient forests, the possible loss of an entire species, the destruction of several complex ecosystems, the blockage of the wild river itself, and the loss of those rocky gorges, are factors to be taken into account only insofar as they adversely affect sentient creatures. Is a more radical break with the traditional position possible? Can some or all of these aspects of the flooding of the valley be shown to have intrinsic value, so that they must be taken into account independently of their effects on human beings or nonhuman animals?

To extend an ethic in a plausible way beyond sentient beings is a difficult task. An ethic based on the interests of sentient creatures is on recognizable ground. Sentient creatures have wants and desires. They prefer some states to others. We can therefore, though with much imaginative effort and no guarantee of success, form an idea of what it might be like to be that creature under particular conditions. (The question "What is it like to be a possum drowning?" at least makes sense, even if it is impossible for us to give a more precise answer than "It must be awful.") In reaching moral decisions affecting sentient creatures, we can attempt to add up the effects of different actions on all the sentient creatures affected by the alternative actions open to us. This provides us with at least some rough guide to what might be the right thing to do. But there is *nothing* that corresponds to what it is like to be a tree dying because its roots have been flooded. Once we abandon the interests of sentient creatures as our source of value, where do we find value? What is good or bad for nonsentient creatures, and why does it matter?

It might be thought that as long as we limit ourselves to living things, the answer is not too difficult to find. After all, we know what is good or bad for the plants in our garden: water, sunlight, and compost are good; extremes of heat or cold are bad. The same applies to plants in any forest or wilderness, so why can we not regard their flourishing as good in itself, independently of its usefulness to sentient creatures?

One problem here is that without conscious interests to guide us, we have no way of assessing the relative weights to be given to the flourishing of different forms of life. Is a 2,000-year-old Huon pine more worthy of preservation than a tussock of grass? Most people will say that it is, but such a judgment seems to have more to do with our feelings of awe for the age, size, and beauty of the tree, or with the length of time it would take to replace it, than with our perception of some intrinsic value in the flourishing of an old tree that is not possessed by a young grass tussock.

If we cease talking in terms of sentience, the boundary between living and inanimate natural objects becomes more difficult to defend. Would it really be worse to cut down an old tree than to destroy a beautiful stalactite that has taken even longer to grow? On what grounds could such a judgment be made? Probably the best-known defence of an ethic that draws the boundaries of ethics around all living things is that of Albert Schweitzer. The phrase he used, "reverence for life," is often quoted; the arguments he offered in support of such a position are less well-known. Here is one of the few passages in which he defended his ethic:

> Just as in my own will-to-live there is a yearning for more life, and for that mysterious exaltation of the will which is called pleasure, and terror in face of annihilation and that injury to the will-to-live which is called pain; so the same obtains in all the will-to-live around me, equally whether it can express itself to my comprehension or whether it remains unvoiced.
>
> Ethics thus consists in this, that I experience the necessity of practising the same reverence for life toward all will-to-live as toward my own. Therein I have already the needed fundamental principle of morality. It is *good* to maintain and cherish life; it is *evil* to destroy and to check life.[12]

A similar view has been defended recently by the contemporary American philosopher Paul Taylor. In his book *Respect for Nature*, Taylor argues that every living thing is "pursuing its own good in its own unique way." Once we see this, we can see all living things "as we see ourselves" and therefore "we are ready to place the same value on their existence as we do on our own."[13]

The problem with the defenses offered by both Schweitzer and Taylor for their ethical views is that they use language metaphorically and then argue as if what they had said was literally true. We may often talk about plants "seeking" water or light so that they can survive, and this way of thinking about plants makes it easier to accept talk of their "will to live," or of them "pursuing" their own good. Once we stop, however, to reflect on the fact that plants are not conscious and cannot engage in any intentional behavior, it is clear that all this language is metaphorical; one might just as well say that a river is pursuing its own good and striving to reach the sea, or that the "good" of a guided missile is to blow itself up along with its target. It is misleading of Schweitzer to attempt to sway us toward an ethic of reverence for all life by referring to "yearning," "exaltation," "pleasure," and "terror." Plants experience none of these.

Moreover, in the case of plants, rivers, and guided missiles, it is possible to give a purely physical explanation of what is happening; and in the absence of consciousness, there is no good reason why we should have greater respect for the physical processes that govern the growth and decay of living things than we have for those that govern nonliving things. This being so, it is at least not obvious why we should have greater reverence for a tree than for a stalactite, or for a single-celled organism than for a mountain; and we can pass silently by Taylor's even more extraordinary claim, that we should be ready not merely to respect every living thing, but that we should place the same value on the life of every living thing as we place on our own.

Deep ecology

More than forty years ago the American ecologist Aldo Leopold wrote that there was a need for a "new ethic," an "ethic dealing with man's relation to land and to the animals and plants which grow upon it." His proposed "land ethic" would enlarge "the boundaries of the community to include soils, waters, plants, and animals, or collectively, the land."[14] The rise of ecological concern in the early 1970s led to a revival of this way of thinking. The Norwegian philosopher Arne Naess wrote a brief but influential article distinguishing between the "shallow" and "deep" forms of ecological thinking. Shallow ecological thinking was limited to the traditional moral framework; those who thought in this way were anxious to avoid pollution to our water supply so that we could have safe water to drink, and they sought to preserve wilderness so that people could continue to enjoy walking through it. Deep ecologists, on the other hand, wanted to preserve the integrity of the biosphere for its own sake, irrespective of the possible benefits to humans that might flow from so doing.[15] Subsequent writers who have attempted to develop some form of deep environmental theory include the Americans Bill Devall and George Sessions, and the Australians Lawrence Johnson, Val Plumwood, and Richard Sylvan.[16]

Where the reverence-for-life ethic emphasizes individual living organisms, proposals for deep ecology ethics tend to take something larger as the object of value: species, ecological systems, even the biosphere as a whole. Leopold summed up the basis of his new land ethic thus: "A thing is right when it tends to preserve the integrity, stability, and beauty of the biotic community. It is wrong when it tends otherwise."[17] In a paper published in 1984, Arne Naess and George Sessions set out several principles for a deep ecological ethic, beginning with the following:

1 The well-being and flourishing of human and nonhuman Life on Earth have value in themselves (synonyms: intrinsic value, inherent value). These values are independent of the usefulness of the nonhuman world for human purposes.
2 Richness and diversity of life forms contribute to the realization of these values and are also values in themselves.
3 Humans have no right to reduce this richness and diversity except to satisfy *vital* needs.[18]

Although these principles refer only to life, in the same paper Naess and Sessions say that deep ecology uses the term "biosphere in a more comprehensive non-technical way to refer also to what biologists classify as 'non-living'; rivers (watersheds), landscapes, ecosystems." Sylvan and Plumwood also extend their ethic beyond living things, including in it an obligation "not to jeopardize the wellbeing of natural objects or systems without good reason."[19]

Behind this application of ethics not only to individuals, but also to species and ecosystems, lies some form of holism – some sense that the species or ecosystem is not just a collection of individuals, but really an entity in its own right. This holism is made explicit in Lawrence Johnson's *A Morally Deep World*, probably the most detailed and carefully argued statement of the case for an ethic of deep ecology yet to appear in print. Lawrence is prepared to talk about the interests of a species in a sense that is distinct from the sum of the interests of each member of the species, and to argue that the interests of a species or an ecosystem ought to be taken into account, with individual interests, in our moral deliberations.

There is, of course, a real philosophical question about whether a species or an ecosystem can be considered as the sort of individual that can have interests; and even if it can, the deep-ecology ethic will face problems similar to those we identified in considering the idea of the reverence-for-life ethic. For it is necessary, not merely that trees, species, and ecosystems can properly be said to have interests, but that they have morally significant interests. We saw in discussing the ethic of reverence for life that one way of establishing that an interest is morally significant is to ask what it would be like for the entity affected to have that interest unsatisfied. This works for sentient beings, but it does not work for trees, species, or ecosystems. There is nothing that corresponds to what it is like to be an ecosystem flooded by a dam. In this respect trees, ecosystems, and species are more like rocks than they are like sentient beings; so the divide between sentient and nonsentient creatures is to that extent a firmer basis for a morally important boundary than the divide between living and nonliving things or holistic entities.

If we were to adopt an ethic that attributed value to nonsentient living things, or to ecosystems as a whole, we would need to have a criterion of what made something more valuable than something else. Naess and Sessions, in common with many other deep ecologists, suggest "richness" and "diversity"; sometimes the term used is "complexity."[20] But what is it for something to be rich, diverse, or complex? Did the introduction of European birds into Australia make our birdlife richer and more diverse? If it could be shown that it did, would that make it a good thing? What if we should discover that allowing effluent from intensive farms to seep into our rivers greatly increases the number of micro-organisms that live in them – thus giving rivers a different, but more diverse and more complex ecosystem than they had before they were polluted? Does that make the pollution desirable?

To seek intrinsic value in diversity or complexity is a mistake. The reason why we may feel more strongly about destruction of diverse and complex ecosystems than about simpler ones (such as a field of wheat) may be the same as the reason why we feel more strongly about preservation of the ceiling of the Sistine Chapel than we do about the preservation of the ceiling of the Lecture Theatre H3 at Monash University (which is painted a uniform white). To break up Michelangelo's fresco into handy-sized chunks for sale to tourists would be lucrative, and no doubt the Vatican could put the money to good use in fighting poverty (better use than that usually made of the returns from damming rivers or clearing forests); but would it be right to do so? The objection, in both cases, is to vandalism: the destruction, for short-term gain, of something that has enduring value to sentient beings, is easy to destroy but once destroyed can never exist again.

If the philosophical basis for a deep-ecology ethic is difficult to sustain, this does not mean that the case for the preservation of wilderness is not strong. All it means is that one kind of argument – the argument for the intrinsic value of the plants, species, or ecosystems – is, at best, problematic. We are on surer ground if we confine ourselves to arguments based on the interests of sentient creatures, present and future, human and nonhuman. In my view the arguments grounded on the interests of present and future human beings, and on the interests of the sentient nonhumans who inhabit wilderness, are quite sufficient to show that, at least in a society where no one needs to destroy wilderness in order to survive, the value of preserving the remaining significant areas of wilderness greatly exceeds the values gained by its destruction.

Notes

1 I have defended this assumption elsewhere: see my *Practical Ethics* (Cambridge: Cambridge University Press, 1989), ch. 1.

2 Genesis 1: 26–28.

3 See Robin Attfield, *The Ethics of Environmental Concern* (Oxford: Blackwell, 1983).

4 Genesis 9: 2.

5 Corinthians 9: 9–10.

6 Augustine, *The Catholic and Manichean Ways of Life*, trans. D. A. Gallagher and I. J. Gallagher (Boston: Catholic University Press, 1966), p. 102. For cursing of the fig tree, see Mark 11: 12–22, and for that of the pigs, Mark 5: 1–13.

7 Aristotle, *Politics* (London: J. M. Dent, 1916), p. 16.

8 Aquinas, *Summa Theologiae*, II, ii, Question 64, article 1; I, ii, Question 72, article 4.

9 For details on the alternative Christian thinkers, see Keith Thomas, *Man and the Natural World* (London: Allen Lane, 1983), pp. 152–3 and Attfield, *The Ethics of Environmental Concern*.

10 Aristotle, *Politics*.

11 Peter Singer, *Animal Liberation*, 2nd edn. (New York: New York Review of Books and Random House, 1990).

12 Albert Schweitzer, *Civilization and Ethics* (Part II of The *Philosophy of Civilization*, trans. C. T. Campion), 2nd edn. (London, 1929), pp. 246–7.

13 Paul Taylor, *Respect for Nature* (Princeton, NJ: Princeton University Press, 1986), pp. 45, 128. My discussion draws on a fine critique of Taylor by Gerald Paske, "The Life Principle: a (metaethical) rejection," *Journal of Applied Philosophy*, 6 (1989), pp. 219–25.

14 A. Leopold, *A Sand County Almanac* (New York: Oxford University Press, 1966; first published 1949), pp. 219, 238.

15 A. Naess, "The Shallow and the Deep, Long-Range Ecology Movement," *Inquiry*, 16 (1973), pp. 95–100.

16 See, for example, the following works: W. Devall and G. Sessions, *Deep Ecology: Living As If Nature Mattered* (Salt Lake City: Gibbs Smith, 1985); L. Johnson, *A Morally Deep World* (Cambridge: Cambridge University Press, 1990); V. Plumwood, "Ecofeminism: an Overview and Discussion of Positions and Arguments: Critical Review," *Australasian Journal of Philosophy*, 64 (Supplement) (1986), pp. 120–38; R. Sylvan, "Three Essays Upon Deeper Environmental Ethics," *Discussion Papers in Environmental Philosophy*, 13 (1986), published by the Australian National University, Canberra; and P. Taylor, *Respect for Nature*.

17 Leopold, *A Sand County Almanac*, p. 262.

18 A. Naess and G. Sessions, "Basic Principles of Deep Ecology," *Ecophilosophy*, 6 (1984), pp. 3–7; quoted from D. Bennet and R. Sylvan, "Australian Perspectives on Environmental Ethics: A UNESCO Project," unpublished, 1989.

19 R. Routley [now R. Sylvan] and V. Routley [now V. Plumwood], "Human Chauvinism and Environmental Ethics," in D. Mannison, M. McRobbie, and R. Routley (eds.), *Environmental Philosophy* (Canberra: Australian National University Research School of Social Sciences, 1980).

20 For a useful survey of the value positions of deep ecologists, see R. Sylvan, *A Critique of Deep Ecology* (Canberra: Australian National University, Department of Philosophy, Discussion Papers in Environmental Philosophy, 12), p. 53.

Twenty-two

Coping with Global Change: The Need for Different Values

What are our ultimate values? What do we take as our goals in life? The problem is that if we *do not* start reflecting seriously on these issues, we are likely to be led by the forces of the free market into a direction that will be individually unsatisfying and collectively self-defeating. The kind of question that I want to ask was nicely put in Oliver Stone's movie *Wall Street*. The movie starred Michael Douglas as a convincingly unpleasant Gordon Gekko, a financial wheeler-dealer and corporate raider. Bud Fox, the ambitious young stockbroker played by Charlie Sheen, is for a time taken in by the prospect of making it big, but when Gekko attempts his usual takeover and asset-stripping procedure on the airline for which Fox's father works as a mechanic, an angry Fox asks: "Tell me, Gordon, when does it all end, huh? How many yachts can you water-ski behind? How much is enough?"

"How much is enough?" is a question that we need to ask more, and we need to discuss with children whose goals are in the process of being formed. It may not sound like an ethical question. It is not a sensitive ethical issue, like abortion or euthanasia. It does not connect with common ethical concerns, like dishonesty. It is not about sexual propriety – or at least, not obviously so. Despite these appearances, however, it is a question that leads us deeply into ethics. That is because we cannot say how much is enough until we know: "enough for *what?*" And this is a value question. I want to explore that question today in the context of global change.

First published in the *Journal of Human Values*, 2 (1996), pp. 37–48. Copyright © Management Centre for Human Values, Institute of Management, Calcutta. Reproduced with permission of the copyright-holders and Sage Publications India, New Delhi.

Since the collapse of communist societies in Eastern Europe and the former Soviet Union, we have been living in a world that has only one dominant social model for developed societies. The hope of resolving the conflict between individual self-interest and the good of all by building an alternative to the free market economy based on collective ownership of the means of production and distribution is now a self-confessed failure. Only a brave few cling to the socialist ideal, rejecting the distortion Lenin and Stalin wrought, and claiming that it has never had a proper trial. It seems that the individualist view of self-interest is the only one we have.

So strongly does the liberal democratic free enterprise model impose itself on our vision of the possibilities that Francis Fukuyama, a former deputy director of policy planning at the US State Department, has been given a respectful, and from some quarters even enthusiastic, hearing for a bold, surprisingly well-defended, but in the end scarcely plausible idea. Fukuyama has revived Hegel's conception of history as a process with a direction and an end. History has an end, according to Hegel and his twentieth-century disciple, not so much in the sense of coming to a full stop, but rather in the sense of a final goal or destination. In *The End of History and the Last Man*, Fukuyama argues that this end is, precisely, the universal acceptance of the liberal, democratic, free enterprise form of society.[1] Yet just when this model has taken so strong a hold on the minds of those who consider themselves politically realistic, we are gradually becoming aware that we are nearing the end of an epoch. Like Daniel Bell, who predicted "The End of Ideology" shortly before the rise of the New Left and the resurgence of radical ideologies in the 1960s,[2] Fukuyama may have predicted the permanence of the liberal free enterprise system just when it is about to prove itself unable to cope with its gravest crisis.

I would like to offer a counterweight to Fukuyama's vision of "The End of History." It is summed up in the title of a book by Bill McKibben: our era is witness to, not the end of history, but rather *the end of nature*. As a writer who lives in the Adirondack Mountains of New York state, McKibben is sharply aware of the fact that for the first time in the history of our species, there is no longer a natural world, unaffected by human beings.[3] Not in the Adirondacks, nor in the rainforests of the Amazon, nor on the Antarctic ice-cap, can one get away from the effects of human civilization. We have depleted the ozone layer that shields our planet from solar radiation. We have added to the amount of carbon dioxide in the atmosphere. Thus the growth of plants, the chemical composition of the rain, and the very forces that form the clouds, are in part our doing. Until now we have used the oceans and the atmosphere as a vast sink for our wastes.

The liberal democratic free enterprise society that Fukuyama proposes as the ultimate outcome of all history is built on the idea that we can keep doing this forever. The body of responsible scientific opinion is telling us that we are passengers on a runaway train that is heading rapidly toward an abyss. We *cannot* continue with business as usual. We shall either change voluntarily, or the climate of our planet will change, and take entire nations with it. Nor are the changes we need to make minor ones. They involve the basic values and ethical outlook that underlie the free enterprise societies of the late twentieth century.

Perhaps the liberal democratic free enterprise society will survive this challenge, and adapt to cope with it; but if it does, it will be a significantly different form of liberal democratic free enterprise society, and the people living in it will need to have very different values and ways of living. So the pressure to reexamine the ethical basis of our lives is upon us in a way that it has never been before.

Jean-Jacques Rousseau or Adam Smith?

If any single man pointed the direction in which the free enterprise economy should march, that man was Adam Smith, and the pointer was his extraordinarily influential work, *The Wealth of Nations*, published in 1776. Smith argued that in a market economy we can each become wealthy only by being more efficient than our competitors at satisfying the wants of our customers or clients – a thought epitomized in his famous sentence: "It is not from the benevolence of the butcher that we expect our dinner but from his regard to his own self-interest." To serve our own interests, we will strive to produce our goods more cheaply than others, or to produce better goods at the same price. If we succeed, the market will reward us with wealth; if we fail, the market will put us out of business. Thus, wrote Smith, the desires of countless individuals for their private interests are drawn together, as if by a hidden hand, to work for the public interest. The collective outcome of the individual desire for wealth is a prosperous nation, which benefits not only the wealthy, but also "the very meanest person in a civilized country." On this last point, Smith waxed lyrical:

> the accommodation of a European prince does not always so much exceed that of an industrious and frugal peasant, as the accommodation of the latter exceeds that of many an African king, the absolute master of the lives and liberties of ten thousand naked savages.[4]

This became a standard justification for the inequality that results from the pursuit of wealth under a free enterprise system. Even the poorest, we are told, have no grounds for complaint, because they are better off than a king in Africa.[5]

Some twenty years before he published *The Wealth of Nations*, Smith wrote a critique of a work that was then causing something of a sensation among intellectuals on the continent: Jean-Jacques Rousseau's *Discourse on Inequality*. Rousseau's essay, which compared modern civilization unfavorably with the life of the "noble savage," was an attack on everything that Smith was later to champion. In Rousseau's vision of the natural state of human beings, the earth was left to "its natural fertility" and was covered with "immense forests whose trees were never mutilated by the axe." These conditions provided "on every side both sustenance and shelter for every species of animal." As for the noble savage himself:

> I see him satisfying his hunger at the first oak, and slaking his thirst at the first brook; finding his bed at the foot of the tree which afforded him a repast; and with that, all his wants supplied.[6]

For taking us out of this idyllic state, Rousseau blamed the institution of private property, which allowed us to accumulate more than we needed, and so made us compare what we had with what others had, and desire to surpass them in wealth. This multiplication of our wants he saw as the source not only of inequality, but also of hatred, civil strife, slavery, crime, war, deceit, and all the other evils of modern life.

Adam Smith, however, took a very different view of the desire to accumulate possessions. Both in his critique of Rousseau and in a larger work, *Theory of the Moral Sentiments*, which he was then delivering as lectures at the University of Glasgow, he defended the multiplication of wants and the desire to accumulate possessions. It was, he thought, our desire to accumulate more and more that led our ancestors to develop the arts and sciences in ways which:

> have entirely changed the whole face of the globe, have turned the rude forests of nature into agreeable and fertile plains, and made the trackless and barren ocean a new fund of subsistence.... The rich ... are led by an invisible hand to make nearly the same distribution of the necessities of life, which would have been made, had the earth been divided into equal portions among all its inhabitants, and thus without intending it, without knowing it, advance the interest of society, and afford means to the multiplication of the species.[7]

A modern reader cannot help being struck by the difference in the attitudes of Rousseau and Smith to the forests and nature generally. Since the world has followed Smith rather than Rousseau, the state of our forests is not surprising. But now it is time to stop and ask: why are we *still* following Smith rather than

Rousseau? It is significant that Smith did not defend the desire to accumulate possessions on the grounds that accumulation is the way to happiness. On the contrary, this belief was, he thought, a "deception." Regarding the grander houses and possessions for which we strive, Smith says:

> If we consider the real satisfaction which all these things are capable of affording, by itself and separated from the beauty of that arrangement which is fitted to promote it, it will always appear in the highest degree contemptible and trifling. But we rarely view it in this abstract and philosophical light.[8]

Instead, when we think about "the pleasures of wealth and greatness," they strike us "as something grand and beautiful and noble, of which the attainment is well worth all the toil and anxiety which we are so apt to bestow upon it." Now comes the punch-line of all this: though we are deceived when we imagine that wealth will bring us real satisfaction, the deception is a fortunate one, because "it is this deception which rouses and keeps in continual motion the industry of mankind."[9] Thus the father of modern economics and the greatest original advocate of the free enterprise society did not believe that it would bring us any real satisfaction!

It is true that all this economic development conformed to the biblical notion that it is good for our species to "be fruitful, and multiply, and replenish the earth, and subdue it, and have dominion over the fish of the sea and over the fowl of the air, and over every living thing that moveth upon the earth."[10] Today, however, the desirability of any further "multiplication of the species" is highly dubious, and there are few who would advocate turning more forests into "agreeable plains." We need to challenge the view of nature that lies behind Adam Smith's economics.

Living on Our Inheritance

As a generation, we have inherited the accumulated resources of our planet: fertile soils, forests, oil, coal, and minerals like iron and bauxite; and an atmosphere and oceans capable of absorbing the wastes we put into them. We began the twentieth century with a relatively clean and stable natural global environment. On this basis, we have built a huge global economy that produces, for the upper- and middle-class citizens of developed nations, an unprecedented standard of luxury, supplemented by an extraordinary range of gadgets. The global economy now produces as much in seventeen days as the economy of our grandparents, around the turn of the century, produced in a year.[11] We assume that this expansion can go on without limit, but the economy we have built depends on using up our inheritance. Since the middle of the century the world has doubled its per capita use of energy, steel, copper, and wood. Consumption of meat has doubled in the same period and car ownership has quadrupled. And these are items that were already being used in large quantities in 1950; the increase for relatively new materials, like plastic and aluminum, is higher still. Since 1940, Americans alone have used up as large a share of the earth's mineral resources as did everyone before them put to-gether.[12] We are eating up capital, rather than living on what we produce. From the food we produce to the exhaust we emit from our cars, the pattern is the same. We take what we want from the earth, and leave behind toxic chemical dumps, polluted streams, oil slicks on the oceans, and nuclear wastes that will be deadly for tens of thousands of years. The economy is a subsystem of the biosphere, and it is rapidly running up against the limits of the larger system.

How an Overflowing Sink Makes Adam Smith Obsolete

Our present economy is simply not sustainable. That is true even if we focus only on the developed countries. But we cannot limit our focus in this way. Jeremy Leggatt, science director of Greenpeace in Britain, has warned that China's plans to increase its coal burning sixfold in the next forty years could mean that China is emitting three times as much of the world's greenhouse gases as the United States does today. Such grim warnings have led to various international conferences that try to get nations to agree first not to increase greenhouse gas emissions, and then to wind them back to the levels of previous years, for example, 1990 levels. But there is a fundamental ethical flaw in this way of dealing with the problem. The average American is responsible for the burning of between 4 and 5 tonnes of carbon per year; the average Indian or Chinese contributes roughly one-tenth of this amount. How can the citizens of rich nations tell China to stop, when even if China's ambitious plans succeed, each Chinese citizen would still be adding less carbon dioxide to the atmos-phere than the citizens of most rich countries do today?

No wonder that Third World economists are starting to see Western concern about the environmental effects of Third World economic develop-ment as a new form of colonialism. Anil Agarwal of the Center for Science and the Environment in New Delhi has put the case forcefully:

India and China today account for more than one-third of the world's popula-tion. The question to be asked is whether we are consuming one-third of the world's resources or contributing one-third of the muck and dirt in the atmos-phere and the oceans. If not, then surely these nations should be lauded for keeping the world in balance because of their parsimonious consumption despite the Western rape and pillage of the world's resources.[13]

Agarwal suggests that we see our planet's facility for dealing with waste as a very large, but finite, global sink. The use of this sink should be shared out equally between the people of the world. Every individual on the planet might be regarded as having an entitlement to dump, say, half a ton of carbon down the sink. On that basis, Americans are now using more than six times their fair share, while most Indians and Chinese are using less than their entitlement. The greediest five countries, seen from this perspective, are the United States, Australia, Canada, Germany, and the bloc that made up the former Soviet Union.

Adam Smith argued that the rich did not deprive the poor of their share of the world's wealth. In another part of the passage cited earlier in this article, he wrote:

> The rich only select from the heap what is most precious and agreeable. They consume little more than the poor, and in spite of their natural selfishness and rapacity, though they mean only their own conveniency, though the sole end which they propose from the labours of all the thousands whom they employ, be the gratification of their own vain and insatiable desires, they divide with the poor the produce of all their improvements.[14]

Smith then refers, as in the section of the passage quoted earlier, to the "invisible hand" which brings about a distribution of the necessities of life that is "nearly the same" as it would have been if the world had been divided up equally among all its inhabitants. Whether this was true even in Smith's day is very doubtful; but if we move to the present time, and consider "the rich" to include all the developed nations, then in the light of the facts to which Agarwal refers it is quite obvious that Smith is wrong. Smith never dreamt that the capacity of the atmosphere to absorb pollutants might be a finite resource. So while he knew that the rich could be selfish and rapacious, he did not imagine that they could take ten times their share of the global atmospheric sink. Far from dividing with the poor the produce of all their improvements, the rich effectively deprive the poor of the opportunity to develop along the lines that the rich themselves have taken; for if the poor were to behave as the rich do, the global sink would overflow, bringing catastrophe on us all.

An Opportunity for Change

It is time to return to the question: "How much is enough?" I have not yet given the answer that Gordon Gekko gives to Bud Fox's question, "How much is enough?" Here it is:

It's not a question of enough, pal. It's a zero-sum game. Somebody wins, somebody loses.

The result of this competitive attitude to life is a striving that can never be satisfied. Consider the real-life case of Ivan Boesky, the multimillionaire arbitrageur to whom the figure of Gordon Gekko bears more than a passing resemblance. Why did Boesky get involved in insider trading when he already had more money than he could ever spend? In 1992, six years after Boesky pleaded guilty to insider trading, his estranged wife Seema broke her silence and spoke about Ivan Boesky's motives in an interview with Barbara Walters for the American ABC network's *20/20* program. Walters asked whether Ivan Boesky was a man who craved for luxury. Seema Boesky thought not, pointing out that he worked around the clock, seven days a week, and never took a day off to enjoy his money. She then recalled that when, in 1982, *Forbes* magazine first listed Boesky among the wealthiest people in the US, he was upset. She assumed he disliked the publicity, and made some remark to that effect. Boesky replied:

> That's not what's upsetting me. We're no one. We're nowhere. We're at the bottom of the list and I promise you I won't shame you like that again ever. We will not remain at the bottom of that list.[15]

We must free ourselves from this absurd conception of success. Not only does it fail to bring happiness even to those who, like Ivan Boesky, do extraordinarily well in the competitive struggle; it also sets a social standard that is a recipe for global injustice and environmental disaster. We cannot continue to see our goal as acquiring more and more wealth, or as consuming more and more goodies, and leaving behind us a larger than ever heap of waste.

The problem is that the dominant conception of the good life today depends on constantly rising levels of consumption. When the celebrated Harvard economist J. K. Galbraith published *The Affluent Society* in 1958, nobody disputed the accuracy of its title as a description of the United States, nor did they disagree with the picture presented in the book of a land, America, that had reached heights of affluence undreamt of by earlier generations. Yet Paul Wachtel pointed out in *The Poverty of Affluence* that America has since become, in terms of material, considerably more affluent than it had been twenty-five years earlier. Wachtel reports that by the early 1980s, Americans owned five times as many air-conditioners per head, four times as many clothes dryers, and seven times as many dish-washers. One can add to Wachtel's figures: in 1960, only 1 percent of American homes had color television; by 1987, this had risen to 93 percent. Microwaves and video cassette recorders entered American homes in the 1970s and 1980s, and within a decade were to be found in nearly two-thirds of all homes.[16] Despite this dramatic increase in material goods, people felt neither more affluent nor happier. The University of Chicago's National Opinion Research Center has for many years been asking Americans how happy they are. The proportion describing themselves as "very happy" has hovered around one-third since the 1950s.[17] Why has it not risen with material levels of affluence? Essentially, because though the society was still becoming more affluent, the rate at which it was doing so had slowed:

> In judging how well off we are economically ... we assimilate new input to our "adaptation level." For many Americans, having one or several color television sets, two or more cars, a home in which there are more rooms than people ... these and other features of their lives are experienced as the "neutral point." They do not excite us or arouse much feeling. Only a *departure* from that level is really noticed. Some pleasure may be afforded by our background level of material comfort, but unless we look elsewhere than the accumulation of goods for the main sources of pleasure and excitement in our lives, we are bound to be on a treadmill – one which, we are increasingly recognizing, can damage our health and shorten our lives.[18]

The message is that no amount of running on a treadmill can lead to personal fulfillment. Whether people compare themselves with their own wealth the year before, or with what their neighbors have, it is clear that for most people, most of the time, the pursuit of material affluence cannot bring happiness. That may be why the glaring disparities of wealth between Nigerians and West Germans, or between Filipinos and Japanese, do not give rise to any differences in how people from these nations rate their level of happiness. Michael Argyle, an Oxford psychologist and author of *The Psychology of Happiness*, sums up the evidence by saying: "There is very little difference in the levels of reported happiness found in rich and very poor countries."[19] Equally obviously, when growth runs into environmental constraints, this attitude is a recipe for disaster.

To say this is not to be anti-growth. There is potential for environmentally sustainable growth. Often ways of doing things that are environmentally friendly are also more labour-intensive than alternatives that consume more fossil fuels or cause more pollution. The Worldwatch Institute has estimated that generating 1,000 gigawatt-hours of electricity per year requires 100 workers in a nuclear power plant, 116 in a coal-fired plant, 248 in a solar thermal plant, and 542 on a wind farm.[20] Those figures partially explain, of course, why the nuclear and coal plants produce electricity that, in straight dollar terms, is cheaper than the more environmentally friendly alternatives; but the cost to our global ecosystem is not included in the dollar figures. The same is true of a comparison between an industry based on the use of a natural resource, such as a forest or a bauxite deposit, and one based on recycling paper or aluminum cans. The use of the natural resource may be cheaper, but it uses up an irreplaceable resource; recycling will be more labour-intensive and therefore costlier, but it is sustainable.

To move toward a sustainable economy would cause unemployment in some industries, but on balance, it would create jobs, not reduce them. Nevertheless, in strictly material terms, it has to be assumed that we would be worse off. Consuming irreplaceable resources is a quick and easy way of enriching ourselves; and we save ourselves a lot more trouble and expense by pouring our wastes down the global sink at a rate that, if continued by future generations, or matched by those in underdeveloped countries, will cause global catastrophe. If we cut back on these cheap ways of enriching ourselves, the economic loss must be felt somewhere. Products now made by consuming irreplaceable resources or polluting the environment will become more expensive, and so we will be able to afford fewer of them. That may include cars, consumer goods, the use of energy for air-conditioning, heating, and transport, and even food, like feedlot beef and intensively farmed pork and poultry, produced by methods that are extravagant of energy, soil, and water.

If we retain our narrow view of our own self-interest, particularly the conception that has been molded by the development of consumerism since World War II, we will see the reduction in material affluence as nothing but a setback. Even if we recognize that it is inevitable, that the present economy cannot be sustained, we will consider it a regrettable necessity, desirable in the interests of the world as a whole, but bad in its impact on our own lives. On a broader view of self-interest, however, we ought to welcome the change, not just for the good of the global environment, but also for ourselves. For a start, although walking, riding bicycles, and using public transport may use fewer resources than sitting in slow-moving traffic in one's own air-conditioned car, it is by no means obvious that the lower use of resources leads to less overall satisfaction for those who walk, cycle, or take the train. This is just one way in which the size of a nation's gross national product is no guide to the level of welfare of the population. This is one reason why we need to change our conception of self-interest; but there is another, which goes deeper.

For centuries Western society has sought satisfaction from the holy grail of material abundance. The search has been exciting, and we have discovered many things that were well worth finding, but insofar as our goal was ever a sensible one, we reached it long ago. Unfortunately we have forgotten that there could be any other goals at all. What is there to live for, other than to be richer than others, and richer than we were before? Many who are outstandingly successful in terms of the materialistic conception of success find that the rewards for which they have worked so hard lose their appeal once they have been achieved. Adam Smith would not have been at all surprised. The search for happiness through material wealth is based on a deception. Considered just from the standpoint of our own real interests the case for changing our conception of the good life is very strong. But as I have argued, this conception has to be changed for quite different reasons. It is constructed and became entrenched during a period when no one thought of limits to material wealth or consumption. As the idea of unlimited growth has become untenable, so too has our conception of the good life. So what should our goals be? The pressing ecological necessity of changing our economy offers us the best opportunity for centuries to reflect on this question, and to find out how much really is enough.

The Importance of a Cause

How then do we find meaning in our lives? How do we choose goals? What should we take to be our ultimate values? In my book *How Are We to Live?* I have suggested that we need to find a cause, or causes, that extend beyond the boundaries of our self.[21] There are many such causes. Footballers are constantly reminded that the club is larger than the individual; so are employees of corporations, especially those that work for corporations that foster group loyalty with songs, slogans, and social activities, in the Japanese manner. To support one's Mafia "family" is to be part of a cause larger than the self. So is being a member of a religious cult, or of the Nazi Party. And so too is working against injustice and exploitation in one of its many specific forms. No doubt, a commitment to each of these causes can be, for some people, a way of finding meaning and fulfillment.

So is it after all arbitrary, whether one chooses an ethical cause or some other cause? No; living an ethical life is certainly not the only way of making a commitment that can give substance and worth to one's life; but for anyone choosing one kind of life rather than another, it is the commitment with the firmest foundation. The more we reflect on our commitment to a football club, a corporation, or any sectional interest, the less point we are likely to see in it. In contrast, no amount of reflection will show a commitment to an ethical life to be trivial or pointless.

We tend to see ethics as opposed to self-interest: we assume that those who make fortunes from insider trading are successfully following self-interest (as long as they do not get caught) and ignoring ethics. We think that it is in our interest to take a more senior and better-paid position with another company, even though it means that we are helping to manufacture or promote a product that does no good at all, or is environmentally damaging. On the other hand, those who pass up opportunities to rise in their career because of ethical "scruples" about the nature of the work, or who give away their wealth to good causes, are thought to be sacrificing their own interests in order to obey the dictates of ethics.

This message is blasted at us from every side of popular culture. We see the same assumption of conflict between ethics and self-interest in the axioms of modern economics. The idea is propagated in popular presentations of sociobiology applied to human nature. Bestselling books like Robert J. Ringer's *Looking Out for No. 1* – which was on the *New York Times* bestseller list for an entire year – tell millions of readers that to put the happiness of anyone else ahead of one's own is "to pervert the laws of Nature."[22] Television, both in its programs and its commercials, conveys materialist images of success that lack ethical content.

The message is coming over strongly, but something is wrong. Today the assertion that life is meaningless no longer comes from existentialist philosophers who treat it as a shocking discovery; it comes from bored adolescents, for whom it is a truism. Perhaps it is the central place of self-interest, and the way in which we conceive of our own interest, that is to blame here. The pursuit of self-interest, as standardly conceived, is a life without any meaning beyond our own pleasure or individual satisfaction. Such a life is often a self-defeating enterprise. The ancients knew of the "paradox of hedonism," according to which the more explicitly we pursue our desire for pleasure, the more elusive we will find its satisfaction. There is no reason to believe that human nature has changed so dramatically as to render this ancient wisdom inapplicable.

Here ethics returns to complete our picture. An ethical life is one in which we identify ourselves with other and larger goals, thereby giving meaning to our lives. If we understand both ethics and self-interest properly, they may not be at odds after all. The view that there is a harmony between ethics and enlightened self-interest is an ancient one, now often scorned. Cynicism is more fashionable than idealism. But such hopes are not groundless, and there are substantial elements of truth in the ancient view that an ethically reflective life is also a good life for the person leading it. Never has it been so urgent that the reasons for accepting this view should be widely understood.

In a society in which the narrow pursuit of material self-interest is the norm, the shift to an ethical stance is more radical than many people realize. In comparison with the needs of people going short of food in Rwanda, the desire to sample the wines of Australia's best vineyards pales into insignificance. The preservation of old-growth forests should override our desire to use disposable paper towels. An ethical approach to life does not forbid having fun or enjoying food and wine; but it changes our sense of priorities. The effort and expense put into fashion, the endless search for more and more refined gastronomic pleasures, the added expense that marks out the luxury car market – all these become disproportionate to people who can shift perspective long enough to take themselves, at least for a time, out of the spotlight. If a higher ethical consciousness spreads, it will fundamentally change the society in which we live.

Radical as this change is, a shift in our goals is absolutely necessary if we are to avoid both social and ecological disaster. My hope is that over the next decade, beginning with a few committed individuals, there will emerge a critical mass of people with new priorities. If these people are seen to do well, in every sense of the term – if their altruism to each other brings reciprocal benefits, and if they manifest greater fulfillment in their lives – then the ethical attitude may gradually spread. I am no utopian, and I do not expect the ethical attitude ever to be adopted universally. There will always be a niche for those who take advantage of others, and the fewer who occupy that niche, the more profitable it will become for those who remain in it. As an initial target, it will be enough if the idea of living an ethical life can be reinstated as a realistic and viable alternative to the present dominance of materialist self-interest.

Notes and References

1 Francis Fukuyama, *The End of History and the Last Man* (New York: Penguin, 1992).
2 Daniel Bell, *The End of Ideology* (Cambridge, MA: Harvard University Press, 1988).
3 Bill McKibben, *The End of Nature* (New York: Random House, 1989).
4 Adam Smith, *The Wealth of Nations*, I.i, ed. R. H. Campbell and A. S. Skinner (Oxford: Clarendon Press, 1976), p. 24.
5 For Locke it was a king in America, not Africa: "And a king of a larger and fruitful territory there feeds, lodges, and is clad worse than a day labourer in England." *Second Treatise on Civil Government* (London: J. M. Dent, 1966), ch. 5, para 41; see also Bernard Mandeville, *The Fable of the Bees*, pt. i.181: "If we trace the most flourishing Nations in their Origin, we shall find that in the remote Beginnings of every Society, the richest and most considerable Men among them were a great while destitute of a great many Comforts of Life that are now enjoy'd by the meanest and most humble Wretches." I owe this reference to R. H. Campbell and A. S. Skinner's edition of *Wealth of Nations* (Oxford: Clarendon Press, 1976), p. 24n.
6 Jean-Jacques Rousseau, *Discourse on Inequality* (London: J. M. Dent, 1958), p. 163.
7 Adam Smith, *Theory of Moral Sentiments* (Oxford: Oxford University Press, 1976), IV.1.10.
8 Ibid.

9 Ibid. I owe these references to Michael Ignatieff, *The Needs of Strangers* (London: Chatto and Windus, 1984), pp. 108ff.

10 Genesis 1: 24–28.

11 Sandra Postel and Christopher Flavin, "Reshaping the Global Economy," in Lester Brown et al. (eds.), *State of the World, 1991: The WorldWatch Institute Report on Progress Towards a Sustainable Society* (London: Allen & Unwin, 1991), p. 186.

12 Alan Durning, "Asking How Much is Enough," in ibid., pp. 154, 157.

13 Anil Agarwal and Sunita Narain, *Global Warming in an Unequal World: A Case of Environmental Colonialism* (New Delhi: Centre for Science and the Environment, 1991), quoted from Fred Pearce, "Ecology and the New Colonialism," *New Scientist* (1 February 1992), pp. 55–6.

14 Smith, *A Theory of the Moral Sentiments* (n. 7 above), IV.i.10.

15 *ABC News 20/20* Transcript #1221, 15 May 1992, p. 5.

16 Alan Durning, "Asking How Much is Enough," in Brown et al., *State of the World, 1991* (n. 1 above), p. 154.

17 Ibid., p. 156, citing a personal communication from Michael Worley of the National Opinion Research Center, September 1990.

18 Paul Wachtel, *The Poverty of Affluence* (New York: Free Press, 1983), p. 11.

19 Michael Argyle, *The Psychology of Happiness* (London: Routledge, 1989), drawing on the work of R. A. Easterlin, "Does Economic Growth Improve the Human Lot: Some Empirical Evidence," in P. A. David and M. Abramovitz (eds.), *Nations and Households in Economic Growth* (New York: Academic Press, 1974), p. 121.

20 Cited by Rosie Beaumont, "Jobs vs. The Trees: Dispelling the Myth," *Habitat Australia*, 20 (1992), p. 31.

21 Peter Singer, *How are We to Live?* (Melbourne: Text Publishing Company, 1993; London: Mandarin, 1995; Buffalo, NY: Prometheus, 1995).

22 Robert J. Ringer, *Looking Out for No. 1* (New York: Fawcett Crest, 1978), p. 22.

Part Eight

Move Over, Marx

Twenty-three

Hegel and Marx:
Dialogue with Peter Singer

Introduction

Bryan Magee Few philosophers have more obviously changed the world than Hegel – both personally, through his influence on German nationalism, and indirectly, through the work of his most famous philosophical disciple, Karl Marx (with whose name a great many governments in our own day actually describe themselves). So, if we want to see some of the practical consequences of Hegel's ideas, all we have to do is look around us. Hegel's influence on philosophy itself was correspondingly great: it has been said that the history of philosophy since Hegel can be seen as a succession of varying reactions against his work.

Georg Wilhelm Friedrich Hegel was born in Stuttgart in 1770. A teacher of one sort or another for most of his life, he eventually became Professor of Philosophy at Heidelberg and then in Berlin. As a philosopher he was a late developer, but by the time of his death in 1831 he was the dominant figure in philosophy throughout the whole of Germany. The titles of some of his most influential works are *The Phenomenology of Mind*, *The Science of Logic*, *The Philosophy of Right*, and *The Philosophy of History*.

Hegel had several followers who themselves became well known, but far and away the most famous of them is Karl Marx. Marx was born in the town of Trier in Germany in 1818, and as a young student of philosophy was very

First published in *The Great Philosophers: An Introduction to Western Philosophy*, by Bryan Magee (London: BBC Books, 1987), pp. 190–208.

much a Hegelian. He did not become a Socialist until his middle twenties, when he began to develop that rich and original mixture of German philosophy, French politics, and British economics which is Marxism. Together with a wealthy young industrialist, Friedrich Engels, he wrote *The Communist Manifesto* in 1848. The ensuing partnership between Marx and Engels is perhaps the most momentous collaboration in the history of ideas. Engels supported Marx for most of his life so that he could produce his writings; and it was a life spent largely in exile because of Marx's political activities: at the age of 31 he went to live in London, and stayed there until his death in 1883. His grave is in Highgate Cemetery. For many years he did his work in the Reading Room of the British Museum, and it was there that he wrote his masterpiece, *Das Kapital*, published in 1867.

Marxism is not exactly philosophy in the accepted meaning of the term, but there is obviously a major philosophical component in it, and that component always remained Hegelian. What I propose to do in this discussion is devote the bulk of the time to Hegel, and then show how some of the most important ideas we shall have discussed were incorporated into Marxism. With me to do this is someone who has published excellent introductions to the works of both thinkers: Peter Singer, [formerly] Professor of Philosophy at Monash University in Melbourne [and now at Princeton University].

Discussion

Magee   Hegel is widely regarded as being the most difficult of all the major philosophers to read and understand, but your little book about him has the unique merit of conveying some of his central ideas in ordinary language, and I look forward to your doing the same in this discussion. Where, from your point of view, is the best place to start?

Singer   I start with *The Philosophy of History*, because Hegel's account of history is quite concrete. Part of the difficulty with Hegel is that his thought is so abstract. But *The Philosophy of History*, because it deals with specific historical events, provides an easy entrée to the more abstract parts of his philosophy.

Magee   That in itself is already a new departure as far as Western philosophy is concerned: to none of the great philosophers before Hegel had history, or the philosophy of history, seemed especially important. One may perhaps make a partial exception of Hume, because of his *History of England*, but Hume never produced philosophy of history as we understand the term. Likewise Leibniz wrote the history of a family but never produced any philosophy of history.

Singer   Yes, it is a departure. Compare it with Kant, for instance: on Kant's view of human nature, human beings are eternally divided between their reason and their brute desires. It's like the old picture of Man as halfway between the apes and the angels. Now for Kant it is just a fact of human nature that we will always be torn between these two aspects of our nature. But Hegel denied that this was immutable. He looked at human nature in historical terms. In ancient Greece, Hegel said, human nature was more harmonious. People were not conscious of any conflict between their desires and their reason. So the division that Kant saw must be something that has occurred historically. In fact, Hegel said, it developed with the rise of individual conscience in Protestant Europe. Because it has happened historically, it need not be a permanent feature. It could, in some other period, again be overcome and harmony restored.

Magee   Hegel looked not just at this but at all important concepts *historically*, didn't he? He saw our concepts as being embedded in ways of life, and thus in societies; and when societies changed, the concepts changed.

Singer   Yes, that's absolutely right. He saw that there was *development* in the way history occurred – that it was always moving forward. It was always a process, never static.

Magee   And he had a name for the way in which it moved forward; "the dialectical process," sometimes just referred to as "the dialectic." Can you explain what, in Hegel's view, this dialectical process was?

Singer   Let's go back to the example I mentioned before. Hegel regarded Greek society as one in which there was a harmony between reason and desire; but this was a simple harmony. It was simple because in ancient Greece people had not developed the modern notion of individual conscience. So there was harmony between the individual and society, because individuals hadn't considered themselves as separate from their city-state, and able to make their own judgments about right and wrong. Then into that simple harmony there came Socrates, whom Hegel considers a world historical figure because it was he who introduced the idea of questioning everything. Socrates went around asking people questions like: "What is justice?" or "What is virtue?" And when people tried to answer, they realized that they had accepted conventional assumptions about these things which Socrates had no trouble in showing could not be sustained. So the simple harmony of Greek society broke down. Incidentally, Hegel thinks that the Athenians were quite right to condemn Socrates to death. Socrates *was* corrupting and subverting Athenian society. But that was an essential part of the historical process, which ultimately led to the rise of individual conscience. This was the second necessary element of historical development. It was the very opposite of the governing principle of Greek society. So we moved from what Hegel calls the "thesis" of simple harmony to the "antithesis" of individual conscience, risen to its height in Protestant Europe. But that too turns out to be unstable. It leads to the destruction carried out by the French Revolution, and the terror that followed the French Revolution; and so that, too, must give way to a "synthesis." This is a third stage which combines harmony and individual conscience. Very often, in this process, the synthesis then again serves as the new thesis from which a further antithesis will arise; and so the process will continue.

Magee   Why does the process get going at all? Why is there such a thing as historical change? It is, after all, perfectly possible to conceive of societies which come close to being static, like ancient Egypt. Why should not a balanced, harmonious state of affairs, such as Hegel thought ancient Greece was, simply go on going on indefinitely? Why should there *necessarily* be some fly in the ointment which precipitates change?

Singer   In the case of ancient Greece it was because it was a simple – perhaps a better word would be "naïve" – harmony, which could not be sustained once the principle of reason had been developed. Hegel traces the development of this principle of reason in Greek thought, and shows how its development was necessary. Rational beings could not remain content with an unquestioning acceptance of social norms. Exactly why that questioning attitude came at this particular point is a detail of the historical story; but at some stage, as rational beings, we would have to question this simple harmony. Once we question it, individual conscience begins to rise and destroys the naïve harmony on which the society is based.

Magee   This notion of "dialectical change" has been so influential ever since Hegel – and is very much so today, among Marxists – that it is important for us to get it clear. The idea is, isn't it, that the reason why we human beings are involved in a process of perpetual change is that every complex situation is bound to contain within itself conflicting elements; and these are, of their nature, destabilizing, so the situation can never continue indefinitely. It breaks down under the strain of these internal conflicts and gives rise to a new situation within which those conflicts are resolved, or at least assuaged. But then, of course, the new situation contains within itself new conflicts. And so it goes on, indefinitely. And that indefinitely continuing process is what constitutes history. Thus the notion of the dialectic is offered to us as the key to the historical process, the underlying explanation of why it is that everything keeps changing. And it tells us what form the change invariably takes: thesis, followed by antithesis, followed by synthesis, which then in its turn becomes a new thesis, to be followed again by its own antithesis, and so on and so forth.

Up to this point in the explanation it has remained open to Hegel to maintain that although change is bound to occur, the actual direction taken by it is indeterminate, the unpredictable outcome of innumerable random conflicts; but he doesn't, does he? On the contrary, he believes it's all actually going somewhere – that it has an aim, a goal.

Singer That's right. The goal for Hegel is the greater development of mind towards freedom. We are moving always towards realizing human freedom; and that is a process of increasing awareness of freedom, and of increasing knowledge of ourselves.

Magee You talk as if concepts like freedom and knowledge are *literally* contained in history, and as if historical change *is* the transmutation of these concepts. One is reminded of Russell's jibe that, according to Hegel, history is "jellied thought."

Singer History represents the development of these concepts, that's true. History is not a chapter of accidents. It is not a story told by an idiot. It is the purposive moving forward of these principles of freedom and knowledge.

Magee What is this process of change happening *to*? I mean, usually when we talk of change, in any context, we assume there to be something that changes. What is it in this case? Hegel surely can't believe that the concrete stuff of history is abstract concepts – concepts are not a substance, not even an abstract substance. What, then, are we talking about? Human individuals? Societies? Who – or what – is undergoing the change?

Singer The short answer is that he is writing neither about individuals, nor about societies, but about what he calls "*Geist*." The German word "*Geist*" is a difficult one to translate. The easiest way perhaps would be to say that Hegel is writing about "mind." "Mind" is one normal translation. The German word "*Geisteskrankheit*," for instance, means "mental illness." So we could say that in Hegel's view history happens to "mind," that is, to your mind and mine, or all our individual minds. But "*Geist*" also has another meaning which goes beyond that, the notion of "spirit." We talk about the "*Zeitgeist*," the "spirit of the times." Or we talk about "*Geist*" when Germans talk about the Father, the Son, and the Holy Ghost. So it has also a spiritual or religious flavor – which suggests that in some sense there's a reality above and beyond my individual mind. You could say it is happening to Mind, but to Mind with a capital "M," not just mind in the sense of individual human minds.

Magee   Is Hegel saying that total reality is a unity and is something mental or spiritual, and therefore that all the processes we have been talking about are processes in that mental or spiritual something?

Singer   Yes, ultimately Hegel's view is that reality is *Geist*. It is ultimately mental, or intellectual. The processes we have been talking about happen to *Geist*, to Mind as it develops in history.

Magee   To some of the people following this discussion it might be beginning to sound bizarre. So I think it's worth pointing out that we are already familiar with ideas very similar to these when it comes to religious beliefs, even though we ourselves may not be religious as individuals. Many religious believers, including many Christians, believe that all reality is ultimately spiritual, and that all reality ultimately has a spiritual significance. I suppose Hegel is saying something closely related to that, though not necessarily religious in the conventional sense.

Singer   The difference is that the orthodox Christian holds that God is spiritual and separate from this world, which is mundane and material. On the Christian view the world has a spiritual significance, certainly, but it is not itself spiritual. So the Christian contrasts God and the world, One from himself. Hegel says that this is wrong. We are in fact part of God, or if you like, we are projecting our qualities into God. The way to overcome this kind of alienation is to realize that we and God are one, and that the qualities we attribute to God are *our* qualities, they are not something separate from, and foreign to, us.

Magee   He wouldn't have said that they were human qualities only, would he, but rather shared ones.

Singer   The claim that they are *only* human was made by one of his later disciples, Ludwig Feuerbach. Hegel wouldn't have said that, but he would have said that we and that kind of Divine Spirit are all part of the same Reality, *Geist*, or Mind.

Magee   You have made it clear that Hegel saw total reality as a process of change, and that he saw this change as moving forward dialectically. A moment ago I took the natural next step and asked what this process of dialectical change was heading towards, but we no sooner started answering the question than we got side-tracked. Can we go back to it? Perhaps we're in a better position now to answer it than we were then. Does historical change have a goal?

Singer The end point of the dialectical process is Mind coming to know itself as the ultimate reality, and thus as seeing everything that it took to be foreign and hostile to itself as in fact part of itself. Hegel calls this Absolute Knowledge. It is also a state of absolute freedom, because now Mind, instead of being controlled by external forces, is able to order the world in a rational way. This can be done only when Mind sees that the world is in fact itself. Then Mind has only to implement its own principle of rationality in the world in order to organize the world rationally.

One remarkable feature of this process arises from the fact that the culmination occurs when for the first time Mind understands that it is the only ultimate reality. Ask yourself: when does this actually happen? The answer must be that it happens when Hegel's own mind, in his philosophical thinking, grasps the idea that Mind is everything that is real. So it's not just that Hegel *describes* the goal, the state of Absolute Knowledge and Absolute Freedom towards which all previous human history had been unconsciously struggling: Hegel's philosophy actually *is* the very culmination of the whole process.

Magee I wonder if that penny ever dropped with Hegel himself – whether he actually realized that what he was doing was putting himself-as-philosopher forward as the culmination of world history? I doubt it.

You say that the culminating state is seen at one and the same time as a state of Absolute Knowledge and a state of Absolute Freedom. It's not at all evident that knowledge and freedom are the same thing. Did Hegel think they were?

Singer Self-knowledge becomes freedom because for Hegel Mind is the ultimate reality of the world. In all human history *before* that great moment in which Mind recognizes itself as the ultimate reality of the world, we have been pawns in the game. We haven't been controlling the historical stage because things have been happening to us without our realizing or understanding why they happened. We could not control our destiny because we thought of aspects of our *own* reality as foreign and hostile elements. Once we come to see that we are everything in the world, then we understand the process; we've grasped, if you like, the laws of historical development. Then we see that those laws are in fact the laws of our own reason, they are the very laws of our mind and our thinking.

Magee   I take it this is the point of the famous citation of Hegel as having said: "The Real is the Rational, and the Rational is the Real."

Singer   That's right. And when we come to see that, then we are free. Freedom consists in knowledge of reality, because when we see the rationality of reality we no longer struggle vainly against it. We understand that the essence of reality is our own rational principle. Then we are free to flow with it, and indeed to order it and direct it, in accordance with those laws of reason.

Magee   One characteristic of Hegel's thought which you have brought out clearly is the way he sees ideas not as existing only in the abstract, nor as being timeless and unchanging (as, say, Plato did), but as always embodied in societies, institutions – historical realities which change. Now, given this fact, what sort of *society* does Hegel see the historical process as culminating in?

Singer   As you would expect from what we have been saying, it is a rationally ordered society. But I must make clear what that is for Hegel, because it is not the society of pure reason. Hegel saw the society of pure reason as typified by the ideals of the French Revolutionaries. They didn't just get rid of the king, the nobles, and religion: they tried to make *everything* rational. They said: why have months with irregular numbers of days? Why not make them all the same? Why have weeks of seven days? Let's make them ten, like our decimal system of measurement. . . . And so on. Hegel saw this as the result of a madly abstract notion of reason. It was the reasoning of the town planner who looks at a map of London and says: "Oh, your streets all run crookedly, and traffic has to make detours. Let's get rid of this mess. Let's tear the buildings down. We'll make nice straight streets and in each block we'll put a big high-rise apartment building. That way we can fit more people in, we can have a smooth green lawn outside for the children to play, and it'll all be beautiful, ordered, and rational."

Magee   We've had that precisely in London. It has been catastrophic.

Singer   Hegel would have predicted that it would be catastrophic, because it was abstract reason taken to an extreme. For Hegel, a truly rational town-planning scheme for London would look at the *real*, that is, London as it exists, find what's *rational* in the real (and of course it has developed the way it did for certain reasons, so there must be a rational element) and then try to follow those reasons through in a way that fulfills the rationale behind London's development. Hegel's rationality would not lead us to raze it down and start anew. It would encourage us to modify some of the arbitrary and capricious aspects of London's development which cause particular problems; but basic-ally Hegelian rationality seeks what's rational in what's real, and enhances it and develops it so as to allow it to fulfill itself.

Magee   One criticism in particular has always been made of this so-called rational conception of the state, especially by liberal-minded philosophers in the Anglo-Saxon tradition. A state which is a single, organic whole, behaving rationally and ordering everything rationally, cannot permit individual enter-prise, initiative, eccentricity, or dissent to operate, because these would keep ruining its plans. So in practice it always turns out to be intolerant of individual initiative, i.e. not free. What's your comment on that?

Singer   I don't think Hegel was opposed to all individual freedom, but it is true that his view of freedom was not the standard Anglo-Saxon liberal view. To grasp the difference between the two, let's look first at the idea of freedom in the economic sphere, in the market. According to one view, the liberal view, freedom consists of people's being able to do as they prefer. If I prefer to wear an orange shirt this spring for instance, then I am free if I am not prevented from buying a shirt of that color. If I prefer to buy a deodorant I am free if I can do that. To decide that I am free, that's all the liberal economist needs to know. But some of the more radical economists have questioned this. They've said that this is a very superficial notion of freedom. They want to know *why* I want to wear an orange shirt this season. Why do I want to use a deodorant? Why do I consider natural body odor to be a problem? The radical economists might decide that the reason is that I've been manipulated. There are people who want to make a profit out of my buying their deodorant, out of my thinking that the colors I wore last season are no longer good enough this season. So I've been manipulated, I'm not free. To know if I am free, the radical economist needs to know not only if I can do what I prefer, but why I prefer what I prefer. Are my preferences rational? Are they preferences that satisfy my needs?

   Hegel would have sympathized with the radical economist. He said that freedom is more than just the ability to follow your own caprice, or to satisfy desires which others have induced you to have so that they can sell you something. Freedom, for Hegel, must consist in fulfilling yourself as a rational individual.

Magee   That sounds all very fine, but just think what it means in practice. I happen to believe that I know what I want: I want, if I like, to be able to wear an orange shirt this spring, and when the weather gets hotter I want to be able to go out and buy a deodorant. But I live under a state which says to me: "No, no, you only *think* you want those things. They are not at all rational preferences on your part. But we, it so happens, know what you would want if your preferences were rational. So we'll decide what you're to have – or, in this case, not to have. You'll be much happier, really, even though you may not realize it."

Hegel's approach, surely, is bound to lead to authoritarianism?

Singer I think in practice you are probably right, and I don't know that Hegel has any reply to that objection. The only thing that he can say is that while it might be very difficult in practice to work out how you can have a society in which individuals genuinely realize their rational natures without an authoritarian state, that doesn't mean that you overcome the problem by the liberal *laissez-faire* notion. We still have to face the problem that people's wants and desires might be being manipulated, and to the extent that they are, it's misleading to say that they are really free.

Magee You are saying that the problem is a real one even if Hegel doesn't have the answer to it.

Singer It's still a problem.

Magee Let us pause for a moment and take stock. I started our whole discussion by asking you what was the easiest way in to Hegel's philosophy, and you replied by saying that it was best to start with his philosophy of history. So we did; and we continued on it – in a straight line, so to speak – to the point we've just reached. Well, are we now in a better position to understand other aspects of his philosophy?

Singer I think we've already grasped many of the essentials of Hegel's philosophy. Take Hegel's *Logic* for instance. We've discussed the dialectic, which is the most famous idea in Hegel's *Logic*, the idea of the thesis, antithesis, synthesis. Or take another point: in the *Logic* Hegel contends that logic is not just a matter of form as separate from content, which is how the traditional logic of Aristotle was interpreted, Hegel says that form and content go to-gether. We can now see why he says that. He thinks that dialectic is something that is realized in the actual process of history. Logic, Hegel said, is "truth without its husk," that is, the eternal, immutable form of truth, irrespective of a particular historical content, though in fact it's always linked to some content. So that's another of the key ideas of the *Logic*. Another point that we've also just touched on is Hegel's idea of ultimate reality and the way in which what is ultimately real is mental rather than material.

Magee   With the *Logic*, then, as with those aspects of Hegel's thought we've discussed, we come up against the notion of reason as being embodied in reality – and embodied, what is more, in a historical reality. One seems unable to escape this idea in Hegel: everything always comes back to Mind and its omnipresence in a historical process. I suppose this is why he is regarded as the Idealist philosopher *par excellence*?

Singer   Yes, Hegel certainly thought that Mind is the ultimate reality. That strikes us as a very peculiar notion. To understand why Hegel thought that, you have to consider the way in which he develops his thought from the philosophy of Kant. Kant held that our mind shapes the way in which we perceive reality, so that we cannot actually see anything except through the concepts of space and time and causation which our mind brings to it. However, Kant still thought that there was an ultimate reality that was not mental: he called it the thing-in-itself. But for Hegel this was nonsense. For Hegel, if there's no way of knowing the thing-in-itself, then we can't really have knowledge.

Hegel also rejected the ideas of the British empiricists. The British empiricists asked how we know that there is a table like this in front of us. They said that there are some kind of sense data that convey the image of the table to our mind, so there's a medium of sense data between mind and material reality. Hegel said that in that case we could still never know the table as it is, we would always know it only through a medium. Hegel used many arguments to show that this doesn't work and that it must lead to skepticism, to the view that we can't really know anything. But Hegel also offered further arguments to demonstrate the impossibility of skepticism. So where is he left? The only solution, Hegel says, is to reject this idea of a knower and what's known, the table for instance, as existing on its own, separate from the mind that knows it. What you have to say is that knowledge, if it's to exist, must be immediate. There must be no medium through which we know things. How can that happen? Only if the knower and the known are one and the same. How can *that* happen? Since the knower is mind, what is known must also be mind, so all of reality must be mental.

Magee   When I consider all the ideas of Hegel that you've put forward up to this point, there seems to me to be one core insight out of which all the most important concepts arise naturally one after another. The core insight is that understanding reality means not understanding a given state of affairs but understanding a process of change. From that it seems to me that all the key notions of Hegel's philosophy then arise naturally in the following way, and in the following order. If we ask: "What is it that changes?" Hegel replies:

"*Geist.*" If we ask: "Why does it change instead of remaining the same?" Hegel replies: "Because, to begin with, it's in a state of alienation." If we ask: "What form does the process of change take?" Hegel replies: "The dialectic." If we ask: "Does the process of change have a goal?" Hegel replies: "Yes, Absolute Knowledge (which is Absolute Freedom) on one level, the Organic Society on another."

Now because it's possible to make Hegel's most basic ideas clear in this way, a question which naturally arises is "Why did Hegel not do it?" His writing is almost uniquely obscure – it positively repels the reader. So obscure is it that many outstanding philosophers from Schopenhauer to Russell have sincerely maintained that it didn't say anything at all, that it was nothing but charlatanry. They were wrong, of course, but it's partly Hegel's own fault that they took that view. One can read page after page of Hegel, racking one's brains and thinking: "What the *hell* does he mean?" So much like gobbledygook is a lot of it that philosophy students read passages aloud to each other just to raise a laugh. Why did Hegel write like that?

Singer   Some of his less charitable critics thought he was deliberately obscure in order to cover the shallowness of his ideas. But I don't think Hegel's ideas are shallow. I think that they are profound, and that in fact the difficulty comes from the nature of the ideas. One of his students said that whereas an eloquent lecturer might have had everything off by heart and trotted it out clearly, Hegel was always dredging up deep ideas as he lectured. He was bringing these ideas to the surface with great effort. His is the style of one who is thinking aloud and having difficulty with the material. We may very well regret that he did not then revise and polish it, but in the context of German philosophical style at the time, it is not so surprising that he didn't feel the need for clarity. After all, Kant, Fichte, and other contemporaries were also very obscure, and they were still regarded as great philosophers.

Magee   Another question all this gives rise to is how it came about that a philosopher so obscure, so difficult to understand, acquired even in his own lifetime such immense influence.

Singer   I think that's partly due to his situation at the University of Berlin, which was the capital of Prussia, the rising state in Germany at the time. It's also due to the fertility of Hegel's ideas in a variety of fields. The influence that Hegel had is not just an influence in philosophy, it's an influence in theology, in history, in politics, in economics, in war. The fact that Hegel's ideas could be applied in these ways shows how useful his approach was, particularly the historical elements of his approach. Hegel's historical vision of everything as having developed, as being the outcome of a process, could fruitfully be applied by scholars in all those different areas.

Magee Can we turn now to the afterlife of these ideas, which has been so important? One of the first things that happened after Hegel's death was that his followers split into two movements: the Young Hegelians and the Old Hegelians, or alternatively the Left Hegelians and the Right Hegelians. Can you explain the distinction?

Singer The Right Hegelians were the people who thought that Hegel's philosophy implied that something like the Prussian state was the organic state to which Hegel's ideas were pointing. They thought that Hegel had himself said this in *The Philosophy of Right*, his most explicitly political work. There he described a state, a constitutional monarchy, not very different from the Prussian state, and so they thought that there was no real need for further change. So they were the Conservative, or Right-Wing, Hegelians.

The Left Hegelians insisted that the basic thrust of Hegel's philosophy was much more radical. Hegel talked, as we said at the very beginning, about overcoming the division between reason and desire, or between morality and self-interest. That's a very fundamental change to bring about. No one could believe that that had occurred in the Prussia of 1830. So, the Left Hegelians said, the thrust of Hegel's philosophy is for a much more far-reaching change, a revolutionary change. They had to admit that in *The Philosophy of Right* Hegel hadn't written as if he were a revolutionary; but they pointed out that Hegel's salary was paid by the state of Prussia. They said Hegel had compromised, had sold out, but they wanted to be truer to Hegel than he had been to himself. They sought to carry his ideas forward to the point at which the thesis and antithesis of reason and desire, morality and self-interest, are overcome – the point at which we reach the synthesis of a harmonious society, in which those gulfs and divisions in human nature are reconciled.

Magee And of course that brings us to Marxism and Marx, who for us today is far and away the most important and interesting of the Young or Left Hegelians. (Incidentally, I thought that last comment of yours was most revealing in showing how extreme right-wing and extreme left-wing diagnoses can both validly be derived from Hegel – something which puzzles many people who have not themselves looked into it. Not only are right-wing and left-wing totalitarianism similar in practice, but their intellectual ancestry is also similar. Hegel is the grandfather of both.)

All but one of Hegel's basic ideas which we have discussed so far was taken over by Marx and made central to Marxism: first, the idea that reality is a historical process; second, the idea that the way this process changes is dialectical: third, the idea that this dialectical process of change has a specific goal: fourth, the idea that this goal is a conflict-free society; fifth, the idea that until that goal is reached we are condemned to remain in one form or another of alienation. The great point of difference is that whereas Hegel saw this process as happening to something mental or spiritual, Marx saw it as happening to something material. With that one difference, however, the whole pattern of ideas remains the same. It's as if Marx took over a long sequence of equations from Hegel and substituted a different value for x but kept the equations themselves all the same.

Singer   Precisely. You can see it, for instance, in Marx's materialist conception of history. This is the central idea in Marx's thought. He saw the development of history as determined by the forces of material production. So the material side, the forces of production, dominate the mental side of our life. Our ideas, our religion, our politics, all flow from the kind of economic structure that we have in our society. That's an inversion of Hegel's view of history. As Marx himself said, he'd stood Hegel on his head. For Hegel, of course, it was the development of Mind that led to the formation of particular societies and particular historical epochs.

Magee   Do you think it can be claimed for Marx that he made an original contribution to philosophy?

Singer   I don't think Marx made important contributions to philosophy in the narrow sense in which we talk about problems of the ultimate nature of reality. Marx was certainly a materialist, but he didn't argue for his materialism as a philosopher; he accepted it as something that was pretty obvious. What mattered was the material world, not something remote like *Geist*, which Marx dismissed as a kind of speculative German metaphysical abstraction. So he didn't argue for materialism, and he therefore didn't make contributions to that philosophical discussion. What he did do was give us a kind of a vision, a vision of a world in which we are controlled by our economic circumstances and are *for that reason* not free. It's still rather like Hegel in that we are pawns in the game of history: to become free we must control the economic forces, which after all are our own forces. What is economics, after all, but our own ways of providing for food, providing for shelter, and so on? So it's a vision in which we are unwittingly controlled by something that is really part of us. If we are to be free, we must control these forces. That's a powerful, and broadly philosophical, vision of the human situation; but it's not an important philosophical discovery in the narrow, academic sense of the word "philosophy."

Magee   Viewing the two closely linked thought-systems of Hegelianism and Marxism together, what would you say has been their most valuable contribution to human thinking since their time?

Singer   Well, it's clear from what we've said that the idea of history as a process which affects every aspect of our thinking and our ideas is a crucial addition to our understanding which has come from Hegel and Marx.

Magee   It became almost the dominant new aspect of all thought in the nineteenth century, didn't it? Of course, it was soon to receive a powerful boost from Darwin's theory of evolution, which taught us to look on all life – not just human life, still less just social life – as having evolved, and therefore as having been involved in a process of perpetual change.

Singer   We can't now imagine looking at societies or ideas as timeless entities, independent of their history. That's something we owe to Hegel and Marx. So that's one very important thing. The other immensely important idea is this notion of freedom, the idea that is so different from the liberal notion. We cannot be free unless we control our destiny, unless we, instead of being blown about by the winds of economic circumstances (for Marx) or steered by the unseen hand of reason (for Hegel), actually take control, realize our own power, realize the capacity of human beings collectively to control our destiny, and do just that. That idea may in practice, as you said, have very dangerous authoritarian tendencies, but it's a very important idea. Now that we've been presented with it by Hegel and Marx, I don't think it can ever be forgotten.

Magee   This brings us to the demerits as well as the merits of these ideas. The chief negative charge against them is that they are, quite simply, the fountainhead of totalitarianism in the modern world. Hegel was always appealed to as the intellectual founder of the idea of the organic state, and more specifically of the kind of German state-worship which culminated in Hitler; and his philosophical disciple Karl Marx has always been appealed to as the intellectual founder of Communism, which produced under Stalin the greatest tyranny of the modern age. Both Hitler's regime and Stalin's murdered many millions of their own citizens. Now I am far from suggesting that either of our two philosophers had anything remotely like this in mind, still less that they would have approved of it. But the fact is that both philosophers regarded the embodiment of ideas in history, in institutions, in social reality, as being the really essential thing about ideas – and yet this is the reality of what happened when their own ideas were so embodied. On their own premises, then, there must have been some fatal flaw in the ideas themselves. What was it?

Singer   Well I think their own ideas were mis-embodied. I don't think you can really trace Hegelian ideas at all in Hitler's kind of racist nationalism. You can't find that kind of racism in Hegel.

Magee   So you think the state-worshipping tradition of German nationalism has completely misrepresented Hegel?

Singer   It was complete misrepresentation of Hegel in that case, certainly. And also, as perhaps the ultimate irony, in what happened to Marx. Marx, as I've been saying, was a philosopher of freedom. He cherished freedom. He hated subordination. He was once asked by his daughter to write down the vice he most detested. He replied: "Servility." Servility, the very thing you needed to survive in Stalin's totalitarianism! And yet it is true that these ideas did get misapplied. They did get distorted.

Magee   Why? What was it about them that lent itself to this wholesale misapplication, if such it was?

Singer   I think in the end there's a faulty view of human nature. There's an attempt to show a greater unity than really exists between human beings. We could trace this to Hegel's notion of Mind or *Geist*, as something which is above and beyond the differences between individual minds. We find it also in Marx, in the idea that if you change the economic circumstances you change human nature, and we will all then overcome the divisions between one and another. The divisions between my interest and your interest, and between our individual interests and the interests of society, will all disappear, Marx says, once we get rid of the economic structure which leads us to compete in the marketplace. It seems, unfortunately, that this is false. You can change the economic basis, but you don't get rid of the divisions between reason and desire, between my interest and yours, or between individual and society. In fact, what happens once you make it impossible, or very difficult, for people to compete with one another for wealth, is that they then start competing for status, or for power. That's no better than it used to be. In the case of Stalin's society it proved to be worse. So I think that Marx was wrong to believe that human nature would change.

   The last word perhaps ought to go to Marx's great nineteenth-century rival, the Russian anarchist Bakunin, because Bakunin criticized just this aspect of Marx's thought. Marx said we should let the workers rule because then they will rule on behalf of the great mass of society, the working class. Bakunin said No. You shouldn't have any rulers, he said, because if the workers are rulers, they will cease to be workers and will become rulers. They will follow the interests of the rulers, not the interests of the working class. Marx thought that was rubbish. Marx thought that people in a different society would be different people, would have different, less self-directed interests, and would work together for the benefit of all. If you look at what's happened in the so-called "Marxist" societies, perhaps Bakunin's view of human nature was right.

Twenty-four

Darwin for the Left

The Left needs a new paradigm. The collapse of communism and the aban-donment by democratic socialist parties of the traditional socialist aim of public ownership have deprived the Left of the goals it cherished over the two centuries in which it grew to a position of great political power and intellectual influence. My focus here is not so much with the Left as a politically organized force, as with the Left as a broad body of thought, a spectrum of ideas about achieving a better society. The Left, in this sense, is urgently in need of new ideas. I want to suggest that one source of such ideas is an approach to human behavior based firmly on a modern understanding of human nature. It is time for the Left to take seriously the fact that we have evolved from other animals; we bear the evidence of this inheritance, not only in our anatomy and our DNA, but in what we want and how we are likely to try to get it. In otherwords, it is time to develop a Darwinian Left.

Can the Left adopt Darwin and still remain Left? That depends on what it considers essential. Let me answer this in a personal way. During the past year, I have completed both a television documentary and a book about Henry Spira. This name will mean nothing to most people, but Spira is the most remarkable person I have ever worked with. When he was 12, his family lived in Panama. His father ran a small store, which was not doing well; to save money the family accepted an offer from a rich friend to stay in his house. The house was a mansion that took up an entire city block. One day, two men who worked for the owner asked Henry if he wanted to come with them when they collected

First published in *Prospect* (June 1998), pp. 26–30.

rents. He went and saw how the luxurious existence of his father's benefactor was financed; they went into the slums, where poor people were menaced by the armed rent collectors. At the time, Henry had no concept of "the Left," but from that day on, he was part of it. Later Spira moved to the US, became a Trotskyist, worked as a seaman, was blacklisted during the McCarthy era, went to the South to support black people, left the Trotskyists because they had lost touch with reality, and taught ghetto kids in New York. As if that wasn't enough, in 1973 he read my essay "Animal Liberation" and decided that here was another group of exploited beings that needed help. He has subsequently become the single most effective activist of the US animal rights movement.

Spira has a knack for putting things plainly. When I asked him why he has spent his life working for these causes, he said simply that he is on the side of the weak, not the powerful, of the oppressed, not the oppressor, of the ridden, not the rider. He spoke of the huge quantity of pain and suffering that exists in our universe, and of his desire to do something to reduce it. This, I think, is what the Left is about. If we shrug our shoulders at the avoidable suffering of the weak and the poor, of those who are getting exploited and ripped off, we are not of the Left. The Left wants to change this situation. There are many different ideas of equality which are compatible with this broad picture of the Left. But in a world in which the 400 richest people have a combined net worth greater than the bottom 45 per cent of the world's population, it is not hard to find some common ground on working toward a more equal distribution of resources.

So much for the Left. What about the politics of Darwinism? One way of answering the question is to invoke the fact–value distinction. Since to be "of the Left" is to hold certain values, and Darwin's theory is a scientific one, the impossibility of deducing values from facts means that evolution has nothing to do with Left or Right. So there can be a Darwinian Left as easily as there can be a Darwinian Right.

It is, of course, the Right which has drawn most on Darwinian thinking. Andrew Carnegie, for example, appealed to evolution to suggest that economic competition will lead to the "survival of the fittest," and so will make most people better off. Darwinian thinking is also invoked in the claim that social policies may be helping the "less fit" to survive, and thus have deleterious genetic consequences. This claim is highly speculative. Its factual basis is strongest in regard to the provision of life-saving medical treatment to people with genetically linked diseases; without treatment, these people would die before they could reproduce. There are, no doubt, many more people with early-onset diabetes being born because of the discovery of insulin. But no one would seriously propose withholding insulin from children with diabetes in order to avoid the genetic consequences of providing insulin.

But there is a more general aspect of Darwinian thinking that does need to be taken seriously. That is the claim that an understanding of human nature in the light of evolutionary theory can help us to assess the price we will have to pay for achieving our social and political goals. This does not imply that any social policy is wrong because it is contrary to Darwinian ideas. Rather, it leaves the ethical decision up to us and merely provides information relevant to that decision.

The core of the Left worldview is a set of values; but there is also a penumbra of factual beliefs that have typically been associated with the Left. We need to ask whether these factual beliefs are at odds with Darwinian thinking; if they are, what would the Left be like without them?

The intellectual Left, and Marxists in particular, have generally been enthusiastic about Darwin's account of the origin of species, as long as its implications for human beings are confined to anatomy and physiology. Marx's materialist theory of history implies that there is no fixed human nature. It changes with each new mode of production. It has already changed in the past – between primitive communism and feudalism, and between feudalism and capitalism – and it could change again in the future.

Belief in the malleability of human nature has been important for the Left because it has provided grounds for hoping that a different kind of society is possible. The real reason why the Left rejected Darwinism is that it dashed the Left's great dream: the perfectibility of man. Even before Plato's *Republic*, the idea of building a perfect society had been present in the Western consciousness. For as long as the Left has existed, it has sought a society in which all human beings live harmoniously and cooperatively with each other in peace and freedom. For Darwin, on the other hand, the struggle for existence, or at least for the existence of one's offspring, is unending.

In the twentieth century, the dream of the perfectibility of humankind turned into the nightmares of Stalinist Russia, China during the Cultural Revolution, and Cambodia under Pol Pot. From these nightmares the Left awoke in turmoil. There have been attempts to create a new and better society with less terrible results – Castro's Cuba, the Israeli kibbutzim – but none are unqualified successes. The dream of perfectibility should be put behind us, and with that, one barrier to a Darwinian Left has been removed.

But what about the malleability of human nature? What do we mean by malleability and how essential is it to the Left? Let us divide human behavior into three categories: that which shows great variation across culture; some variation across culture; and little or no variation across culture.

In the first category, showing great variation, I would include the way we produce our food – by gathering and hunting, by grazing domestic animals, or by growing crops. To these differences would correspond differences in lifestyles – nomadic or settled – as well as differences in the kinds of food we eat. This first category would also include economic structures, religious practices and forms of government – but not, significantly, the existence of some form of government, which seems to be nearly universal.

In the second category, showing some variation, I would include sexuality. Victorian anthropologists were very impressed by the differences between attitudes to sexuality in their own society and those in the societies they studied; as a result, we tend to exaggerate the extent to which sexual morality is relative to culture. There are, of course, important differences between societies that allow men to have one wife and those that allow men to have more than one wife; but almost every society has a system of marriage that implies restrictions on sexual intercourse outside marriage. Moreover, while men may be allowed one wife or more, according to the culture, systems of marriage in which women are allowed more than one husband are rare. Whatever the rules of marriage may be, and no matter how severe the sanctions, infidelity and sexual jealousy seem to be universal elements of human sexual behavior.

In this second category I would also include ethnic identification and its opposite, xenophobia and racism. I live in a multicultural society with a relatively low level of racism; but I know that racist feelings do exist among Australians, and they can be stirred up by demagogues. The tragedy of Bosnia has shown how ethnic hatred can be revived among people who have lived peacefully with each other for decades. Racism can be learned and unlearned, but racist demagogues hold their torches over highly flammable material.

In the third category, showing little variation across cultures, I would include the fact that we are social beings and that we are concerned for the interests of our kin. Our readiness to form cooperative relationships and to recognize reciprocal obligations is another universal. More controversially, I would claim that the existence of a hierarchy or system of rank is an almost universal human tendency. There are very few human societies without differences in social status; when attempts are made to abolish such differences, they tend to reemerge rapidly. Finally, gender roles also show relatively little variation. Women almost always play the main role in caring for young children, while men are much more likely than women to be involved in physical conflict, both within the social group and in warfare between groups. Men also tend to have a disproportionate role in the political leadership of the group.

Of course, culture does have an influence in sharpening or softening even those tendencies that are most deeply rooted in our human nature. And there can be variations between individuals. Nothing I have said is contradicted by the existence of individuals who do not care for their kin, or couples where the man looks after the children while the woman serves in the army. I must also stress that my rough classification of human behavior carries no evaluative overtones. I am not saying that because male dominance is characteristic of almost all societies, that it is therefore good, or acceptable, or that we should not attempt to change it. My point is not about deducing an "ought" from an "is," but about estimating the price we may have to pay for achieving our goals.

For example, if we live in a society with a hierarchy based on a hereditary aristocracy, and we abolish that aristocracy, as the French and American revolutionaries did, we are likely to find that a new hierarchy emerges, based perhaps on military power or wealth. When the Bolshevik revolution in Russia abolished both the hereditary aristocracy and private wealth, a hierarchy soon developed on the basis of rank and influence within the Communist party; this became the basis for all sorts of privileges. The tendency to form hierarchies shows itself in all sorts of petty ways in corporations and bureaucracies, where people place enormous importance on how big their office is, and how many windows it has. None of this shows that hierarchy is good, or desirable, or even inevitable; but it does show that getting rid of it is not going to be as easy as previous revolutionaries thought.

The Left has to accept and understand our nature as evolved beings. But there are different ways of working with the tendencies inherent in human nature. The market economy is based on the idea that human beings can be relied upon to work hard and show initiative only if by doing so they will further their own economic interests. To serve our own interests we will strive to produce better goods than our competitors, or to produce similar goods more cheaply. Thus, as Adam Smith said, the self-interested desires of a multitude of individuals are drawn together, as if by a hidden hand, to work for the benefit of all. Garrett Hardin summarized this view in *The Limits of Altruism* when he wrote that public policies should be based on "an unwavering adherence to the cardinal rule: never ask a person to act against his own self-interest." In theory – abstract theory that is, free from any assumptions about human nature – a state monopoly should be able to provide the cheapest and most efficient utility services, transport services or, for that matter, bread supply; indeed, such a monopoly would have huge advantages of scale and would not have to make profits for its owners. However, when we take into account the popular assumption that self-interest – more specifically, the desire to enrich oneself – drives human beings to work well, the picture changes. If the community owns an enterprise, its managers do not profit from its success. Their own economic interest and that of the enterprise pull in different directions. The result is, at best, inefficiency; at worst, widespread corruption and theft. Privatizing the enterprise will ensure that the owners will take steps to reward management in accordance with performance; in turn, the managers will take steps to ensure that the enterprise runs as efficiently as possible.

This is one way of tailoring our institutions to human nature, or at least to one view of human nature. But it is not the only way. Even within the terms of Hardin's cardinal rule, we still have to ask what we mean by "self-interest." The acquisition of material wealth, beyond a relatively modest level, has little to do with self-interest in the biological sense of maximizing the number of descendents one leaves in future generations. There is no reason to assume that increasing personal wealth must, either consciously or unconsciously, be the goal that people set for themselves. It is often said that money cannot buy happiness. This may be trite, but it implies that it is more in our interests to be happy than to be rich. Properly understood, self-interest is broader than economic self-interest. Most people want their lives to be happy, fulfilling, or meaningful; they recognize that money is at best a means of achieving part of these ends. Public policy does not have to rely on self-interest in this narrow economic sense.

Modern Darwinian thought embraces both competition and reciprocal altruism (a more technical term for cooperation). Focusing on the competitive element, modern market economies are premised on the idea that we are driven by acquisitive and competitive desires. Free market economies are designed to channel our acquisitive and competitive desires so that they work for the good of all. Undoubtedly, this is better than a situation in which they work only for the good of a few. But even when competitive consumer societies work at their best, they are not the only way of harmonizing our nature with the common good. Instead we should seek to encourage a broader sense of self-interest, in which we seek to build on the social and cooperative side of our nature rather than the individualistic and competitive side.

Robert Axelrod's work on the prisoner's dilemma provides a basis for building a more cooperative society. The prisoner's dilemma describes a situation in which two people can each choose whether or not to cooperate with the other. The catch is that each does better, individually, by not cooperating; but if both make this choice, they will both be worse off than they would have been if they had both chosen to cooperate. The outcome of rational, self-interested choices by two or more individuals can make all of them worse off than they would have been if they had not pursued their own interest. The individual pursuit of self-interest can be collectively self-defeating.

People who commute to work by car face this kind of situation every day. They would all be better off if, instead of sitting in heavy traffic, they abandoned their cars and used the buses, which would then travel swiftly down uncrowded roads. But it is not in the interests of any individual to switch to the bus, because as long as most people continue to drive, the buses will be even slower than cars.

Axelrod is interested in which strategy, of cooperating or not cooperating, would bring about the best results for parties who face repeated situations of this type. Should they always cooperate? Should they always defect, as the noncooperative strategy suggests? Or should they adopt some mixed strategy, varying cooperation and defection in some way? Axelrod invited people to suggest strategies which would produce the best payoff for the person using it, if they were in repeated prisoner's dilemma situations.

When he received the answers, Axelrod ran them against each other on a computer, in a kind of round-robin tournament in which each strategy was pitted against every other strategy 200 times. The winner was a simple strategy called "tit for tat." It opened every encounter with a new player by cooperating. After that, it simply did whatever the other player had done the previous time. So if the other cooperated, it cooperated; and it continued to do so unless the other defected. Then it defected too, and continued to do so unless the other player again cooperated. Tit for tat also won a second tournament that Axelrod organized, even though the people sending in strategies this time knew that it had won the previous tournament.

Axelrod's results, which have been supported by subsequent work in the field, can serve as a basis for social planning that should appeal to the Left. Anyone on the Left should welcome the fact that the strategy with the best payoff always begins with a cooperative move, and is never the first to abandon the cooperative strategy or seek to exploit the "niceness" of the other party. But members of the more idealistic Left may regret that tit for tat does not continue to cooperate no matter what. A Left that understands Darwin must realize that this is essential to its success. By being provokable, tit for tat creates a virtuous spiral in which life gets harder for cheats, and so there are fewer of them. In Richard Dawkins's terms, if there are "suckers," then there will also be "cheats" who can prosper by taking advantage of them. It is only by refusing to be played for a sucker that tit for tat can make it possible for cooperators to do better than cheats. A non-Darwinian Left would blame the existence of cheats on poverty, or a lack of education, or the legacy of reactionary ways of thinking. A Darwinian Left will realize that while all these factors may make a difference to the level of cheating, the only permanent solution is to change the payoffs so that cheats do not prosper.

The question we need to address is: under what conditions will tit for tat be a successful strategy for everyone to adopt? The first problem is one of scale. Tit for tat cannot work in a society of strangers who will never encounter each other again. This is why people living in big cities do not always show the consideration to each other that is the norm in rural villages in which people have known each other all their lives. We need to find structures that can overcome the anonymity of the huge, highly mobile societies in which we live, and which show every sign of increasing in size.

The next problem is even more difficult. If nothing you do really makes much difference to me, tit for tat will not work. So while equality is not required, too great a disparity in power or wealth will remove the incentive for mutual cooperation. If you leave a group of people so far outside the social commonwealth that they have nothing to contribute to it, you alienate them from the social practices and institutions of which they are part; and they will almost certainly become adversaries who pose a threat to those institutions. The political lesson of twentieth-century Darwinian thinking is entirely different from that of nineteenth-century Social Darwinism. Social Darwinists saw the fact that those who are less fit will fall by the wayside as nature's way of weeding out the unfit – an inevitable result of the struggle for existence. To try to overcome it was futile, if not positively harmful. A Darwinian Left which understands the prerequisites for mutual cooperation and its benefits would strive to avoid economic conditions that create outcasts.

Let me draw some threads together. What distinguishes a Darwinian Left from previous versions of the Left? First, a Darwinian Left would not deny the existence of a human nature, nor insist that human nature is inherently good, nor infinitely malleable. Second, it would not expect to end all conflict and strife between human beings. Third, it would not assume that all inequalities are due to discrimination, prejudice, oppression, or social conditioning. Some will be, but not all. For example, the fact that there are fewer women chief executives than men may be due to men being more willing to subordinate their personal lives and other interests to their career goals; biological differences between men and women may be a factor in that greater readiness to sacrifice everything for the sake of getting to the top.

What about those things that a Darwinian Left would support? First, it would recognize that there is such a thing as human nature. It would seek to find out more about it so that it can be grounded on the best available evidence of what human beings are. Second, it would expect that, under many different social and economic systems, many people will act competitively in order to enhance their own status, gain power, and advance their interests and those of their kin. Third, it would expect that irrespective of the social and economic system in which they live, most people will respond positively to invitations to enter into mutually beneficial forms of cooperation, as long as the invitations are genuine. Fourth, it would promote structures that foster cooperation rather than competition, and attempt to channel competition into socially desirable ends. Fifth, it would recognize that the way in which we exploit nonhuman animals is a legacy of a pre-Darwinian past which exaggerated the gulf between humans and other animals, and therefore work towards a higher moral status for nonhuman animals. Sixth, it would stand by the traditional values of the Left by being on the side of the weak, poor, and oppressed, but think very carefully about what will really work to benefit them.

In some ways, this is a sharply deflated vision of the Left, its utopian ideas replaced by a coolly realistic view of what can be achieved. But in the longer term, we do not know to what extent our capacity to reason can take us beyond the conventional Darwinian constraints on the degree of altruism that a society may be able to foster. We are reasoning beings. Once we start reasoning, we may be compelled to follow a chain of argument to a conclusion that we did not anticipate. Reason provides us with the capacity to recognize that each of us is simply one being among others, all of whom have wants and needs that matter to them, as our needs and wants matter to us. Can this insight ever overcome the pull of other elements in our evolved nature that act against the idea of an impartial concern for all of our fellow humans, or better still, for all sentient beings?

No less a champion of Darwinian thought than Richard Dawkins holds out the prospect of "deliberately cultivating and nurturing pure, disinterested altruism – something that has no place in nature, something that has never existed before in the whole history of the world." Although "we are built as gene machines," he tells us, "we have the power to turn against our creators." There is an important truth here. We are the first generation to understand not only that we have evolved, but also the mechanisms by which we have evolved. In his philosophical epic, *The Phenomenology of Mind*, Hegel portrayed the culmination of history as a state of absolute knowledge, in which the mind knows itself for what it is, and thus achieves its own freedom. We don't have to accept Hegel's metaphysics to see that something similar really has happened in the last fifty years. For the first time since life emerged from the primeval soup, there are beings who understand how they have come to be what they are. In a more distant future we can still barely glimpse, it may turn out to be the prerequisite for a new kind of freedom: the freedom to shape our genes so that instead of living in societies constrained by our evolutionary origins, we can build the kind of society we judge best.

Note

This is an edited version of the Second Annual Darwin Public Lecture given at the London School of Economics on May 12, 1998. The full version was published in October 1999 by Weidenfeld and Nicolson in London (and in 2000 by Yale University Press, New Haven) as part of the "Darwinism Today" series of small books.

Peter Singer:
Selected Publications, 1970–2000

Books

Democracy and Disobedience, Oxford: Clarendon Press, 1973; New York: Oxford University Press, 1974; reprint, Aldershot, Hampshire: Gregg Revivals, 1994.

Animal Liberation: A New Ethics for our Treatment of Animals, New York: New York Review/Random House, 1975; London: Jonathan Cape, 1976; New York: Avon, 1977; London: Paladin, 1977; London: Thorsons, 1983; 2nd edn., New York: New York Review/Random House, 1990; London: Jonathan Cape, 1990; New York: Avon, 1991; London: Thorsons, 1991.

Thomas Regan and Peter Singer (eds.): *Animal Rights and Human Obligations: An Anthology*, Englewood Cliffs, NJ: Prentice-Hall, 1976; 2nd edn., rev. 1989.

Practical Ethics, Cambridge: Cambridge University Press, 1979; 2nd edn., 1993.

Marx, Oxford: Oxford University Press, 1980; New York: Hill and Wang, 1980; reissued as *Marx: A Very Short Introduction*, Oxford: Oxford University Press, 2000. Also included in full in K. Thomas (ed.), *Great Political Thinkers: Machiavelli, Hobbes, Mill, and Marx*, Oxford: Oxford University Press, 1992.

James Mason and Peter Singer: *Animal Factories*, New York: Crown, 1980; 2nd, rev. edn., New York: Harmony, 1990.

The Expanding Circle: Ethics and Sociobiology, New York: Farrar, Straus and Giroux, 1981; Oxford: Oxford University Press, 1981; New York: New American Library, 1982.

Hegel, Oxford and New York: Oxford University Press, 1982; also included in full in *German Philosophers: Kant, Hegel, Schopenhauer, Nietzsche*, Oxford: Oxford University Press, 1997.

William Walters and Peter Singer: *Test-Tube Babies: A Guide to Moral Questions, Present Techniques, and Future Possibilities*, Melbourne: Oxford University Press, 1982.

Peter Singer and Deane Wells: *The Reproduction Revolution: New Ways of Making Babies*, Oxford: Oxford University Press, 1984; rev. American edn., *Making Babies*, New York: Scribner's, 1985.

Helga Kuhse and Peter Singer: *Should the Baby Live? The Problem of Handicapped Infants*, Oxford: Oxford University Press, 1985; New York: Oxford University Press, 1986; reprint, Aldershot, Hampshire: Gregg Revivals, 1994.

In Defence of Animals (ed.): Oxford: Blackwell, 1985; New York: Harper and Row, 1986.

Applied Ethics (ed.): Oxford: Oxford University Press, 1986.

Peter Singer, Helga Kuhse, Stephen Buckle, Karen Dawson, and Pascal Kasimba (eds.): *Embryo Experimentation*, Cambridge: Cambridge University Press, 1990; paperback edn., updated, 1993.

A Companion to Ethics (ed.): Oxford: Blackwell, 1991; paperback edn., 1993.

Paola Cavalieri and Peter Singer: *The Great Ape Project: Equality Beyond Humanity*, London: Fourth Estate, 1993; New York: St. Martin's Press, 1994 (hardback); New York: St. Martin's Press, 1995 (paperback).

How Are We to Live? Ethics in an Age of Self-interest, Melbourne: Text Publishing, 1993; London: Mandarin, 1995; Buffalo, NY: Prometheus, 1995; Oxford: Oxford University Press, 1997.

Ethics (ed.): Oxford: Oxford University Press, 1994.

Helga Kuhse and Peter Singer: *Individuals, Humans, and Persons: Questions of Life and Death*, Sankt Augustin, Germany: Academia Verlag, 1994.

Rethinking Life and Death: The Collapse of Our Traditional Ethics, Melbourne: Text Publishing, 1994; New York: St. Martin's Press, 1995; Oxford: Oxford University Press, 1995.

John McKie, Jeff Richardson, Peter Singer, and Helga Kuhse: *The Allocation of Health Care Resources: An Ethical Evaluation of the "QALY" Approach*, Aldershot: Ashgate/ Dartmouth, 1998.

Helga Kuhse and Peter Singer: *A Companion to Bioethics*, Oxford: Blackwell, 1998.

Ethics into Action: Henry Spira and the Animal Rights Movement, Lanham, MD: Rowman and Littlefield, 1998; Melbourne: Melbourne University Press, 1999.

Helga Kuhse and Peter Singer (eds.): *Bioethics: An Anthology*, Oxford: Blackwell, 1999.

A Darwinian Left, London: Weidenfeld and Nicolson, 1999; New Haven: Yale University Press, 2000.

Writings on an Ethical Life, New York: Ecco, 2000.

Articles in Professional Journals

"Is Act-Utilitarianism Self-Defeating?" *Philosophical Review*, 81 (1972), pp. 94–104.

"Famine, Affluence, and Morality," *Philosophy and Public Affairs*, 1 (1972), pp. 229–43.

"Moral Experts," *Analysis*, 32 (1972), pp. 115–17.

"The Triviality of the Debate over 'Is-Ought' and the Definition of 'Moral'," *American Philosophical Quarterly*, 10 (1973), pp. 51–6.

"Altruism and Commerce: A Reply to Arrow," *Philosophy and Public Affairs*, 2 (1973), pp. 312–20.

"Sidgwick and Reflective Equilibrium," *The Monist*, 58 (1974), pp. 490–517.

"All Animals are Equal," *Philosophical Exchange*, 1 (Summer 1974), pp. 103–16.

"Is Racial Discrimination Arbitrary?" *Philosophia*, 8 (1978), pp. 185–203.

"Killing Humans and Killing Animals," *Inquiry*, 22 (1979), pp. 145–56.

"Animals and Human Beings are Equals," *Animal Regulation Studies*, 2 (1979/80), pp. 165–74.

"Utilitarianism and Vegetarianism," *Philosophy and Public Affairs*, 9 (1980), pp. 325–37.

"Animal Liberation," *Connecticut Scholar*, Occasional Papers no. 3 (1980), pp. 70–88.

Peter Singer and Yew-Kwang Ng: "An Argument for Utilitarianism," *Canadian Journal of Philosophy*, 11 (1981), pp. 229–39.

"Ethics and Sociobiology," *Philosophy and Public Affairs*, 11 (1982), pp. 40–64.

"The Oxford Vegetarians – A Personal Account," *International Journal for the Study of Animal Problems*, 3 (1982) pp. 6–9.

"Can We Avoid Assigning Greater Value to Some Lives Than to Others?" *Community Health Studies*, supplementary issue (May 1982), pp. 39–44.

Peter Singer, Helga Kuhse, and Cora Singer: "The Treatment of Newborn Infants with Major Handicaps: A Survey of Obstetricians and Paediatricians in Victoria," *Medical Journal of Australia* (Sept. 17, 1983), pp. 274–8.

Peter Singer and Deane Wells: "*In Vitro* Fertilisation: the Major Issues," *Journal of Medical Ethics*, 9 (1983), pp. 192–5, 198–9.

"The Ethics of the Reproduction Revolution," *Annals of the New York Academy of Sciences*, 442 (1985), pp. 588–94.

"Making Laws about Making Babies," *Hastings Center Report*, 15 no. 4 (August 1985), pp. 5–6.

Peter Singer and Helga Kuhse: "Ethics and the Handicapped Newborn Infant," *Social Research*, 52 (1985), pp. 505–42.

Helga Kuhse and Peter Singer: "Resources and Hard Choices in Aged Care," *Proceedings of the 20th Annual Conference of the Australian Association of Gerontology* (1985), pp. 38–41.

"Animal Liberation: A Personal View," *Between the Species*, 2 (1986), pp. 148–54.

Peter Singer and Helga Kuhse: "The Ethics of Embryo Research," *Law, Medicine, and Health Care*, 14 (1986), pp. 133–8.

Helga Kuhse and Peter Singer: "For Sometimes Letting – and Helping – Die", *Law, Medicine, and Health Care*, 14 (1986), pp. 149–54.

"Animal Liberation or Animal Rights?" *The Monist*, 70 (1987), pp. 3–14.

C. De Garis, H. Kuhse, P. Singer, and V. Y. H. Yu: "Attitudes of Australian Neonatal Paediatricians to the Treatment of Extremely Preterm Infants," *Australian Paediatric Journal*, 23 (1987), pp. 223–6.

"Which Babies are too Expensive to Treat?" *Bioethics*, 1 (1987), pp. 275–83.

Helga Kuhse and Peter Singer: "Age and the Allocation of Medical Resources," *Journal of Medicine and Philosophy*, 13 (1988), pp. 101–16.

Peter Singer and Karen Dawson: "IVF and the Argument from Potential," *Philosophy and Public Affairs*, 17 (1988) pp. 87–104.

Helga Kuhse and Peter Singer: "Doctors' Practices and Attitudes Regarding Voluntary Euthanasia," *Medical Journal of Australia*, (June 20, 1988), pp. 623–7.

H. Kuhse, J. Mackenzie, and P. Singer: "Allocating Resources in Perinatal Medicine: A Proposal," *Australian Paediatric Journal*, 24 (1988), pp. 235–9.

Carl Wood and Peter Singer: "Whither Surrogacy?" *Medical Journal of Australia* (October 17, 1988), pp. 426–9.

"Can Bioethics be both Rigorous and Practical?" *Reseaux*, 53–4 (1987–8), pp. 121–30.

Stephen Buckle, Karen Dawson, Peter Singer: "The Syngamy Debate: When *Precisely* Does a Human Life Begin?" *Law, Medicine and Health Care*, 17 (1989), pp. 174–81.

Pascal Kasimba and Peter Singer: "Australian Commissions and Committees on Issues in Bioethics," *Journal of Medicine and Philosophy*, 144 (1989), pp. 403–24.

Helga Kuhse and Peter Singer: "The Quality/Quantity-of-Life Distinction and its Moral Importance for Nurses," *International Journal of Nursing Studies*, 26 (1989), pp. 203–12.

"To Do or Not to Do?" *Hastings Center Report*, 19 no. 6 (November/December 1989), pp. 42–4.

"Il concetto di morte tra etica filosofica e medicina," *Politeia* (Milan), 5 no. 16 (1989), pp. 4–13.

"Bioetica: dilucidazioni e problemi" ("Bioethics: Elucidations and Problems"), *Iride* (Rome), 3 (1989), pp. 167–81 (an interview with M. Mori).

"Bioethics and Academic Freedom," *Bioethics*, 4 (1990), pp. 33–44.

Karen Dawson and Peter Singer: "Should fertile people have access to in vitro fertilisation?" *British Medical Journal*, 300 (January 20, 1990), pp. 167–70.

Karen Dawson and Peter Singer: "The Human Genome Project: for better or for worse?" *Medical Journal of Australia*, 152 (May 7, 1990) pp. 484–6.

Peter Singer and Helga Kuhse: "Zwischen Leben entscheiden: Eine Verteidigung," *Analyse & Kritik*, 12 (1990), pp. 119–30.

"The 'Singer-Affair' and Practical Ethics: A Response," *Analyse & Kritik*, 12 (1990), pp. 245–64.

"The Ethics of Patenting Life-Forms," *Intellectual Property Forum*, 14 (1991), pp. 31–8.

"A Philosopher Among the Test-Tubes," *Meanjin*, 50 (1991), pp. 493–500.

"Euthanasia and Academic Freedom in the German-Speaking World," *Kriterion*, 1 (1991), pp. 8–10.

"Applied Ethics in a Hostile Environment," *Theoria*, 67 (1991), pp. 111–14.

Helga Kuhse and Peter Singer: "Euthanasia: A Survey of Nurses' Attitudes and Practices," *Australian Nurses' Journal*, 21 no. 8 (March 1992), pp. 21–2.

"A German Attack on Applied Ethics," *Journal of Applied Philosophy*, 9 (1992), pp. 85–91.

"Xenotransplantation and Speciesism," *Transplantation Proceedings*, 24 (1992), pp. 728–32.

"L'éthique appliquée," *Cahiers antispécistes lyonnais*, 4 (1992), pp. 5–12.

"Bioethics at Monash University," *International Journal of Bioethics*, 2 (1992), pp. 111–15.

"The International Association of Bioethics," *Medical Journal of Australia*, 158 (March 1, 1993), pp. 298–9.

Helga Kuhse and Peter Singer: "Voluntary Euthanasia and the Nurse: An Australian Survey," *International Journal of Nursing Studies*, 30 (1993), pp. 311–22.

Peter Singer and Helga Kuhse: "More on Euthanasia: A Response to Pauer-Studer," *The Monist*, 76 (1993), pp. 158–74.

"Bioethics and the Limits of Tolerance," *Journal of Medicine and Philosophy*, 19 (1994), pp. 129–45.

"Die Ethik der Embryonenforschung," *Aufklärung und Kritik*, Sonderheft 1 (1995), pp. 83–7.

"Feminism and Vegetarianism: A Response," *Philosophy in the Contemporary World*, 1 (1994), pp. 36–9.

Peter Singer, John McKie, Helga Kuhse, Jeff Richardson: "Double Jeopardy and the Use of QALYs in Health Care Allocation," *Journal of Medical Ethics*, 21 (1995), pp. 144–50.

"Is the Sanctity of Life Ethic Terminally Ill?" *Bioethics*, 9 (1995), pp. 327–43.

Peter Singer, Leslie Cannold, Helga Kuhse: "William Godwin and the Defence of Impartialist Ethics", *Utilitas*, 7 (1995), pp. 67–86.

Alison Hutchinson and Peter Singer: "Xenotransplantation: Is it Ethically Defensible?" *Xeno*, 3 no. 4 (August 1995), pp. 58–60.

"The Legalisation of Voluntary Euthanasia in the Northern Territory," *Bioethics*, 9 (1995), pp. 419–24.

Eric Nord, Jeff Richardson, Andrew Street, Helga Kuhse, Peter Singer: "Maximizing Health Benefits vs. Egalitarianism: An Australian Survey of Health Issues," *Social Science and Medicine*, 41 (1995), pp. 1429–37.

Helga Kuhse and Peter Singer: "Active Voluntary Euthanasia, Morality, and the Law," *Journal of Law and Medicine*, 3 (1995), pp. 129–35.

Paola Cavalieri and Peter Singer: "The Great Ape Project: Premises and Implications," *ATLA*, 23 (1995), pp. 626–31.

"Coping with Global Change," *Critical and Creative Thinking*, 3 no. 2 (1995), pp. 1–12.

"Is there a Universal Moral Sense?" *Critical Review*, 9 (1995), pp. 325–39.

Eric Nord, Jeff Richardson, Andrew Street, Helga Kuhse, Peter Singer: "Who Cares about Cost? Does Economic Analysis Impose or Reflect Social Values?" *Health Policy*, 34 (1995), pp. 79–94.

"Coping with Global Change: The Need for Different Values," *Journal of Human Values*, 2 (1996), pp. 37–48.

Leslie Cannold, Peter Singer, Helga Kuhse, Lori Gruen: "What is the Justice-Care Debate *Really* About?" *Midwest Studies in Philosophy*, 20 (1996), pp. 357–77.

Helga Kuhse and Peter Singer: "Ethics and the Limits of Scientific Freedom," *The Monist*, 79 (1996), pp. 218–29.

"Dilemma von Leben und Tod," *Universitas*, 51 (May 1996), pp. 432–7.

Eric Nord, Andrew Street, Jeff Richardson, Helga Kuhse, Peter Singer: "The Significance of Age and Duration of Effect in Social Evaluation of Health Care," *Health Care Analysis*, 4 (1996), pp. 103–11.

Maurice Rickard, Helga Kuhse, Peter Singer: "Caring and Justice: A Study of Two Approaches to Health Care Ethics," *Nursing Ethics*, 3 (1996), pp. 212–23.

"O Naravi Bioetike" ("On the Nature of Bioethics"), *Drustvena Istrazivanja* (Zagreb), 5 (1996), pp. 523–32.

John McKie, Helga Kuhse, Jeff Richardson, Peter Singer: "Allocating Healthcare by QALYs: The Relevance of Age," *Cambridge Quarterly of Healthcare Ethics*, 5 (1996), pp. 534–45.

Helga Kuhse, Peter Singer, Peter Baume, Malcolm Clark, Peter Baume: "End-of-life Decisions in Australian Medical Practice," *Medical Journal of Australia*, 166 (February 17, 1997), pp. 191–6.

"Neither Human nor Natural: Ethics and Feral Animals," *Reproduction, Fertility, and Development*, 9 (1997), pp. 157–62.

Helga Kuhse, Peter Singer, Maurice Rickard, Leslie Cannold, Jessica van Dyk: "Partial and Impartial Ethical Reasoning in Health Care Professionals," *Journal of Medical Ethics*, 23 (1997), pp. 226–32.

Helga Kuhse, Peter Singer, Peter Baume, Malcolm Clark: "Medical End-of-life Decisions: Australia and the Netherlands," *Mature Medicine Canada*, 1 no. 3 (May-June 1998), pp. 37–8.

Hartmut Kuhlmann and Peter Singer: "Die alte Ethik bröckelt," *Universitas*, 53 (1998), pp. 665–80.

Helga Kuhse, Peter Singer, Maurice Rickard: "Reconciling Impartial Morality and a Feminist Ethic of Care," *Journal of Value Inquiry*, 32 (1998), pp. 451–63.

Arlene Klotzko and Peter Singer: "Learning from Henry Spira," *Cambridge Quarterly of Healthcare Ethics*, 8 (1999), pp. 3–6.

"Ética más allá de los límites de la especie," *teorema*, 18 no. 3 (1999), pp. 5–16.

Peter Singer and Paula Casal: "El 'Proyecto Gran Simio' y el concepto de persona," *Laguna*, 7 (2000), pp. 333–47.

Discussion Notes in Professional Journals

"A Note on an Objection to Determinism," *Philosophy*, 45 (1970), pp. 156–7.

"Neil Cooper's Concepts of Morality," *Mind*, 80 (1971), pp. 421–3.

"Why Nozick is Not So Easy to Refute," *Western Political Quarterly*, 29 (1976), pp. 191–2.

"Utility and the Survival Lottery," *Philosophy*, 52 (1977), pp. 218–22.

"Can Ethics Be Taught in a Hospital?" *Pediatrics*, 60 (1977), pp. 253–5.

"The Fable of the Fox and The Unliberated Animals," *Ethics*, 88 (1978), pp. 119–25.

"Anglin on the Obligation to Create Extra People," *Canadian Journal of Philosophy*, 8 (1978), pp. 583–5.

"Regan's Critique of Singer," *Analysis*, 39 (1979), pp. 118–19.

"Advocacy, Objectivity and the Draize Test," *International Journal for the Study of Animal Problems*, 1 (1980), pp. 212–13.

"Reply to Dr. Harris," *Philosophical Books*, 22 (1981), pp. 198–200.

"How do we Decide?" *Hastings Center Report*, 12 no. 3 (June 1982), pp. 9–11.

"Sanctity of Life or Quality of Life?" *Pediatrics*, 72 (1983), pp. 128–9.

"A Comment on the Animal Rights Debate," *International Journal of Applied Philosophy*, 1 (1983), pp. 89–90.

Y.-K. Ng and Peter Singer: "Ng & Singer on Utilitarianism: A Reply," *Canadian Journal of Philosophy*, 13 (1983), pp. 241–2.

"In Reply," *Pediatrics*, 73 (1984), pp. 261–3.

"The Moral Status of Embryos: Response," *Journal of Medical Ethics*, 10 (1984), pp. 80–1.

"Neonatal Intensive Care: How Much, and Who Decides?" *Medical Journal of Australia*, 142 (March 18, 1985), pp. 335–6.

"The Expanding Circle: A Reply to Munevar," *Explorations in Knowledge*, 9 (1987), pp. 51–4.

"Australian Developments in Reproductive Technology," *Hastings Center Report*, 18 no. 2 (April/May 1988), p. 4.

"Comment on Frey, 'Moral Standing, the Value of Lives, and Speciesism'," *Between the Species*, 4 (1988), pp. 202–3.

Helga Kuhse and Peter Singer: "Resolving Arguments about the Sanctity of Life: A Response to Long," *Journal of Medical Ethics*, 14 (1988), pp. 198–9.

"Experiments on Animals," *British Medical Journal*, 299 (November 18, 1989), pp. 1238–9.

"The Significance of Animal Suffering," *Behavioral and Brain Sciences*, 13 (1990), pp. 9–12.

"Ethics and Animals," *Behavioral and Brain Sciences*, 13 (1990), pp. 45–9.

Yew-Kwang Ng: "An Argument for Utilitarianism: A Defence," *Australasian Journal of Philosophy*, 68 (1990), pp. 448–54.

Peter Singer and Helga Kuhse: "Viel Wind um Nichts" ("A lot of wind about nothing"), *Ethik und Sozialwissenschaften*, 2 (1990), pp. 411–14.

"Speciesism, Morality, and Biology," *Psychologist*, 4 (1991), pp. 199–200.

Helga Kuhse and Peter Singer: "Prolonging Dying is the same as Prolonging Living – One More Response to Long," *Journal of Medical Ethics*, 17 (1991), pp. 205–6.

"The Pervasiveness of Species Bias," *Behavioral and Brain Sciences*, 14 (1991), pp. 759–60.

"How to Argue with Egg Producers," *Behavioral and Brain Sciences*, 17 (1994), p. 749.

"Straw Men with Broken Legs: A Reply to Per Sandström," *Journal of Medical Ethics*, 21 (1995), pp. 89–90.

Helga Kuhse and Peter Singer: "Euthanasia: Kuhse and Singer respond," *Australian Nursing Journal* (September 1995), p. 26.

"Blind Hostility: A Response to Russell and Nicoll," *Proceedings of the Society for Experimental Biology and Medicine*, 211 (1996), pp. 139–46.

Peter Singer, John McKie, Helga Kuhse, Jeff Richardson: "Double Jeopardy, the Equal Value of Lives and the Veil of Ignorance: A Rejoinder to Harris," *Journal of Medical Ethics*, 22 (1996), pp. 204–8.

John McKie, Helga Kuhse, Jeff Richardson, Peter Singer: "Another Peep behind the Veil," *Journal of Medical Ethics*, 22 (1996), pp. 216–21.

"Morte cerebrale ed etica della sacralità della vita," *Bioetica*, 8 (2000), pp. 31–49.

Articles Contributed to Books

"A Utilitarian Population Policy" in *Ethics and Population*, ed. M. Bayles (Cambridge, MA: Schenkman, 1976), pp. 81–99.

"Freedoms and Utilities in Health Care" in *Markets and Morals,* ed. G. Dworkin, G. Bermant, P. Brown (New York: Halstead Press, 1977), pp. 149–73.

"Unsanctifying Human Life" in J. Ladd (ed.), *Ethical Issues Relating to Life and Death*, (New York: Oxford University Press, 1978), pp. 41–61.

"Reconsidering the Famine Relief Argument" in *Food Policy: U.S. Responsibility in the Life and Death Choices*, ed. P. Brown and H. Shue (New York: Free Press, 1977), pp. 36–53.

"Animal Experimentation" in *The Encyclopedia of Bioethics*, ed. W. T. Reich (New York: Macmillan, 1978), pp. 79–83.

"Life: Value of Life" in *The Encyclopedia of Bioethics*, ed. W. T. Reich (New York: Macmillan, 1978), pp. 822–8.

"Rights and the Market" in J. Arthur and W. Shaw (eds.), *Justice and Economic Distribution* (Englewood Cliffs, NJ: Prentice-Hall, 1978), pp. 207–21.

"Animals and the Value of Life" in T. Regan (ed.), *Matters of Life and Death* (New York: Random House, 1980; rev. edns., Random House, 1986, McGraw-Hill, 1993), pp. 280–321.

"Not for Humans Only: The Place of Nonhumans in Environmental Issues" in K. E. Goodpastor and K. M. Sayre (eds.), *Ethics and Problems of the 21st Century* (Notre Dame, IN: University of Notre Dame Press, 1979), pp. 191–206.

"Preface" to H. S. Salt, *Animal Rights* (first published in 1892, reissued 1980), Clarks Summit, PA: Society for Animal Rights, 1980), pp. v–x.

Helga Kuhse and Peter Singer: "The Moral Status of the Embryo" in William Walters and Peter Singer (eds.), *Test-Tube Babies* (Melbourne: Oxford University Press, 1982), pp. 57–67.

William Walters and Peter Singer: "Conclusions – and Costs" in William Walters and Peter Singer (eds.), *Test-Tube Babies* (Melbourne: Oxford University Press, 1982), pp. 128–41.

"The Concept of Moral Standing" in A. Caplan and D. Callahan (eds.), *Ethics in Hard Times* (New York: Plenum Press, 1981), pp. 31–45.

"Contemporary Theories of Morality: A Secularist Perspective" in T. J. Connolly (ed.), *Health Care in Crisis: A Bioethical Perspective* (Sydney: Laurdel Bioethics Foundation, 1982), pp. 101–15.

"The Ethics of Animal Use" in L. Peel and D. E. Tribe (eds.) *World Animal Science, Vol. A1: Domestication, Conservation and Use of Animal Resources* (Amsterdam: Elsevier, 1983), pp. 153–65.

"Arguments against Markets: Two Cases from the Health Field," in C. L. Buchanan and E. W. Prior (eds.), *Medical Care and Markets* (Sydney: Allen and Unwin, 1985), pp. 2–19.

"Ethics," *Encyclopaedia Britannica*, 1986 and subsequent printings, vol. 18 pp. 627–48.

"Creating Embryos" in W. B. Weil and M. Benjamin (eds.), *Ethical Issues at the Outset of Life* (Boston: Blackwell Scientific Publications, 1987), pp. 43–62.

"Hegel and Marx" (a dialogue with Bryan Magee) in B. Magee, *The Great Philosophers* (London: BBC Books, 1987), pp. 190–208. (Portuguese translation: Lisbon: Presenca, 1989.)

Helga Kuhse and Peter Singer: "Ethical Issues raised by Treatment of Extremely Preterm Infants" in V. Y. H. Yu and E. C. Wood (eds.), *Prematurity* (Edinburgh: Churchill Livingstone, 1987), pp. 257–73.

"Life's Uncertain Voyage" in P. Pettit, R. Sylvan, and J. Norman (eds.), *Metaphysics and Morality: Essays in Honour of J. J. C. Smart* (Oxford: Blackwell, 1987), pp. 154–72.

Helga Kuhse and Peter Singer: "Ethical Issues in Reproductive Alternatives for Genetic Indications" in F. Vogel and K. Sperling (eds.), *Human Genetics* (Berlin: Springer, 1987), pp. 683–91.

"Reasoning towards Utilitarianism" in D. Seanor and N. Fotion (eds.), *Hare and Critics* (Oxford: Clarendon Press, 1988), pp. 147–59.

"Ethical Experts in a Democracy" D. Rosenthal and F. Shehadi (eds.), *Applied Ethics and Ethical Theory* (Salt Lake City: University of Utah Press, 1988), pp. 149–61.

Peter Singer and Renata Singer: "The Ethics of Refugee Policy" in M. Gibney (ed.), *Open Borders? Closed Societies?* (New York: Greenwood Press, 1988), pp. 111–30.

Karen Dawson and Peter Singer: "Some Consequences of Regulating Reproductive Medicine in Australia" in C. Byk (ed.), *Procréation artificielle: où en sont l'éthique et le droit?* (Lyon: Lacassagne, 1989), pp. 185–92.

"Animal Liberation?" (interview with Robyn Williams) in Robyn Williams, *The Uncertainty Principle* (Sydney: ABC Books, 1989), pp. 139–50.

"Il Dibattito Bioetico in Australia" ("The Bioethics Debate in Australia") in O. Polleggioni and M. Russo (eds.), *Il bambino bionico* (Florence: La Nuova Italia, 1989), pp. 139–43.

Helga Kuhse and Peter Singer: "Should All Seriously Disabled Infants Live?" in Geoffrey Scarre (ed.), *Children, Parents and Politics* (Cambridge: Cambridge University Press, 1989), pp. 168–81.

"IVF and Australian Law" in D. Bromham, M. Dalton, and J. Jackson (eds.), *Philosophical Ethics in Reproductive Medicine* (Manchester: Manchester University Press, 1990), pp. 31–47.

Helga Kuhse and Peter Singer: "Introduction: The Nature of Ethical Argument" in Peter Singer, Helga Kuhse, Stephen Buckle, Karen Dawson, and Pascal Kasimba, *Embryo Experimentation* (Cambridge: Cambridge University Press, 1990), pp. 37–42.

Helga Kuhse and Peter Singer: "Individuals, Humans, and Persons: The Issue of Moral Status" in Peter Singer, Helga Kuhse, Stephen Buckle, Karen Dawson, and Pascal Kasimba, *Embryo Experimentation* (Cambridge: Cambridge University Press, 1990), pp. 65–75.

"Je mehr wir fuer andere leben, desto zufriedener leben wir" in K. Deschner (ed.), *Woran ich Glaube* (Guetersloh: Gerd Mohn, 1990), pp. 267–71.

"Introduction" and "Afterword" in P. Singer (ed.), *A Companion to Ethics* (Oxford: Blackwell, 1991), pp. v–vi and 543–5.

"Research into Aging: Should it be Guided by the Interests of Present Individuals, Future Individuals, or the Species?" in Frederic C. Ludwig (ed.), *Life Span Extension: Consequences and Open Questions* (New York: Springer, 1991), pp. 132–45.

"Environmental Values" in Ian Marsh (ed.), *The Environmental Challenge* (Melbourne: Longman Cheshire, 1991), pp. 3–24.

P. Singer, C. Fehige, G. Merkel: "Mir leuchtet nicht ein, wie man so Werte bewahren will" in R. Hegselmann and R. Merkel (eds.), *Zur Debatte ueber Euthanasie* (Frankfurt am Main: Suhrkamp, 1991), pp. 153–77.

Helga Kuhse and Peter Singer: "Hard Choices: Ethical Questions Raised by the Birth of Handicapped Infants" in Paul Badham (ed.), *Ethics on the Frontiers of Human Existence* (New York: Paragon House, 1992), pp. 153–77.

"Embryo Experimentation and the Moral Status of the Embryo" in E. Matthews and M. Menlowe (eds.), *Philosophy and Health Care* (Aldershot: Avebury, 1992), pp. 81–91.

Helga Kuhse and Peter Singer: "Allocating Health Care Resources and the Problem of the Value of Life" in D. Cockburn (ed.), *Death and the Value of Life* (Lampeter: Trivium, 1992), pp. 7–23.

"Beyond Traditional Religion" in Georg Feuerstein and Trisha Lamb Feuerstein (eds.), *Voices on the Threshold of Tomorrow* (Wheaton, IL: Quest, 1993), pp. 251–2.

Peter Singer and Edgar Dahl: "Das gekreuzigte Tier" in Edgar Dahl (ed.), *Die Lehre des Unheils: Fundamentalkritik am Christentum* (Hamburg: Carlsen, 1993), pp. 280–9.

Helga Kuhse and Peter Singer: "Abortion and Contraception: The Moral Significance of Fertilization" in Fritz Beller and Robert F. Weir (eds.), *The Beginning of Human Life* (Dordrecht: Kluwer, 1994), pp. 145–61.

"On the Nature of Bioethics" in Helga Kuhse and Peter Singer, *Individuals, Humans, Persons* (Sankt Augustin: Academia Verlag, 1994), pp. 21–32.

Paola Cavalieri and Peter Singer: "The Great Ape Project" in Raymond Corbey and Bert Theunissen (eds.), *Ape, Man, Apeman: Changing Views since 1600* (Leiden: Department of Prehistory, Leiden University, 1995), pp. 367–76.

"Animal Research: Philosophical Issues" in W. T. Reich (ed.), *Encyclopedia of Bioethics* (New York: Macmillan and Simon & Schuster, 1995), vol. I, pp. 147–53.

"Kirche und Embryonenforschung" in Edgar Dahl (ed.), *Die Lehre des Unheils: Fundamentalkritik am Christentum* (Hamburg: Goldmann, 1995), pp. 276–85.

"Taking Sides on the Right to Die" in Simon Chapman and Stephen Leeder (eds.), *The Last Right: Australians take Sides on the Right to Die* (Melbourne: Mandarin, 1995), pp. 142–4.

"Abortion" in Ted Honderich (ed.), *A Companion to Philosophy* (Oxford: Oxford University Press, 1995), pp. 2–3.

"Animals" in Ted Honderich (ed.), *A Companion to Philosophy* (Oxford: Oxford University Press, 1995), pp. 35–6.

"Applied Ethics" in Ted Honderich (ed.), *A Companion to Philosophy* (Oxford: Oxford University Press, 1995), pp. 42–3.

"Dialectic" in Ted Honderich (ed.), *A Companion to Philosophy* (Oxford: Oxford University Press, 1995), p. 198.

"Fertilization *in vitro*" in Ted Honderich (ed.), *A Companion to Philosophy* (Oxford: Oxford University Press, 1995), p. 275.

"Hegel" in Ted Honderich (ed.), *A Companion to Philosophy* (Oxford: Oxford University Press, 1995), pp. 339–43.

"Killing" in Ted Honderich (ed.), *A Companion to Philosophy* (Oxford: Oxford University Press, 1995), pp. 445–6.

"Owl of Minerva" in Ted Honderich (ed.), *A Companion to Philosophy* (Oxford: Oxford University Press, 1995), p. 638.

"Vegetarianism" in Ted Honderich (ed.), *A Companion to Philosophy* (Oxford: Oxford University Press, 1995), p. 897.

"World-soul" in Ted Honderich (ed.), *A Companion to Philosophy* (Oxford: Oxford University Press, 1995), p. 919.

"This I Believe" in John Marsden (ed.), *This I Believe* (Sydney: Random House, 1996), pp. 293–6.

"How are we to live?" in Geoff Mulgan (ed.), *Life After Politics: New Thinking for the Twenty-first Century* (London: Fontana, 1997), pp. 49–55.

"On Comparing the Value of Human and Nonhuman Life" in Edgar Morscher, Otto Neumaier, and Peter Simons (eds.), *Applied Ethics in a Troubled World* (Dordrecht: Kluwer, 1998), pp. 93–104.

"Possible Preferences" in Christoph Fehige and Ulla Wessels (eds.), *Preferences* (Berlin: Walter de Gruyter, 1998), pp. 383–98.

"A Vegetarian Philosophy" in Sian Griffiths and Jennifer Wallace (eds.), *Consuming Passions: Food in the Age of Anxiety* (Manchester: Manchester University Press, 1998), pp. 71–80.

"Utilitarianism" in Marc Bekoff, *Encyclopedia of Animal Rights and Animal Welfare* (Westport, CT: Greenwood Press, 1998), pp. 343–4.

"A Response" in Dale Jamieson (ed.), *Singer and His Critics* (Oxford: Blackwell, 1999), pp. 269–335.

"Reflections" in Amy Gutman (ed.), *The Lives of Animals* (Princeton, NJ: Princeton University Press, 1999), pp. 85–91.

"Ethics across the Species Boundary" in Nicholas Low (ed.), *Global Ethics and Environment* (London: Routledge, 1999), pp. 146–57.

"Embryos and Animals: Can we Justify their Use in Research and Treatment?" in Adam Zeman and Linda Emmanuel (eds.), *Ethical Dilemmas in Neurology* (London: W. B. Saunders, 2000), pp. 122–8.

"Foreword" in Richard B. Brandt, *A Theory of the Good and the Right* (Amherst, NY: Prometheus, 1998).

"Animals" in Dale Jamieson (ed.), *A Companion to Environmental Philosophy* (Oxford: Blackwell, 2001), pp. 416–25.

Articles in Nonprofessional Publications
(including review articles):

"Animal Liberation," *New York Review of Books* (April 5, 1973).

"Discovering Karl Popper," *New York Review of Books* (May 2, 1974).

"Philosophers are Back on the Job," *New York Times Sunday Magazine* (July 7, 1974).

"Looking Backwards," *New York Review of Books* (July 18, 1974).

"Should We Let Them Starve?" *New Humanist* (June 1974).

"The Right to Be Rich or Poor," *New York Review of Books* (March 6, 1975).

"Making Monkeys Neurotic, Dogs Shriek, Etc. Etc.," *New York Times* (December 27, 1975).

"The Case for Animal Liberation," *The Age* (Melbourne) (March 13, 1976).

"Bio-Ethics and The Case of the Fetus," *New York Review of Books* (August 15, 1976).

"Philosophy," *New York Times* (May 8, 1977).

"Philosophical Vegetarianism: A Reply," *Humanist*, 37 (July/August 1977).

"Human Prospecting," *New York Review of Books* (March 22 1979), pp. 30–2.

"Forswearing Secrecy," *Nation* (May 5, 1979), pp. 488–91.

"Why The Whale Should Live," *Habitat*, 6 no. 3 (June 1978), pp. 8–9.

"Do Animals Have Equal Rights?" *Animal Industry Today*, 2 (July/August 1979), pp. 4–8.

"On Your Marx," *New York Review of Books* (December 20, 1979), pp. 44–7.

"Dictator Marx," *New York Review of Books* (September 25, 1980).

"The Case for Prostitution," *The Age* (Melbourne), (September 18, 1980).

"Revolution and Religion," *New York Review of Books* (November 6, 1980), pp. 51–4.

"How the Bunny Lobby Terrorized Revlon," *The Age* (Melbourne), (February 21, 1981).

"Genes and Dominance," *The Age Monthly Review*, 1 no. 1 (May 4, 1981).

"The Real Marx," *The Age Monthly Review*, 1 no. 4 (August 3, 1981).

"Marx and The Real World," *The Age Monthly Review*, 1 no. 5 (September 1981).

"The Control of Cures," *The Age Monthly Review*, 1 no. 7 (November 1981).

"Animal Liberation and Changing the Role of the Modern Zoo," *Thylacinus* (Journal of the Australasian Society of Zookeepers), 7 (1982), pp. 26–30.

"Dim Seer," *The Age Monthly Review*, 2 no. 4 (August 1982).

"Preferences, Pleasure and Happiness," *Times Literary Supplement* (August 27, 1982).

"Whales and the Japanese: A Lesson in Ethics," *The Age Monthly Review*, 2 no. 8 (December 1982).

"The Whitlam Experiment Revisited," *Sydney Morning Herald* (December 1, 1982).

"In Vitro Veritas," *The Age Monthly Review*, 2 no. 12 (April 1983).

"The Horizon Lecture: A Covenant for the Ark?" *The Listener* (April 14, 1983), pp. 11–14.

"The Politics of Procreation," *Australian Penthouse* (October 1983), pp. 156–7.

"Thinking About Animals," *Habitat*, 11 (October 1983), pp. 15–16.

"The Animal Liberation Movement," *Current Affairs Bulletin*, 60 no. 3 (1983), pp. 15–21.

"Misleading Arguments on the Right to Die," *The Age* (Melbourne) (December 15, 1983).

Peter Singer and Helga Kuhse: "The Future of Baby Doe," *New York Review of Books* (March 1, 1984), pp. 17–22.

"Mind Over Manure: Changing Thoughts on Man and Animals" (review of *Man and the Natural World*, by Keith Thomas, and *Animal Thought*, by Stephen Walker), *The Age Monthly Review* (April 1984), pp. 17–18.

"Ten Years of Animal Liberation: A Review of Ten Recent Books," *New York Review of Books* (January 17, 1985), pp. 46–52.

Helga Kuhse and Peter Singer: "Handicapped Babies: A Right to Life?" *Nursing Mirror* (February 20, 1985), pp. 17–20.

"Animal Rights and Wrongs," *The Times Higher Education Supplement* (March 29, 1985).

"Technology and Procreation: How Far Should We Go?" *Technology Review*, 88 no. 2 (February/March 1985), pp. 22–30.

"Ethics and Intensive Farming," *60 Days* (October 1985), pp. 7–9.

"After Live Aid: How Much is Enough?" *The Age Monthly Review* (December 1985/ January 1986).

"Reductio ad Embryo," *The Age Monthly Review* (May 1986).

"Animal Welfare and Scientific Inquiry," *Times Higher Education Supplement* (September 12, 1986).

"Acting on Kant," *The Age Monthly Review* (October 1986).

"Embryo Report is Just the Beginning of the Debate", *The Age* (Melbourne) (November 17, 1986).

"Carrying the White Man's Burden," *The Age* (Melbourne) (March 7, 1987).

"The Vatican Viewpoint on IVF: Stop it, you will go blind," *Sydney Morning Herald* (March 19, 1987).

"The Dog in the Lifeboat: An Exchange," *New York Review of Books* (April 25, 1987), pp. 57–8.

"As the World's Numbers Rise, Our Aid Falls," *Herald* (Melbourne) (June 3, 1987).

"Public Life and Private Morality," *Herald* (Melbourne) (August 13, 1987).

"A Question of Mice and Men," *Herald* (Melbourne) (October 14, 1987).

Renata Singer and Peter Singer: "How Many and Who? Australia's Refugee Policy," *The Age Monthly Review* (April 1988), pp. 18–21.

Renata Singer and Peter Singer: "Migration Policy: Nasty, Brutish and Short-sighted," *The Age* (Melbourne) (August 4, 1988).

"Why Anorexics Lose Their Right to Die," *Herald* (Melbourne) (September 9, 1988).

"Do Blacks Need Extra Help?" *Herald* (Melbourne) (November 15, 1988).

Peter Singer and Helga Kuhse: "Survey shows Australian Professionals Seek Change," *New South Wales Doctor* (September 20, 1988).

"Defending my Right to Put Pin-ups on my Walls," *Herald* (Melbourne) (December 16, 1988).

"Your Freedom of Speech is Under Threat," *Herald* (Melbourne) (January 24, 1989).

"Unkind to Animals," *New York Review of Books* (February 2, 1989), pp. 36–8.

"Absence of Malice," *The Animals' Voice* (February 1989), pp. 8–9.

Peter Singer and Pascal Kasinba: "Through an IVF Glass Darkly," *The Age* (Melbourne) (April 8, 1989).

"Stutters are still good for a laugh," *Herald* (Melbourne) (May 3, 1989).

"Salt of the Earth," *New York Review of Books* (February 15, 1990), pp. 41–2.

"The Great Research Grant Caper," *The Age* (Melbourne) (July 2, 1990).

"New Attitudes Needed on Animal Testing," *New Scientist* (August 11, 1990), p. 4.

"Viewpoint: Animal Experimentation," *Scientific European* (December 1990), pp. 8–9.

"Tutti gli animali sono uguali," *Cenobio* (Lugano, Switzerland and Varese, Italy), 40 (1991), pp. 5–11.

"The Philosopher and the Future" (interview with Terry Lane), *21C* (autumn 1991), pp. 43–7.

"Remember: Dogs and Cats are People too, you know," The *Sunday Age* (Melbourne) (July 7, 1991).

"On Being Silenced in Germany," *New York Review of Books* (August 15, 1991), pp. 36–42.

"Thinking about Suicide," *The Independent Monthly* (October 1991), p. 16.

"Über das Recht, Fragen zu stellen," *Zitty* (Berlin) 22 (October 1991), pp. 18–19.

"Greed is Stupid," *Australian Business Monthly* (March 1992), pp. 78–81.

"Not what you Produce, but how much you Spend," *Modern Times* (March 1992), pp. 16–17.

"The Last Rights," *The Age* (Melbourne) (March 6, 1992).

"That Dangerous Animal," *Modern Times* (April 1992), pp. 10–12.

"Bandit and Friends," *New York Review of Books* (April 9, 1992), pp. 9–13.

"It's all a Question of Ethics," *Australian* (June 4, 1992), p. 6.

"Can Free Trade Make You Happy?" *Australian Business Monthly* (June 1992), pp. 98–100.

"A Response to David DeGrazia," *Between the Species*, 8 (winter 1992), pp. 51–3.

"Animal Liberation: An Exchange," *New York Review of Books* (November 5, 1992), pp. 60–1.

"Has Capitalism Reached its Limits?" *Australian Business Monthly* (November 1992), pp. 112–13.

"Be Radical: Let's Try Self-Reliance," *Australian Business Monthly* (January 1993), pp. 56–9.

"Animal Liberation," *Island*, 54 (autumn 1993), pp. 62–6.

Peter Singer and Helga Kuhse: "Holding Back on a Question of Life or Death," *Australian* (May 7, 1993), p. 15.

"The Rights of Ape," *BBC Wildlife* (June 1993), pp. 28–32.

"Cultural Clash sets Rite against Reason," *Australian* (June 9, 1993).

"The Great Ape Project and its Implications for Scientific and Biomedical Research," *Genetic Engineering News* (November 1, 1993).

"Is there a God?" *The Age* (Melbourne) (December 24, 1993).

"Address to Council," *RACS Bulletin*, 14 no. 3 (November 1994), pp. 23–6.

"The RACS Code and the Patient Who Asks for Help in Dying," *RACS Bulletin*, 14 no. 3 (November 1994), p. 29.

"What Price a Human Life?" *The Sunday Age* (Melbourne), (January 8, 1995).

"To Live Ethical Lives," *The Age* (Melbourne) (January 16, 1995).

"Brave New Territory," *The Sunday Age* (Melbourne) (February 4, 1995).

"Equality: Why it Matters," *Australian Business Monthly* (February 1995), pp. 36–9.

"Menschenrechte für Menschenaffen," *Geo* (April 1995), pp. 176–9.

"Is our Changing Definition of Death for the Better?" *USA Today* (May 18, 1995), p. 15A.

"Taking Note of the Quality of the Life that Chooses Death," *The Age* (Melbourne) (June 7, 1995).

"Final Frontiers," *Times Higher Education Supplement* (August 18, 1995), p. 15.

"Killing Babies isn't always Wrong," *Spectator* (London) (September 16, 1995), pp. 20–2.

"Sentenced to Life," *The Sunday Age* (Melbourne) (October 22, 1995), p. 14.

"Abortion: A Woman's Right," *Beat* (November 1, 1995), p. 10.

"A Christmas Roast," *The Sunday Age* (Melbourne) (December 24, 1995), p. 10.

"The Ethics of Commercialising Wild Animals," *Animals Today*, 4 (1996), pp. 20–3.

"Meaning of Life," *Resurgence* (March/April 1996), pp. 14–15.

"Unnatural Practices," *The Sunday Age* (Melbourne) (April 7, 1996).

"Natural Classic," *BBC Wildlife*, 14 (June 1996), p. 89.

"The Great Ape Project," *Animals' Agenda*, 16 no. 3 (July/August 1996), pp. 12–13.

"Time to Bid Farewell to the Politics of Fear," *The Age* (Melbourne) (October 10, 1996), p. A15.

"Standing for the Greens," *Generation*, 6 nos. 1 and 2 (October 1996), pp. 3–6.

"On Authenticity," *Australian Book Review*, no. 187 (December 1996/January 1997), p. 49.

"Humanismen maste överskrida gränserna," *Dagens Nyheter* (Sweden) (February 9, 1997).

"The Drowning Child and the Expanding Circle," *New Internationalist* (April 1997), pp. 28–30.

Helga Kuhse, Peter Singer, Peter Baume, Malcolm Clark: "Euthanasia: No Time for Hastened Conclusions," *Australian* (February 24, 1997).

"Cloning the News," *The Republican* (April 4, 1997), p. 16.

Helga Kuhse, Peter Singer, Peter Baume, Malcolm Clark: "Muddled Commentary on End-of-life Study," *Australian Doctor* (April 18, 1997), p. 23.

"Angling for Equality of Consideration," *Times Higher Education Supplement* (February 28, 1997), p. 22.

"Research Babies: Another Case of the Stolen Children?" *Sydney Morning Herald* (June 11, 1997).

"To Give or Not to Give?" *Horizons*, 6 no. 2 (spring 1997), pp. 10–11.

"Evolutionary Workers' Party," *Times Higher Education Supplement* (May 15, 1998), pp. 15, 17.

"The Great Ape Project," *Biologist*, 45 no. 2 (April 1998), pp. 87–8.

"Darwin for the Left," *Prospect* (June 1998), pp. 26–30.

"Should an Environmentalist eat Meat?" *Renew*, 64 (July–September 1998), pp. 44–6.

"A Conception to Come to Terms with," *The Sunday Age* (Melbourne) (July 26, 1998), p. 15.

"Zur Natur der Bioethik," *Der Blaue Reiter*, no. 7 (1998), pp. 101–6.

"An Ethical Storm," *The Age* (Melbourne) (February 19, 1999), p. 15.

"Should we Breach the Species Barrier and Grant Rights to the Apes?" *Prospect* (May 1999), pp. 17–19.

"Rights for Chimps," *Guardian* (London) (July 29, 1999), p. 19.

"Sense and Sentience," *Guardian* (London) (August 21, 1999), p. 24.

"The Singer Solution to World Poverty," *New York Times Sunday Magazine* (September 5, 1999), pp. 60–3.

"A New Ethic for Living and Dying," *Daily News* (New York) (October 7, 1999), p. 57.

"Not Right: American Apathy Influences Health Policy," *Daily Princetonian* (October 19, 1999).

"Beastly Behaviour," *The Age Magazine* (October 23, 1999), pp. 56–7.

"Response from Dr Peter Singer," *Yeshiva University Commentator* (November 23, 1999), p. 5.

"Ethics Beyond the Species Barrier," *Earth Matters* (winter 1999/2000), pp. 28–9.

"Stem Cells and Immortal Souls," *Free Inquiry*, 20 no. 2 (spring 2000), p. 9.

"'The Freest Nation in the World'?" *Free Inquiry*, 20 no. 3 (summer 2000), p. 16.

"Everyday Ethics: Racial Slurs; Donating for Dollars," *Prince Magazine* (supplement to *The Daily Princetonian*), (September 25, 2000).

"Everyday Ethics: Cheating; Investment Banking," *Prince Magazine* (supplement to *The Daily Princetonian*) (October 9, 2000).

"Everyday Ethics: Sexual Ethics: Charity Balls," *Prince Magazine* (supplement to *The Daily Princetonian*) (October 23, 2000).

Index